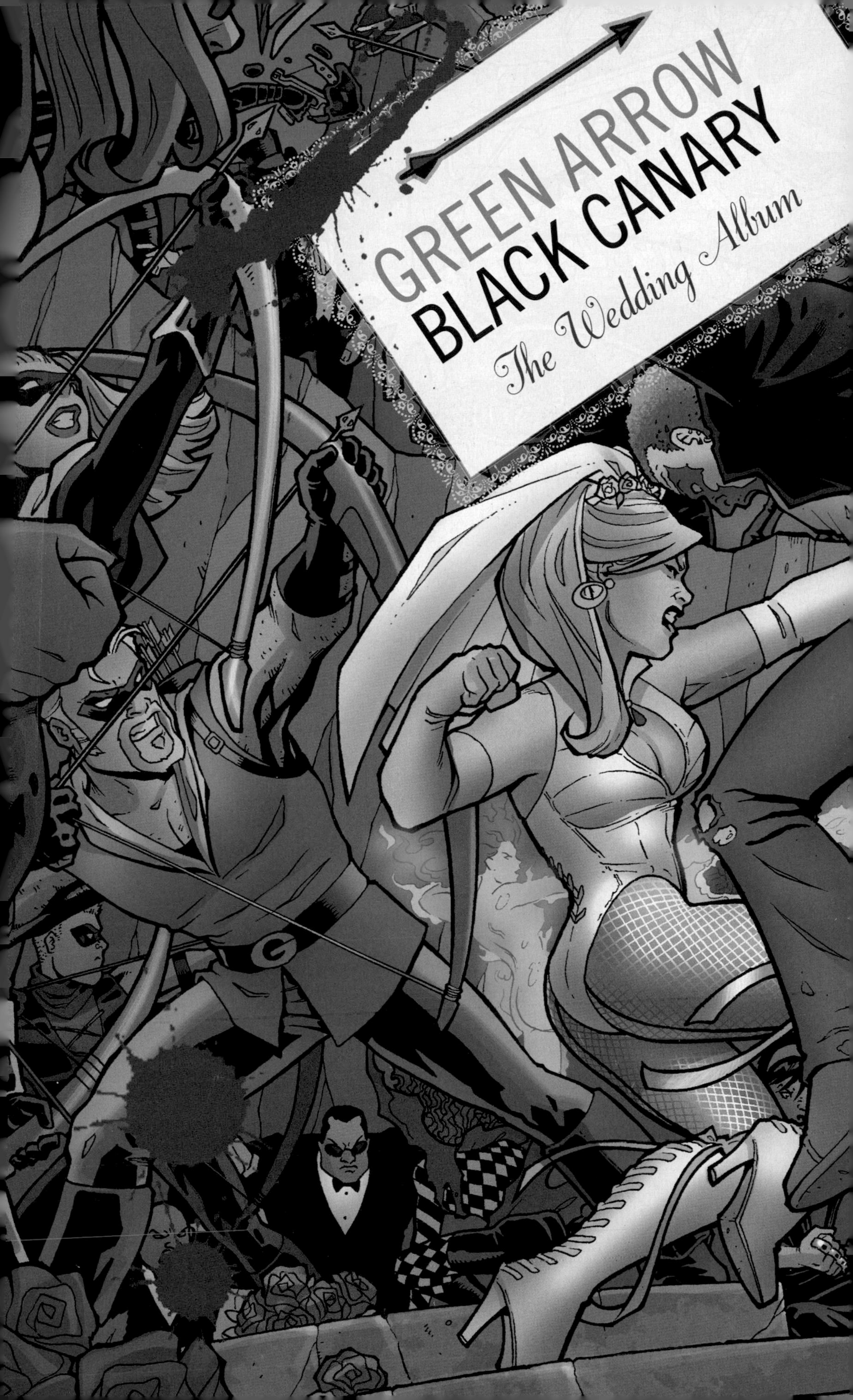
GREEN ARROW
BLACK CANARY
The Wedding Album

DAN DIDIO Senior VP-Executive Editor / **MIKE CARLIN** Editor-original series / **ELISABETH GEHRLEIN** Assistant Editor-original series
BOB JOY Editor-collected edition / **ROBBIN BROSTERMAN** Senior Art Director / **PAUL LEVITZ** President & Publisher
GEORG BREWER VP-Design & DC Direct Creative / **RICHARD BRUNING** Senior VP-Creative Director
PATRICK CALDON Executive VP-Finance & Operations / **CHRIS CARAMALIS** VP-Finance / **JOHN CUNNINGHAM** VP-Marketing
TERRI CUNNINGHAM VP-Managing Editor / **ALISON GILL** VP-Manufacturing / **DAVID HYDE** VP-Publicity
HANK KANALZ VP-General Manager, WildStorm / **JIM LEE** Editorial Director-WildStorm / **PAULA LOWITT** Senior VP-Business & Legal Affairs
MARYELLEN McLAUGHLIN VP-Advertising & Custom Publishing / **JOHN NEE** Senior VP-Business Development
GREGORY NOVECK Senior VP-Creative Affairs / **SUE POHJA** VP-Book Trade Sales / **STEVE ROTTERDAM** Senior VP-Sales & Marketing
CHERYL RUBIN Senior VP-Brand Management / **JEFF TROJAN** VP-Business Development, DC Direct / **BOB WAYNE** VP-Sales

Cover art by Cliff Chiang. Publication design by Amelia Grohman.

GREEN ARROW / BLACK CANARY: THE WEDDING ALBUM
Published by DC Comics. Cover and compilation Copyright © 2008 DC Comics. All Rights Reserved.

Originally published in single magazine form in GREEN ARROW AND BLACK CANARY WEDDING SPECIAL 1,
GREEN ARROW AND BLACK CANARY 1-5 Copyright © 2007, 2008 DC Comics. All Rights Reserved.
All characters, their distinctive likenesses and related elements featured in this publication are trademarks of DC Comics.
The stories, characters and incidents featured in this publication are entirely fictional.
DC Comics does not read or accept unsolicited submissions of ideas, stories or artwork.

DC Comics, 1700 Broadway, New York, NY 10019 / A Warner Bros. Entertainment Company
Printed in USA. First Printing.   HC ISBN-13: 978-1-4012-1841-6   SC ISBN-13: 978-1-4012-2219-2

GREEN ARROW BLACK CANARY
The Wedding Album

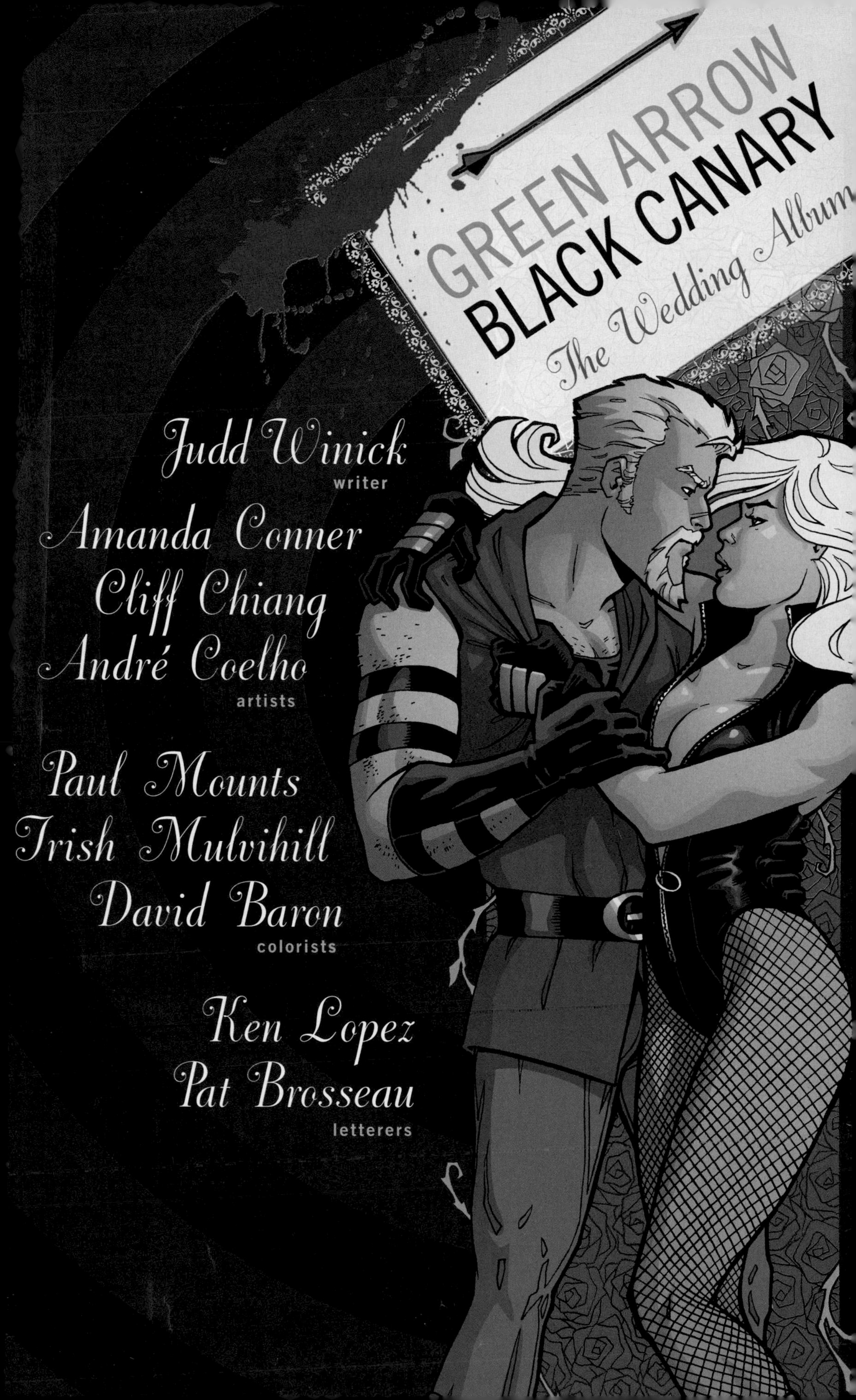

Judd Winick
writer

Amanda Conner
Cliff Chiang
André Coelho
artists

Paul Mounts
Trish Mulvihill
David Baron
colorists

Ken Lopez
Pat Brosseau
letterers

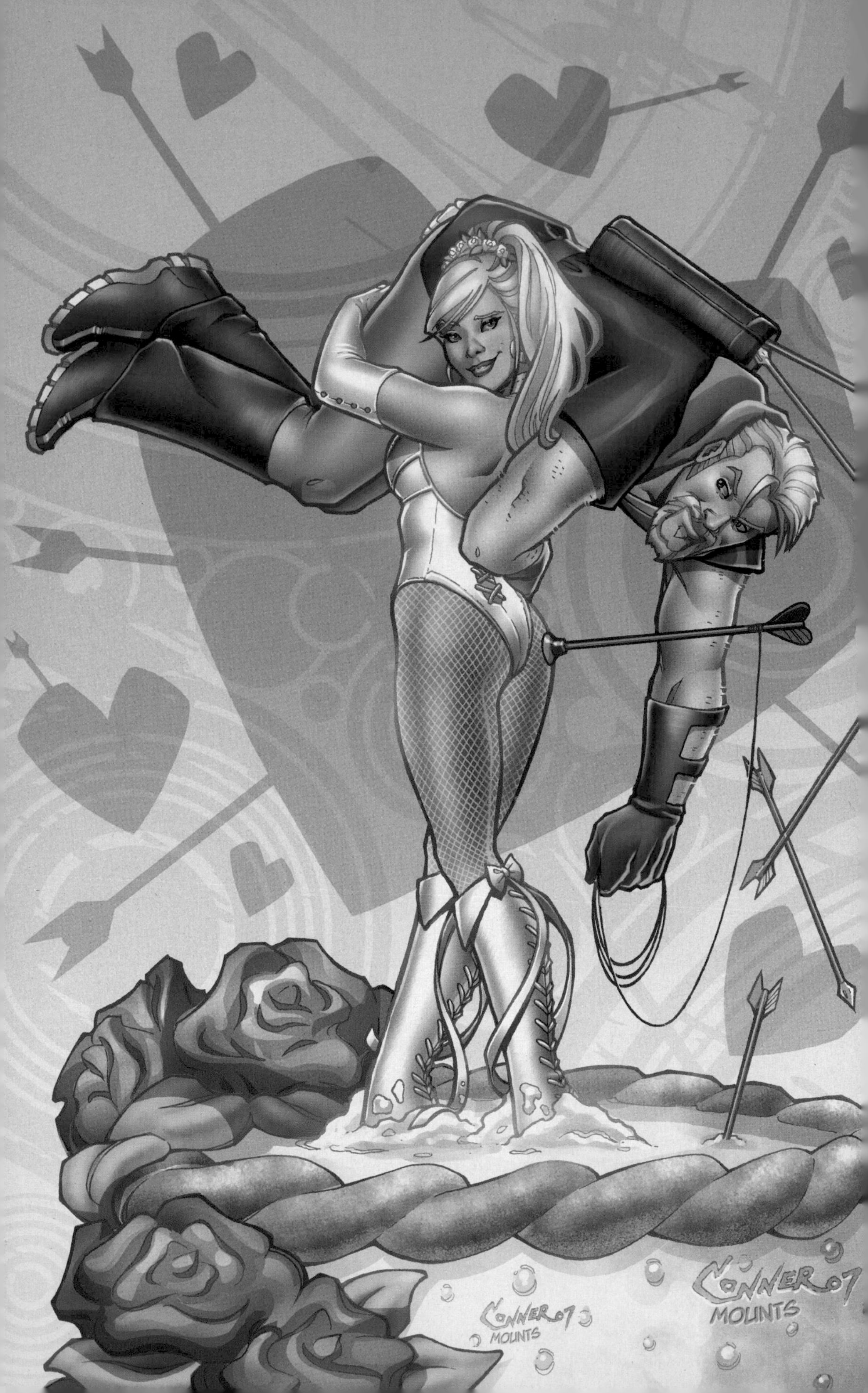
CONNER 07
MOUNTS
CONNER 07
MOUNTS

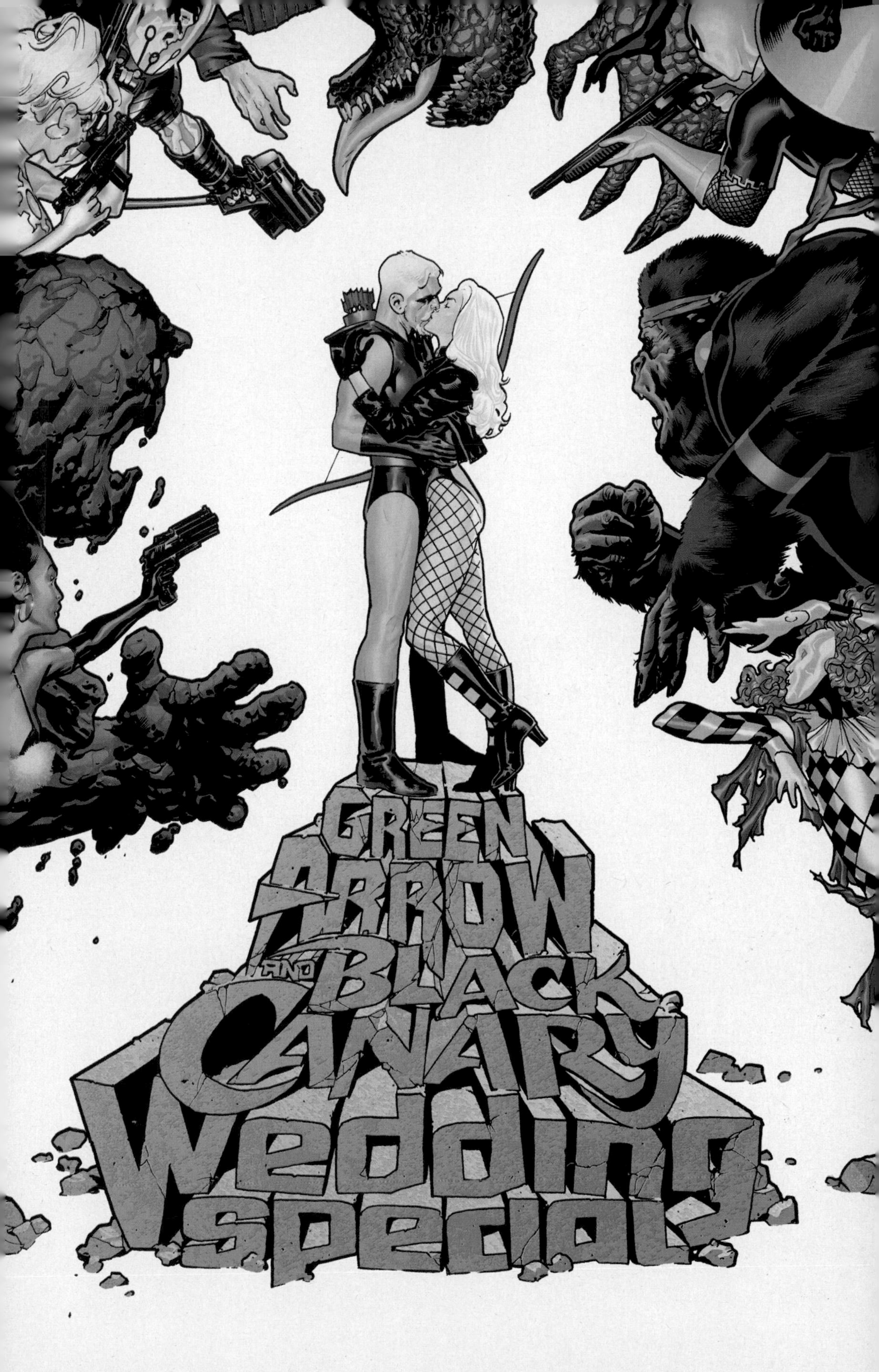
GREEN
ARROW
AND
BLACK
CANARY
Wedding
special

GREEN ARROW AND BLACK CANARY WEDDING SPECIAL *Ryan Sook*

AND THEY SAID IT WOULDN'T LAST

THE WEDDING OF GREEN ARROW
AND BLACK CANARY

Story: **Judd Winick**   *Art:* **Amanda Conner**   *Color:* **Paul Mounts**

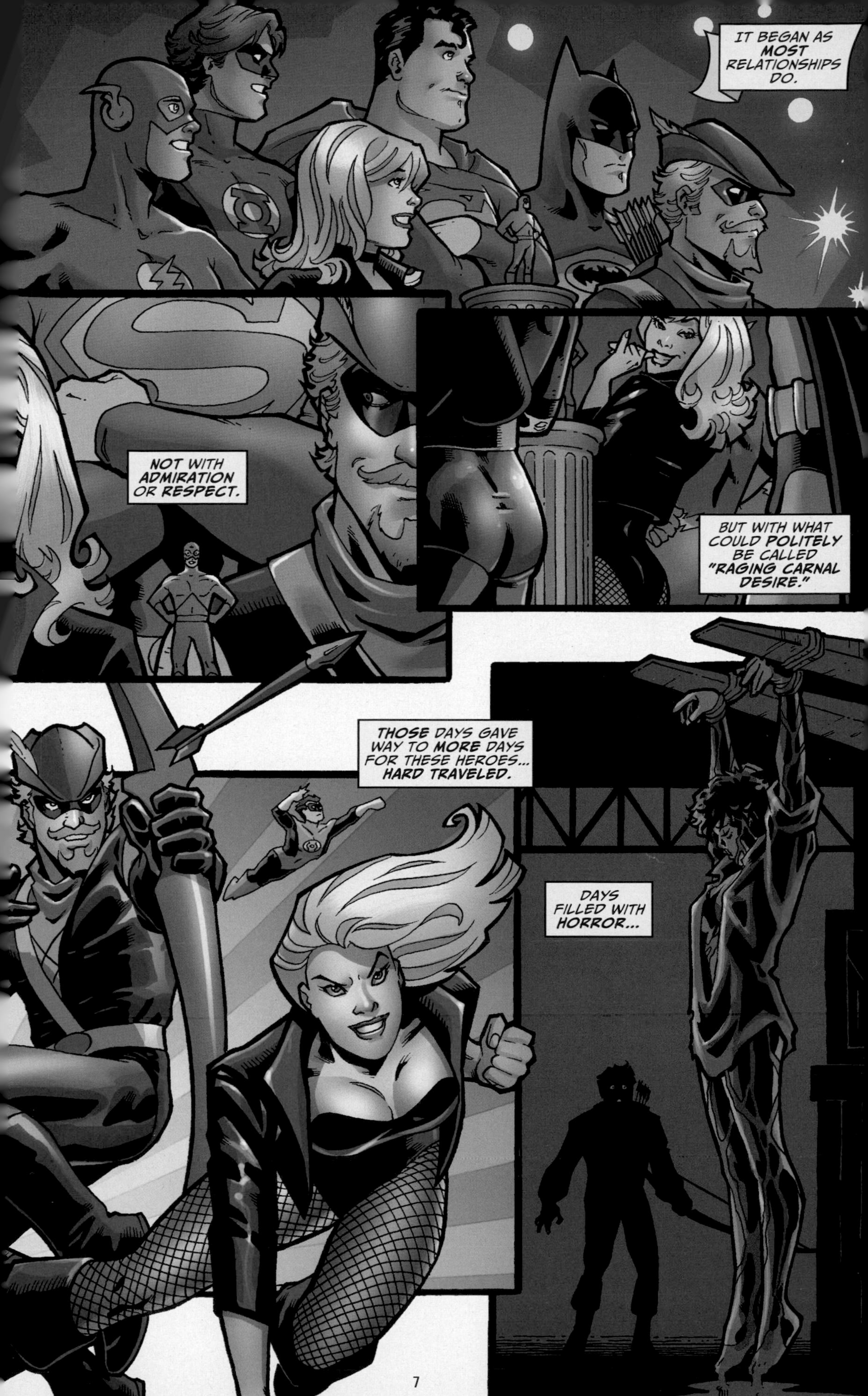
IT BEGAN AS MOST RELATIONSHIPS DO.
NOT WITH ADMIRATION OR RESPECT.
BUT WITH WHAT COULD POLITELY BE CALLED "RAGING CARNAL DESIRE."
THOSE DAYS GAVE WAY TO MORE DAYS FOR THESE HEROES... HARD TRAVELED.
DAYS FILLED WITH HORROR...

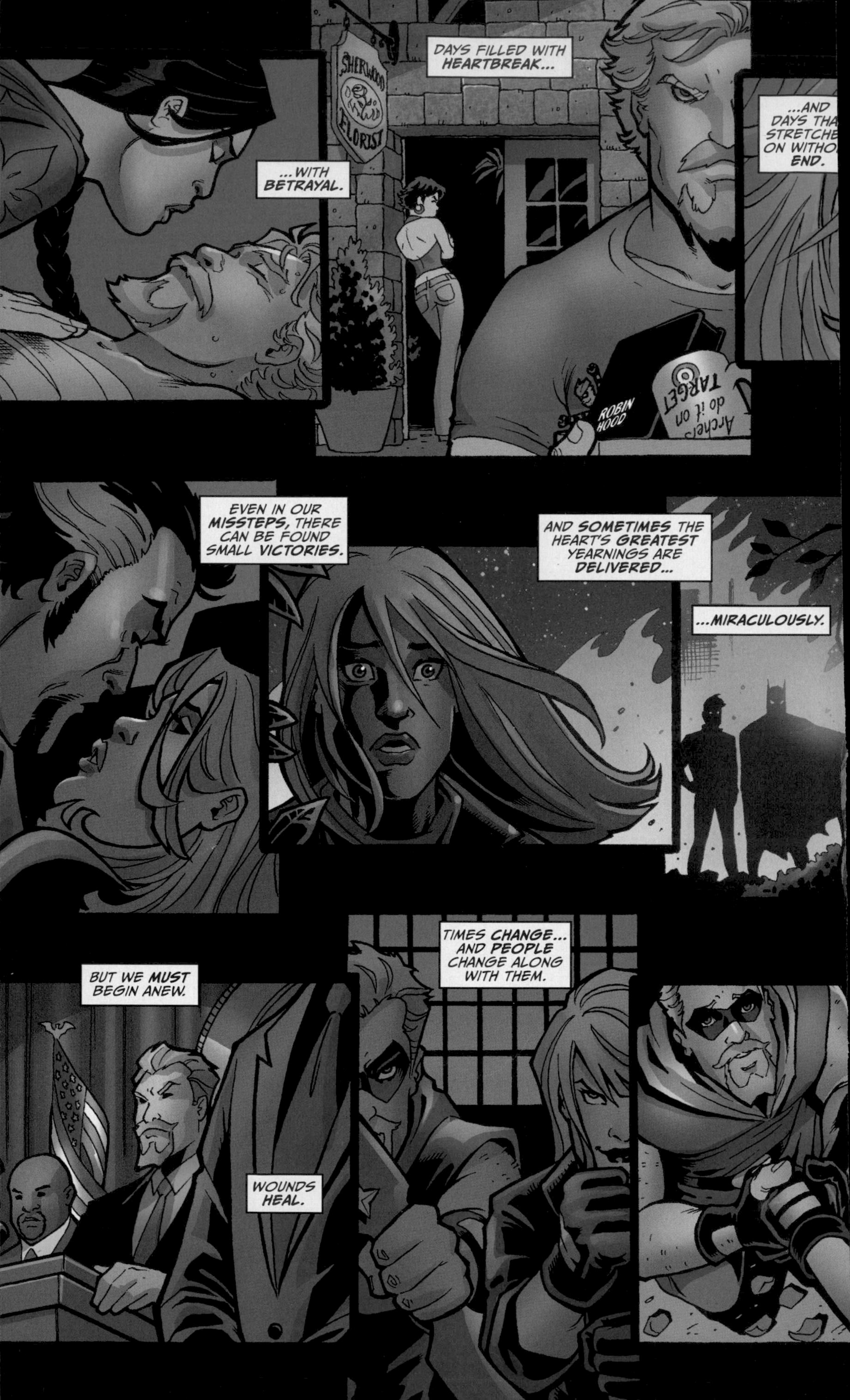

...WITH BETRAYAL.
DAYS FILLED WITH HEARTBREAK...
SHERWOOD FLORIST
...AND DAYS THA STRETCHE ON WITHO END.
ROBIN HOOD
Archers do it on TARGET
EVEN IN OUR MISSTEPS, THERE CAN BE FOUND SMALL VICTORIES.
AND SOMETIMES THE HEART'S GREATEST YEARNINGS ARE DELIVERED...
...MIRACULOUSLY.
BUT WE MUST BEGIN ANEW.
WOUNDS HEAL.
TIMES CHANGE... AND PEOPLE CHANGE ALONG WITH THEM.

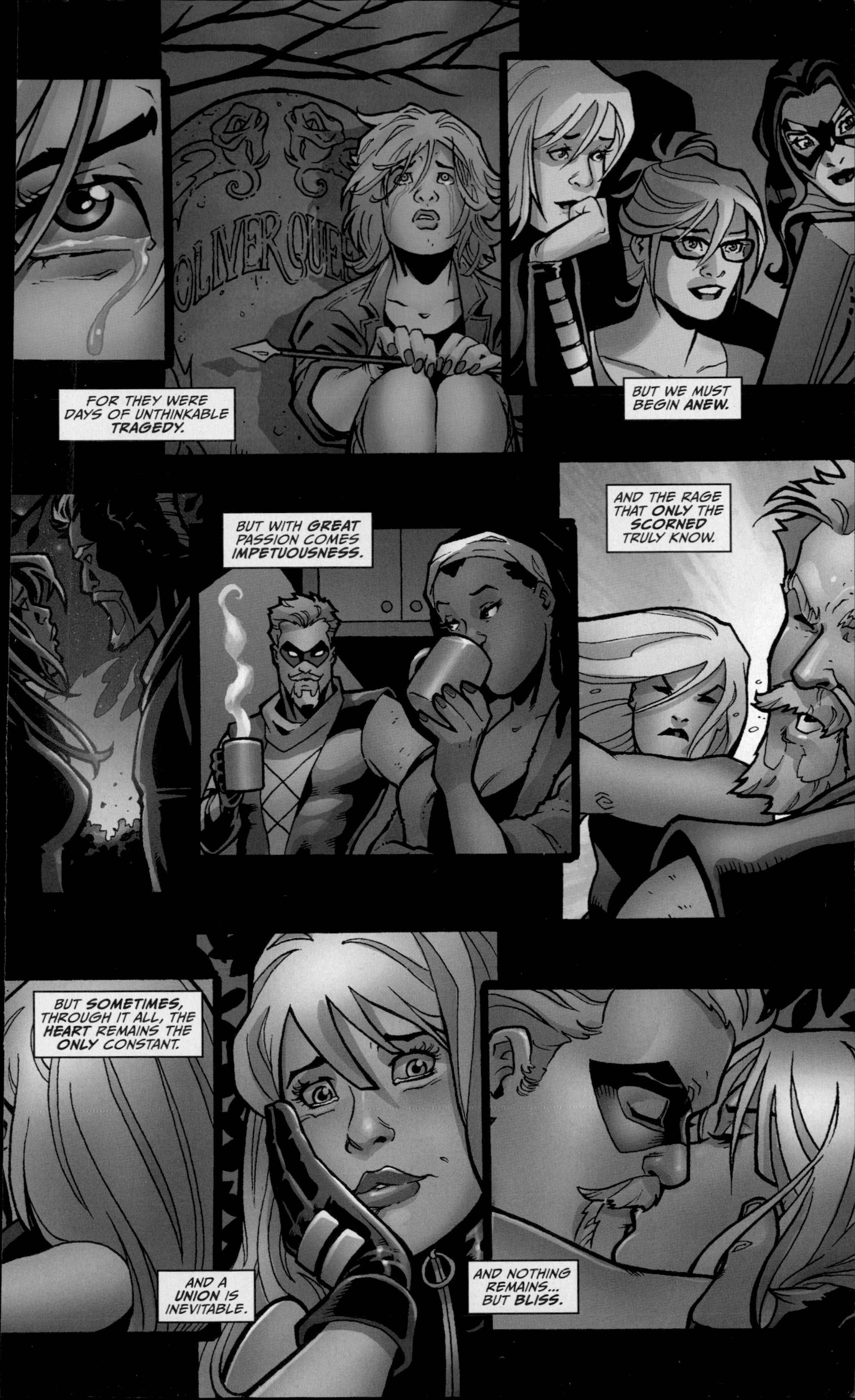
OLIVER QUE
FOR THEY WERE DAYS OF UNTHINKABLE TRAGEDY.
BUT WE MUST BEGIN ANEW.
BUT WITH GREAT PASSION COMES IMPETUOUSNESS.
AND THE RAGE THAT ONLY THE SCORNED TRULY KNOW.
BUT SOMETIMES, THROUGH IT ALL, THE HEART REMAINS THE ONLY CONSTANT.
AND A UNION IS INEVITABLE.
AND NOTHING REMAINS... BUT BLISS.

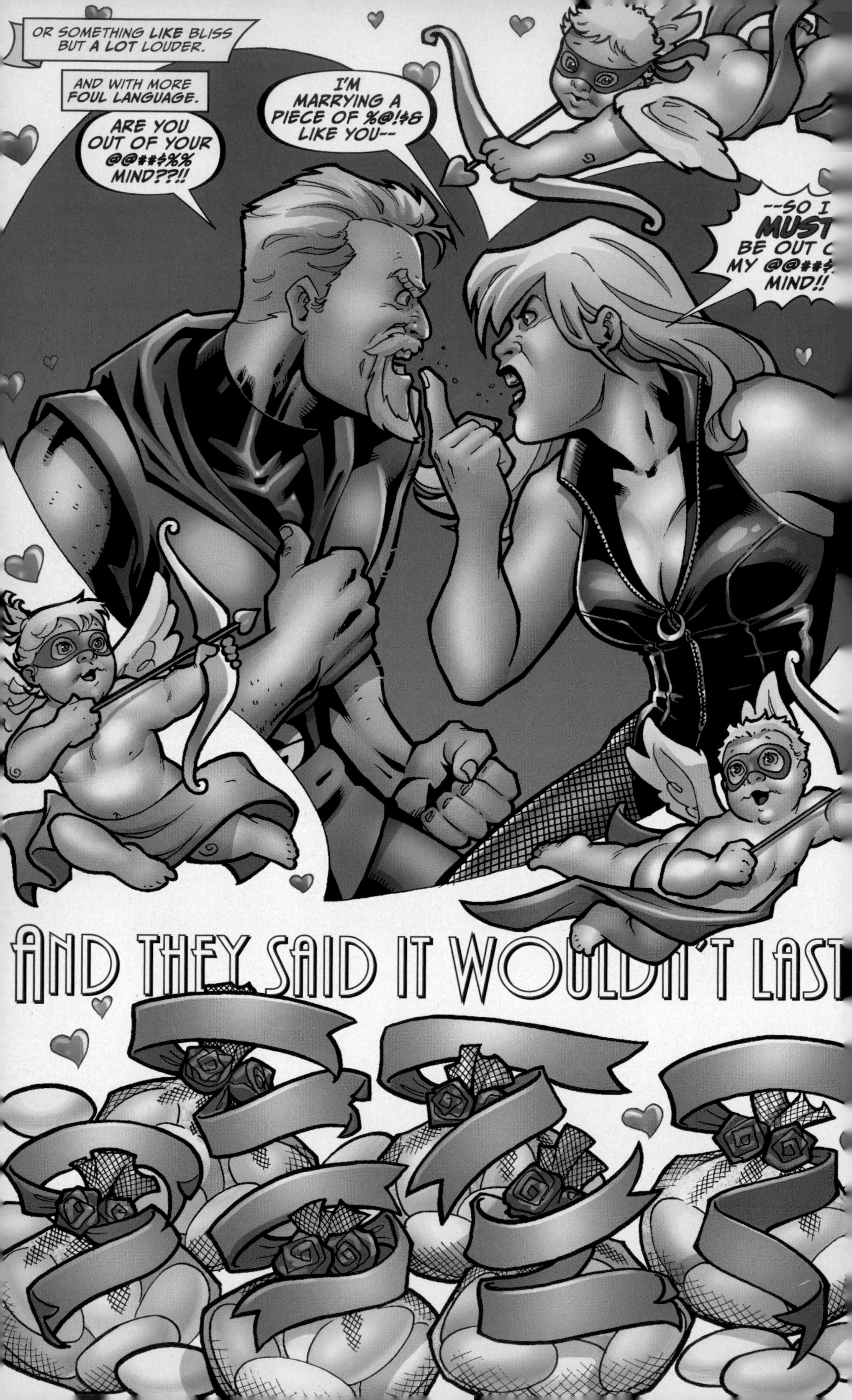
OR SOMETHING LIKE BLISS BUT A LOT LOUDER.
AND WITH MORE FOUL LANGUAGE.
ARE YOU OUT OF YOUR @@##$%% MIND??!!
I'M MARRYING A PIECE OF %@!$& LIKE YOU--
--SO I MUST BE OUT OF MY @@##$ MIND!!
AND THEY SAID IT WOULDN'T LAST

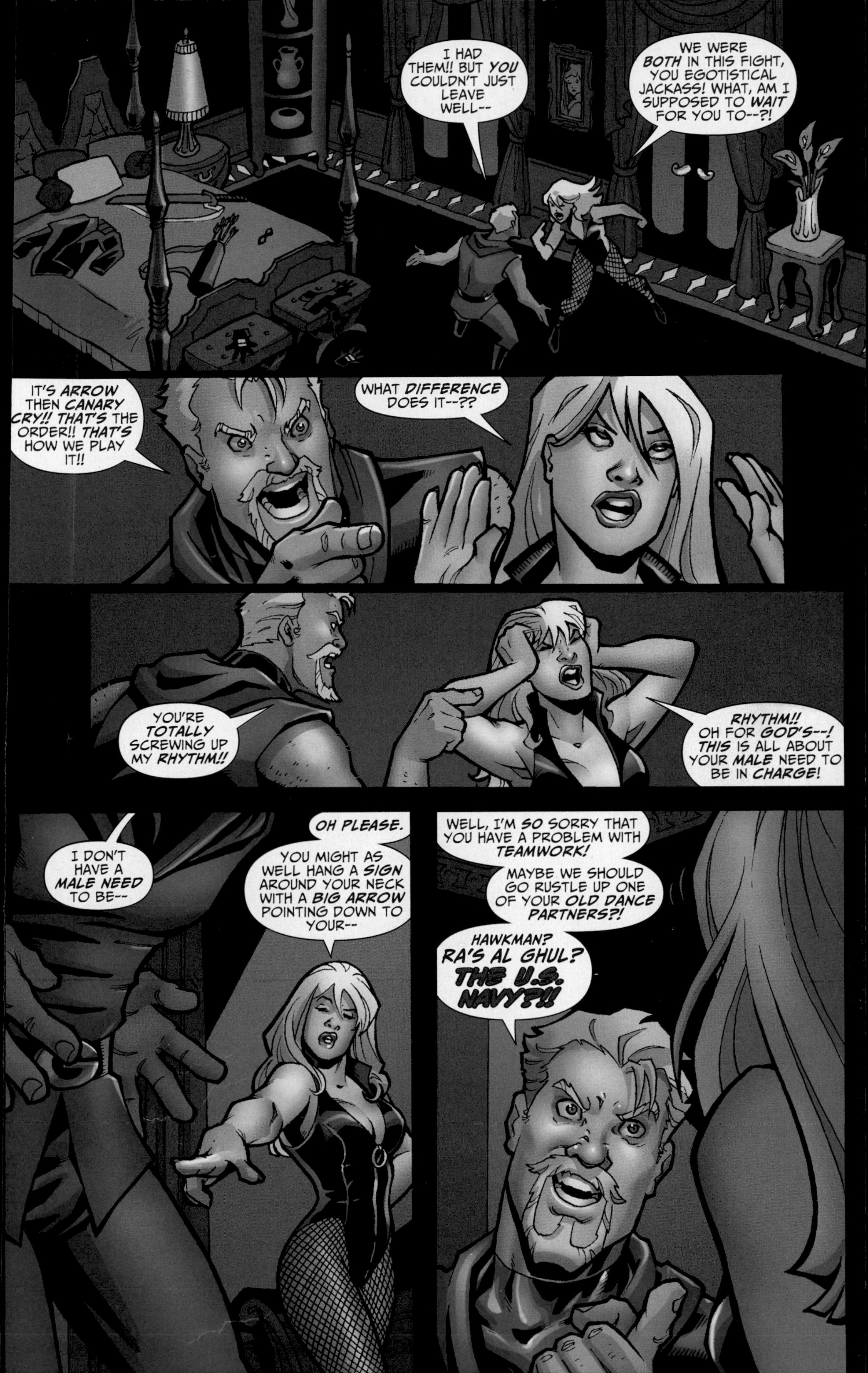
I HAD THEM!! BUT YOU COULDN'T JUST LEAVE WELL--
WE WERE BOTH IN THIS FIGHT, YOU EGOTISTICAL JACKASS! WHAT, AM I SUPPOSED TO WAIT FOR YOU TO--?!
IT'S ARROW THEN CANARY CRY!! THAT'S THE ORDER!! THAT'S HOW WE PLAY IT!!
WHAT DIFFERENCE DOES IT--??
YOU'RE TOTALLY SCREWING UP MY RHYTHM!!
RHYTHM!! OH FOR GOD'S--! THIS IS ALL ABOUT YOUR MALE NEED TO BE IN CHARGE!
I DON'T HAVE A MALE NEED TO BE--
OH PLEASE.
YOU MIGHT AS WELL HANG A SIGN AROUND YOUR NECK WITH A BIG ARROW POINTING DOWN TO YOUR--
WELL, I'M SO SORRY THAT YOU HAVE A PROBLEM WITH TEAMWORK!
MAYBE WE SHOULD GO RUSTLE UP ONE OF YOUR OLD DANCE PARTNERS?!
HAWKMAN? RA'S AL GHUL? THE U.S. NAVY?!!

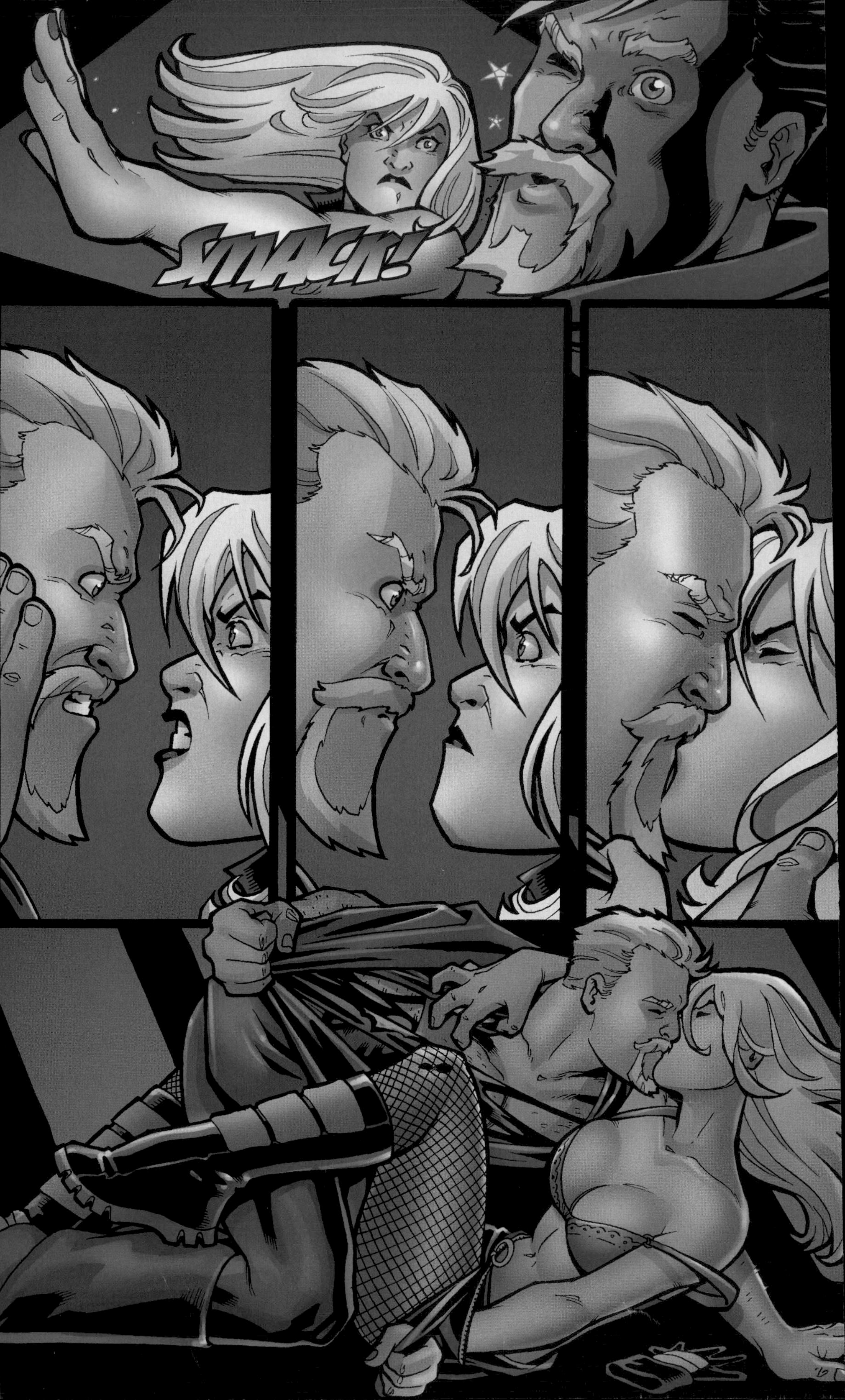
SMACK!

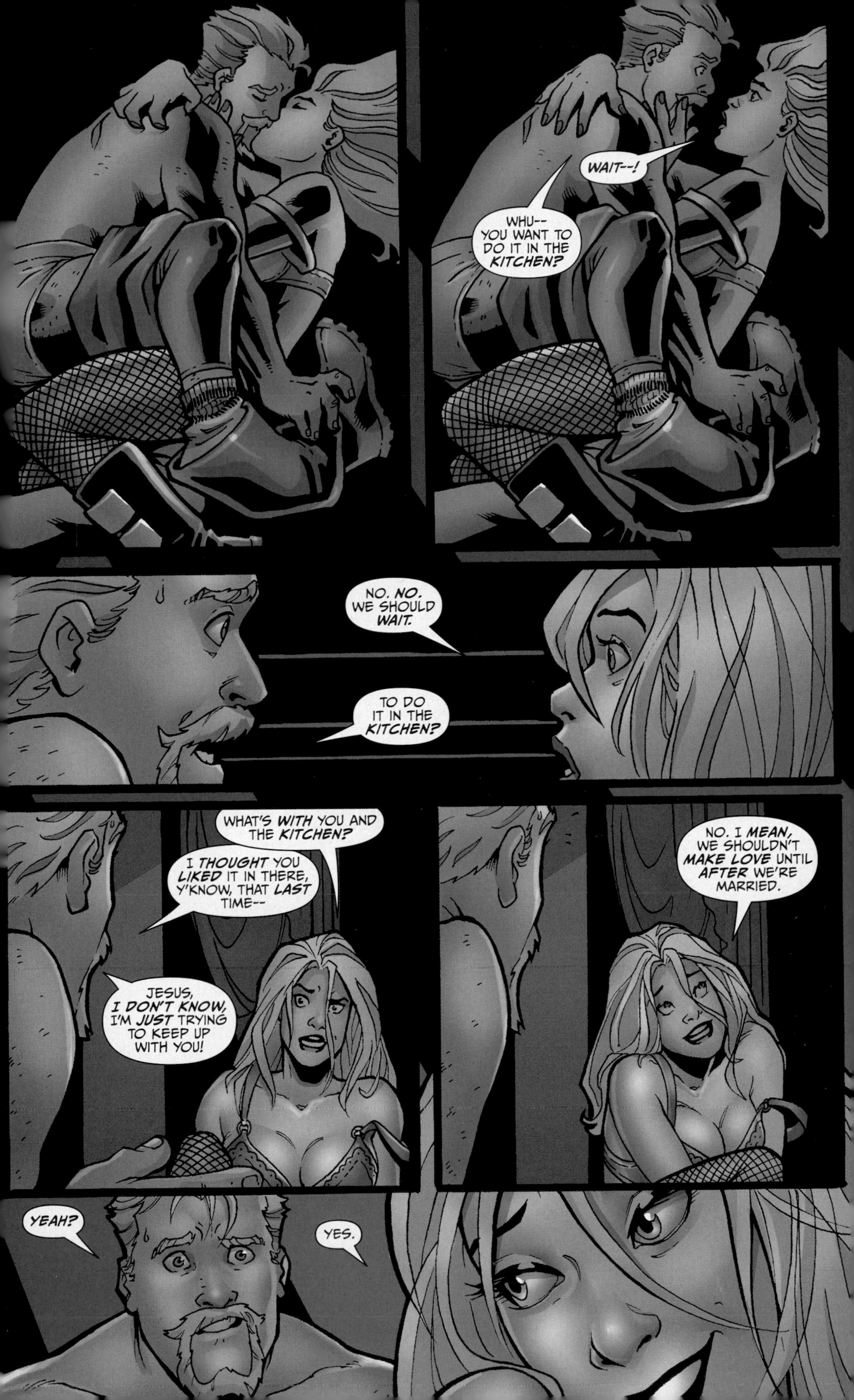
WAIT--!
WHU-- YOU WANT TO DO IT IN THE KITCHEN?
NO. NO. WE SHOULD WAIT.
TO DO IT IN THE KITCHEN?
WHAT'S WITH YOU AND THE KITCHEN?
I THOUGHT YOU LIKED IT IN THERE, Y'KNOW, THAT LAST TIME--
JESUS, I DON'T KNOW, I'M JUST TRYING TO KEEP UP WITH YOU!
NO. I MEAN, WE SHOULDN'T MAKE LOVE UNTIL AFTER WE'RE MARRIED.
YEAH?
YES.

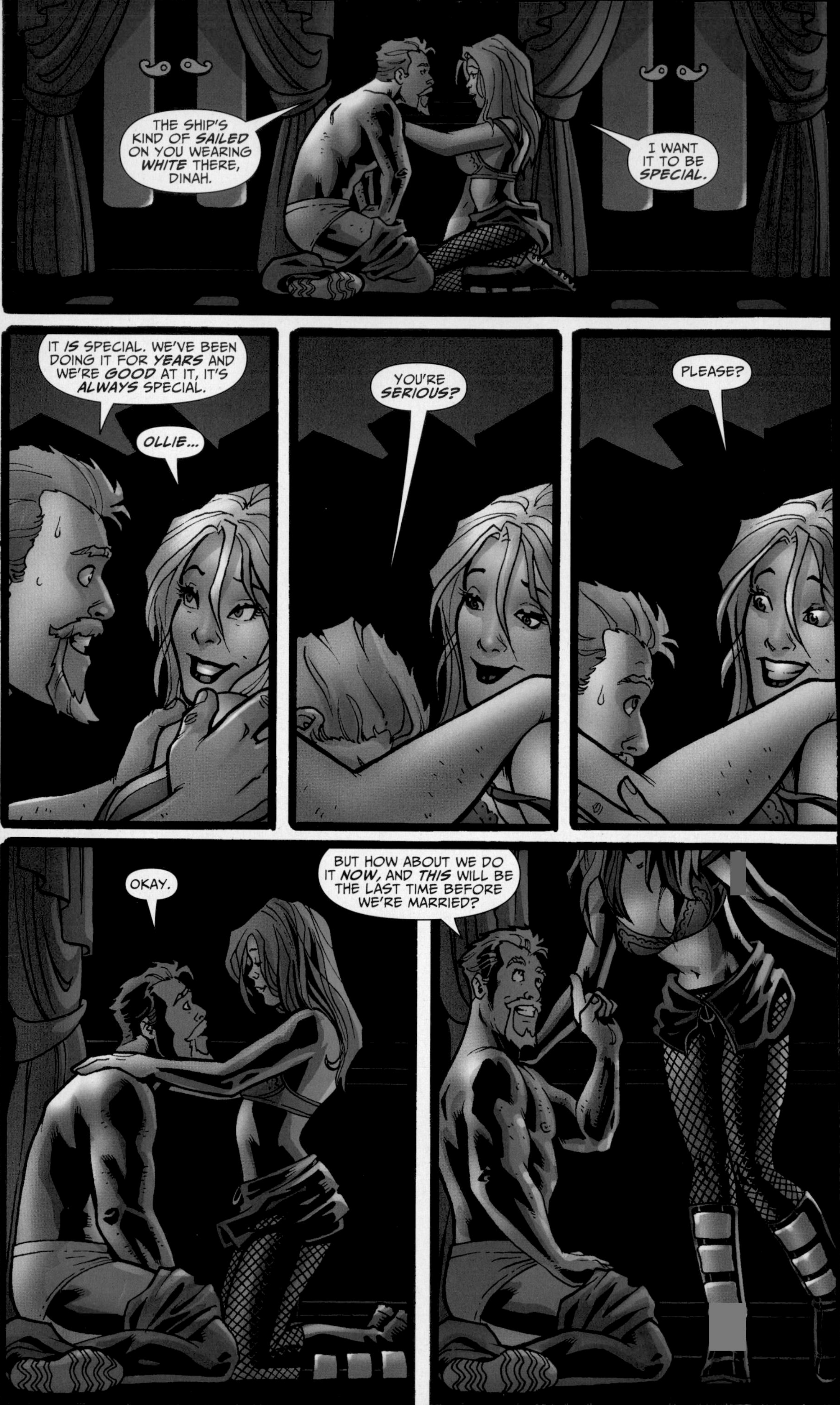
THE SHIP'S KIND OF *SAILED* ON YOU WEARING *WHITE* THERE, DINAH.
I WANT IT TO BE *SPECIAL.*
IT *IS* SPECIAL. WE'VE BEEN DOING IT FOR *YEARS* AND WE'RE *GOOD* AT IT, IT'S *ALWAYS* SPECIAL.
OLLIE...
YOU'RE *SERIOUS?*
PLEASE?
OKAY.
BUT HOW ABOUT WE DO IT *NOW,* AND *THIS* WILL BE THE LAST TIME BEFORE WE'RE MARRIED?

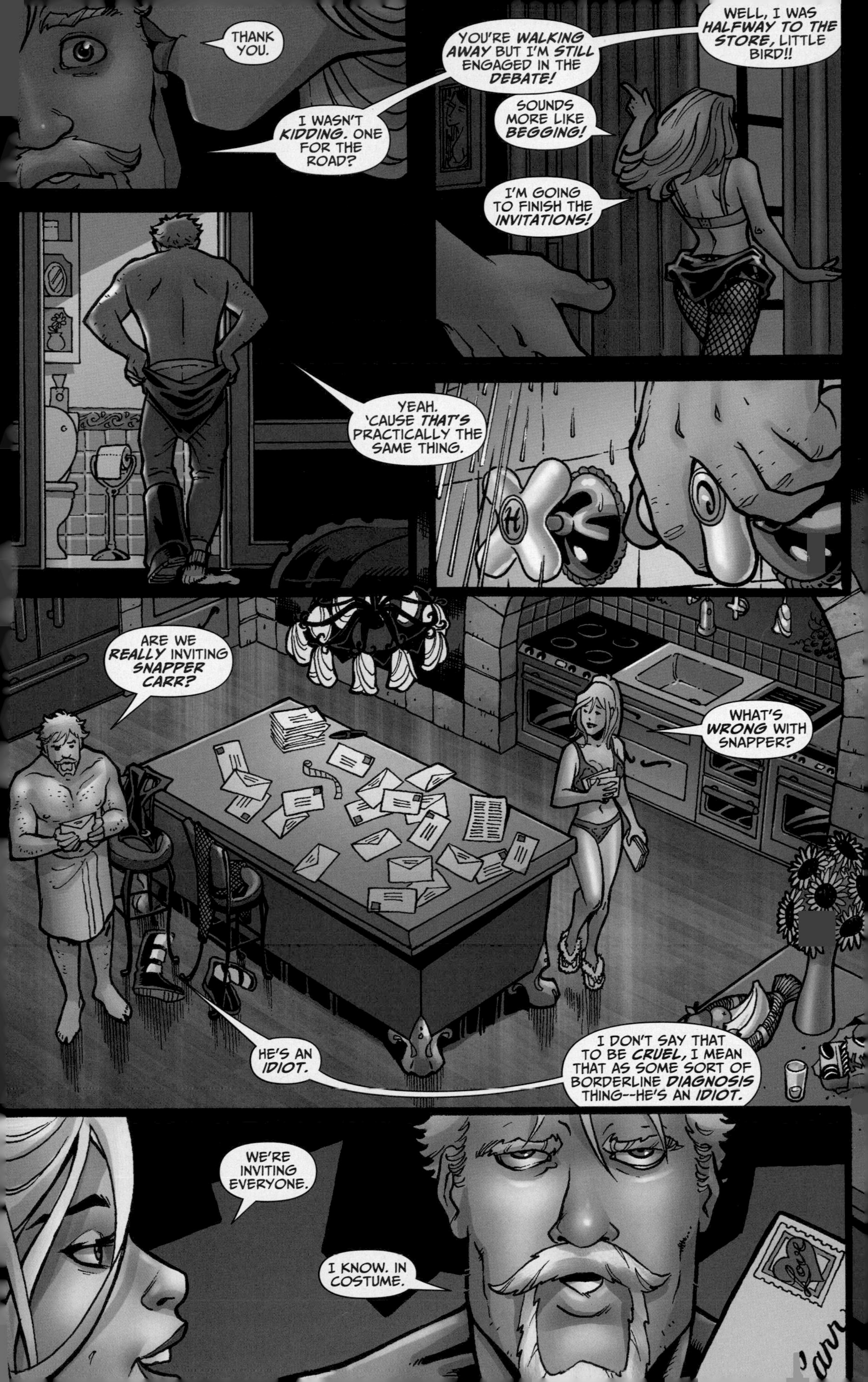

THANK YOU.
I WASN'T KIDDING. ONE FOR THE ROAD?
YOU'RE WALKING AWAY BUT I'M STILL ENGAGED IN THE DEBATE!
WELL, I WAS HALFWAY TO THE STORE, LITTLE BIRD!!
SOUNDS MORE LIKE BEGGING!
I'M GOING TO FINISH THE INVITATIONS!
YEAH. 'CAUSE THAT'S PRACTICALLY THE SAME THING.
ARE WE REALLY INVITING SNAPPER CARR?
WHAT'S WRONG WITH SNAPPER?
HE'S AN IDIOT.
I DON'T SAY THAT TO BE CRUEL, I MEAN THAT AS SOME SORT OF BORDERLINE DIAGNOSIS THING--HE'S AN IDIOT.
WE'RE INVITING EVERYONE.
I KNOW. IN COSTUME.

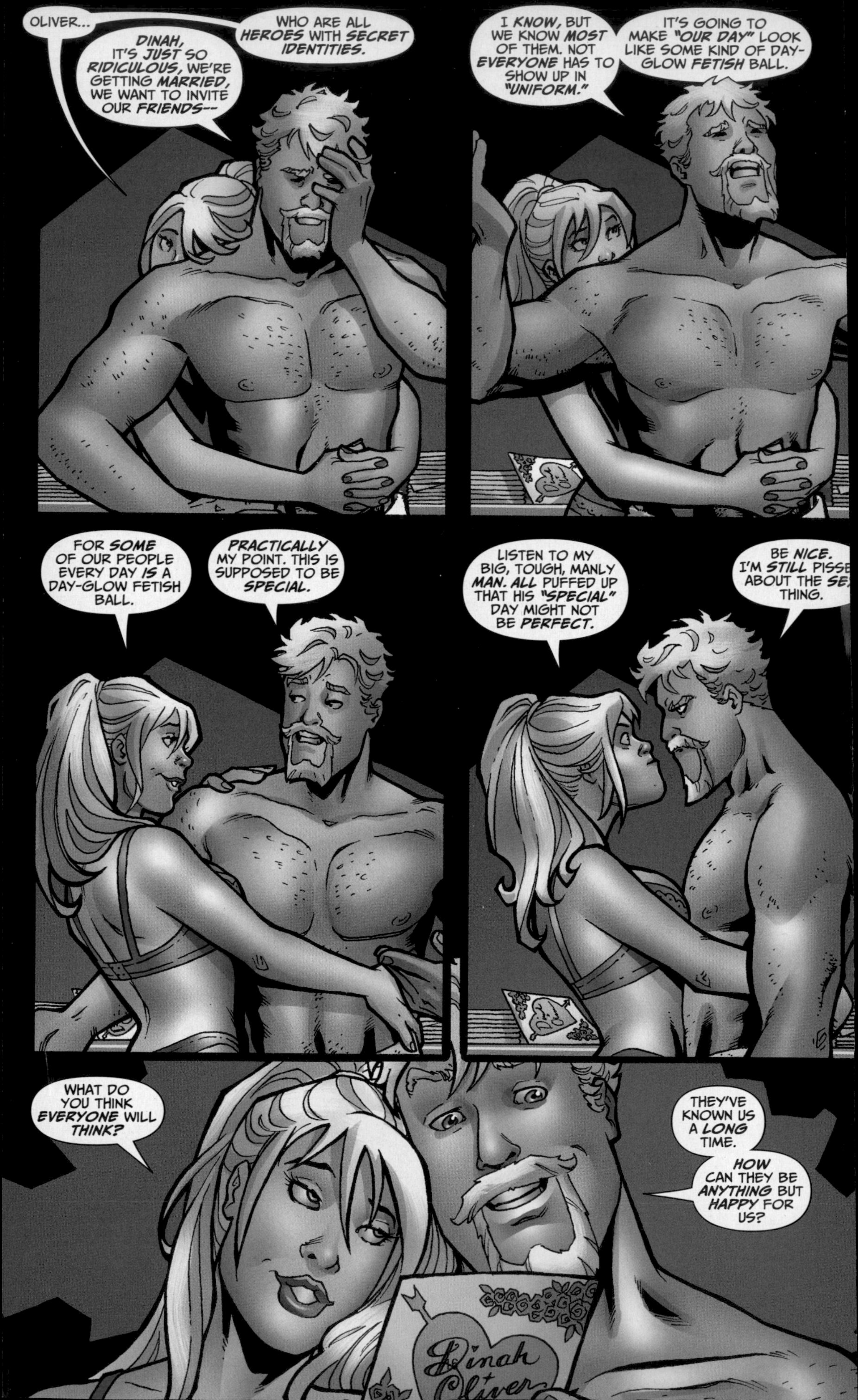
OLIVER...
DINAH, IT'S JUST SO RIDICULOUS, WE'RE GETTING MARRIED, WE WANT TO INVITE OUR FRIENDS--
WHO ARE ALL HEROES WITH SECRET IDENTITIES.
I KNOW, BUT WE KNOW MOST OF THEM. NOT EVERYONE HAS TO SHOW UP IN "UNIFORM."
IT'S GOING TO MAKE "OUR DAY" LOOK LIKE SOME KIND OF DAY-GLOW FETISH BALL.
FOR SOME OF OUR PEOPLE EVERY DAY IS A DAY-GLOW FETISH BALL.
PRACTICALLY MY POINT. THIS IS SUPPOSED TO BE SPECIAL.
LISTEN TO MY BIG, TOUGH, MANLY MAN. ALL PUFFED UP THAT HIS "SPECIAL" DAY MIGHT NOT BE PERFECT.
BE NICE. I'M STILL PISSE ABOUT THE SE THING.
WHAT DO YOU THINK EVERYONE WILL THINK?
THEY'VE KNOWN US A LONG TIME.
HOW CAN THEY BE ANYTHING BUT HAPPY FOR US?
Dinah + Oliver

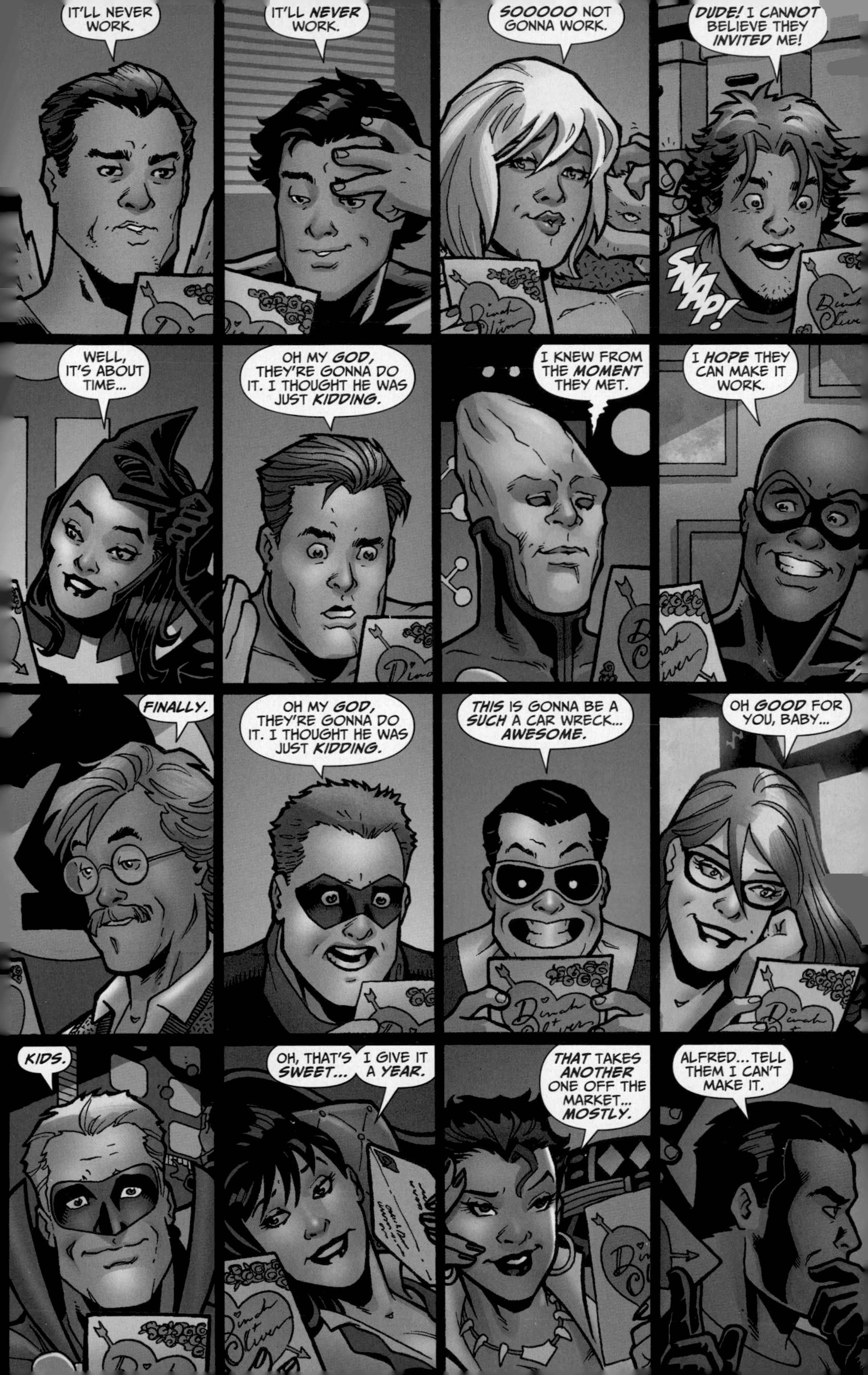
IT'LL NEVER WORK.
IT'LL NEVER WORK.
SOOOOO NOT GONNA WORK.
DUDE! I CANNOT BELIEVE THEY INVITED ME!
SNAP!
WELL, IT'S ABOUT TIME...
OH MY GOD, THEY'RE GONNA DO IT. I THOUGHT HE WAS JUST KIDDING.
I KNEW FROM THE MOMENT THEY MET.
I HOPE THEY CAN MAKE IT WORK.
FINALLY.
OH MY GOD, THEY'RE GONNA DO IT. I THOUGHT HE WAS JUST KIDDING.
THIS IS GONNA BE A SUCH A CAR WRECK... AWESOME.
OH GOOD FOR YOU, BABY...
KIDS.
OH, THAT'S SWEET...
I GIVE IT A YEAR.
THAT TAKES ANOTHER ONE OFF THE MARKET... MOSTLY.
ALFRED...TELL THEM I CAN'T MAKE IT.

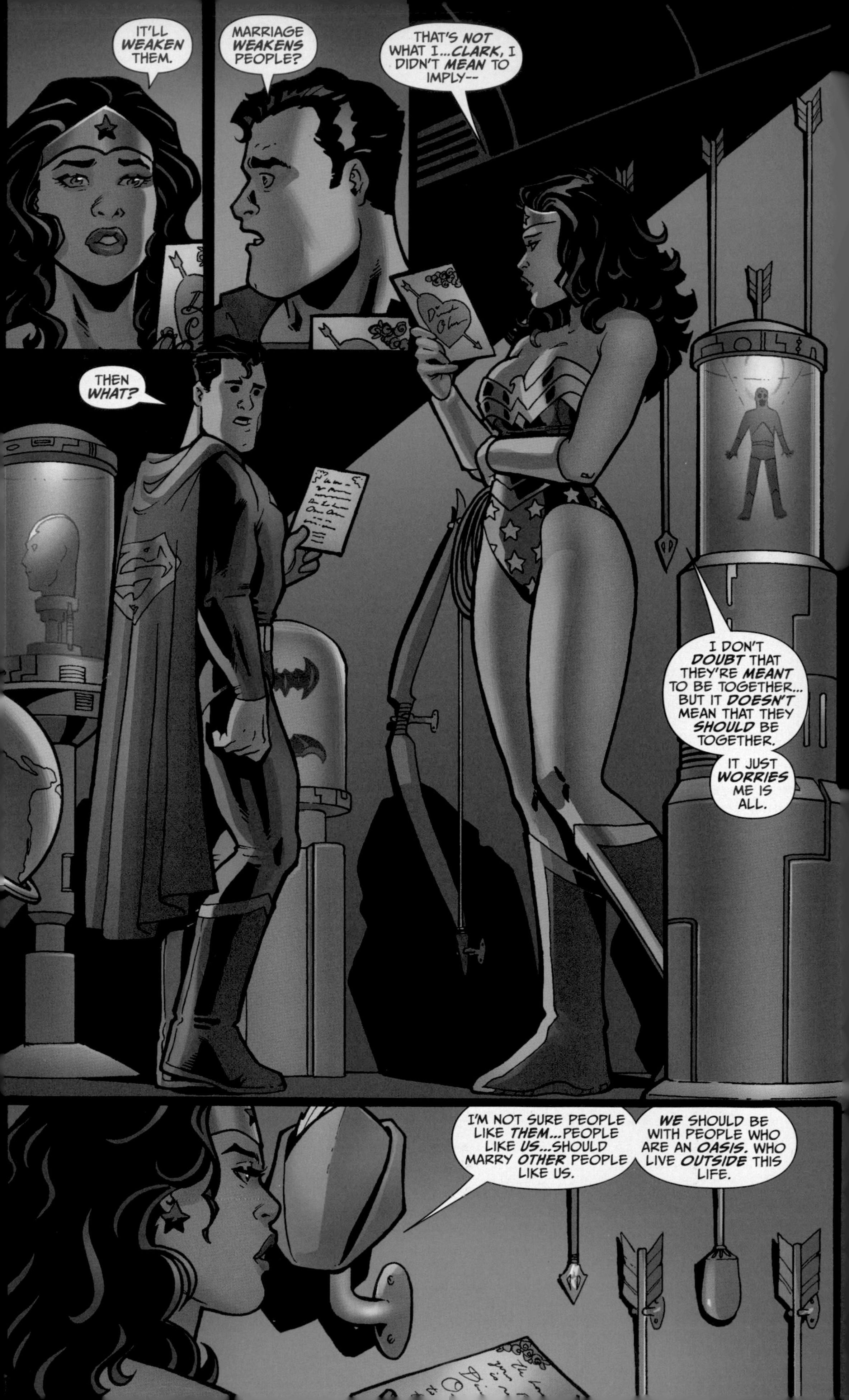
IT'LL WEAKEN THEM.
MARRIAGE WEAKENS PEOPLE?
THAT'S NOT WHAT I...CLARK, I DIDN'T MEAN TO IMPLY--
THEN WHAT?
I DON'T DOUBT THAT THEY'RE MEANT TO BE TOGETHER... BUT IT DOESN'T MEAN THAT THEY SHOULD BE TOGETHER.
IT JUST WORRIES ME IS ALL.
I'M NOT SURE PEOPLE LIKE THEM...PEOPLE LIKE US...SHOULD MARRY OTHER PEOPLE LIKE US.
WE SHOULD BE WITH PEOPLE WHO ARE AN OASIS. WHO LIVE OUTSIDE THIS LIFE.

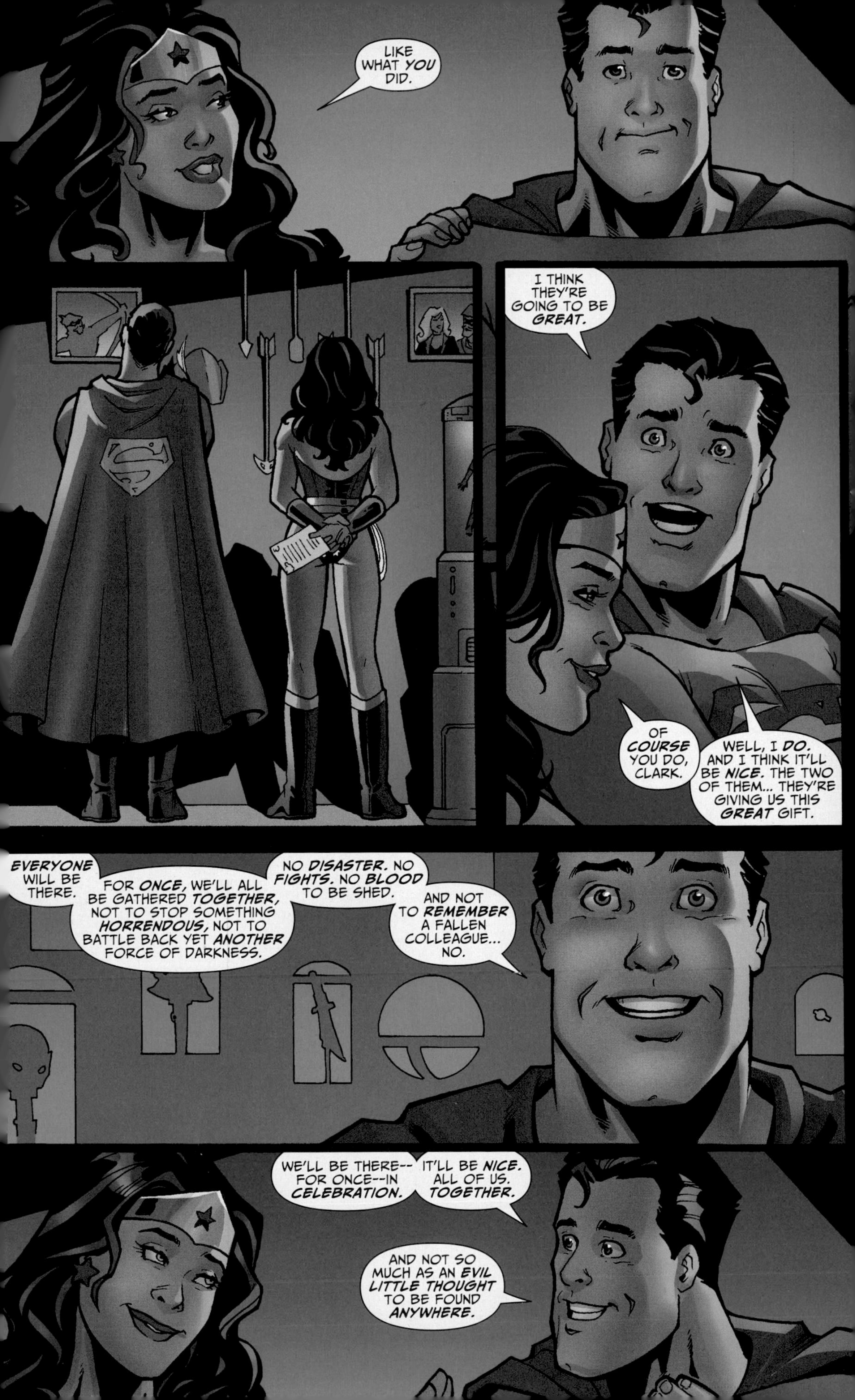
LIKE WHAT YOU DID.
I THINK THEY'RE GOING TO BE GREAT.
OF COURSE YOU DO, CLARK.
WELL, I DO. AND I THINK IT'LL BE NICE. THE TWO OF THEM... THEY'RE GIVING US THIS GREAT GIFT.
EVERYONE WILL BE THERE.
FOR ONCE, WE'LL ALL BE GATHERED TOGETHER, NOT TO STOP SOMETHING HORRENDOUS, NOT TO BATTLE BACK YET ANOTHER FORCE OF DARKNESS.
NO DISASTER. NO FIGHTS. NO BLOOD TO BE SHED.
AND NOT TO REMEMBER A FALLEN COLLEAGUE... NO.
WE'LL BE THERE-- FOR ONCE--IN CELEBRATION.
IT'LL BE NICE. ALL OF US. TOGETHER.
AND NOT SO MUCH AS AN EVIL LITTLE THOUGHT TO BE FOUND ANYWHERE.

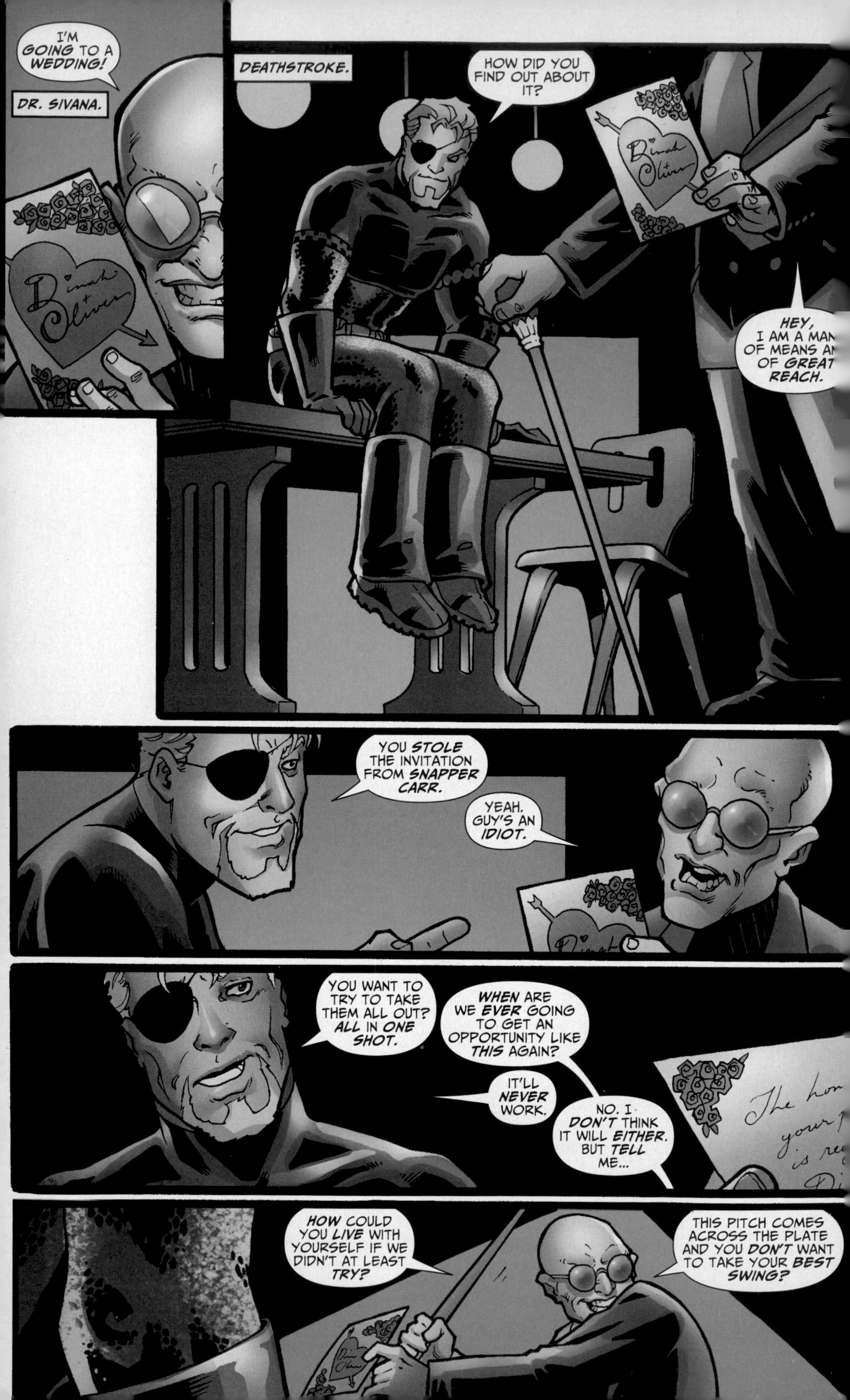
I'M GOING TO A WEDDING!
DR. SIVANA.
DEATHSTROKE.
HOW DID YOU FIND OUT ABOUT IT?
HEY, I AM A MAN OF MEANS AN OF GREAT REACH.
YOU STOLE THE INVITATION FROM SNAPPER CARR.
YEAH. GUY'S AN IDIOT.
YOU WANT TO TRY TO TAKE THEM ALL OUT? ALL IN ONE SHOT.
WHEN ARE WE EVER GOING TO GET AN OPPORTUNITY LIKE THIS AGAIN?
IT'LL NEVER WORK.
NO. I DON'T THINK IT WILL EITHER. BUT TELL ME...
HOW COULD YOU LIVE WITH YOURSELF IF WE DIDN'T AT LEAST TRY?
THIS PITCH COMES ACROSS THE PLATE AND YOU DON'T WANT TO TAKE YOUR BEST SWING?

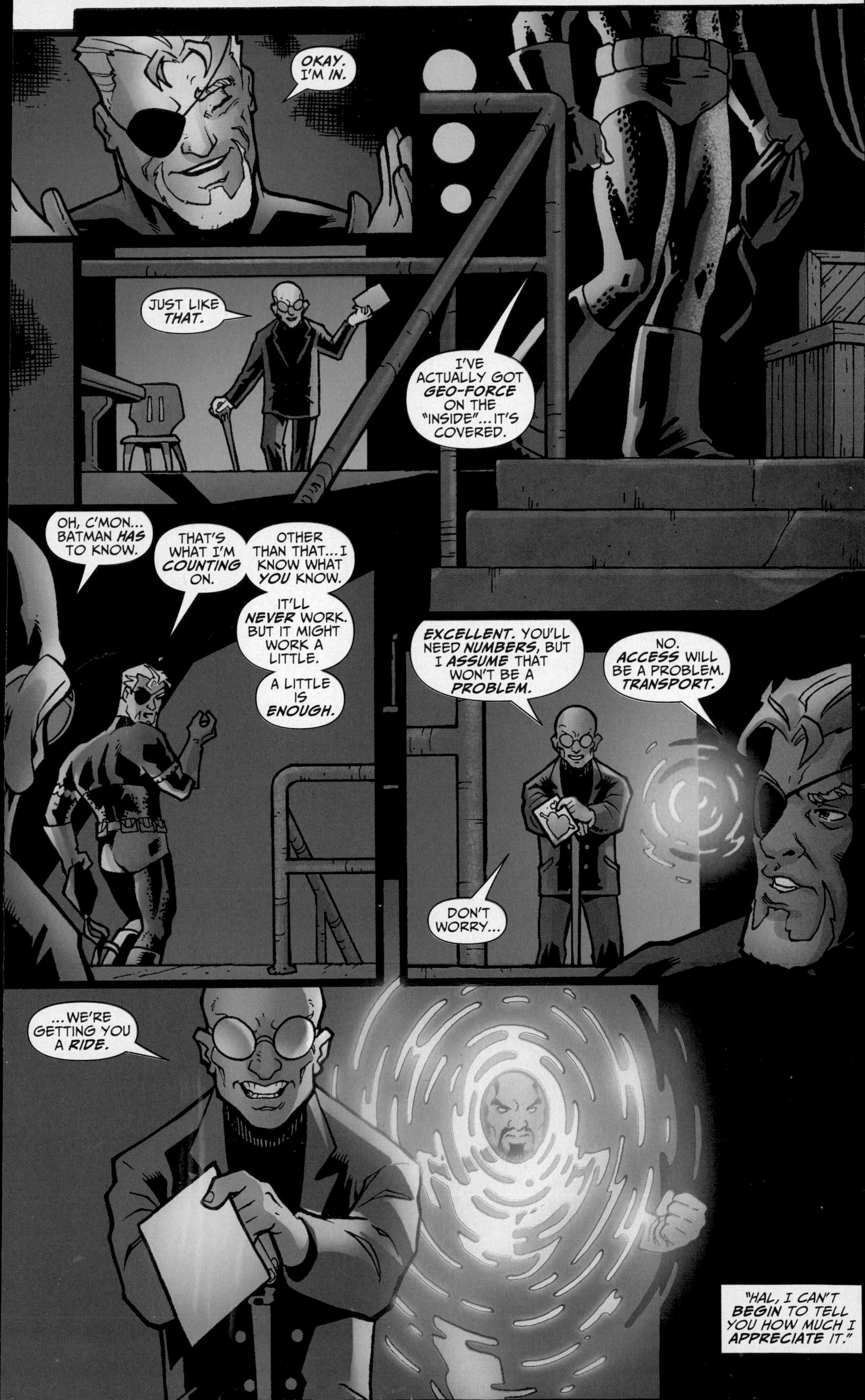
OKAY. I'M IN.
JUST LIKE THAT.
I'VE ACTUALLY GOT GEO-FORCE ON THE "INSIDE"... IT'S COVERED.
OH, C'MON... BATMAN HAS TO KNOW.
THAT'S WHAT I'M COUNTING ON.
OTHER THAN THAT... I KNOW WHAT YOU KNOW.
IT'LL NEVER WORK. BUT IT MIGHT WORK A LITTLE.
A LITTLE IS ENOUGH.
EXCELLENT. YOU'LL NEED NUMBERS, BUT I ASSUME THAT WON'T BE A PROBLEM.
NO. ACCESS WILL BE A PROBLEM. TRANSPORT.
DON'T WORRY...
...WE'RE GETTING YOU A RIDE.
"HAL, I CAN'T BEGIN TO TELL YOU HOW MUCH I APPRECIATE IT."

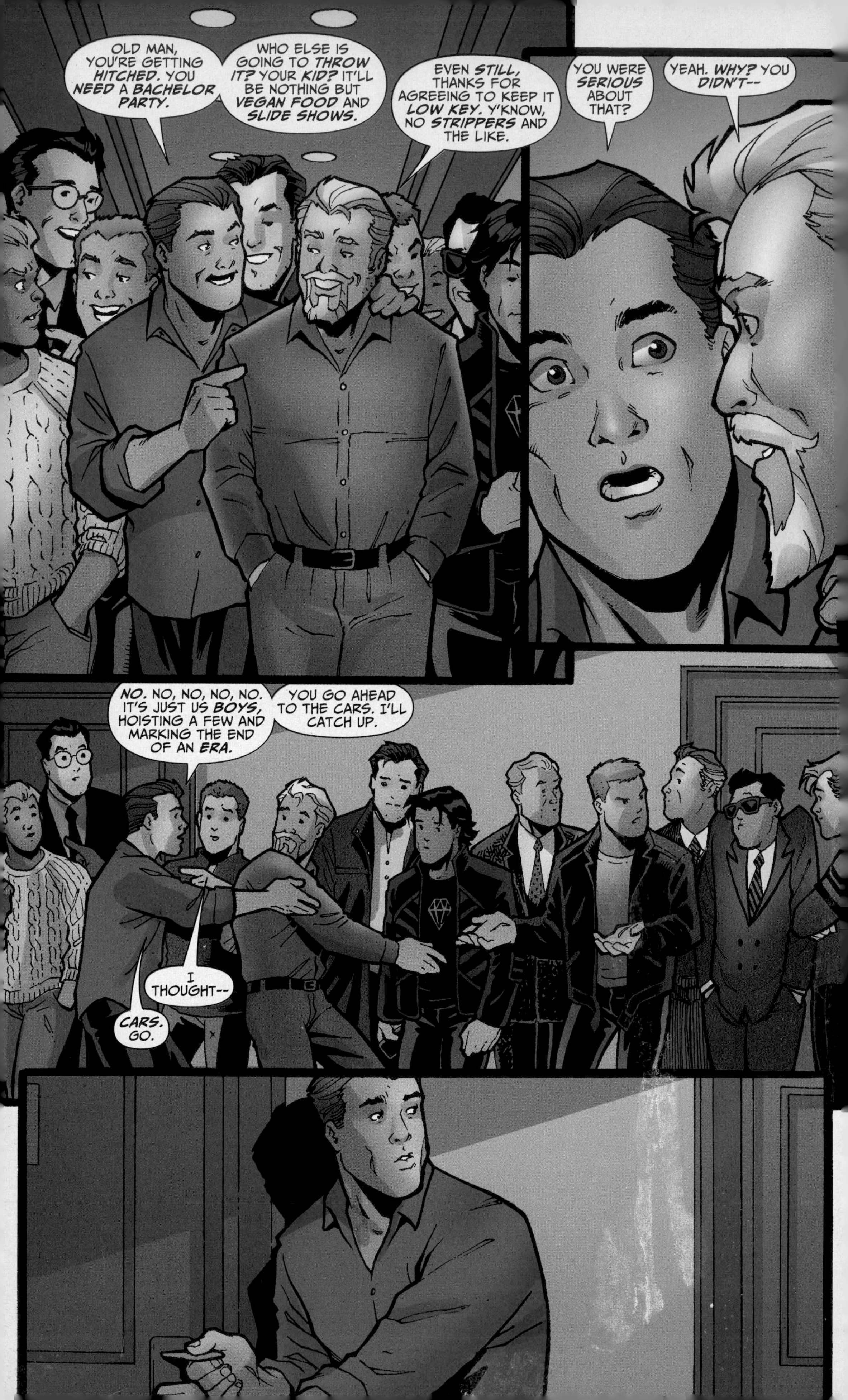
OLD MAN, YOU'RE GETTING HITCHED. YOU NEED A BACHELOR PARTY.
WHO ELSE IS GOING TO THROW IT? YOUR KID? IT'LL BE NOTHING BUT VEGAN FOOD AND SLIDE SHOWS.
EVEN STILL, THANKS FOR AGREEING TO KEEP IT LOW KEY. Y'KNOW, NO STRIPPERS AND THE LIKE.
YOU WERE SERIOUS ABOUT THAT?
YEAH. WHY? YOU DIDN'T--
NO. NO, NO, NO, NO. IT'S JUST US BOYS, HOISTING A FEW AND MARKING THE END OF AN ERA.
YOU GO AHEAD TO THE CARS. I'LL CATCH UP.
I THOUGHT--
CARS. GO.

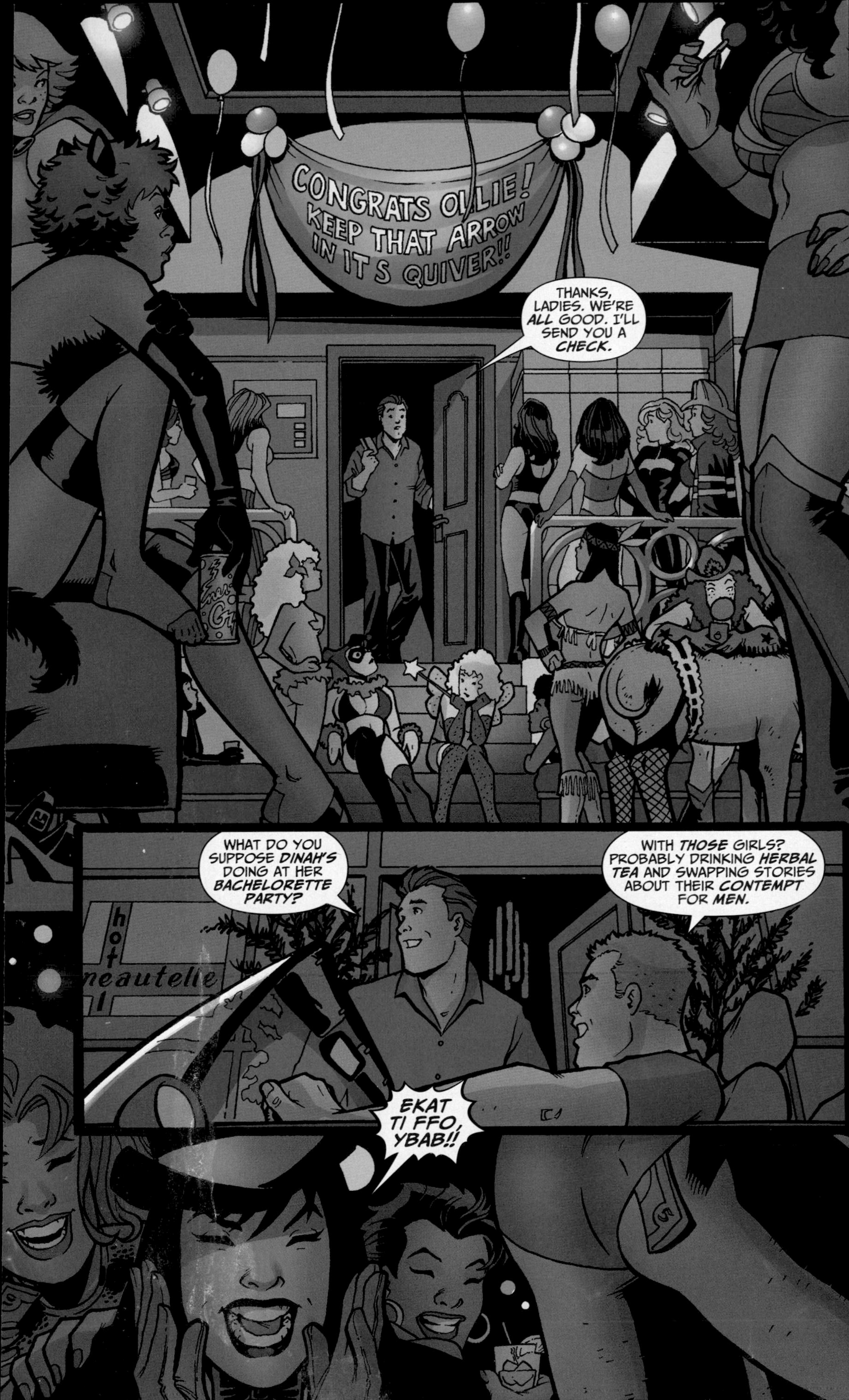
CONGRATS OLLIE! KEEP THAT ARROW IN IT'S QUIVER!!
THANKS, LADIES. WE'RE ALL GOOD. I'LL SEND YOU A CHECK.
WHAT DO YOU SUPPOSE DINAH'S DOING AT HER BACHELORETTE PARTY?
WITH THOSE GIRLS? PROBABLY DRINKING HERBAL TEA AND SWAPPING STORIES ABOUT THEIR CONTEMPT FOR MEN.
EKAT TI FFO, YBAB!!

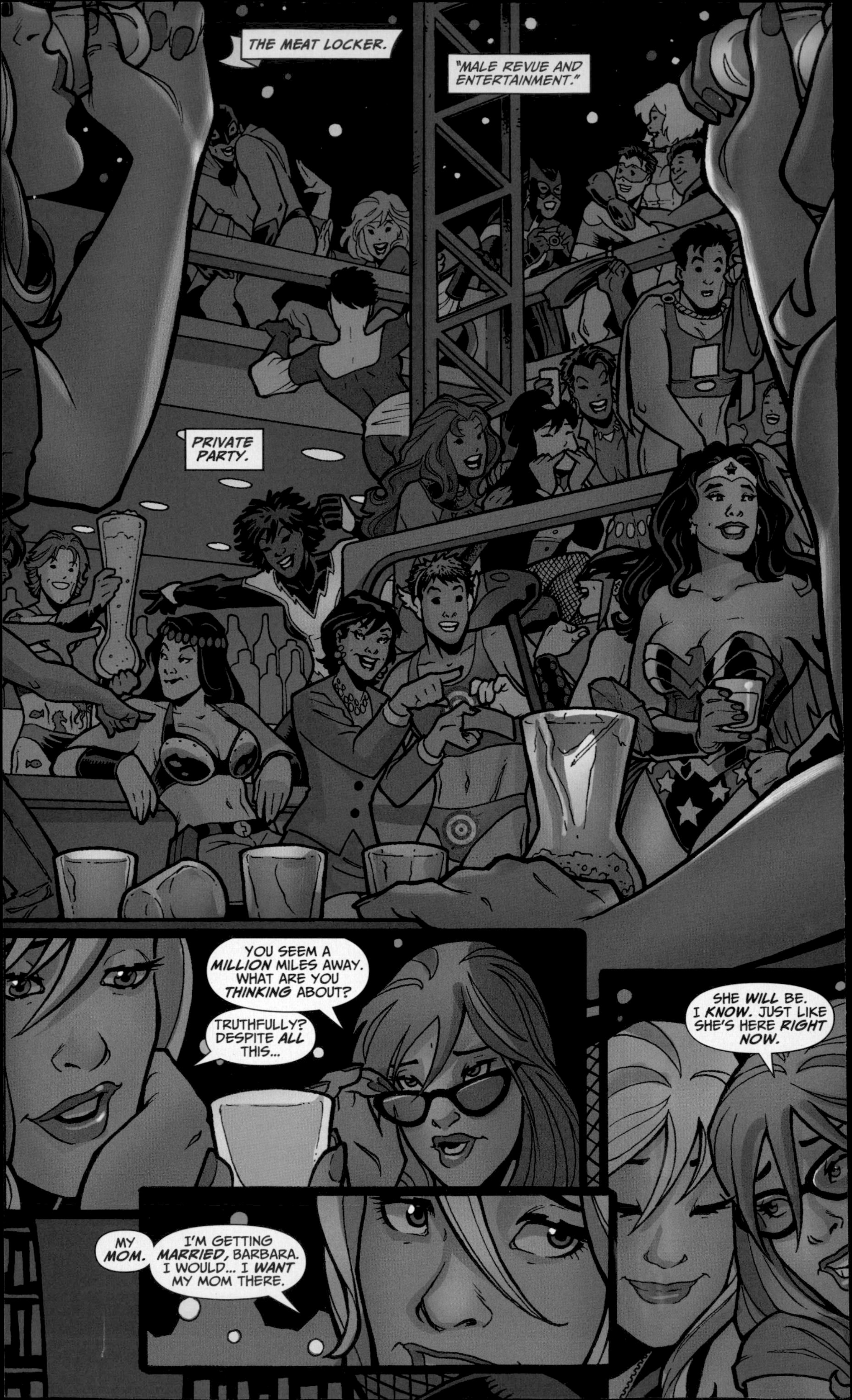
THE MEAT LOCKER.
"MALE REVUE AND ENTERTAINMENT."
PRIVATE PARTY.
YOU SEEM A MILLION MILES AWAY. WHAT ARE YOU THINKING ABOUT?
TRUTHFULLY? DESPITE ALL THIS...
MY MOM.
I'M GETTING MARRIED, BARBARA. I WOULD... I WANT MY MOM THERE.
SHE WILL BE. I KNOW. JUST LIKE SHE'S HERE RIGHT NOW.

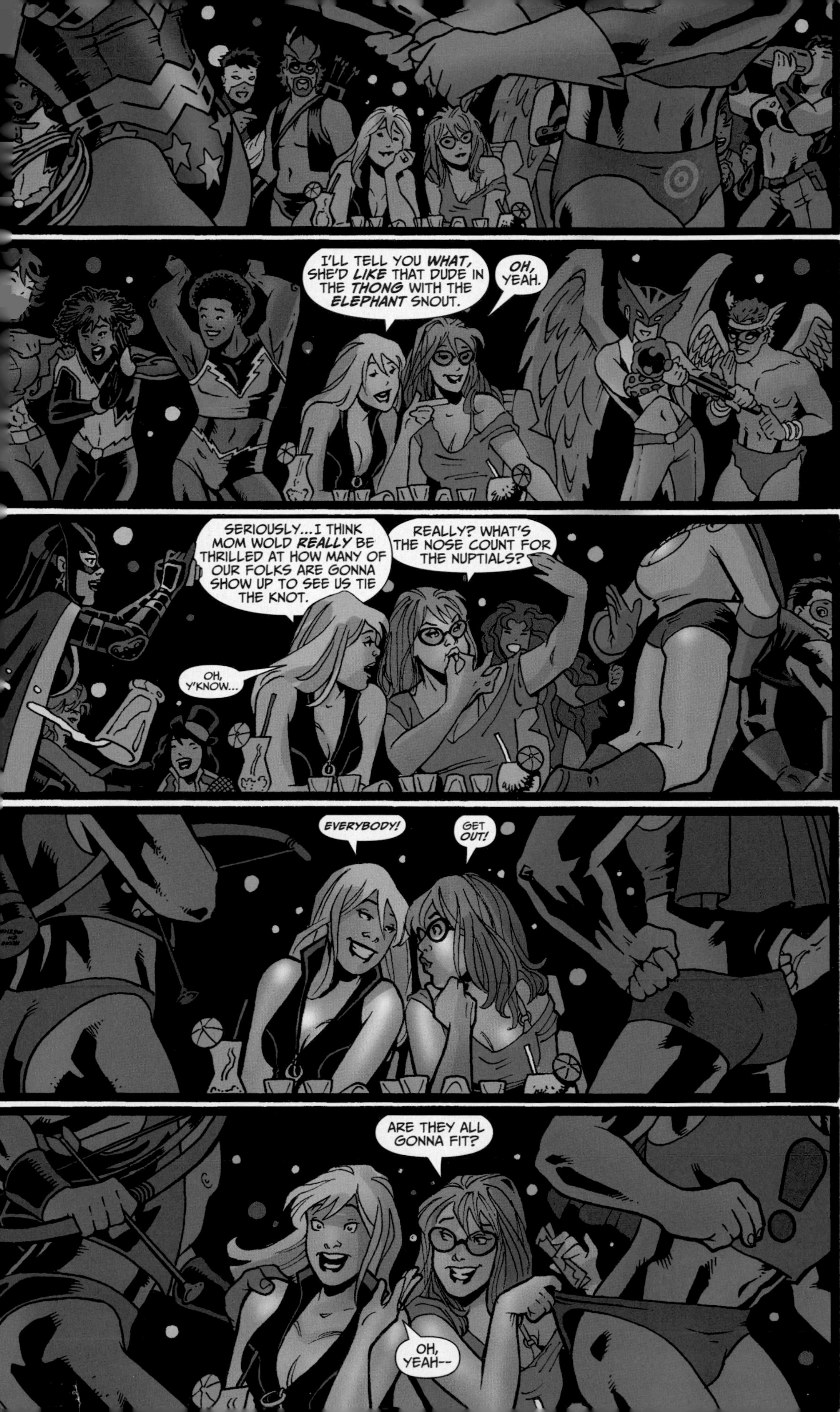
I'LL TELL YOU WHAT, SHE'D LIKE THAT DUDE IN THE THONG WITH THE ELEPHANT SNOUT.
OH, YEAH.
SERIOUSLY...I THINK MOM WOLD REALLY BE THRILLED AT HOW MANY OF OUR FOLKS ARE GONNA SHOW UP TO SEE US TIE THE KNOT.
REALLY? WHAT'S THE NOSE COUNT FOR THE NUPTIALS?
OH, Y'KNOW...
EVERYBODY!
GET OUT!
ARE THEY ALL GONNA FIT?
OH, YEAH--

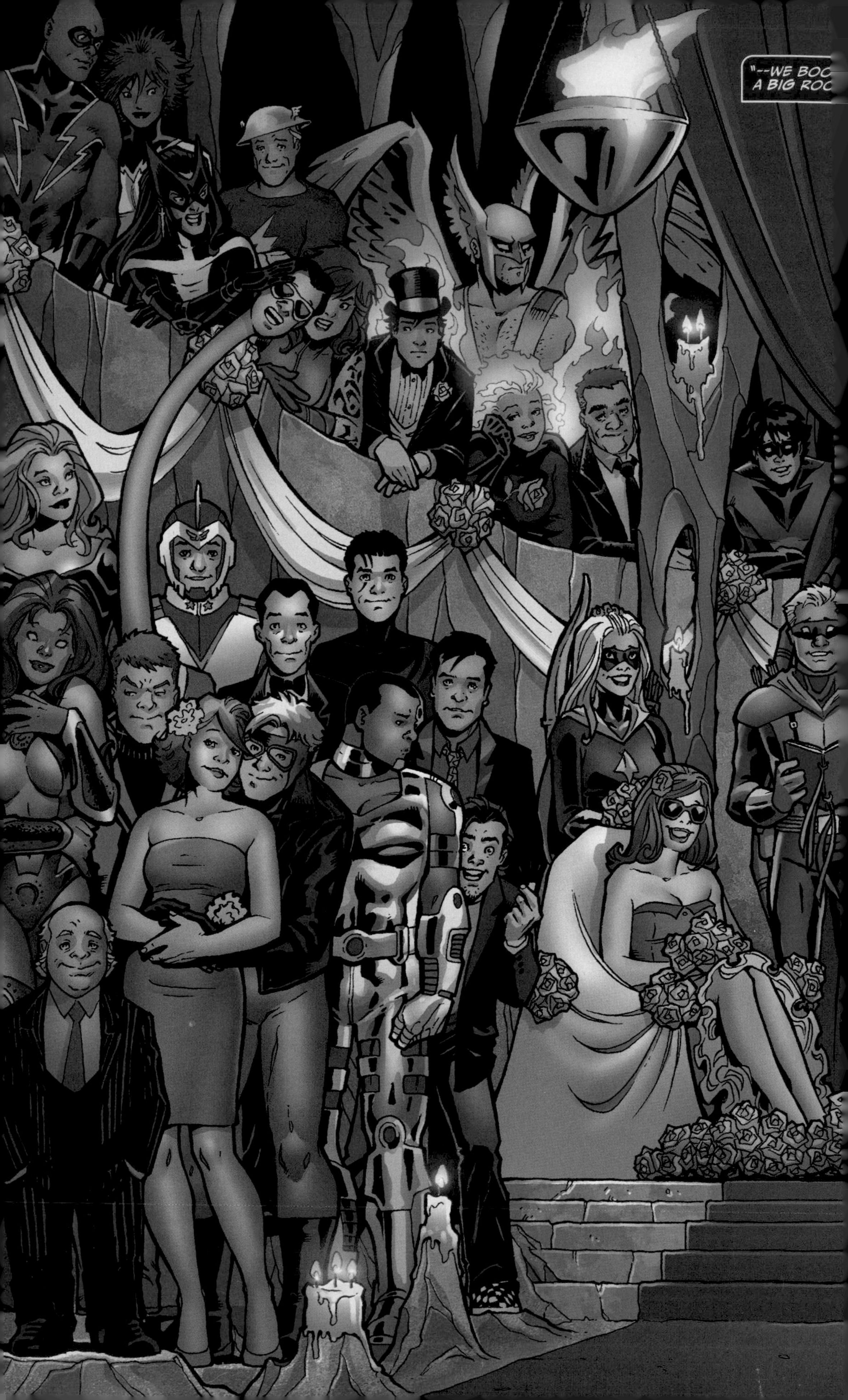
"--WE BOO
A BIG ROC

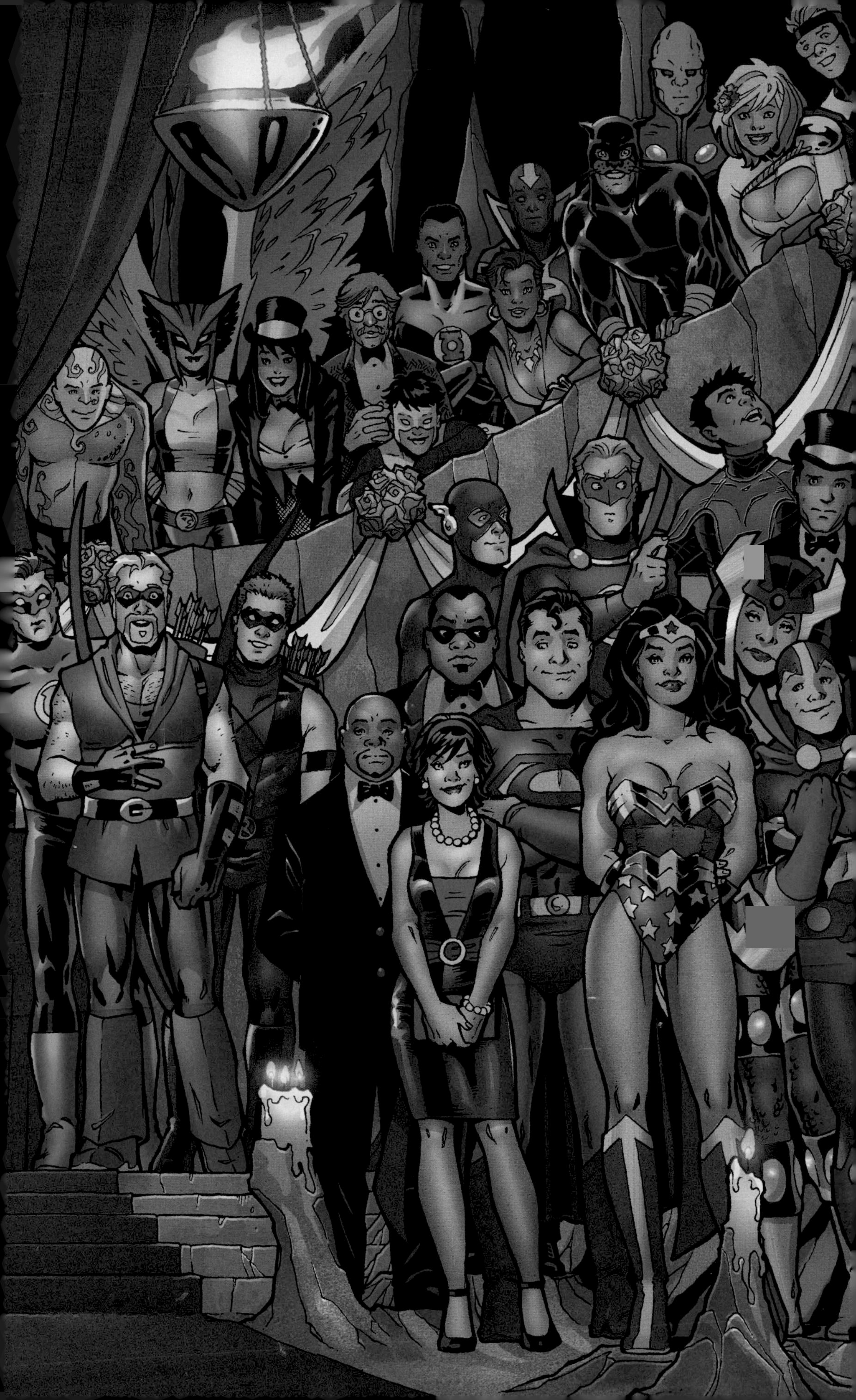

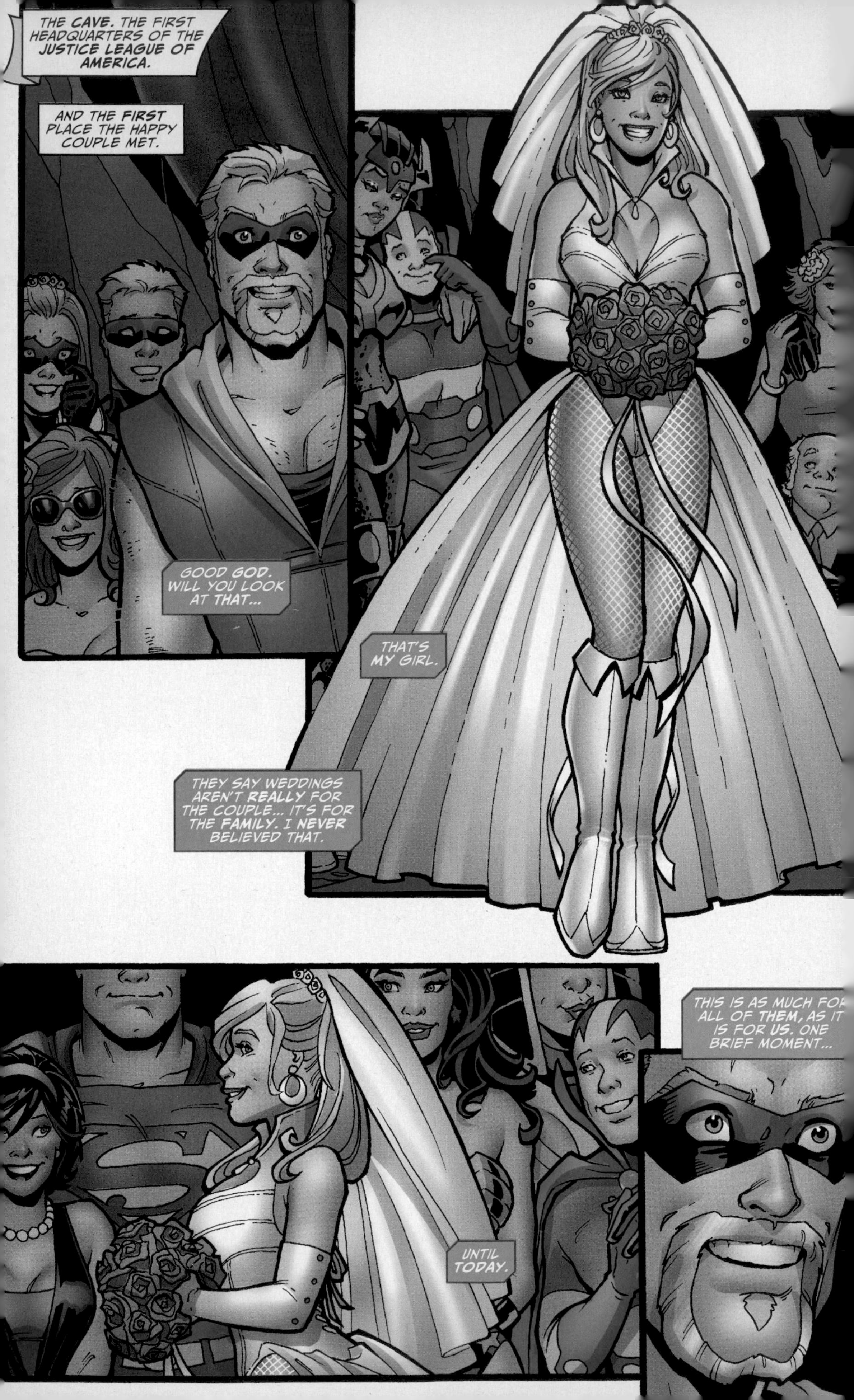
THE CAVE. THE FIRST HEADQUARTERS OF THE JUSTICE LEAGUE OF AMERICA.
AND THE FIRST PLACE THE HAPPY COUPLE MET.
GOOD GOD. WILL YOU LOOK AT THAT...
THAT'S MY GIRL.
THEY SAY WEDDINGS AREN'T REALLY FOR THE COUPLE... IT'S FOR THE FAMILY. I NEVER BELIEVED THAT.
UNTIL TODAY.
THIS IS AS MUCH FOR ALL OF THEM, AS IT IS FOR US. ONE BRIEF MOMENT...

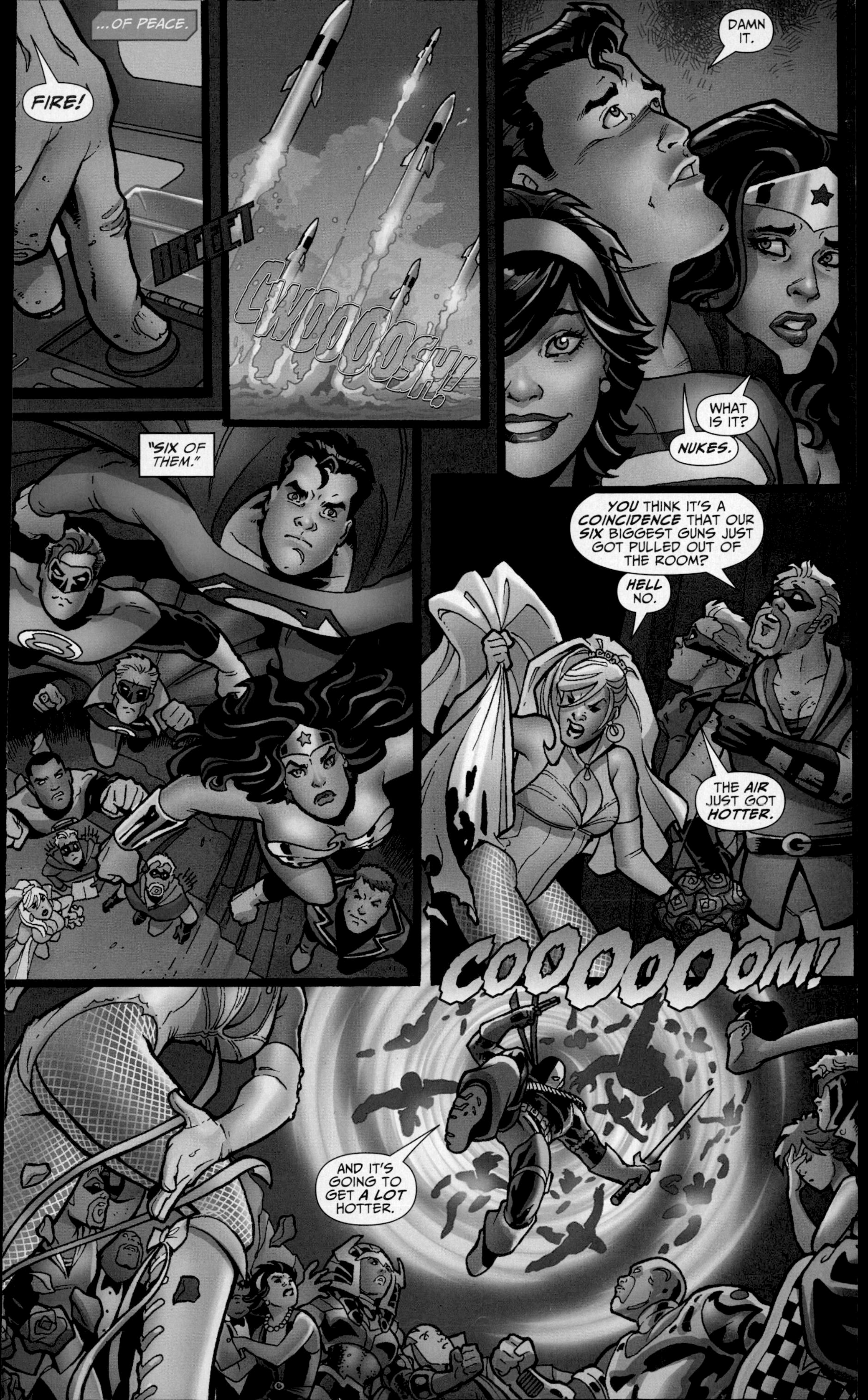
...OF PEACE.
FIRE!
BREEET
CWOOOOSH!!
DAMN IT.
WHAT IS IT?
NUKES.
"SIX OF THEM."
YOU THINK IT'S A COINCIDENCE THAT OUR SIX BIGGEST GUNS JUST GOT PULLED OUT OF THE ROOM?
HELL NO.
THE AIR JUST GOT HOTTER.
COOOOOOOM!
AND IT'S GOING TO GET A LOT HOTTER.

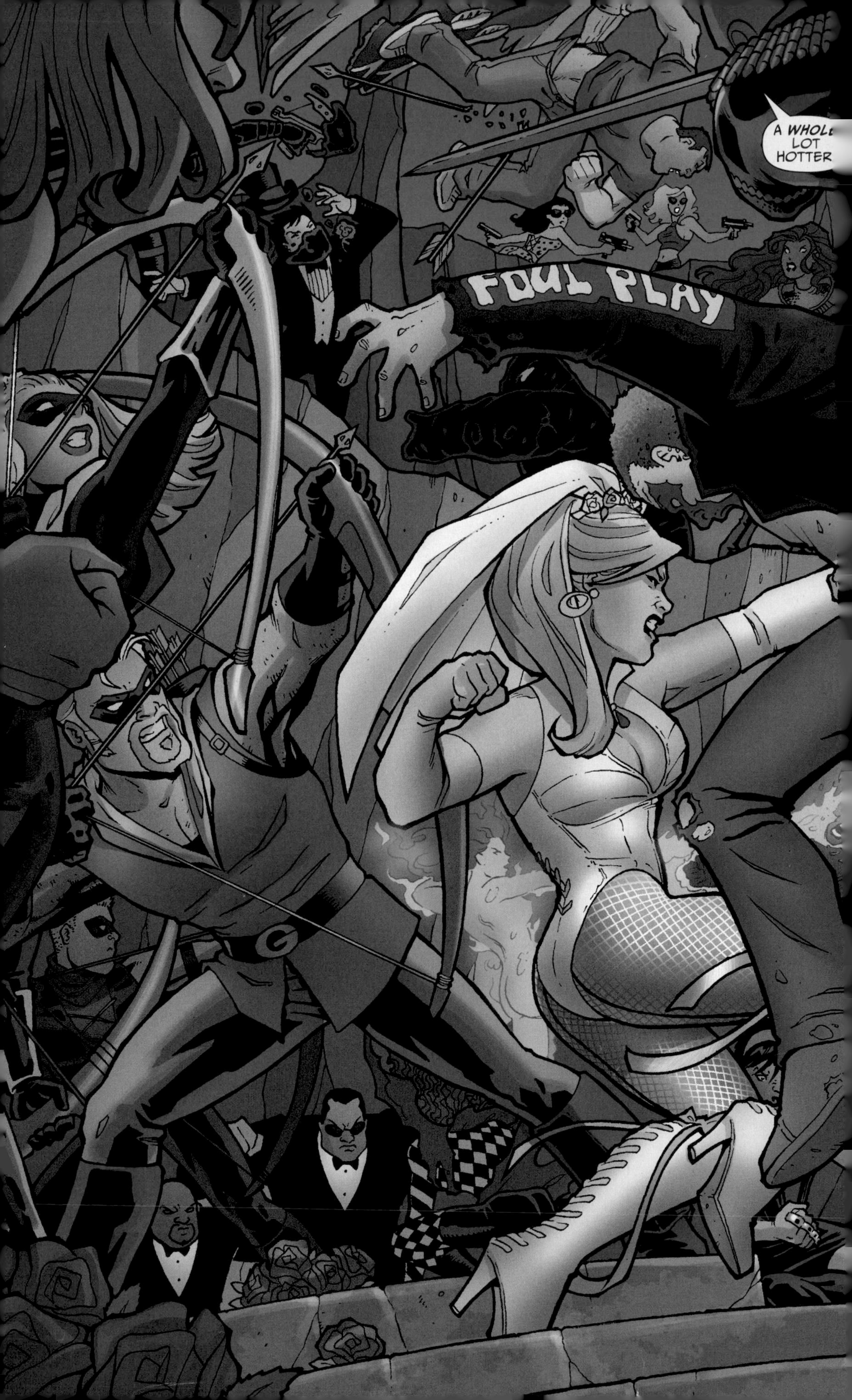
A WHOL
LOT
HOTTER
FOUL PLAY

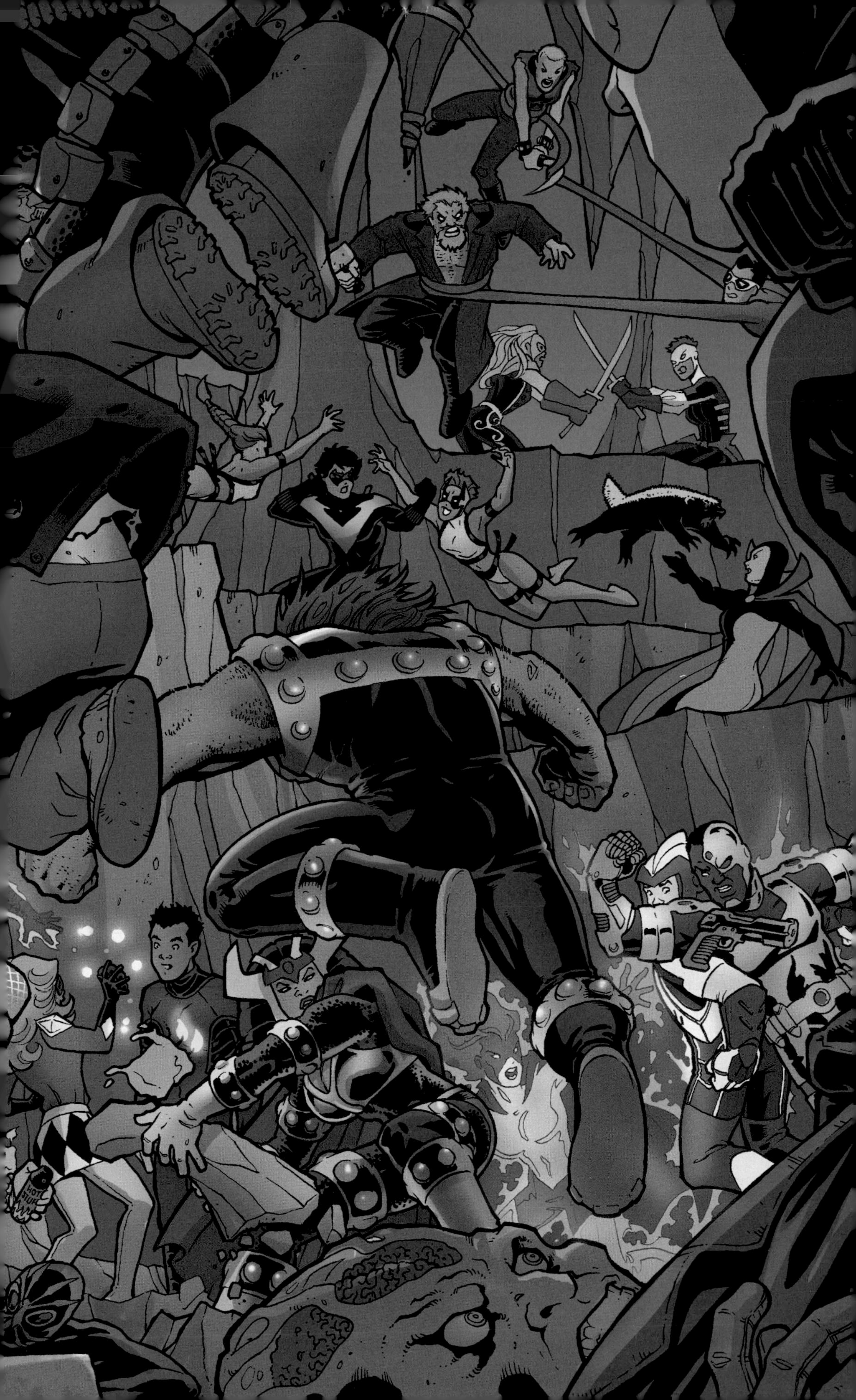

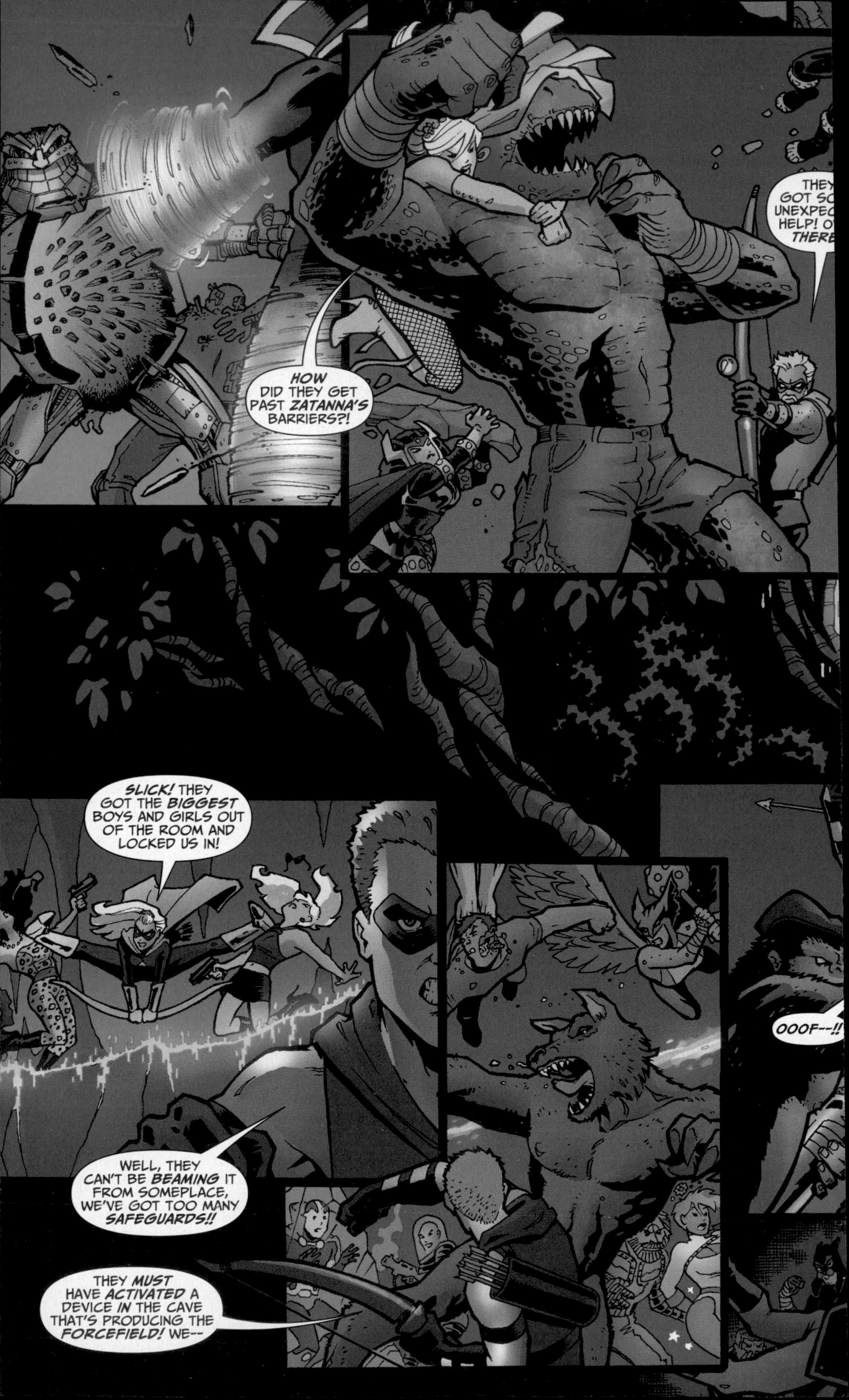
HOW DID THEY GET PAST ZATANNA'S BARRIERS?!
THEY GOT SO UNEXPEC HELP! O THERE
SLICK! THEY GOT THE BIGGEST BOYS AND GIRLS OUT OF THE ROOM AND LOCKED US IN!
WELL, THEY CAN'T BE BEAMING IT FROM SOMEPLACE, WE'VE GOT TOO MANY SAFEGUARDS!!
THEY MUST HAVE ACTIVATED A DEVICE IN THE CAVE THAT'S PRODUCING THE FORCEFIELD! WE--
OOOF--!!

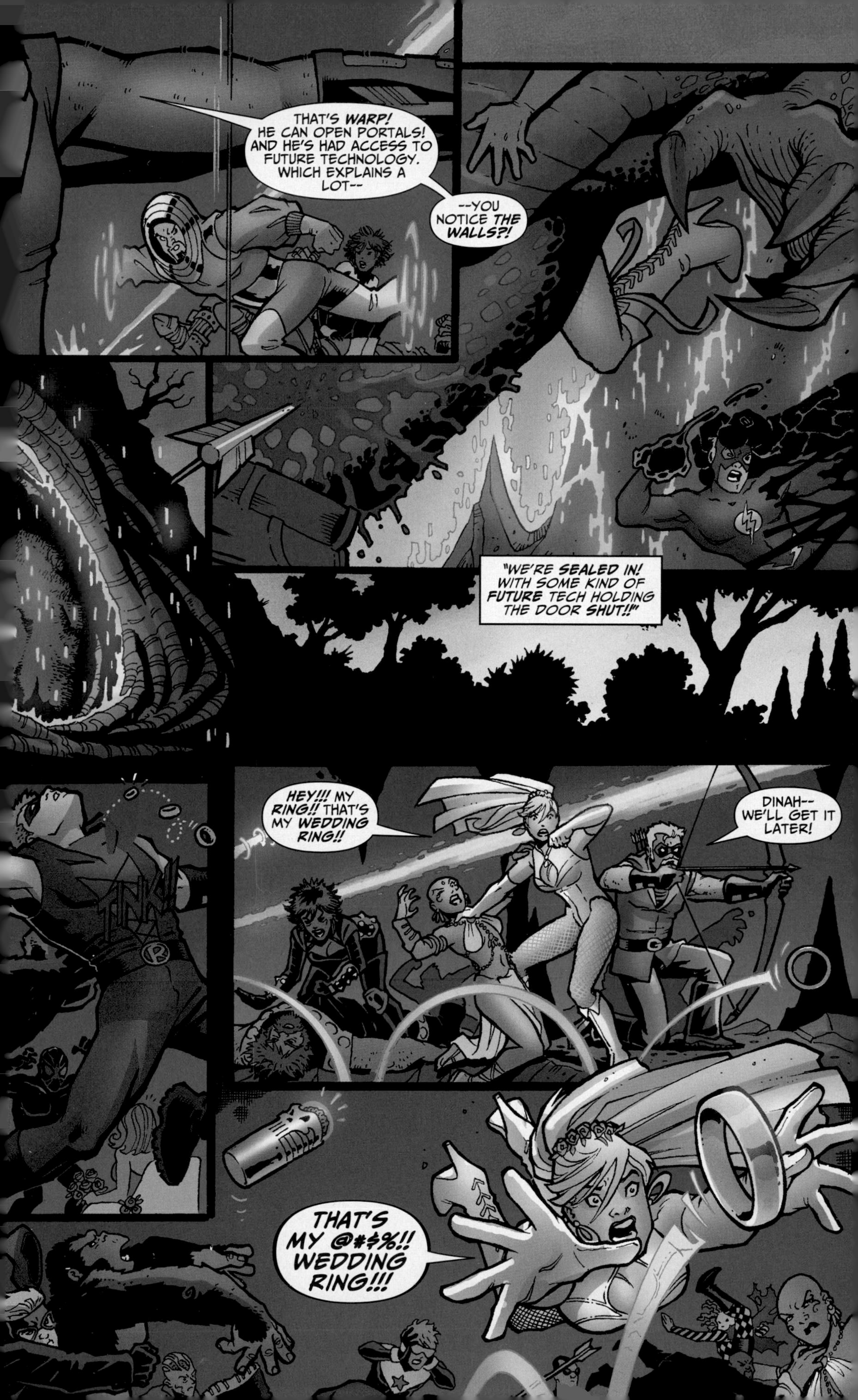
THAT'S WARP! HE CAN OPEN PORTALS! AND HE'S HAD ACCESS TO FUTURE TECHNOLOGY. WHICH EXPLAINS A LOT--
--YOU NOTICE THE WALLS?!
"WE'RE SEALED IN! WITH SOME KIND OF FUTURE TECH HOLDING THE DOOR SHUT!!"
HEY!!! MY RING!! THAT'S MY WEDDING RING!!
DINAH-- WE'LL GET IT LATER!
THAT'S MY @#$%!! WEDDING RING!!!

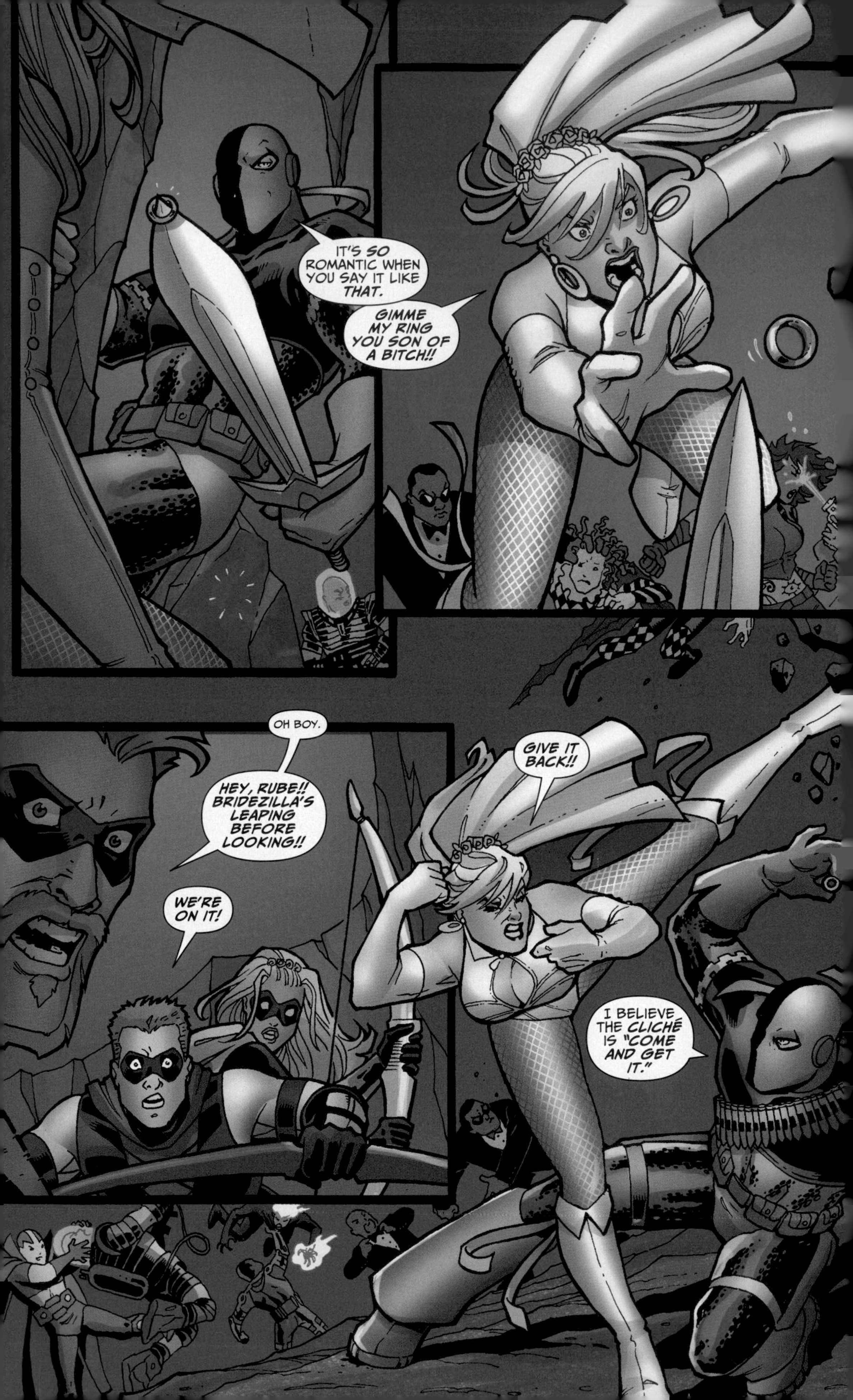
IT'S SO ROMANTIC WHEN YOU SAY IT LIKE THAT.
GIMME MY RING YOU SON OF A BITCH!!
OH BOY.
HEY, RUBE!! BRIDEZILLA'S LEAPING BEFORE LOOKING!!
WE'RE ON IT!
GIVE IT BACK!!
I BELIEVE THE CLICHÉ IS "COME AND GET IT."

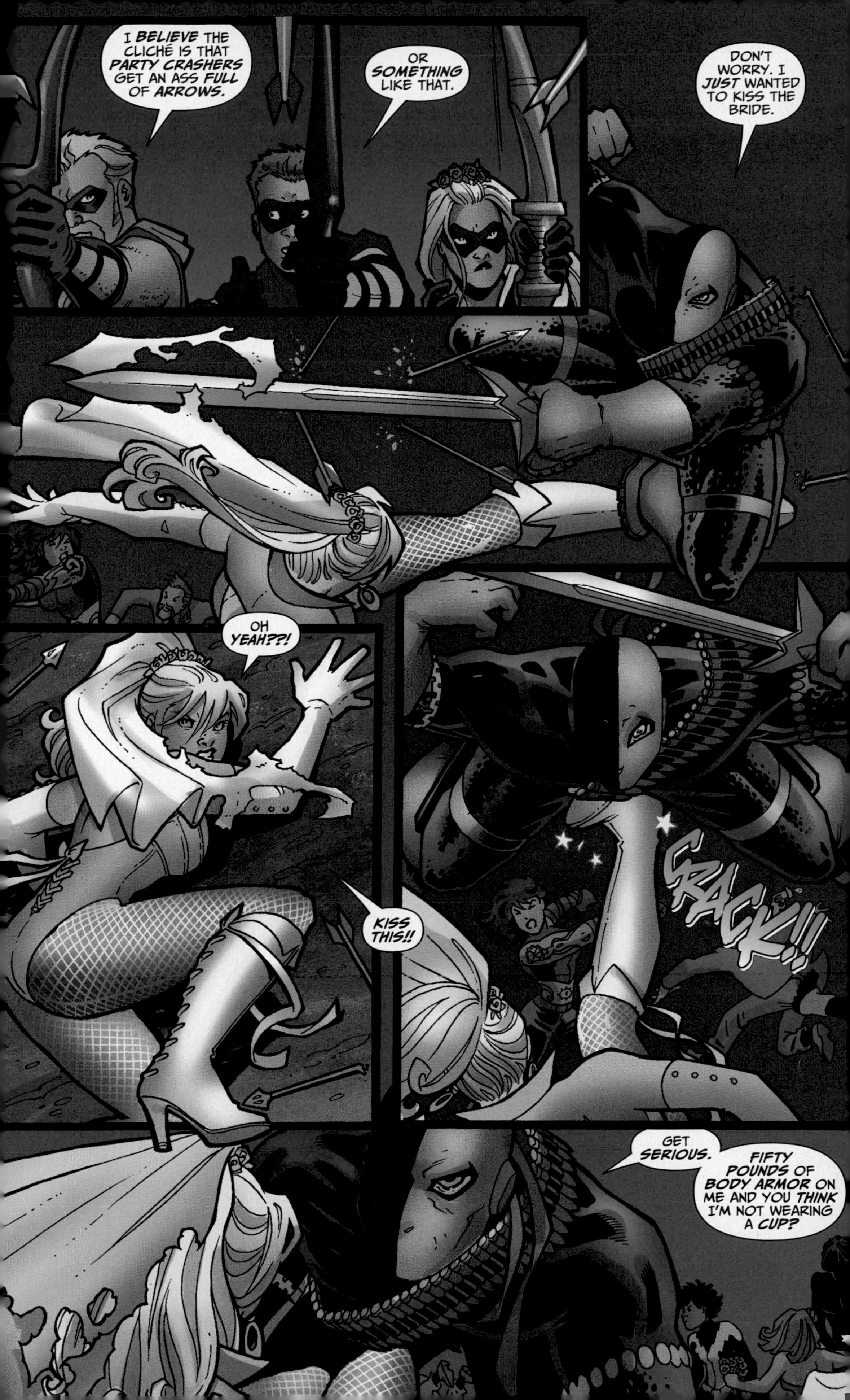

I BELIEVE THE CLICHÉ IS THAT PARTY CRASHERS GET AN ASS FULL OF ARROWS.
OR SOMETHING LIKE THAT.
DON'T WORRY. I JUST WANTED TO KISS THE BRIDE.
OH YEAH??!
KISS THIS!!
CRACK!!!
GET SERIOUS.
FIFTY POUNDS OF BODY ARMOR ON ME AND YOU THINK I'M NOT WEARING A CUP?

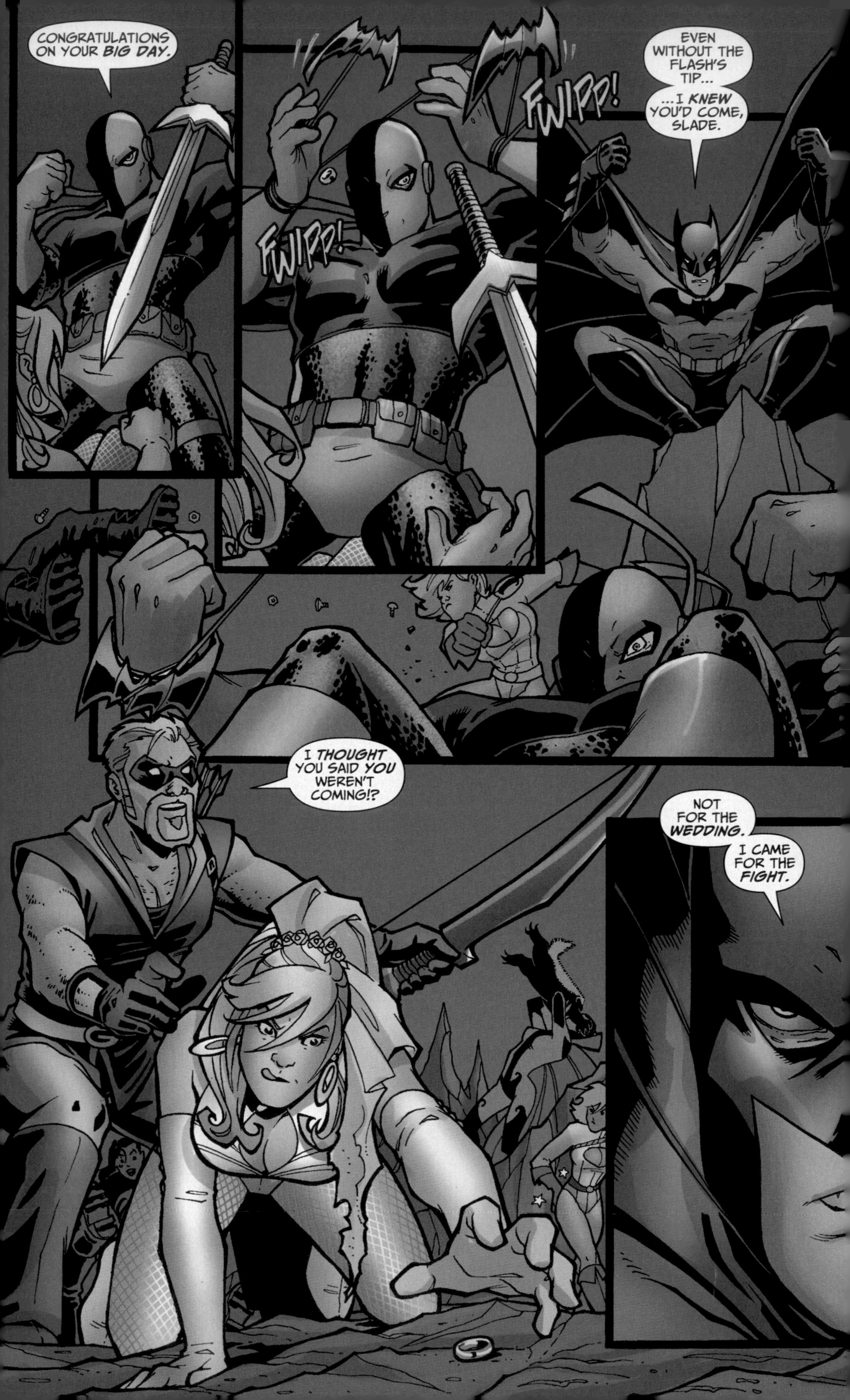
CONGRATULATIONS ON YOUR BIG DAY.
FWIPP!
FWIPP!
EVEN WITHOUT THE FLASH'S TIP...
...I KNEW YOU'D COME, SLADE.
I THOUGHT YOU SAID YOU WEREN'T COMING!?
NOT FOR THE WEDDING.
I CAME FOR THE FIGHT.

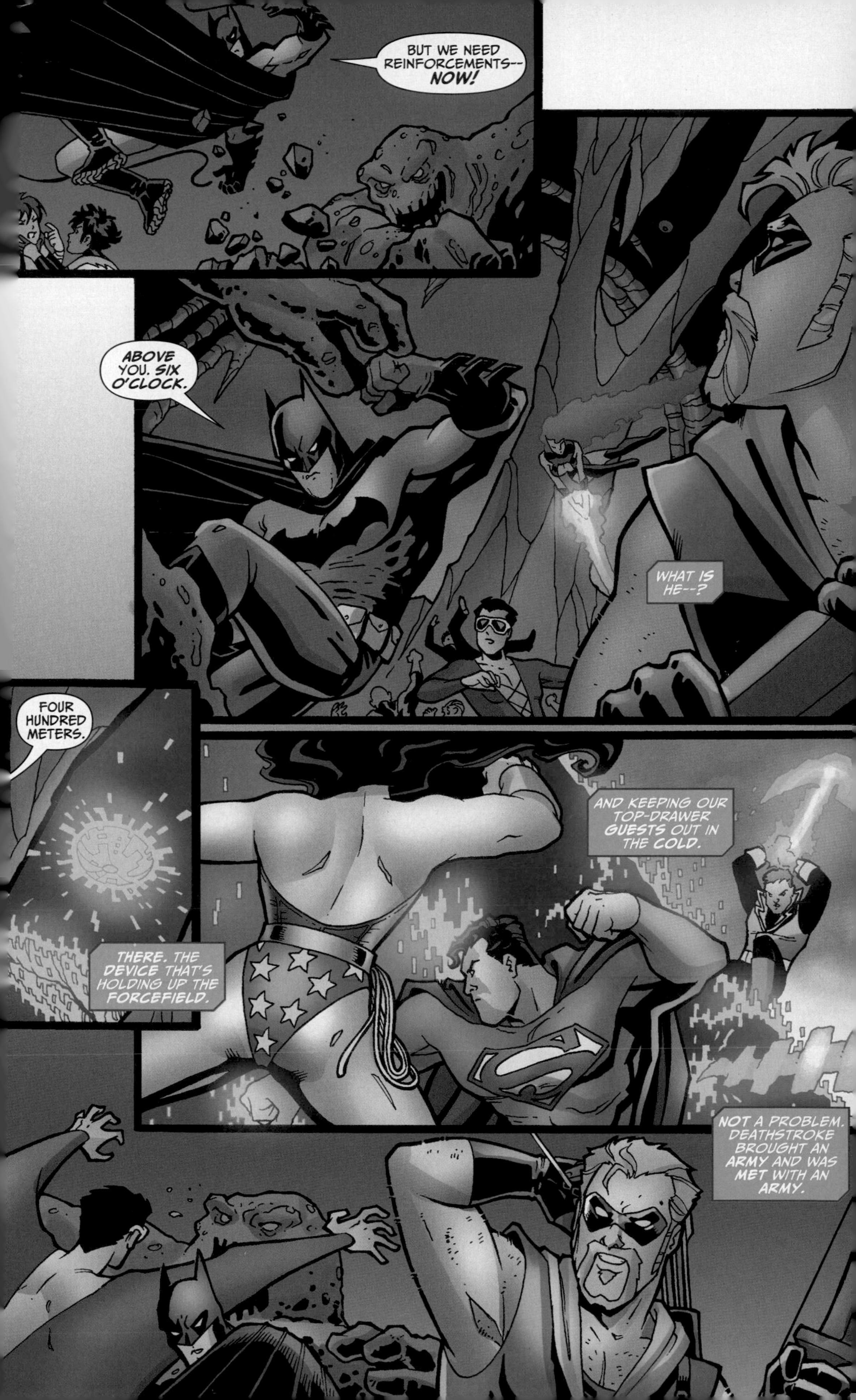
BUT WE NEED REINFORCEMENTS-- NOW!
ABOVE YOU. SIX O'CLOCK.
WHAT IS HE--?
FOUR HUNDRED METERS.
THERE. THE DEVICE THAT'S HOLDING UP THE FORCEFIELD.
AND KEEPING OUR TOP-DRAWER GUESTS OUT IN THE COLD.
NOT A PROBLEM. DEATHSTROKE BROUGHT AN ARMY AND WAS MET WITH AN ARMY.

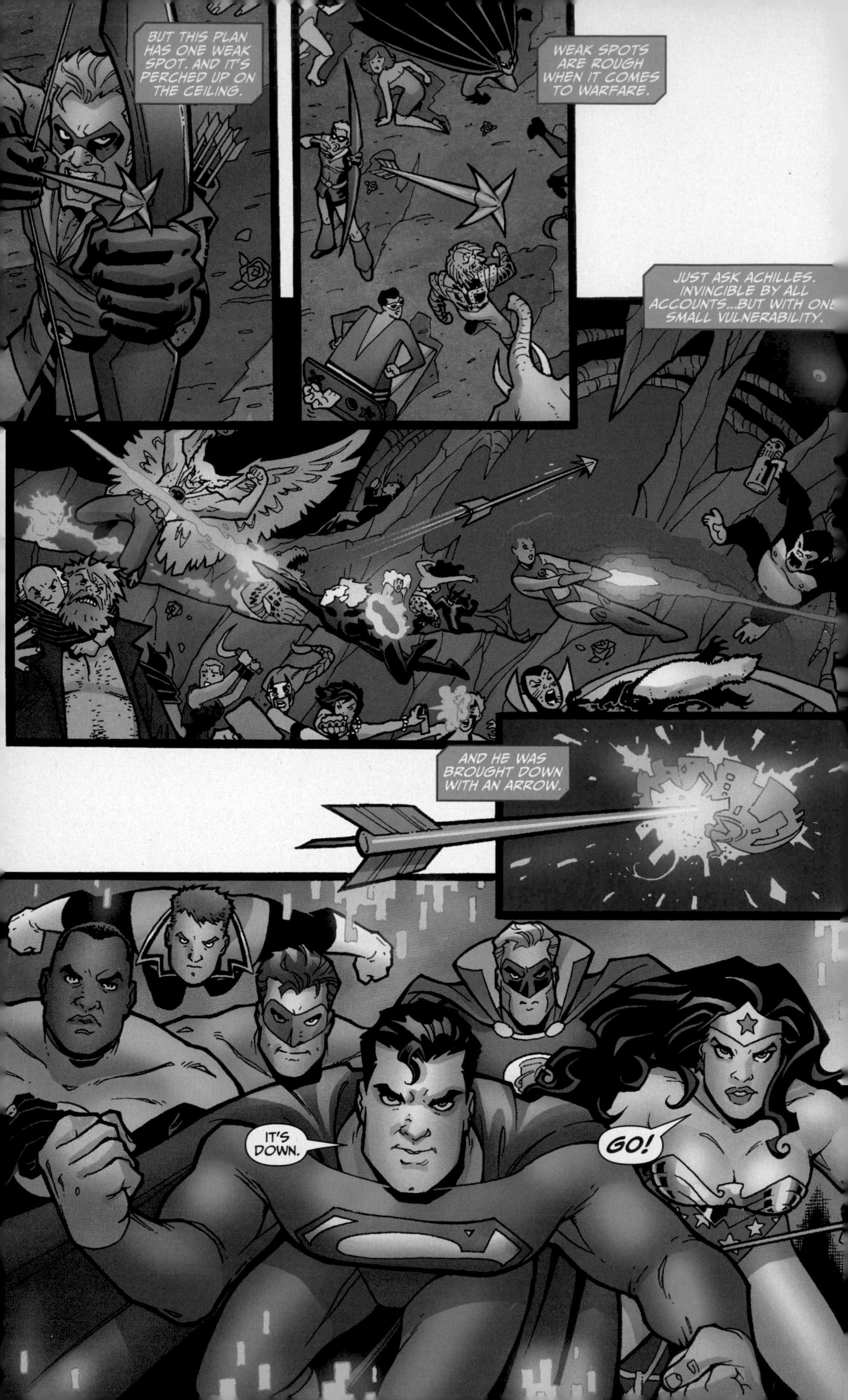
BUT THIS PLAN HAS ONE WEAK SPOT. AND IT'S PERCHED UP ON THE CEILING.
WEAK SPOTS ARE ROUGH WHEN IT COMES TO WARFARE.
JUST ASK ACHILLES. INVINCIBLE BY ALL ACCOUNTS...BUT WITH ONE SMALL VULNERABILITY.
AND HE WAS BROUGHT DOWN WITH AN ARROW.
IT'S DOWN.
GO!

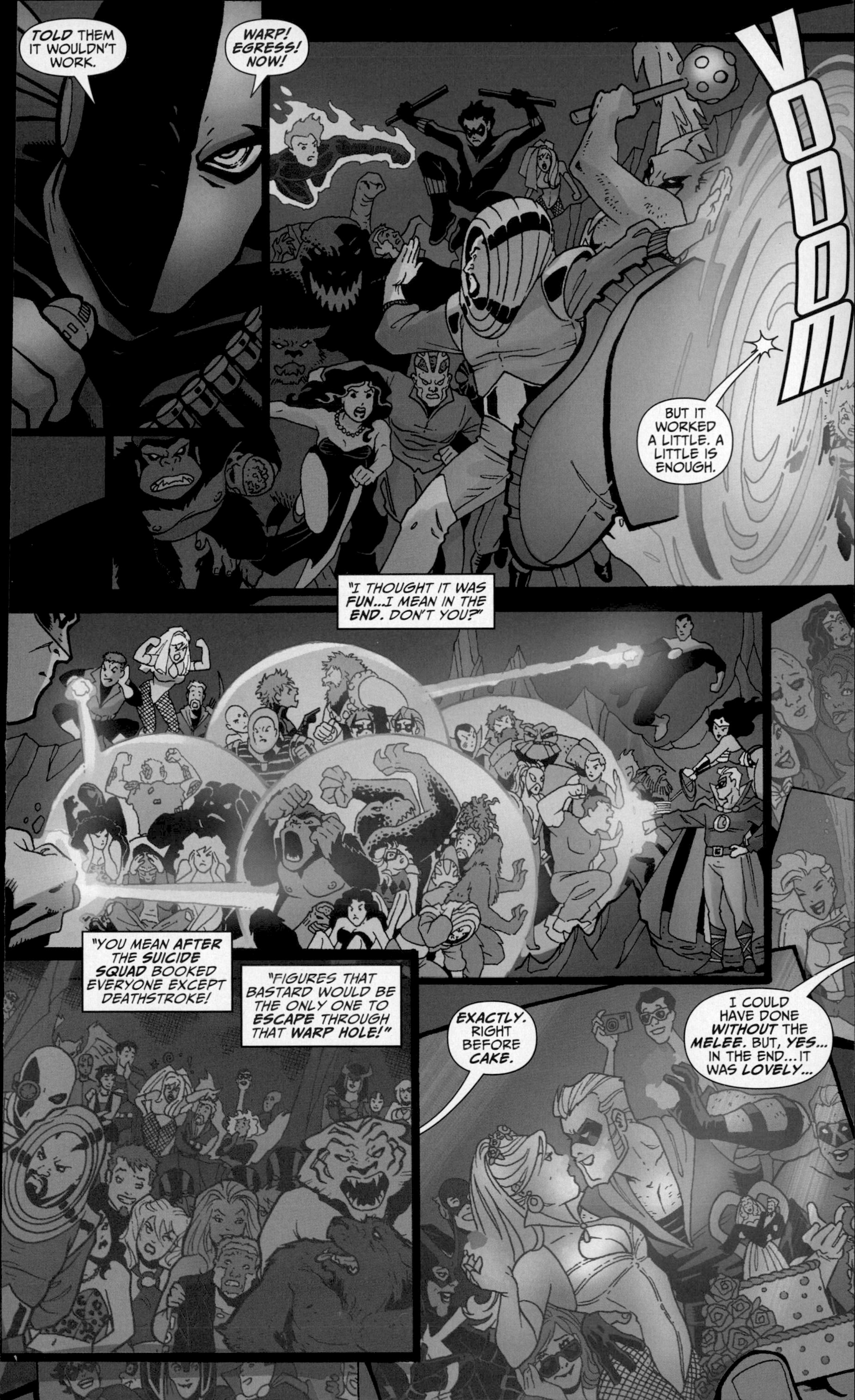

TOLD THEM IT WOULDN'T WORK.
WARP! EGRESS! NOW!
VOOOM
BUT IT WORKED A LITTLE. A LITTLE IS ENOUGH.
"I THOUGHT IT WAS FUN...I MEAN IN THE END. DON'T YOU?"
"YOU MEAN AFTER THE SUICIDE SQUAD BOOKED EVERYONE EXCEPT DEATHSTROKE!
"FIGURES THAT BASTARD WOULD BE THE ONLY ONE TO ESCAPE THROUGH THAT WARP HOLE!"
EXACTLY. RIGHT BEFORE CAKE.
I COULD HAVE DONE WITHOUT THE MELEE. BUT, YES... IN THE END...IT WAS LOVELY...

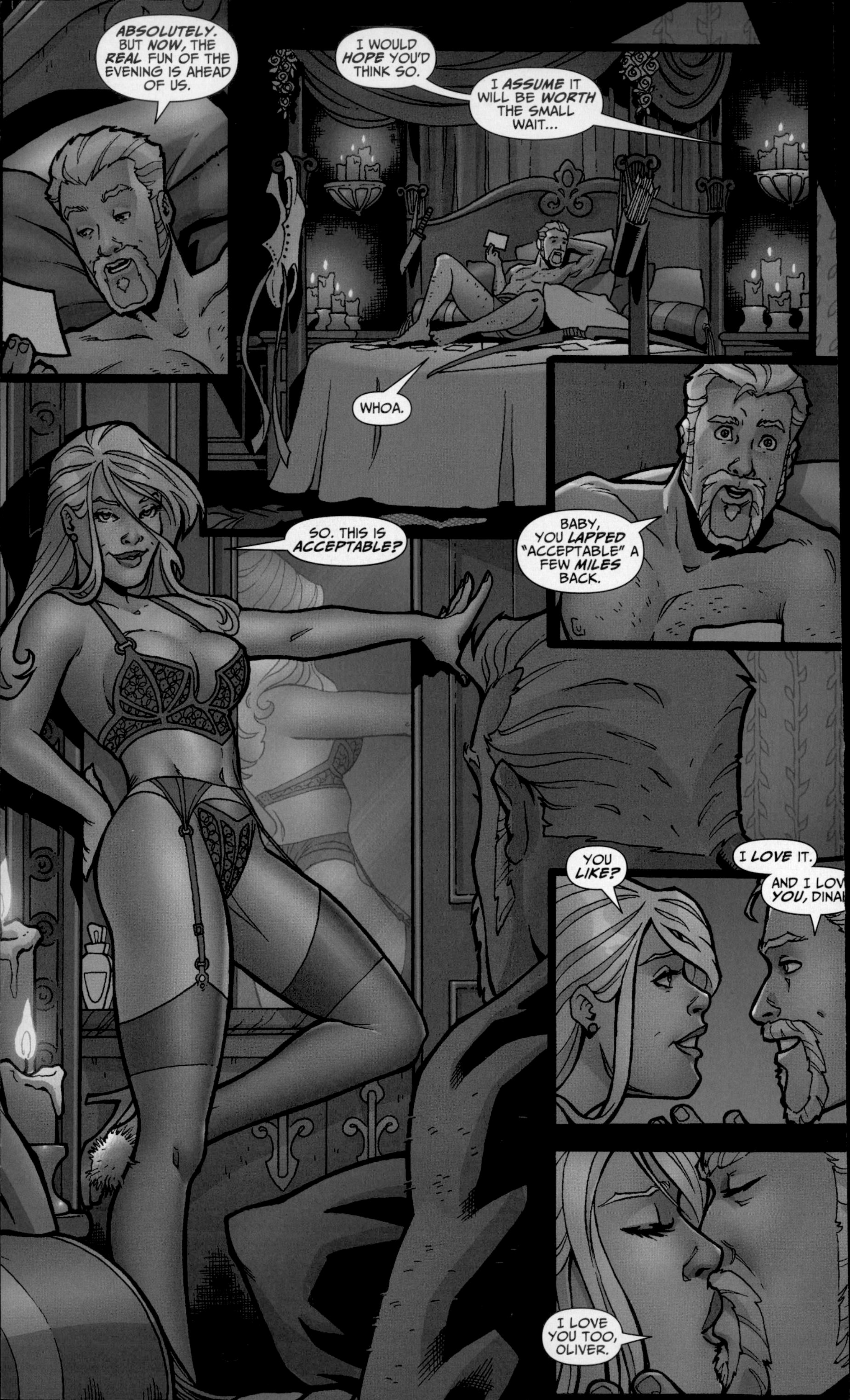
ABSOLUTELY. BUT NOW, THE REAL FUN OF THE EVENING IS AHEAD OF US.
I WOULD HOPE YOU'D THINK SO.
I ASSUME IT WILL BE WORTH THE SMALL WAIT...
WHOA.
SO. THIS IS ACCEPTABLE?
BABY, YOU LAPPED "ACCEPTABLE" A FEW MILES BACK.
YOU LIKE?
I LOVE IT.
I LOVE YOU TOO, OLIVER.

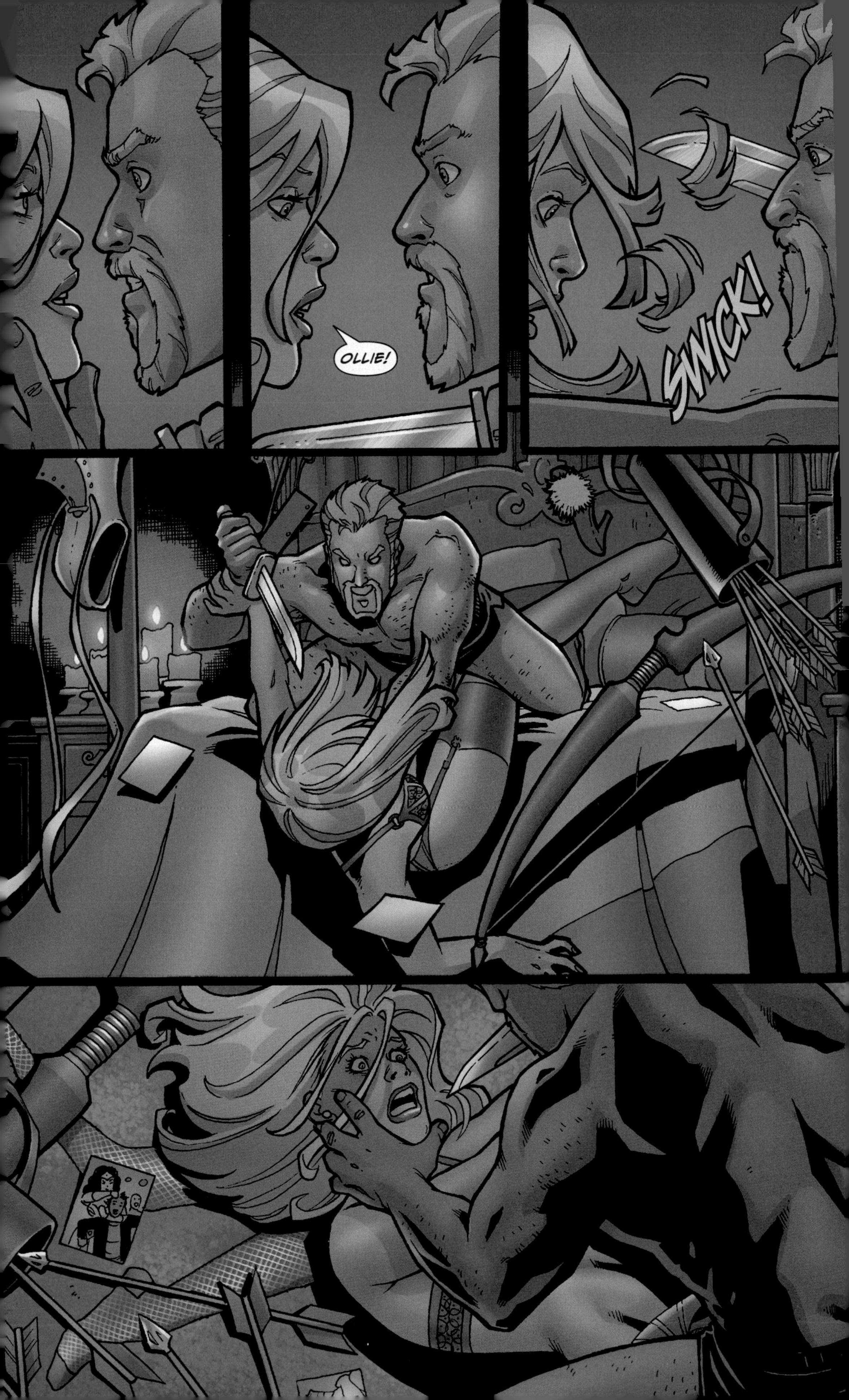
OLLIE!
SWICK!

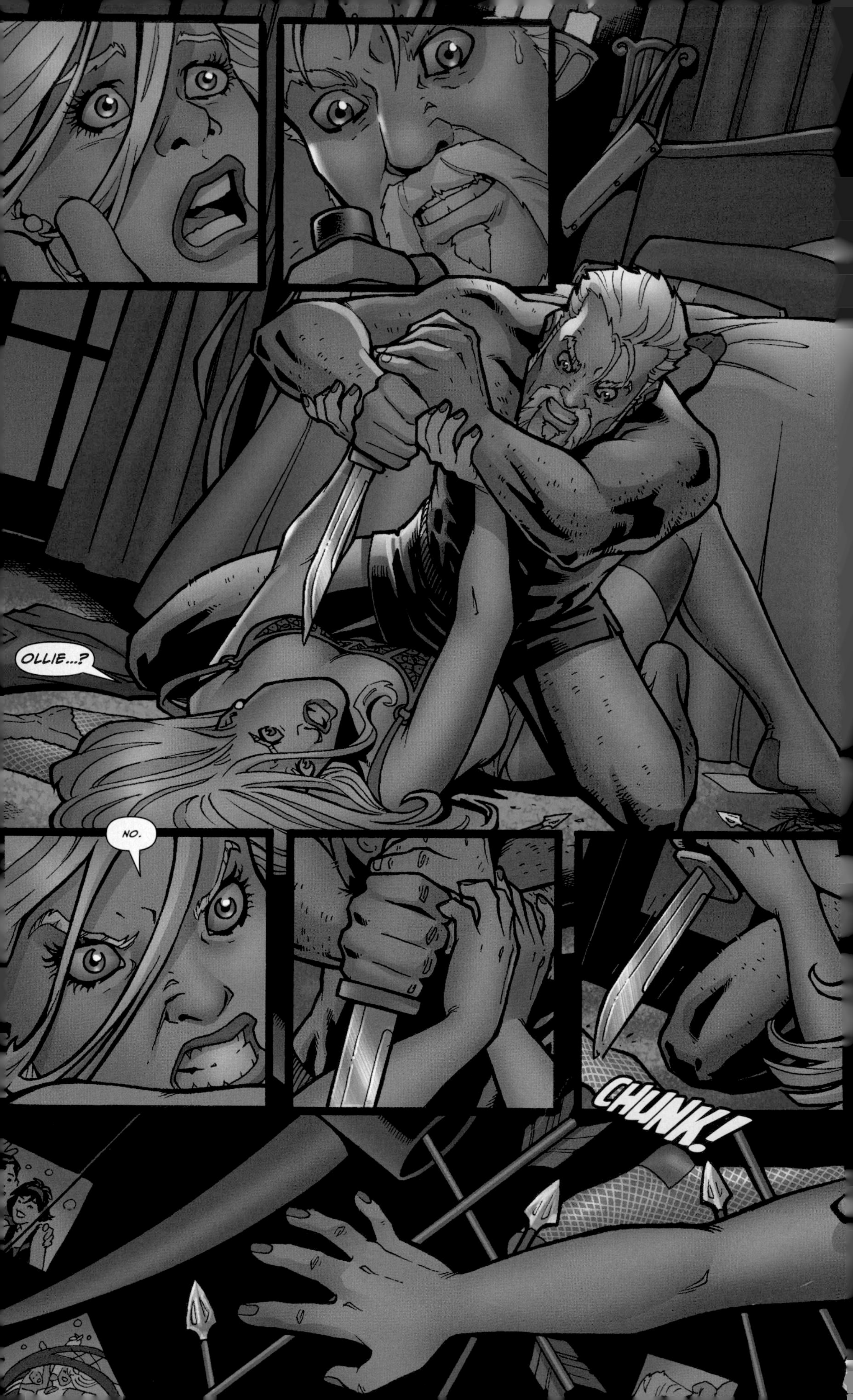
OLLIE...?
NO.
CHUNK!

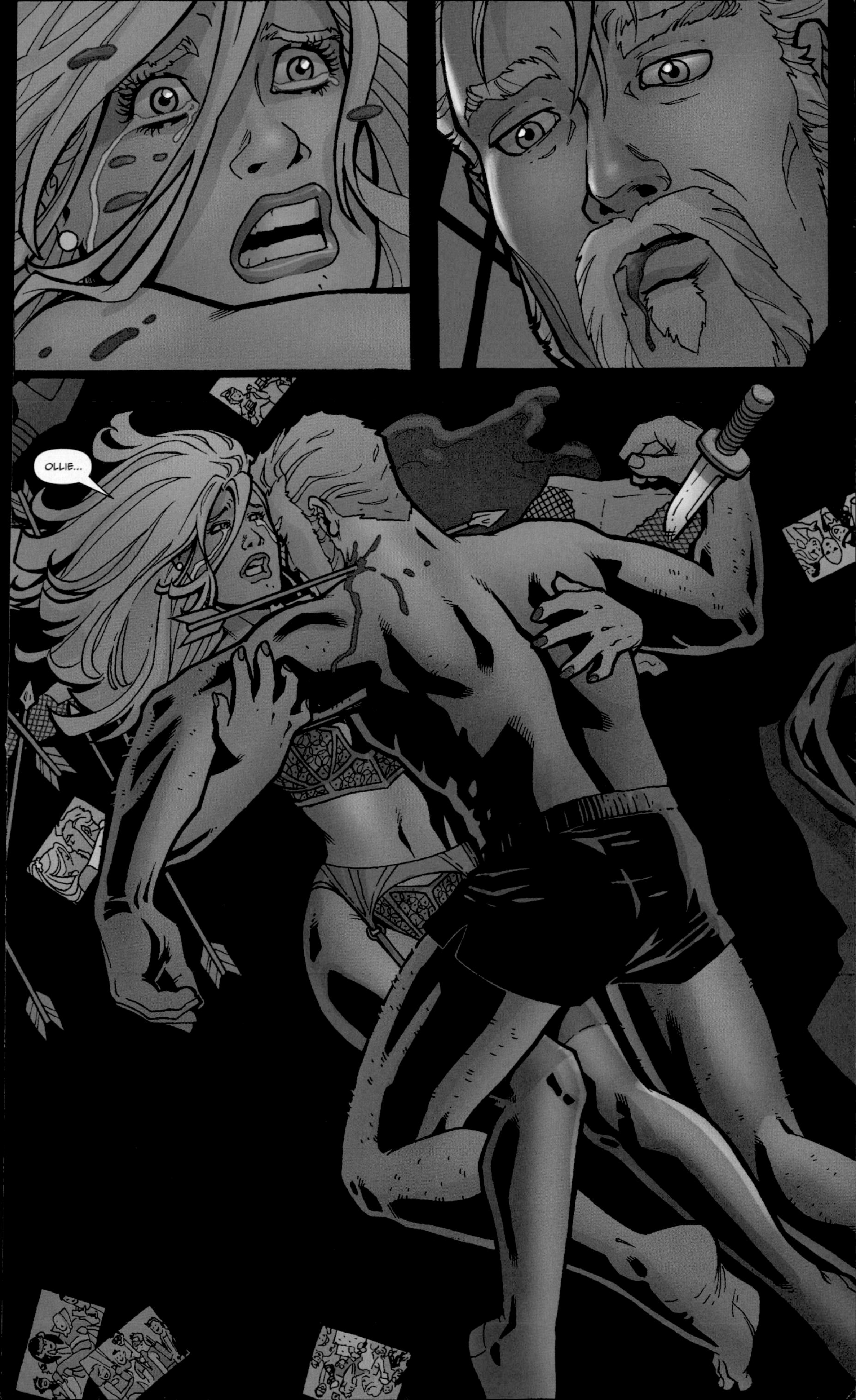
OLLIE...

GREEN ARROW AND BLACK CANARY #1 Cliff Chiang

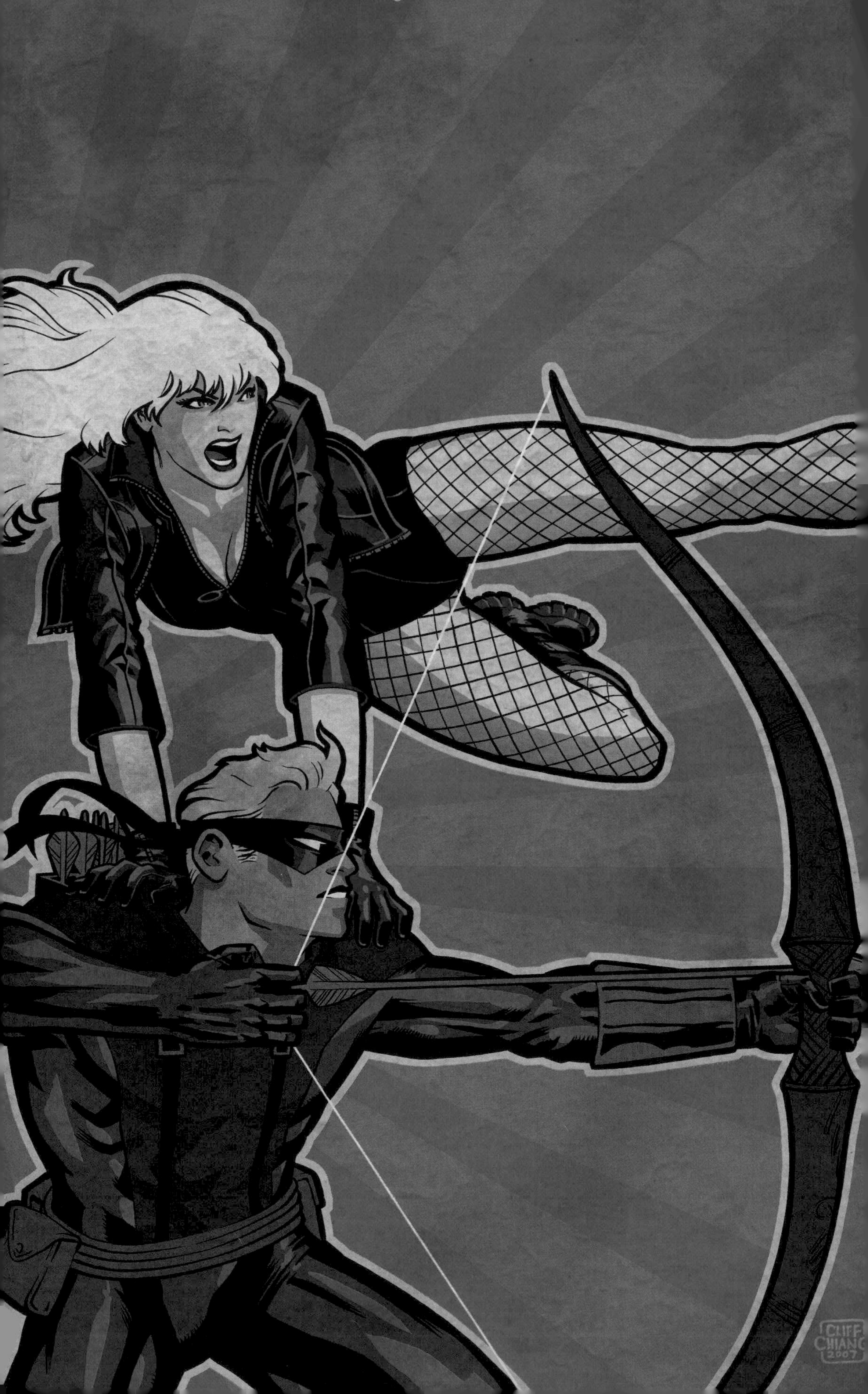
CLIFF
CHIANG
2007

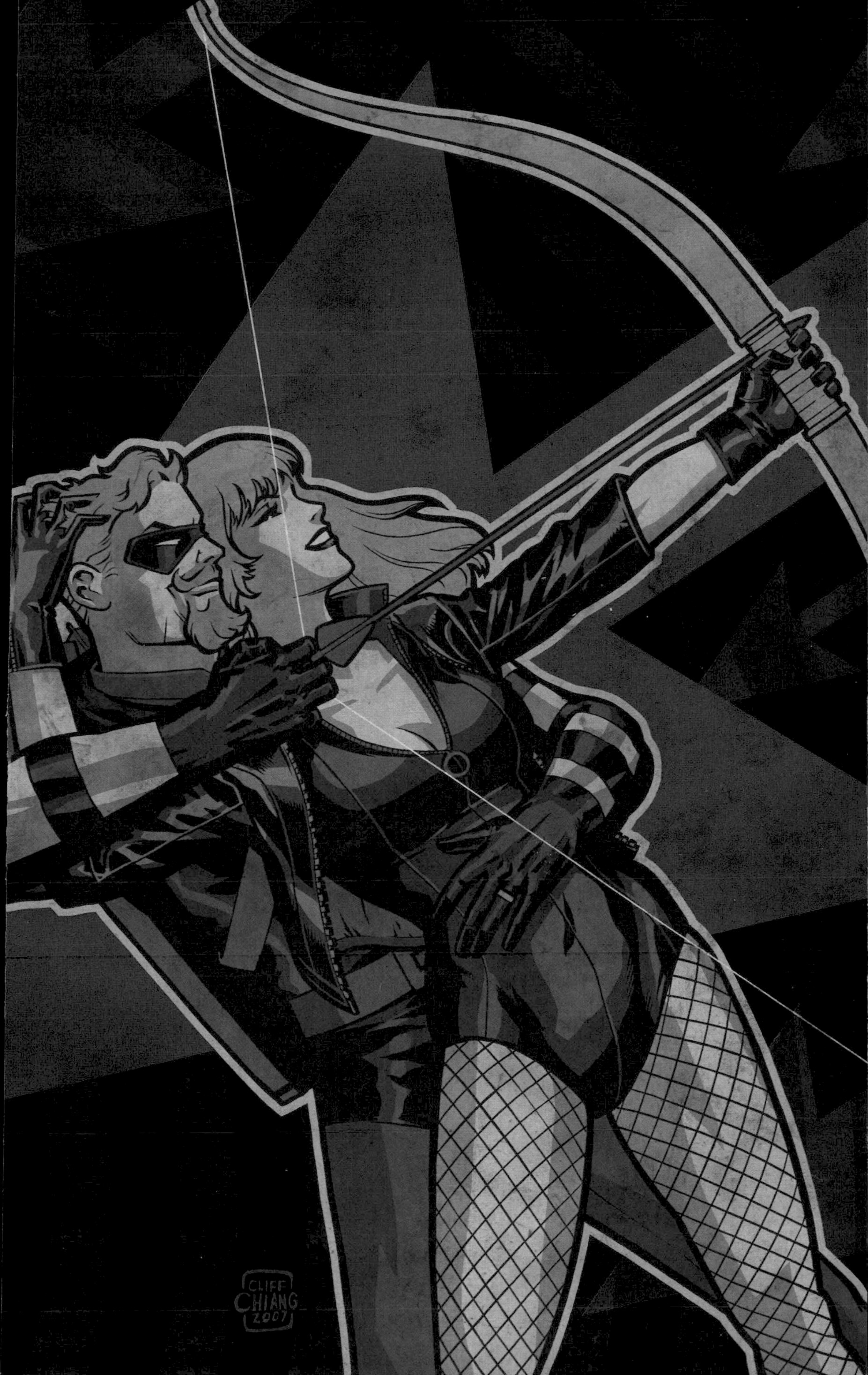
CLIFF
CHIANG
2007

DEAD AGAIN PART ONE: HERE COMES THE BRIDE

Story: **Judd Winick**   *Art:* **Cliff Chiang**   *Color:* **Trish Mulvihill**

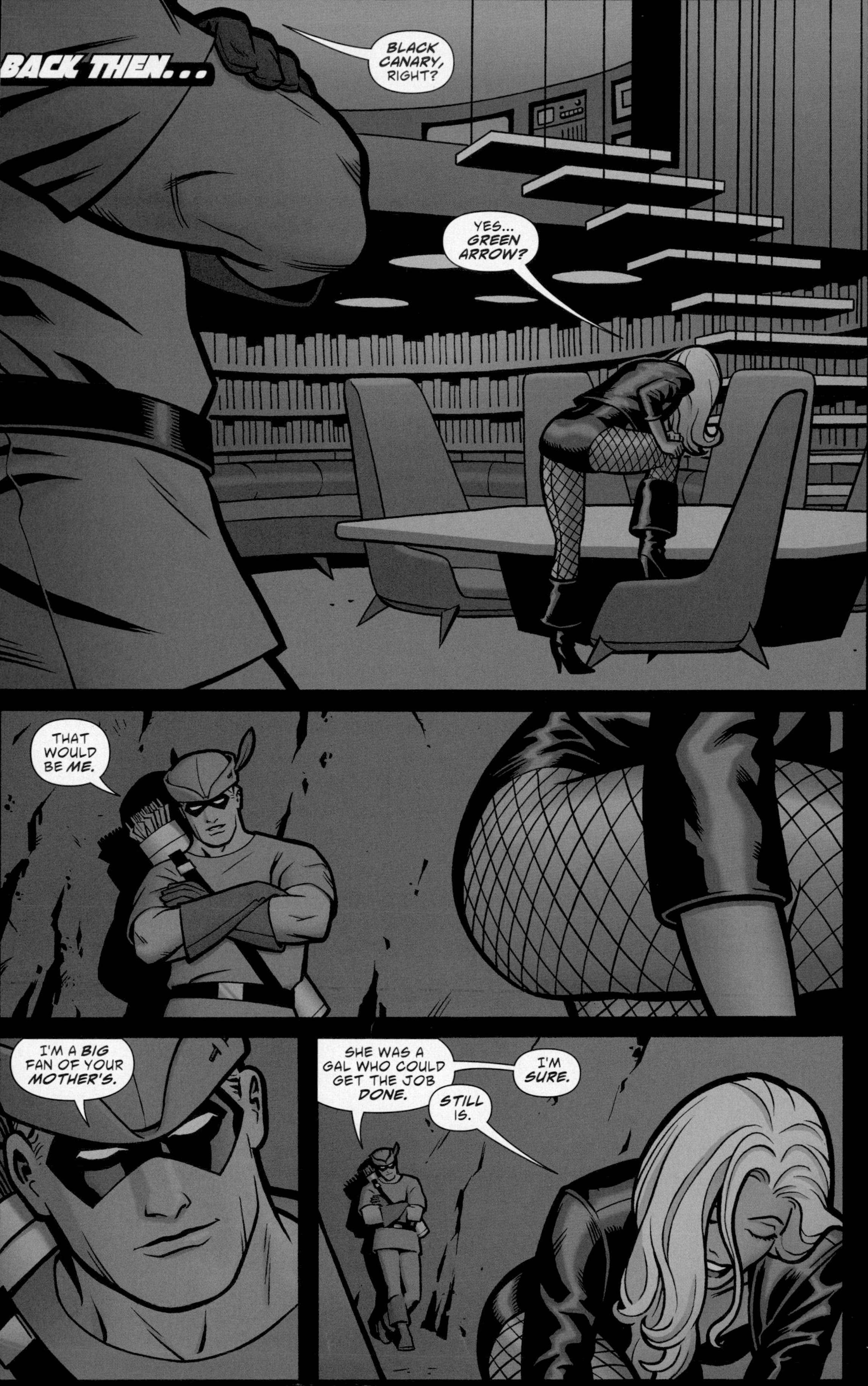
BACK THEN. . .
BLACK CANARY, RIGHT?
YES... GREEN ARROW?
THAT WOULD BE ME.
I'M A BIG FAN OF YOUR MOTHER'S.
SHE WAS A GAL WHO COULD GET THE JOB DONE.
I'M SURE.
STILL IS.

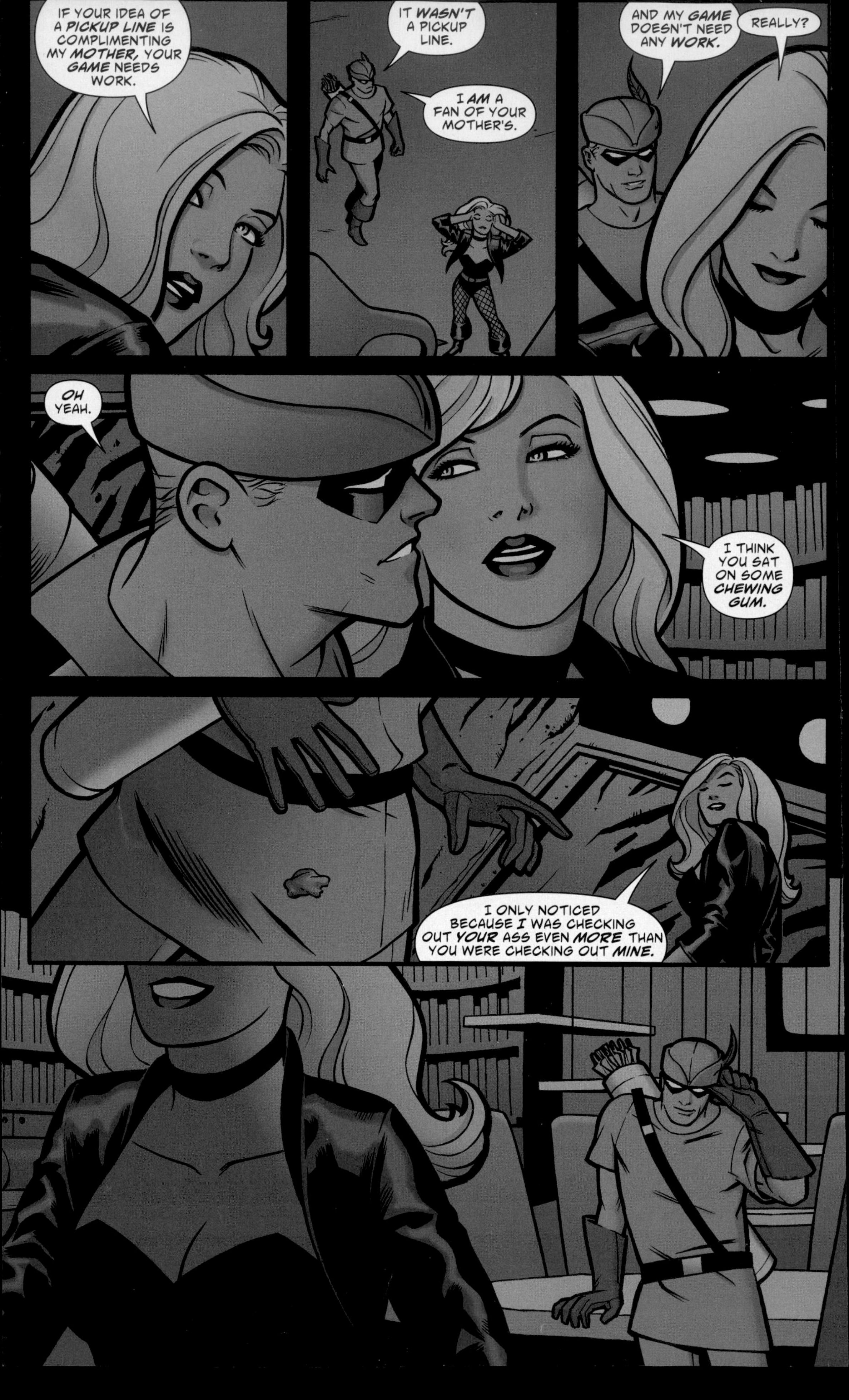
IF YOUR IDEA OF A PICKUP LINE IS COMPLIMENTING MY MOTHER, YOUR GAME NEEDS WORK.
IT WASN'T A PICKUP LINE.
I AM A FAN OF YOUR MOTHER'S.
AND MY GAME DOESN'T NEED ANY WORK.
REALLY?
OH YEAH.
I THINK YOU SAT ON SOME CHEWING GUM.
I ONLY NOTICED BECAUSE I WAS CHECKING OUT YOUR ASS EVEN MORE THAN YOU WERE CHECKING OUT MINE.

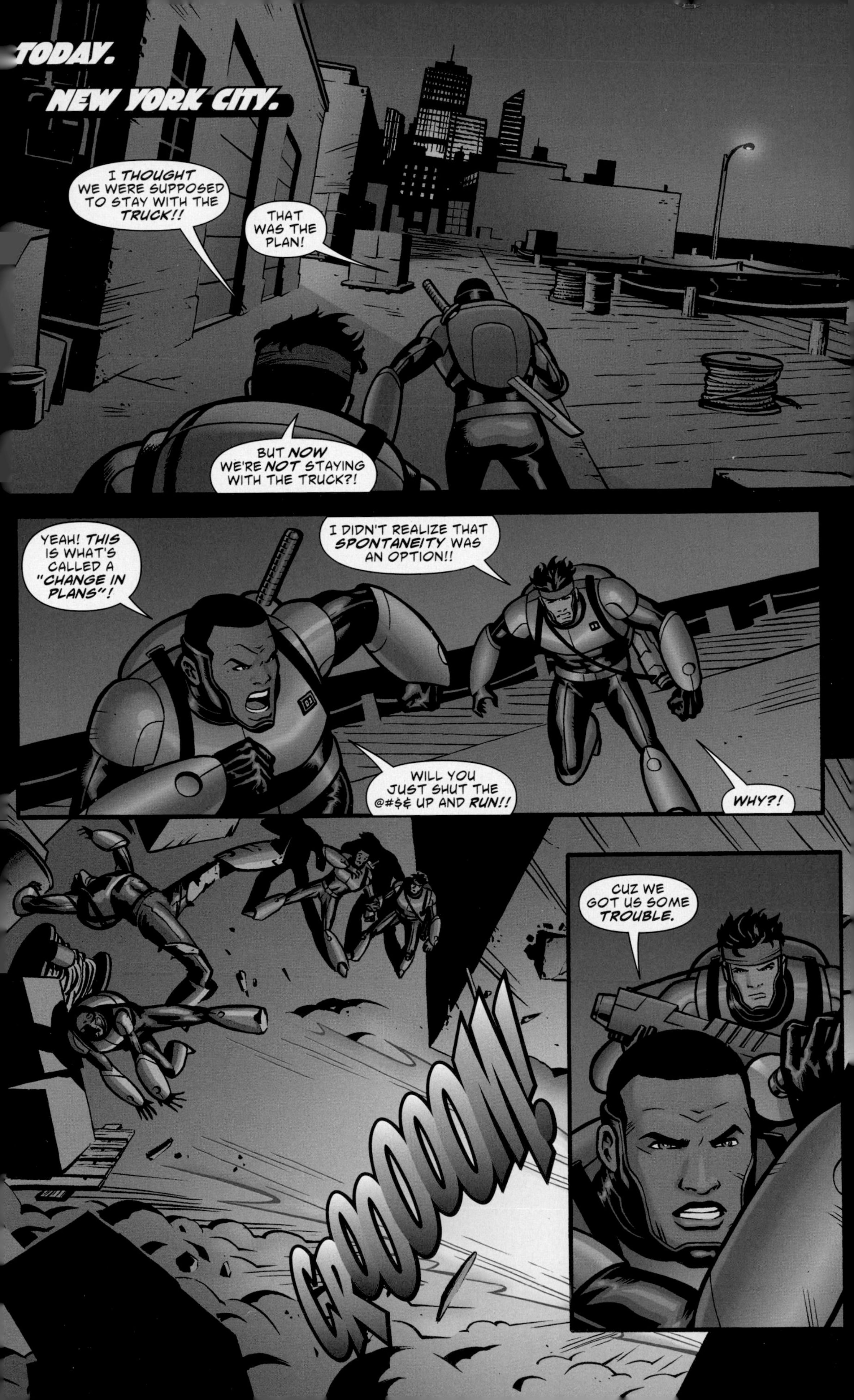
TODAY.
NEW YORK CITY.
I THOUGHT WE WERE SUPPOSED TO STAY WITH THE TRUCK!!
THAT WAS THE PLAN!
BUT NOW WE'RE NOT STAYING WITH THE TRUCK?!
YEAH! THIS IS WHAT'S CALLED A "CHANGE IN PLANS"!
I DIDN'T REALIZE THAT SPONTANEITY WAS AN OPTION!!
WILL YOU JUST SHUT THE @#$& UP AND RUN!!
WHY?!
CUZ WE GOT US SOME TROUBLE.
GROOOOOM!

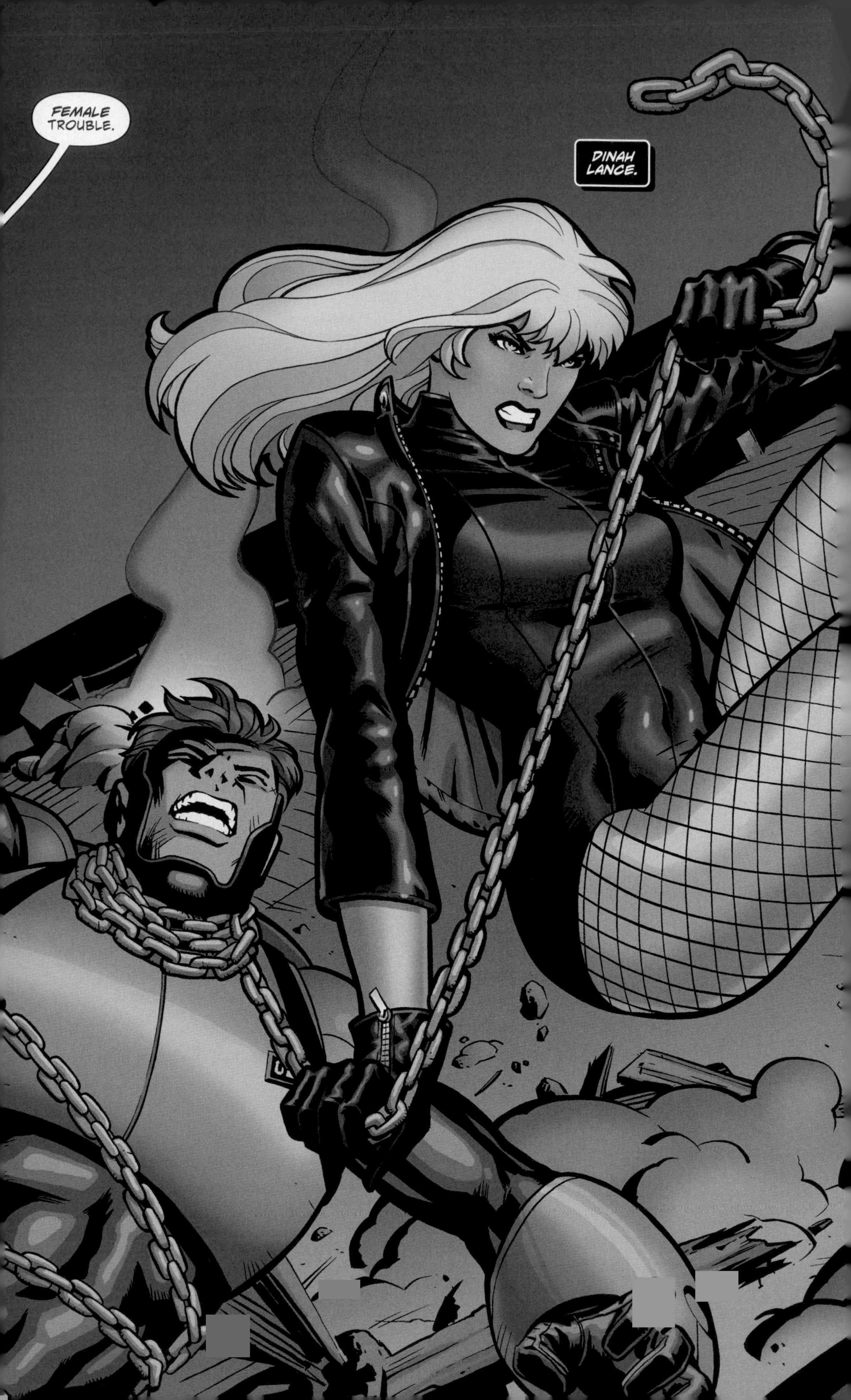
FEMALE TROUBLE.
DINAH LANCE.

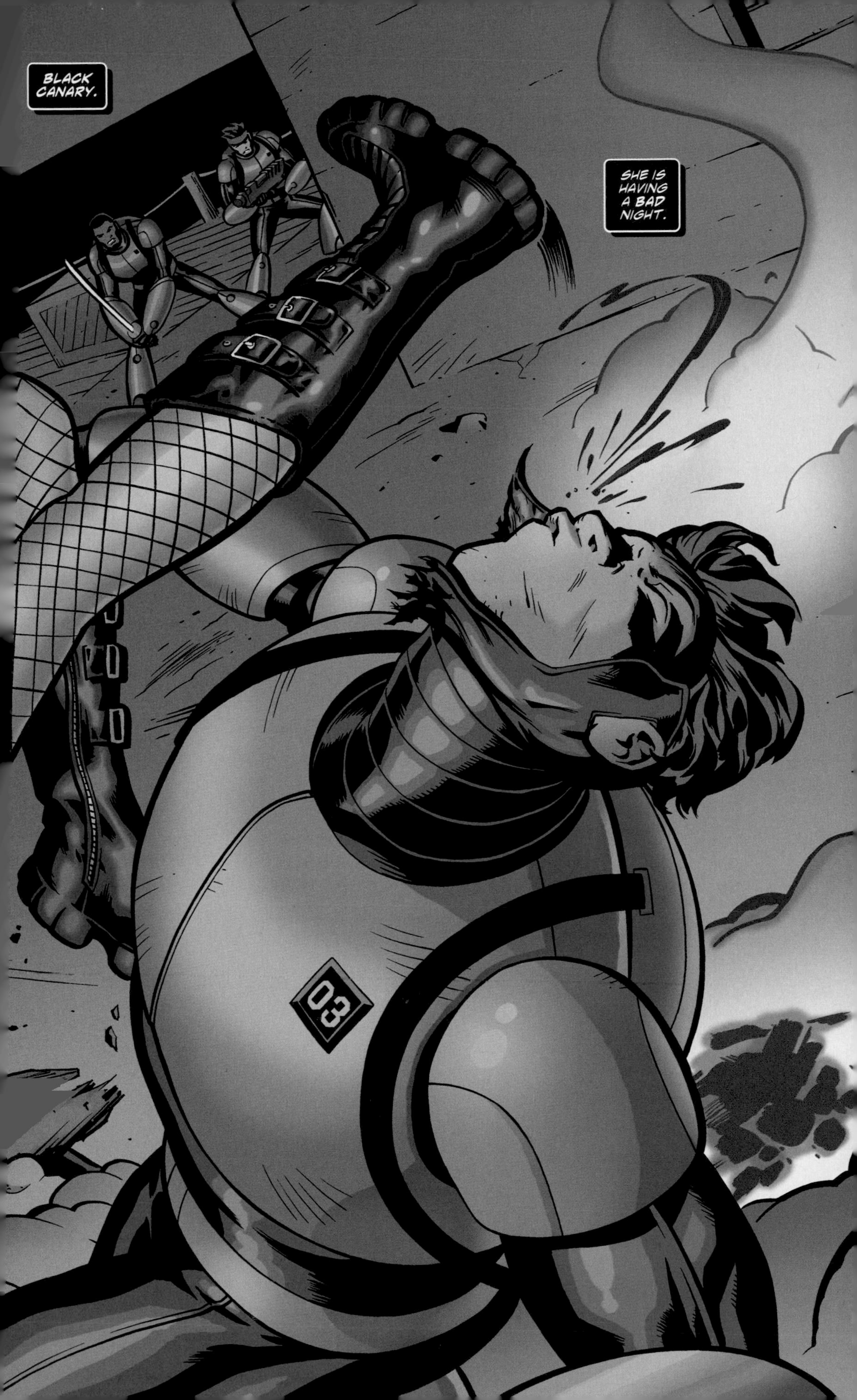
BLACK CANARY.
SHE IS HAVING A BAD NIGHT.
03

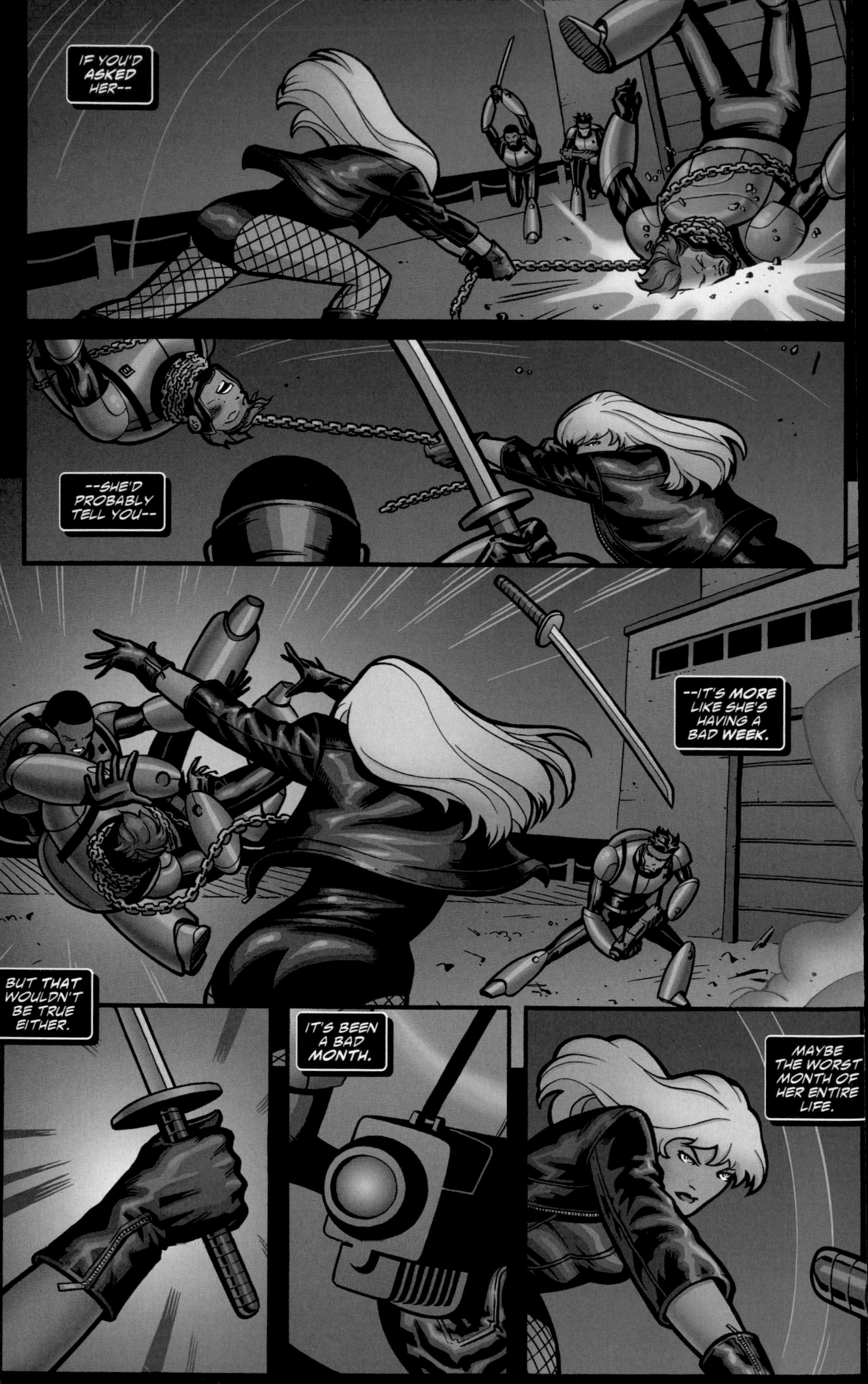
IF YOU'D ASKED HER--
--SHE'D PROBABLY TELL YOU--
--IT'S MORE LIKE SHE'S HAVING A BAD WEEK.
BUT THAT WOULDN'T BE TRUE EITHER.
IT'S BEEN A BAD MONTH.
MAYBE THE WORST MONTH OF HER ENTIRE LIFE.

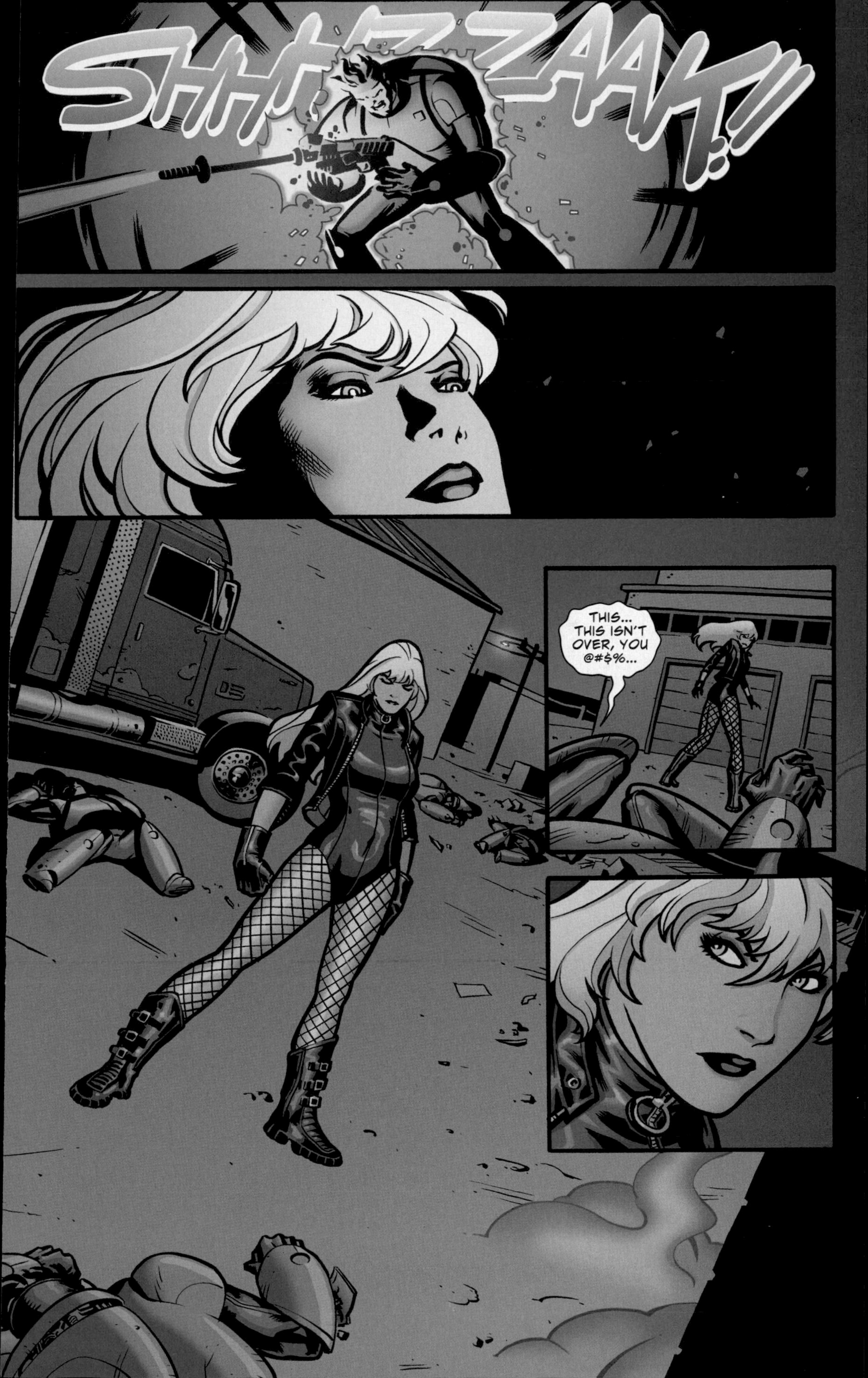
SHHKZZAAK!!
THIS... THIS ISN'T OVER, YOU @#$%...

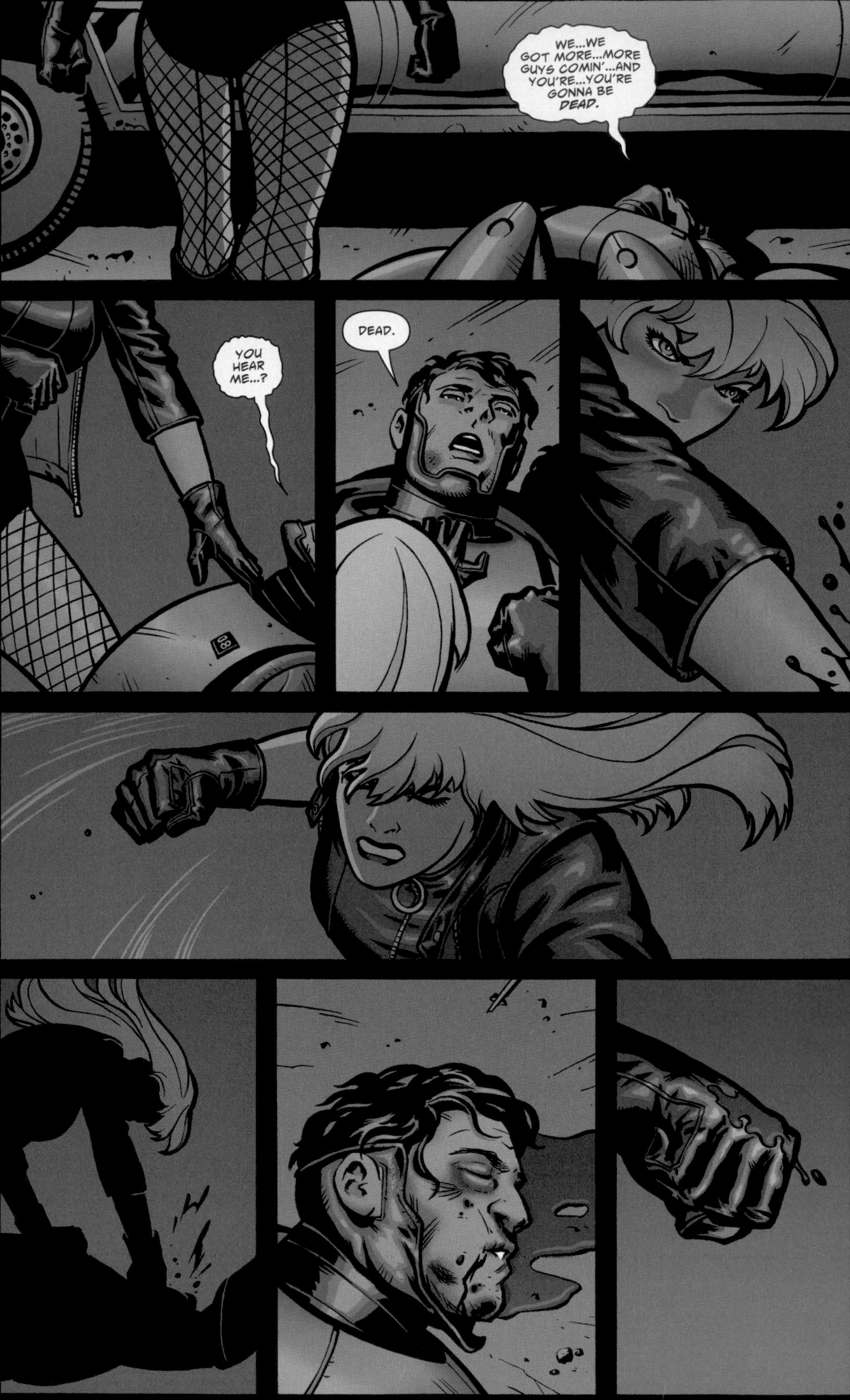
WE...WE GOT MORE...MORE GUYS COMIN'...AND YOU'RE...YOU'RE GONNA BE DEAD.
YOU HEAR ME...?
DEAD.

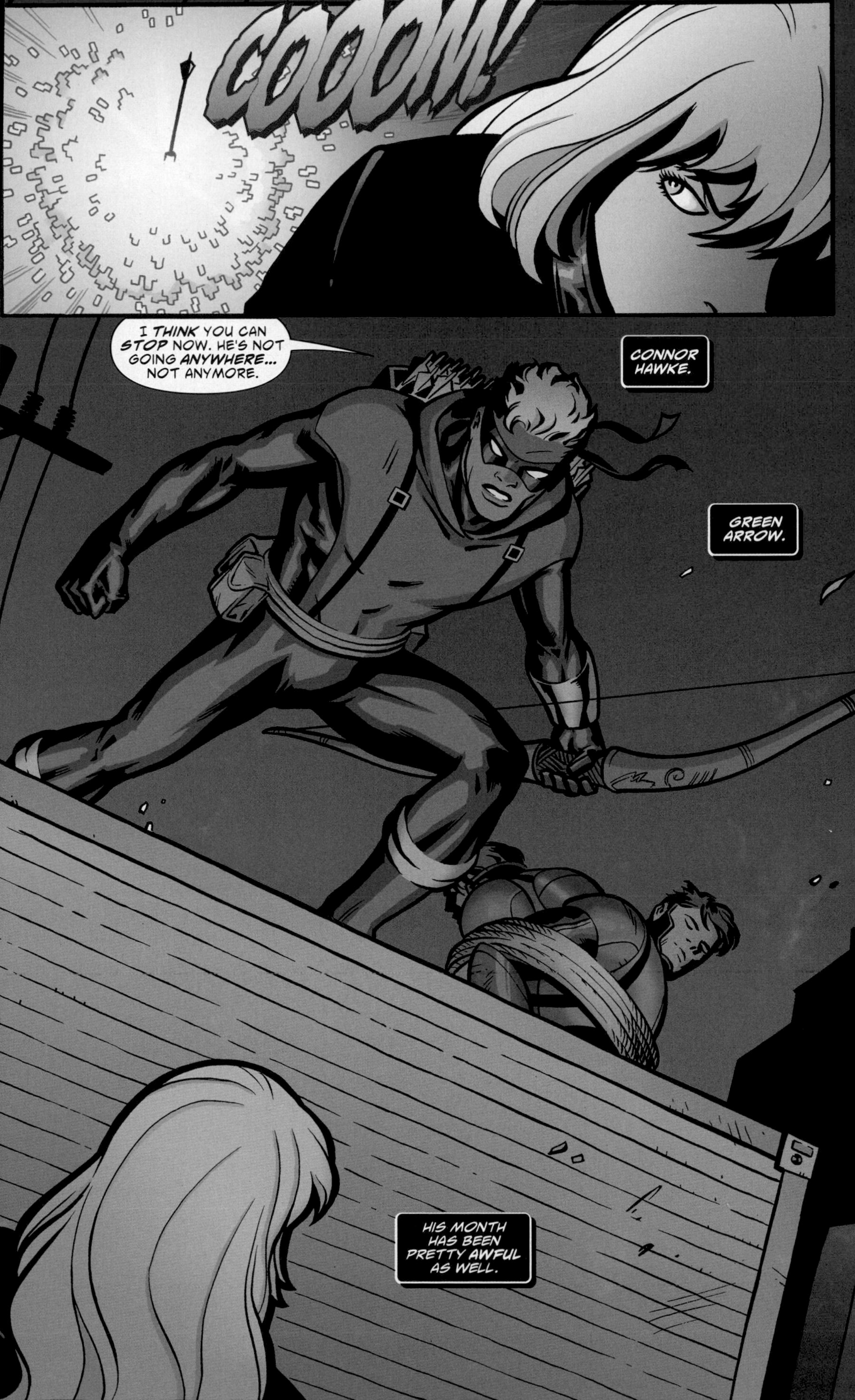
COOOM!
I THINK YOU CAN STOP NOW. HE'S NOT GOING ANYWHERE... NOT ANYMORE.
CONNOR HAWKE.
GREEN ARROW.
HIS MONTH HAS BEEN PRETTY AWFUL AS WELL.

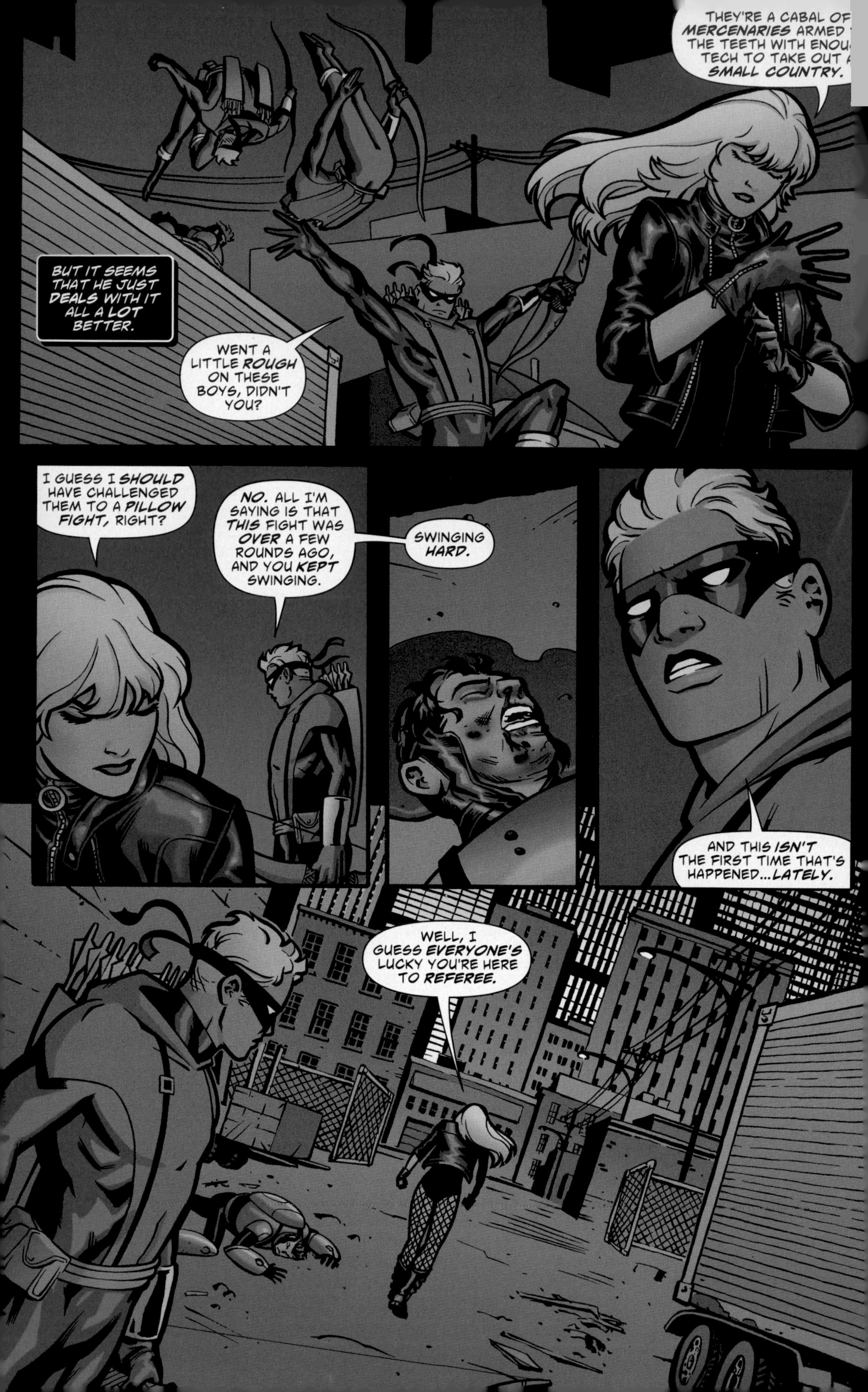
THEY'RE A CABAL OF MERCENARIES ARMED T THE TEETH WITH ENOU TECH TO TAKE OUT A SMALL COUNTRY.
BUT IT SEEMS THAT HE JUST DEALS WITH IT ALL A LOT BETTER.
WENT A LITTLE ROUGH ON THESE BOYS, DIDN'T YOU?
I GUESS I SHOULD HAVE CHALLENGED THEM TO A PILLOW FIGHT, RIGHT?
NO. ALL I'M SAYING IS THAT THIS FIGHT WAS OVER A FEW ROUNDS AGO, AND YOU KEPT SWINGING.
SWINGING HARD.
AND THIS ISN'T THE FIRST TIME THAT'S HAPPENED...LATELY.
WELL, I GUESS EVERYONE'S LUCKY YOU'RE HERE TO REFEREE.

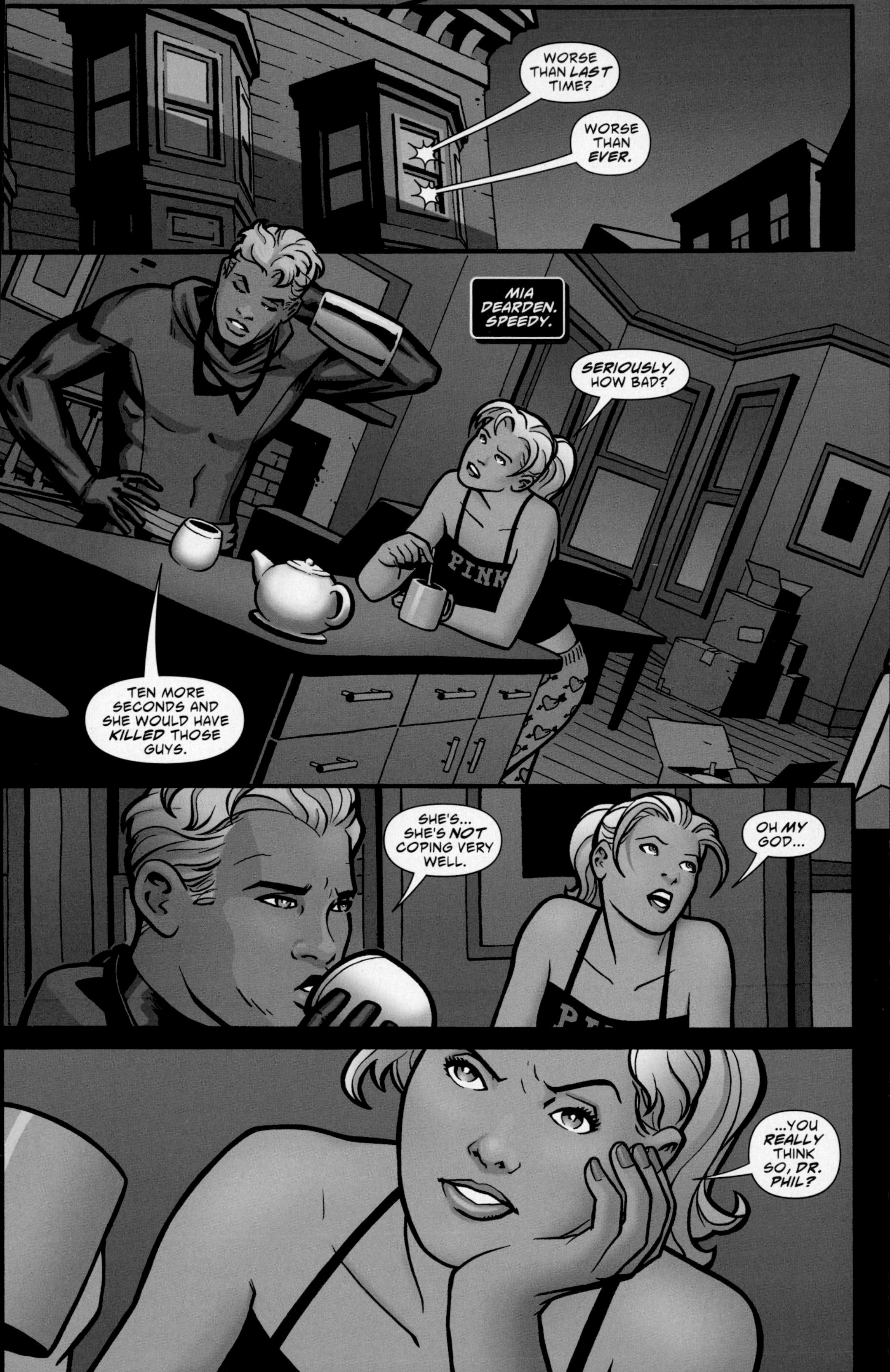
WORSE THAN LAST TIME?
WORSE THAN EVER.
MIA DEARDEN. SPEEDY.
SERIOUSLY, HOW BAD?
TEN MORE SECONDS AND SHE WOULD HAVE KILLED THOSE GUYS.
SHE'S... SHE'S NOT COPING VERY WELL.
OH MY GOD...
...YOU REALLY THINK SO, DR. PHIL?

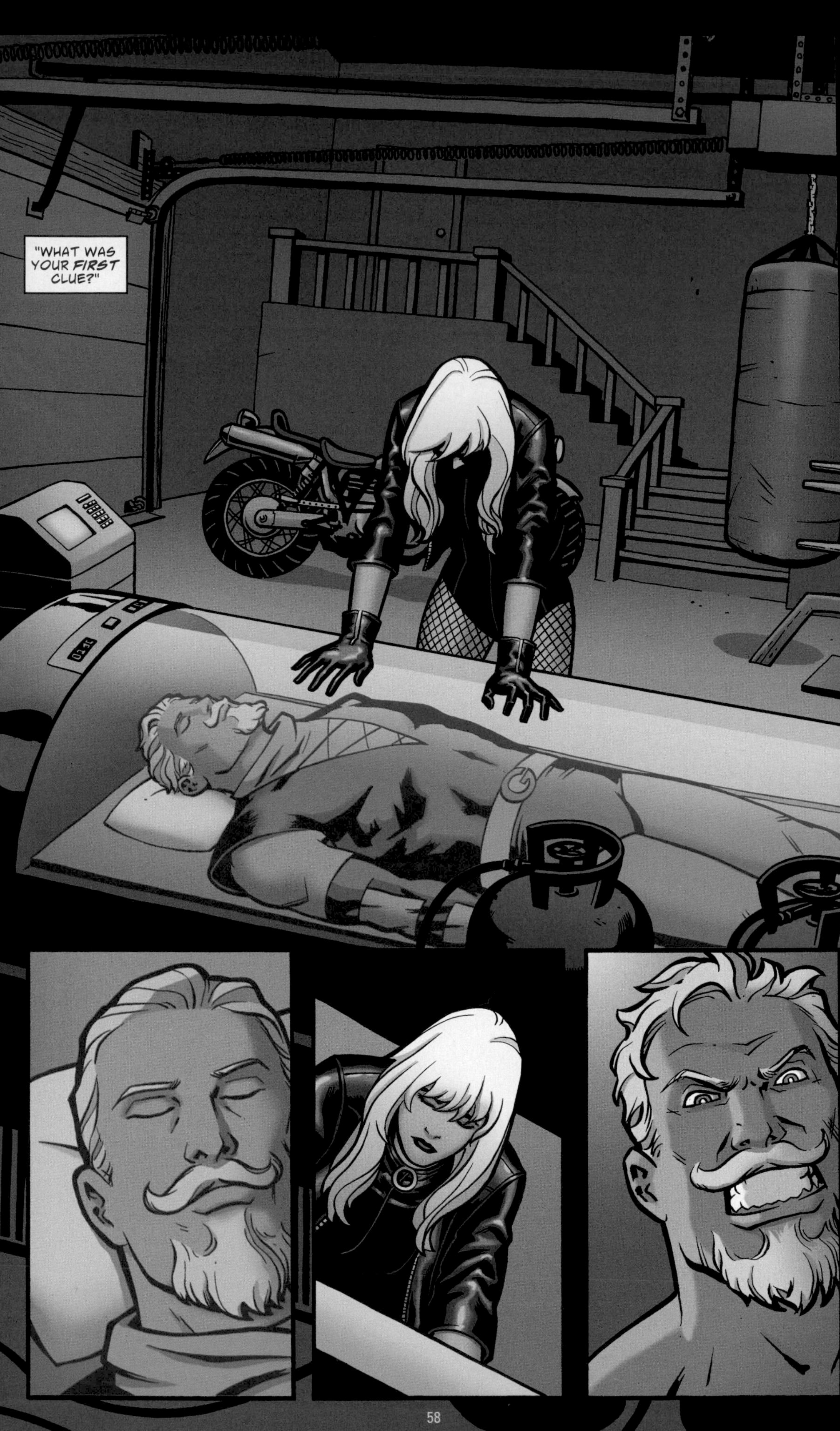
"WHAT WAS YOUR FIRST CLUE?"

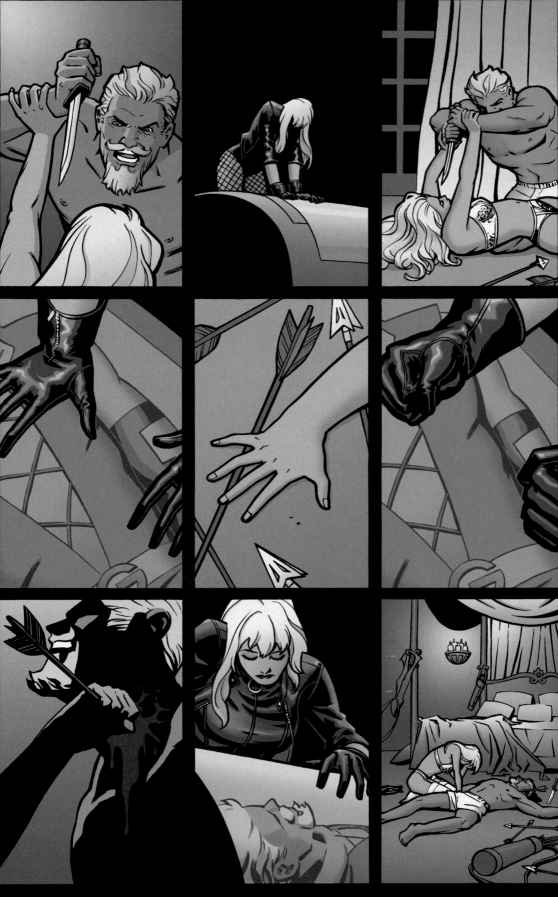

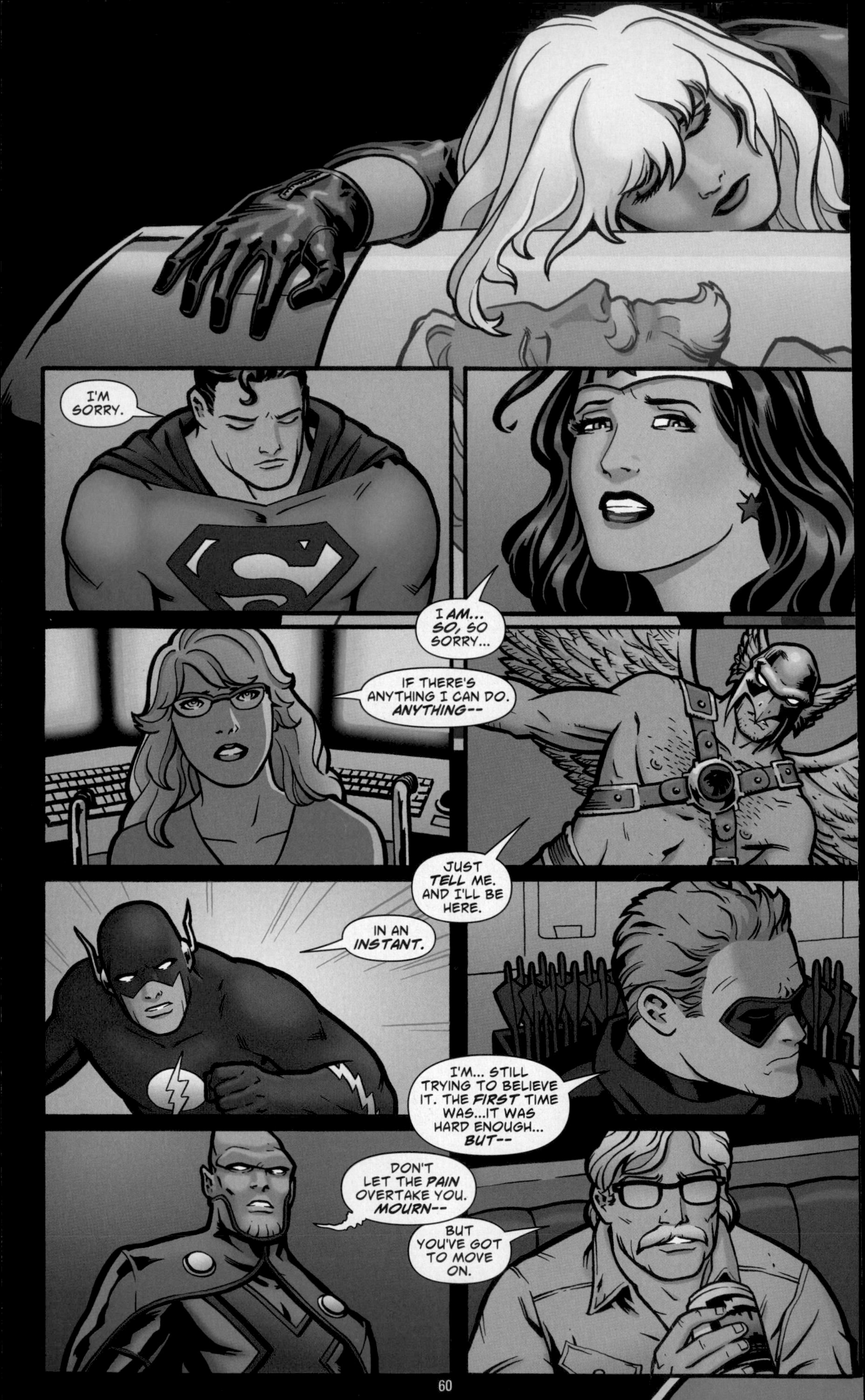
I'M SORRY.
I AM... SO, SO SORRY...
IF THERE'S ANYTHING I CAN DO. ANYTHING--
JUST TELL ME. AND I'LL BE HERE.
IN AN INSTANT.
I'M... STILL TRYING TO BELIEVE IT. THE FIRST TIME WAS...IT WAS HARD ENOUGH... BUT--
DON'T LET THE PAIN OVERTAKE YOU. MOURN--
BUT YOU'VE GOT TO MOVE ON.

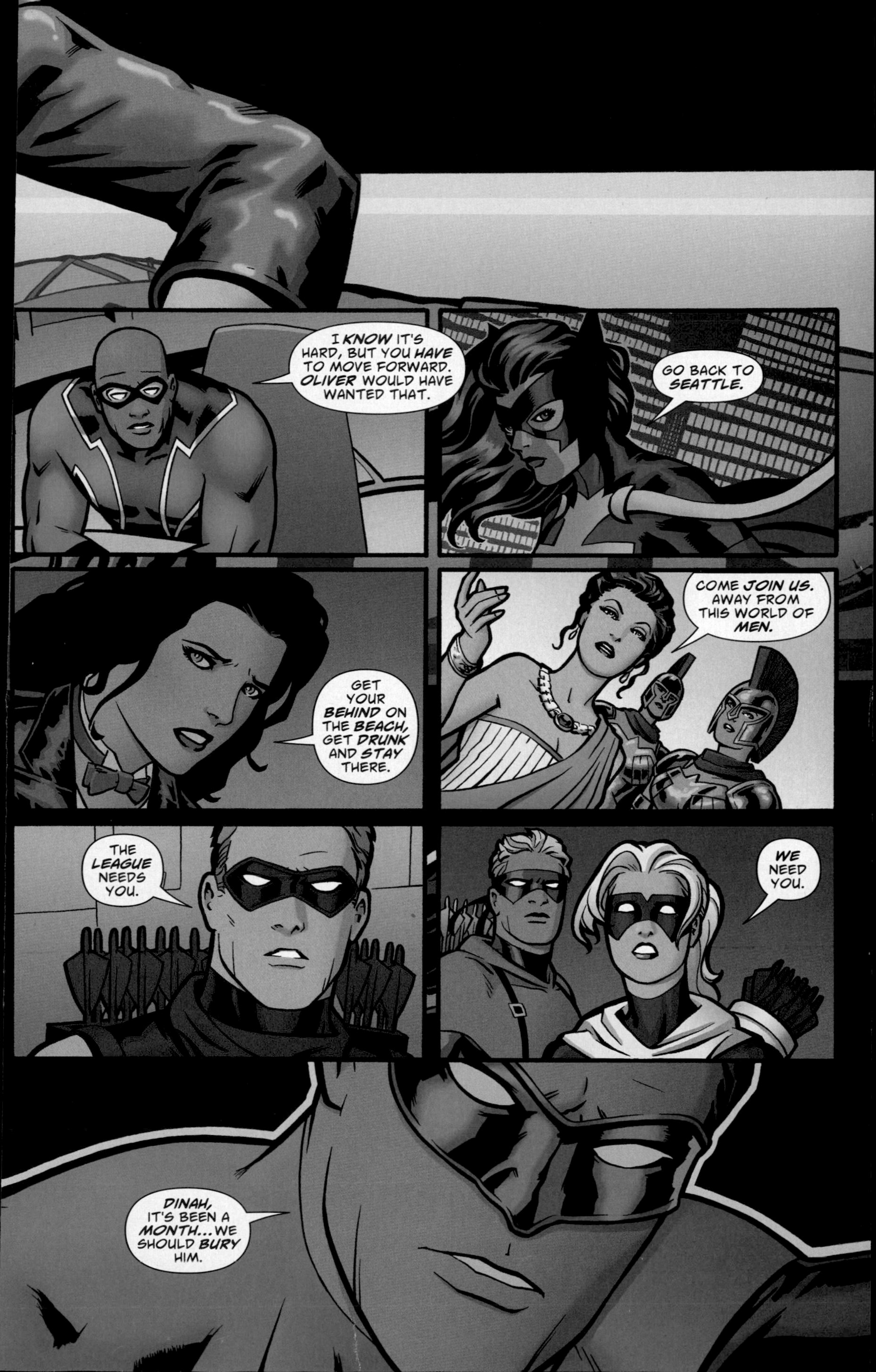
I KNOW IT'S HARD, BUT YOU HAVE TO MOVE FORWARD. OLIVER WOULD HAVE WANTED THAT.
GO BACK TO SEATTLE.
GET YOUR BEHIND ON THE BEACH, GET DRUNK AND STAY THERE.
COME JOIN US. AWAY FROM THIS WORLD OF MEN.
THE LEAGUE NEEDS YOU.
WE NEED YOU.
DINAH, IT'S BEEN A MONTH...WE SHOULD BURY HIM.

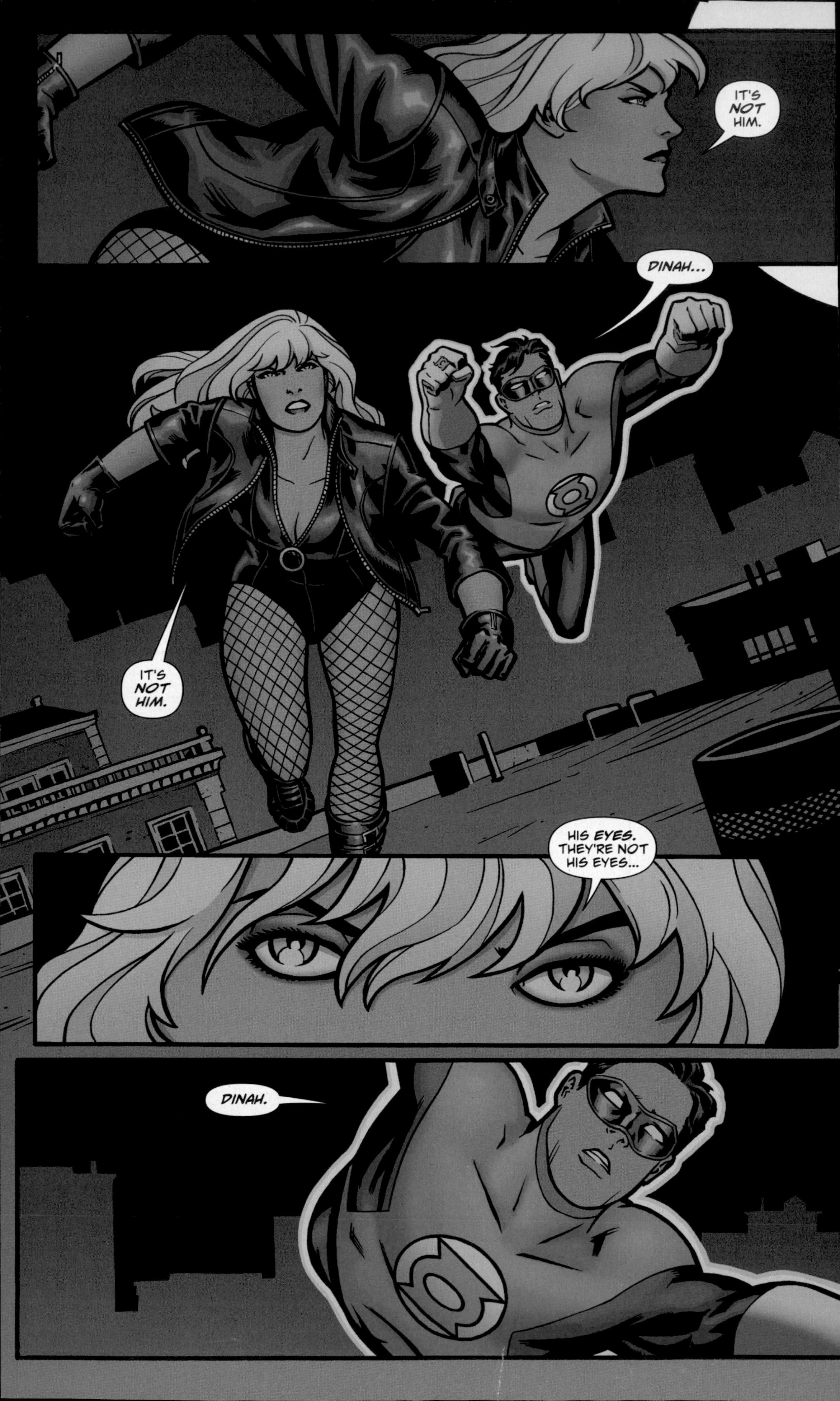

IT'S NOT HIM.
DINAH...
IT'S NOT HIM.
HIS EYES. THEY'RE NOT HIS EYES...
DINAH.

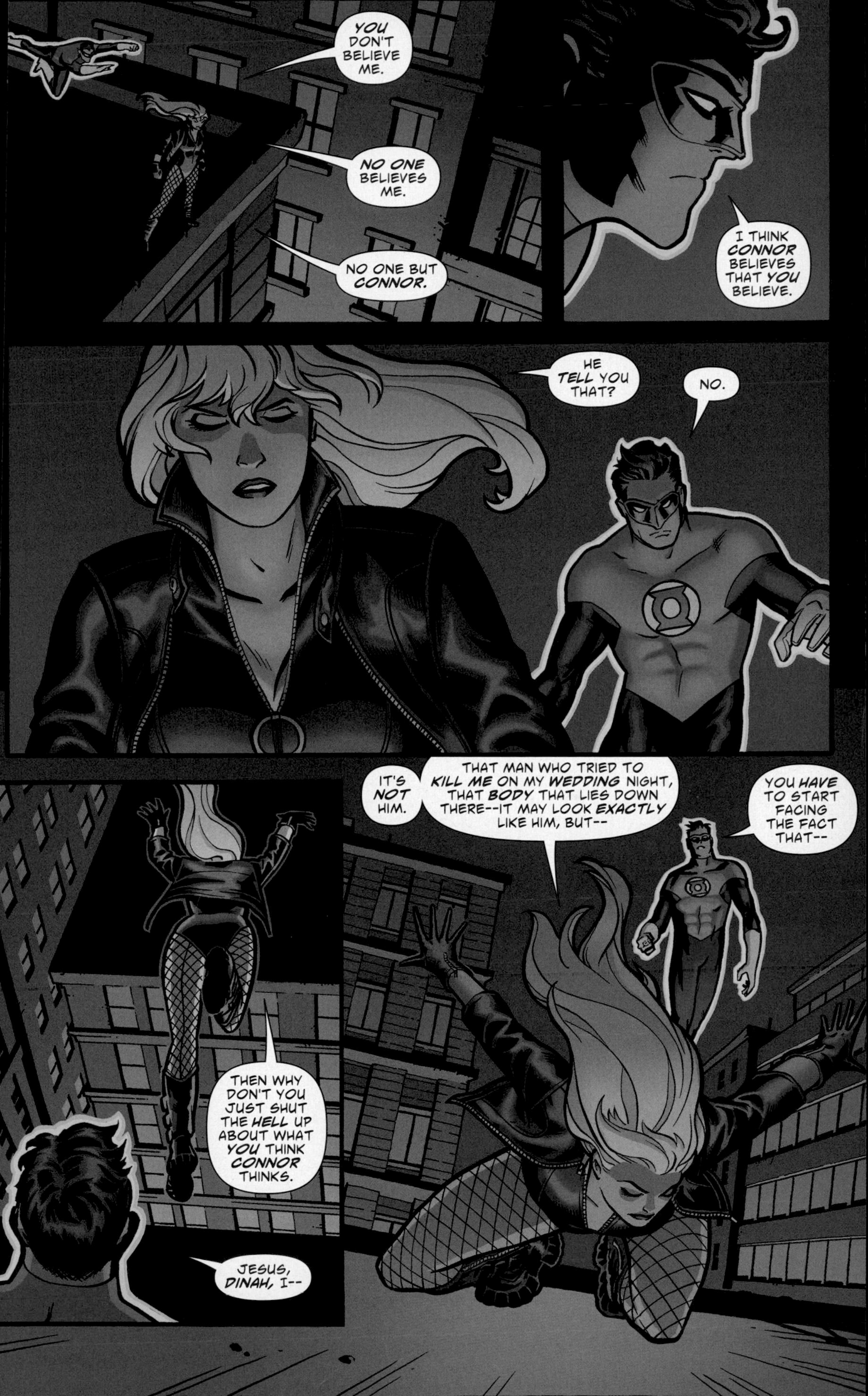
YOU DON'T BELIEVE ME.
NO ONE BELIEVES ME.
NO ONE BUT CONNOR.
I THINK CONNOR BELIEVES THAT YOU BELIEVE.
HE TELL YOU THAT?
NO.
IT'S NOT HIM.
THAT MAN WHO TRIED TO KILL ME ON MY WEDDING NIGHT, THAT BODY THAT LIES DOWN THERE--IT MAY LOOK EXACTLY LIKE HIM, BUT--
YOU HAVE TO START FACING THE FACT THAT--
THEN WHY DON'T YOU JUST SHUT THE HELL UP ABOUT WHAT YOU THINK CONNOR THINKS.
JESUS, DINAH, I--

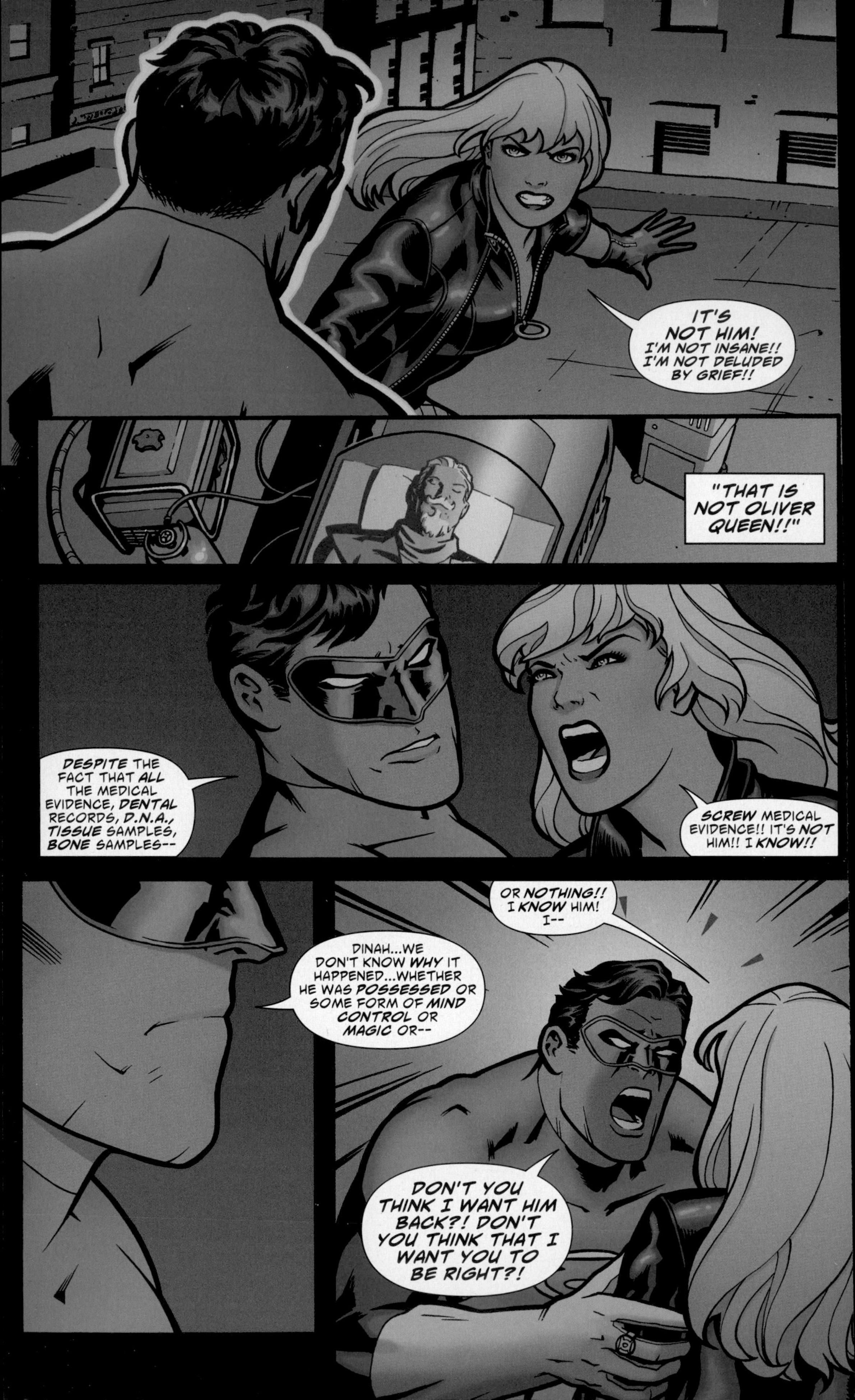
IT'S NOT HIM! I'M NOT INSANE!! I'M NOT DELUDED BY GRIEF!!
"THAT IS NOT OLIVER QUEEN!!"
DESPITE THE FACT THAT ALL THE MEDICAL EVIDENCE, DENTAL RECORDS, D.N.A., TISSUE SAMPLES, BONE SAMPLES--
SCREW MEDICAL EVIDENCE!! IT'S NOT HIM!! I KNOW!!
DINAH...WE DON'T KNOW WHY IT HAPPENED...WHETHER HE WAS POSSESSED OR SOME FORM OF MIND CONTROL OR MAGIC OR--
OR NOTHING!! I KNOW HIM! I--
DON'T YOU THINK I WANT HIM BACK?! DON'T YOU THINK THAT I WANT YOU TO BE RIGHT?!

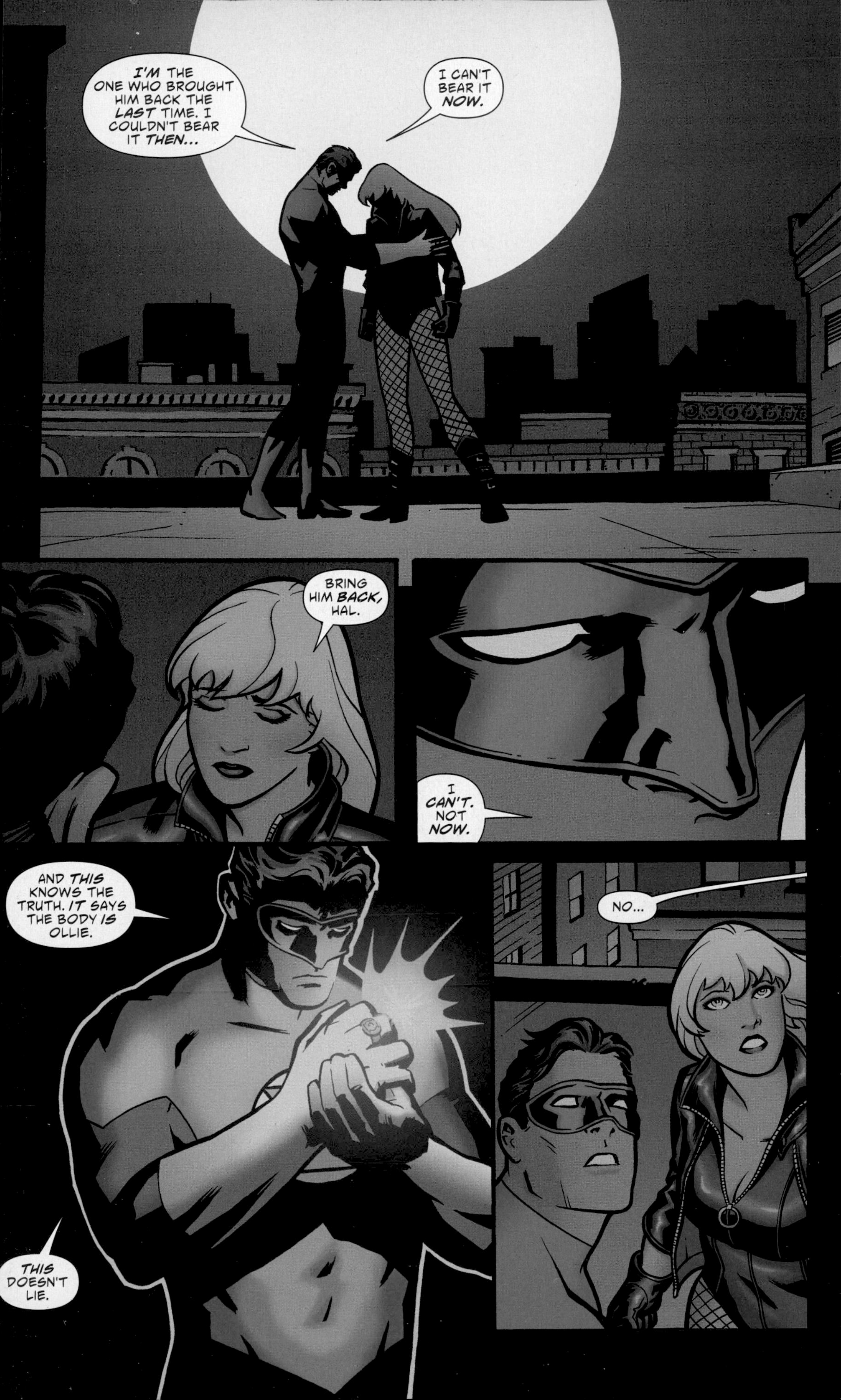
I'M THE ONE WHO BROUGHT HIM BACK THE LAST TIME. I COULDN'T BEAR IT THEN...
I CAN'T BEAR IT NOW.
BRING HIM BACK, HAL.
I CAN'T. NOT NOW.
AND THIS KNOWS THE TRUTH. IT SAYS THE BODY IS OLLIE.
THIS DOESN'T LIE.
NO...

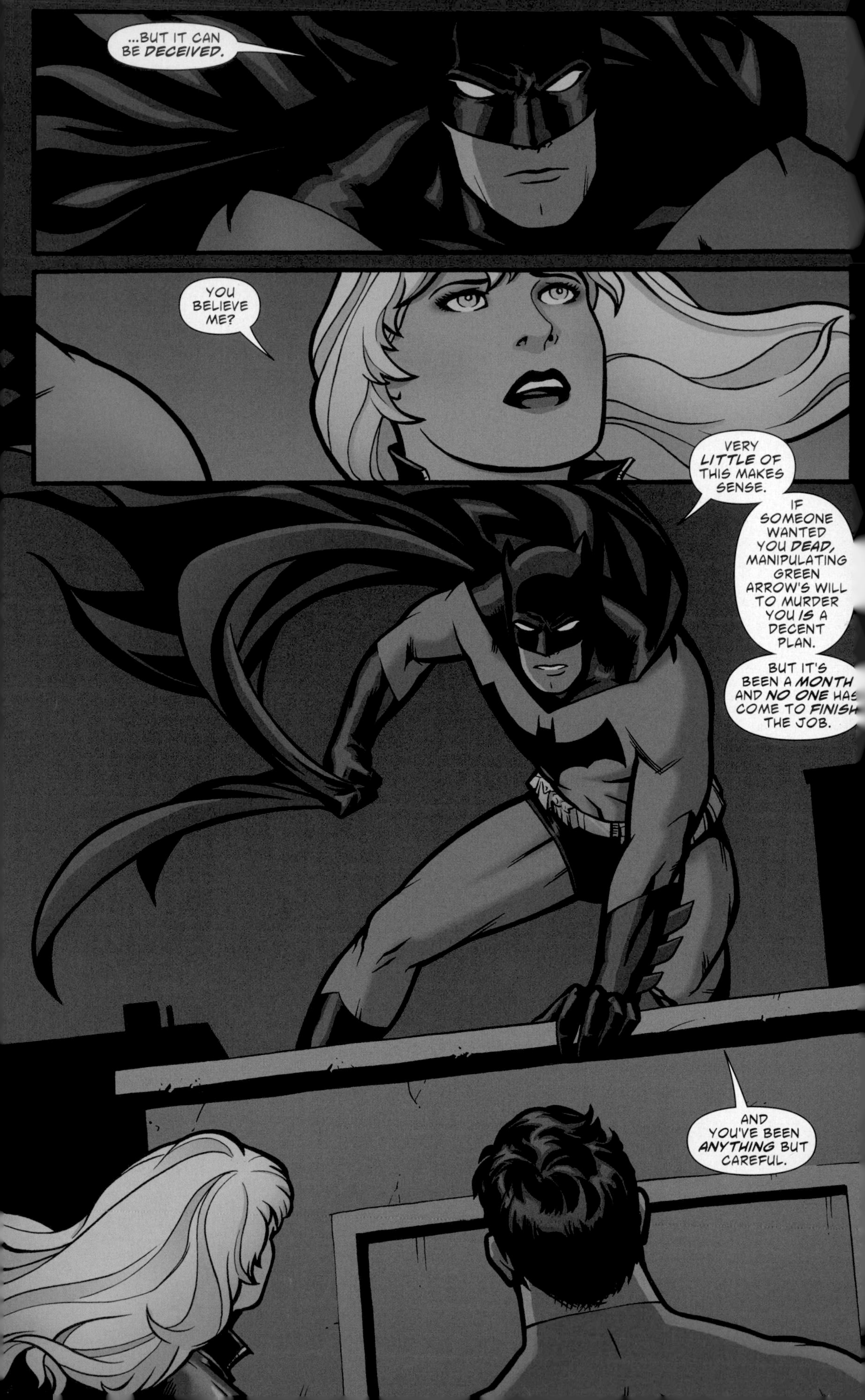
...BUT IT CAN BE DECEIVED.
YOU BELIEVE ME?
VERY LITTLE OF THIS MAKES SENSE.
IF SOMEONE WANTED YOU DEAD, MANIPULATING GREEN ARROW'S WILL TO MURDER YOU IS A DECENT PLAN.
BUT IT'S BEEN A MONTH AND NO ONE HAS COME TO FINISH THE JOB.
AND YOU'VE BEEN ANYTHING BUT CAREFUL.

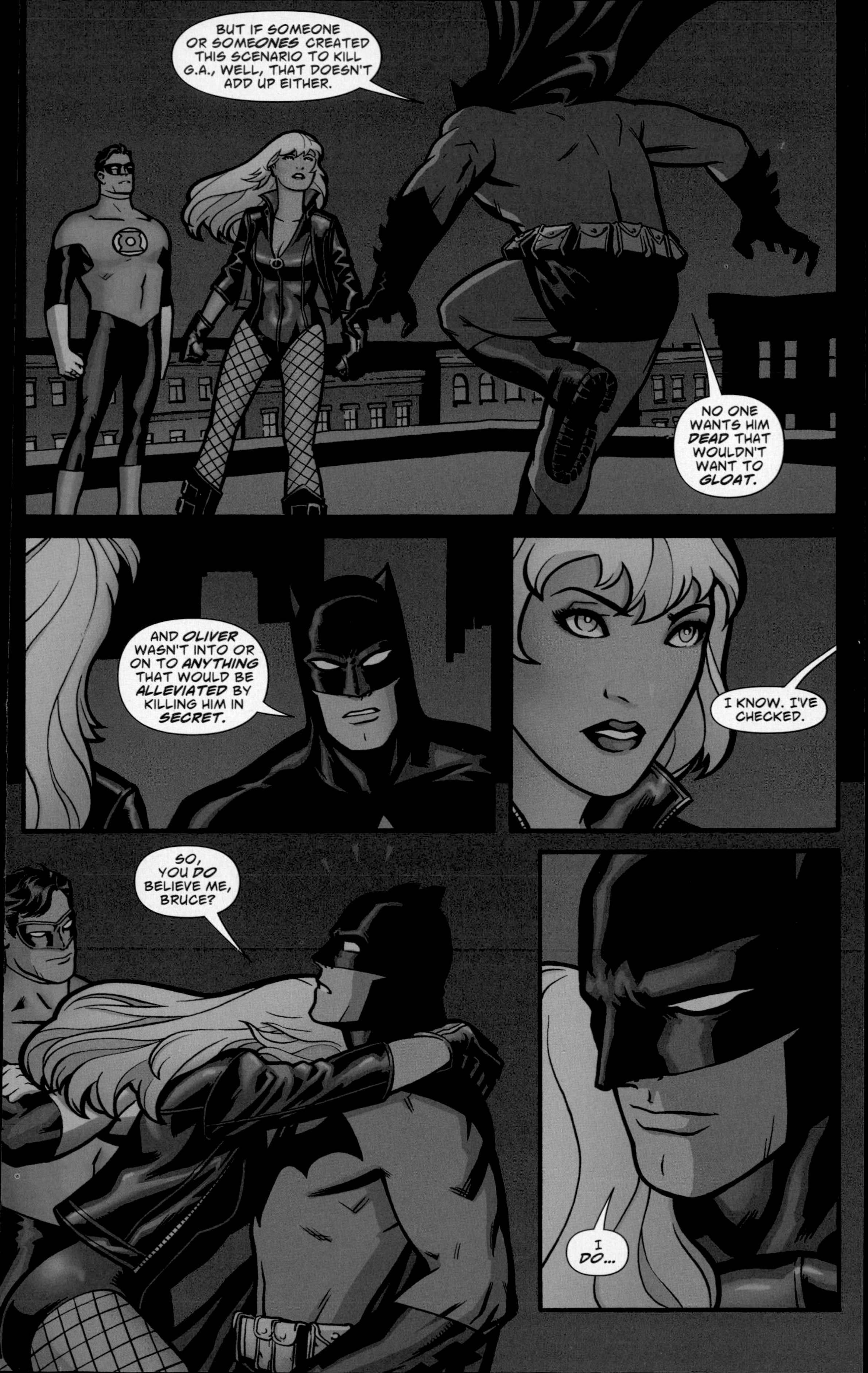
BUT IF SOMEONE OR SOMEONES CREATED THIS SCENARIO TO KILL G.A., WELL, THAT DOESN'T ADD UP EITHER.
NO ONE WANTS HIM DEAD THAT WOULDN'T WANT TO GLOAT.
AND OLIVER WASN'T INTO OR ON TO ANYTHING THAT WOULD BE ALLEVIATED BY KILLING HIM IN SECRET.
I KNOW. I'VE CHECKED.
SO, YOU DO BELIEVE ME, BRUCE?
I DO...

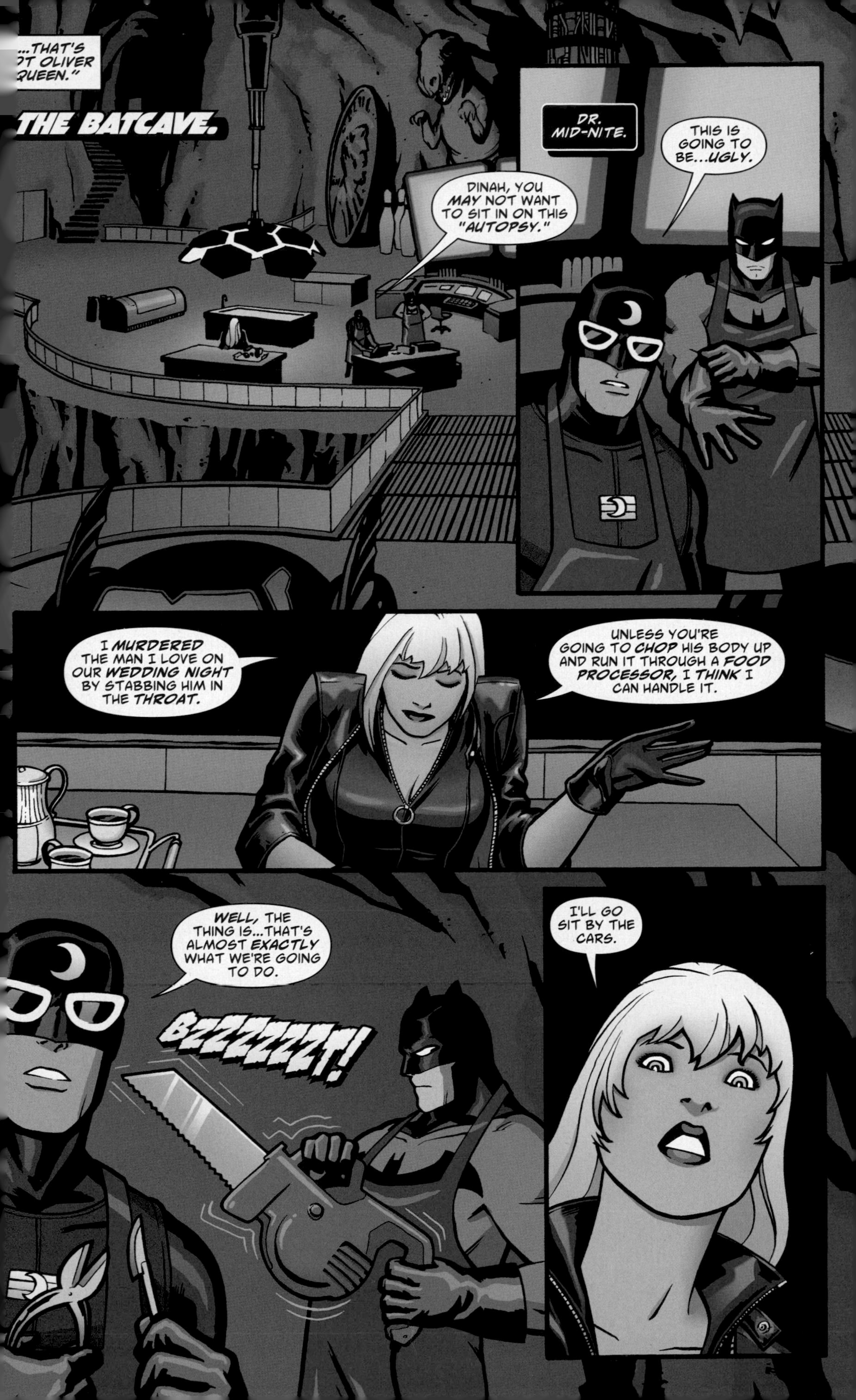
...THAT'S
OT OLIVER
QUEEN."
THE BATCAVE.
DR. MID-NITE.
DINAH, YOU MAY NOT WANT TO SIT IN ON THIS "AUTOPSY."
THIS IS GOING TO BE...UGLY.
I MURDERED THE MAN I LOVE ON OUR WEDDING NIGHT BY STABBING HIM IN THE THROAT.
UNLESS YOU'RE GOING TO CHOP HIS BODY UP AND RUN IT THROUGH A FOOD PROCESSOR, I THINK I CAN HANDLE IT.
WELL, THE THING IS...THAT'S ALMOST EXACTLY WHAT WE'RE GOING TO DO.
BZZZZZZT!
I'LL GO SIT BY THE CARS.

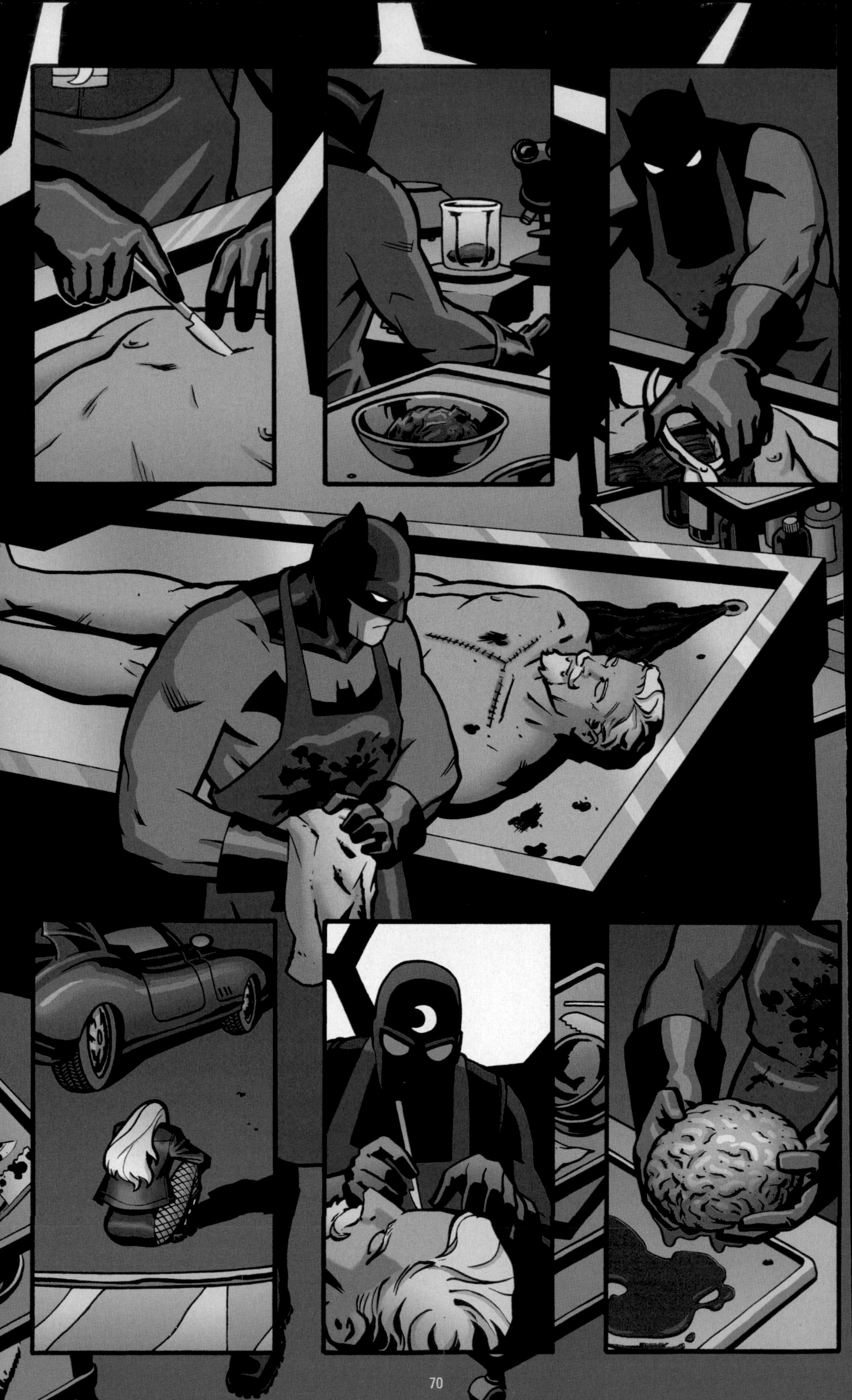

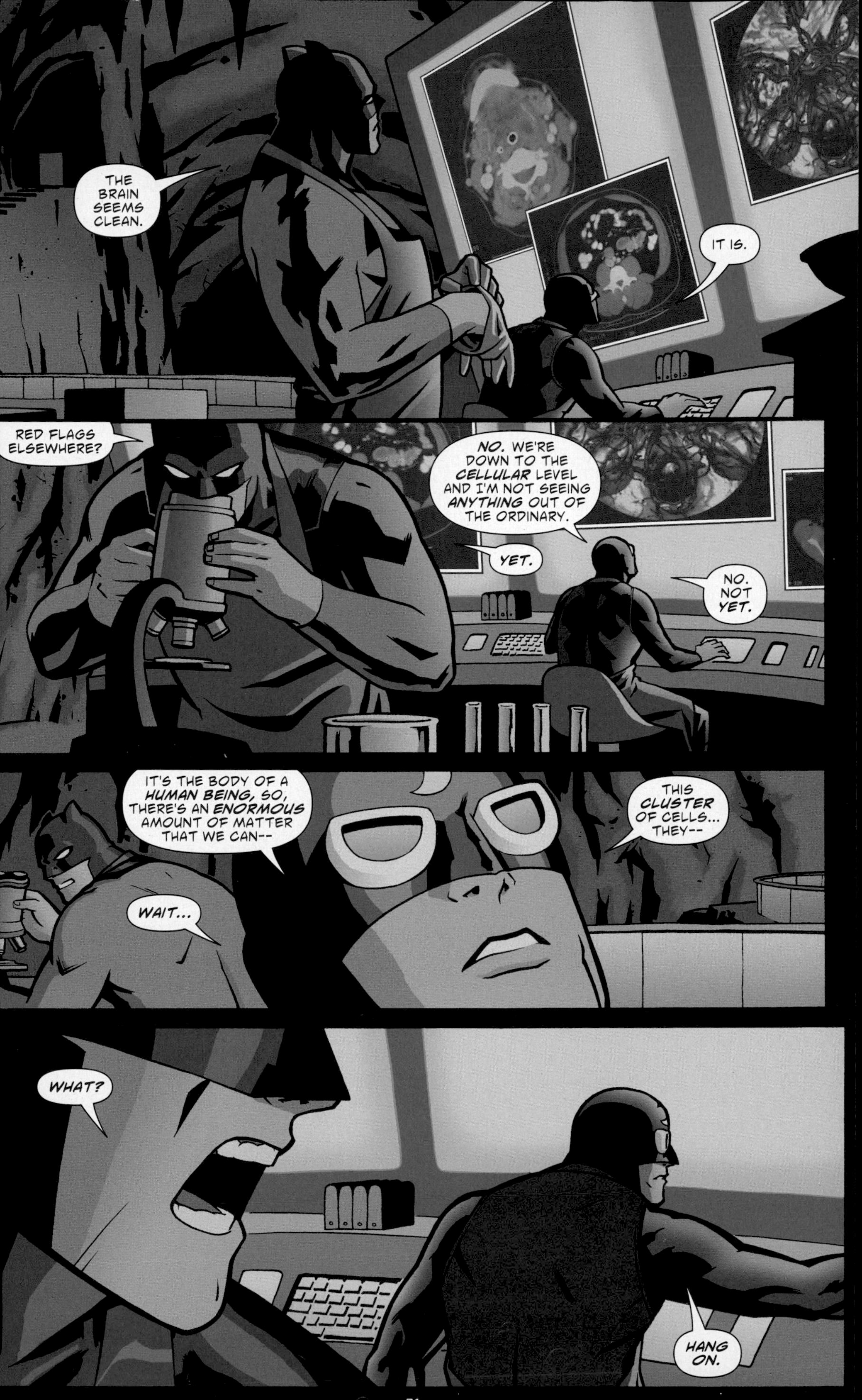
THE BRAIN SEEMS CLEAN.
IT IS.
RED FLAGS ELSEWHERE?
NO. WE'RE DOWN TO THE CELLULAR LEVEL AND I'M NOT SEEING ANYTHING OUT OF THE ORDINARY.
YET.
NO. NOT YET.
IT'S THE BODY OF A HUMAN BEING, SO, THERE'S AN ENORMOUS AMOUNT OF MATTER THAT WE CAN--
THIS CLUSTER OF CELLS... THEY--
WAIT...
WHAT?
HANG ON.

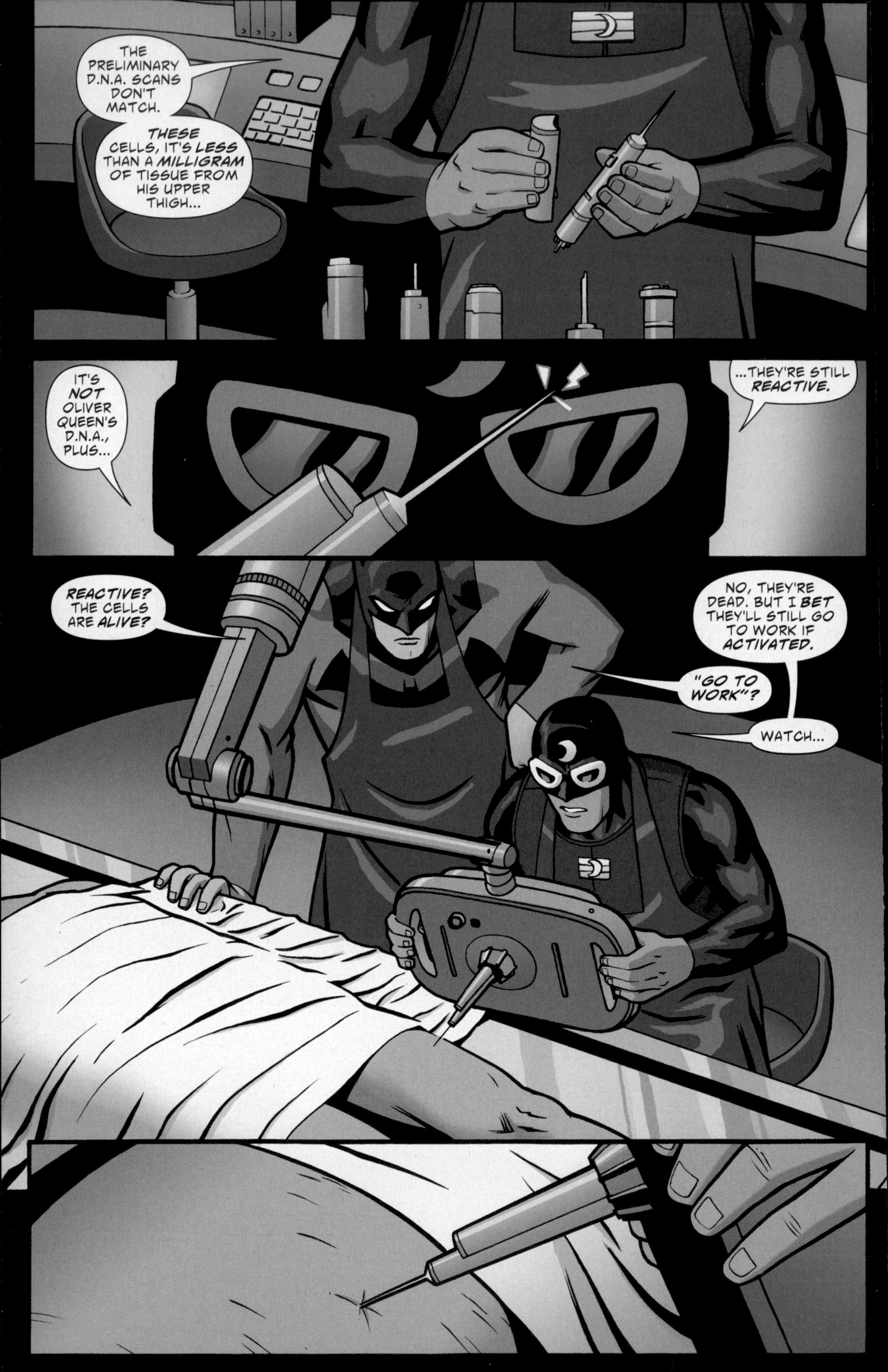

THE PRELIMINARY D.N.A. SCANS DON'T MATCH.
THESE CELLS, IT'S LESS THAN A MILLIGRAM OF TISSUE FROM HIS UPPER THIGH...
IT'S NOT OLIVER QUEEN'S D.N.A., PLUS...
...THEY'RE STILL REACTIVE.
REACTIVE? THE CELLS ARE ALIVE?
NO, THEY'RE DEAD. BUT I BET THEY'LL STILL GO TO WORK IF ACTIVATED.
"GO TO WORK"?
WATCH...

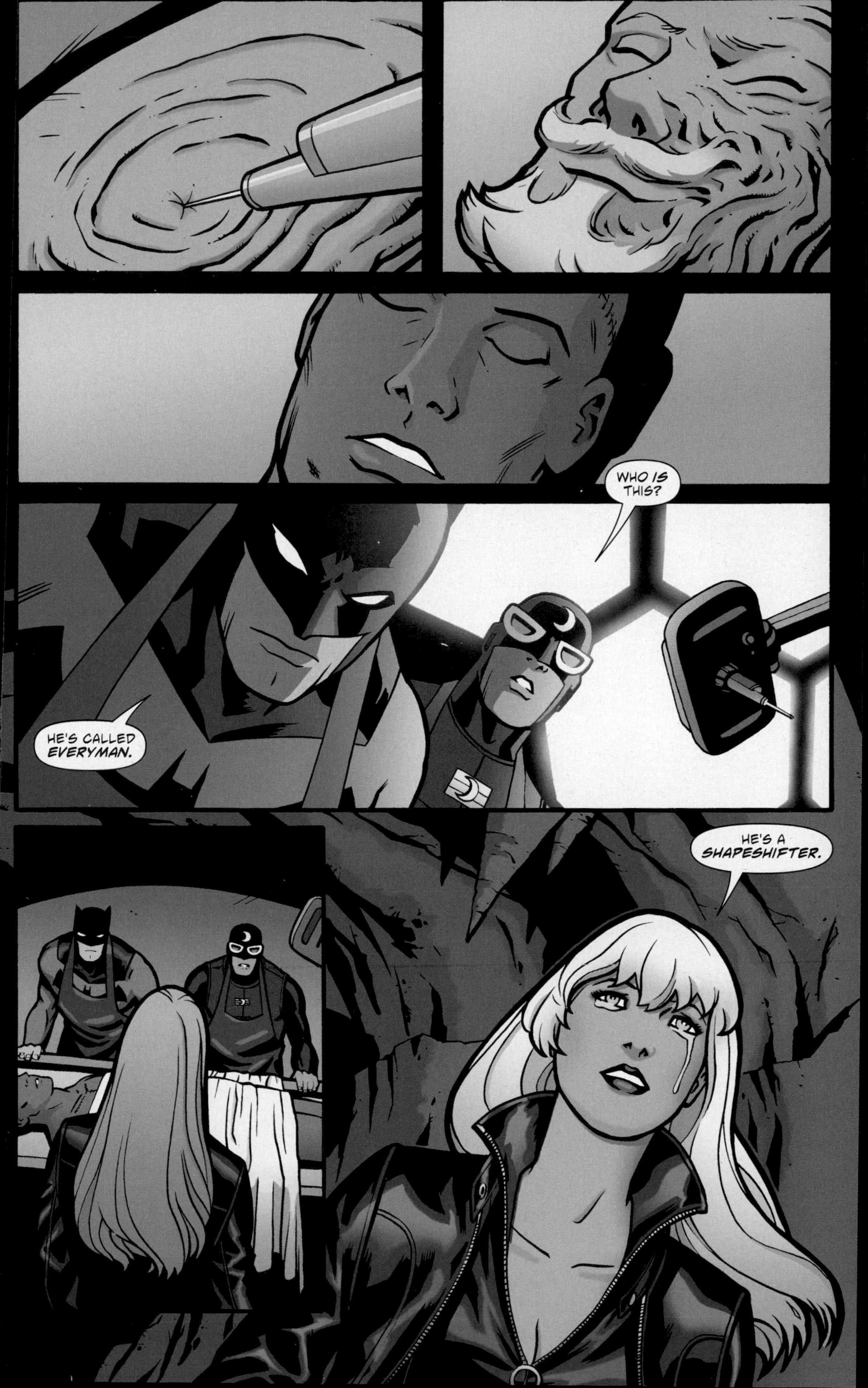
WHO IS THIS?
HE'S CALLED EVERYMAN.
HE'S A SHAPESHIFTER.

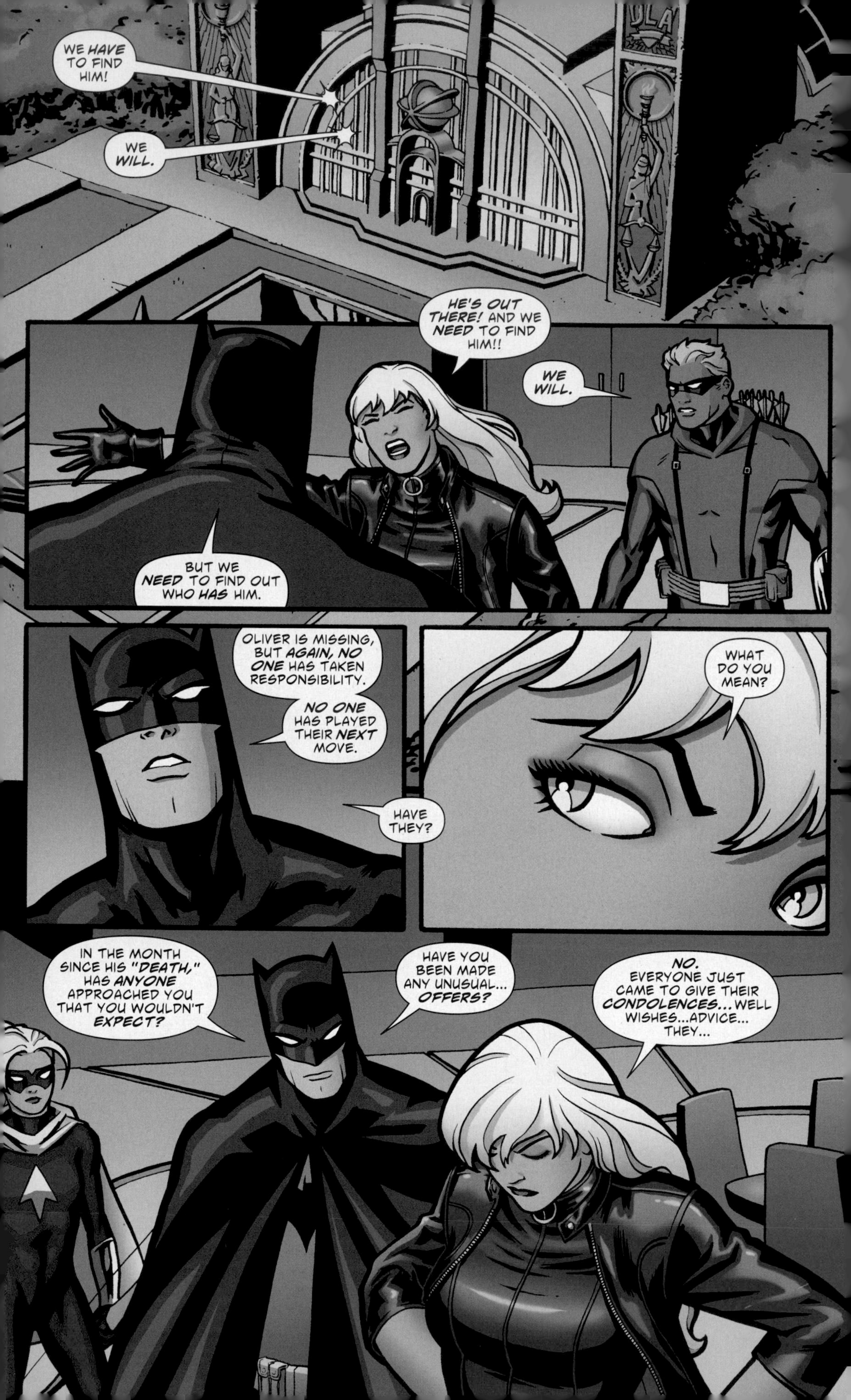
WE HAVE TO FIND HIM!
WE WILL.
HE'S OUT THERE! AND WE NEED TO FIND HIM!!
WE WILL.
BUT WE NEED TO FIND OUT WHO HAS HIM.
OLIVER IS MISSING, BUT AGAIN, NO ONE HAS TAKEN RESPONSIBILITY.
NO ONE HAS PLAYED THEIR NEXT MOVE.
HAVE THEY?
WHAT DO YOU MEAN?
IN THE MONTH SINCE HIS "DEATH," HAS ANYONE APPROACHED YOU THAT YOU WOULDN'T EXPECT?
HAVE YOU BEEN MADE ANY UNUSUAL... OFFERS?
NO. EVERYONE JUST CAME TO GIVE THEIR CONDOLENCES...WELL WISHES...ADVICE... THEY...

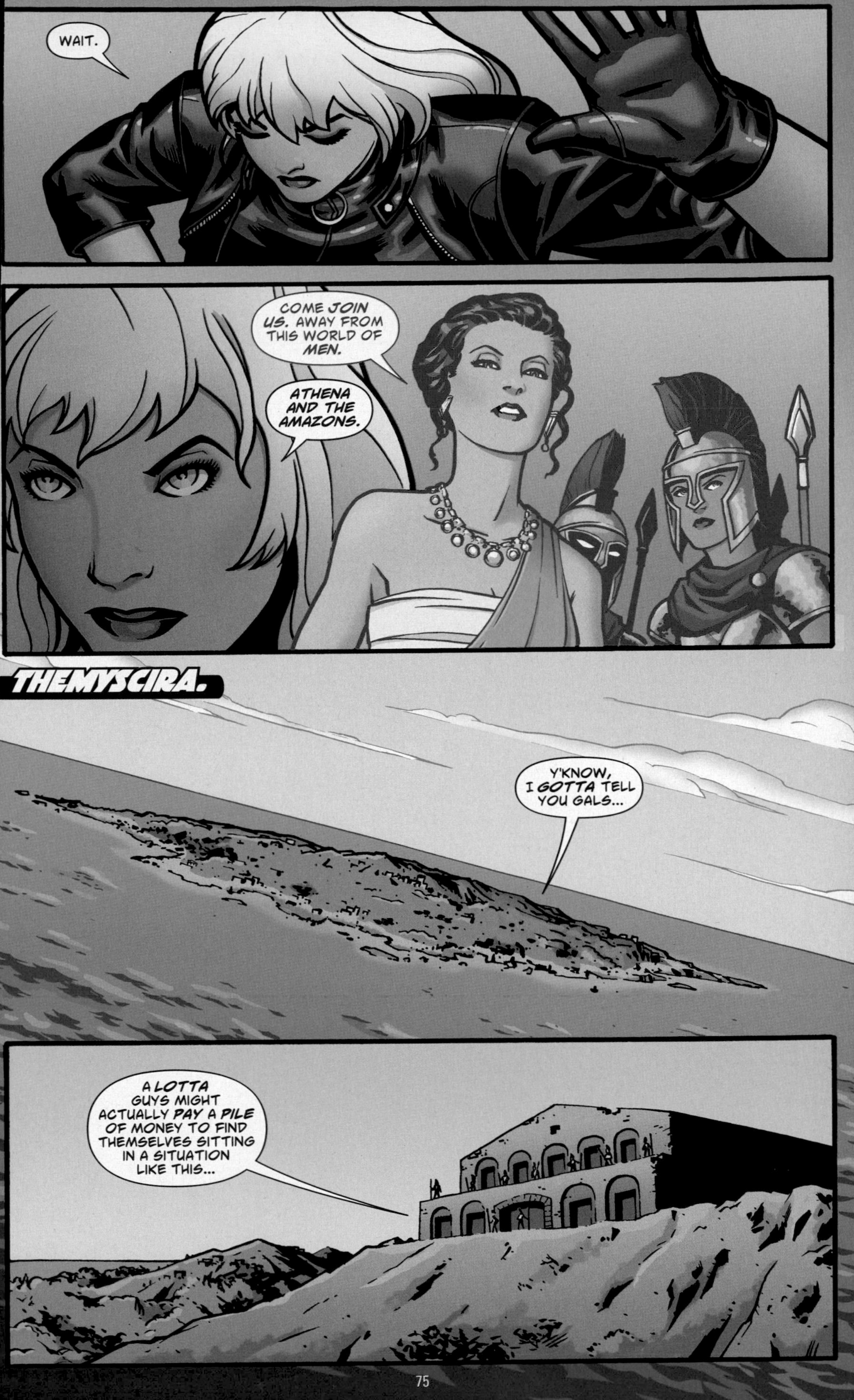
WAIT.
COME JOIN US. AWAY FROM THIS WORLD OF MEN.
ATHENA AND THE AMAZONS.
THEMYSCIRA.
Y'KNOW, I GOTTA TELL YOU GALS...
A LOTTA GUYS MIGHT ACTUALLY PAY A PILE OF MONEY TO FIND THEMSELVES SITTING IN A SITUATION LIKE THIS...

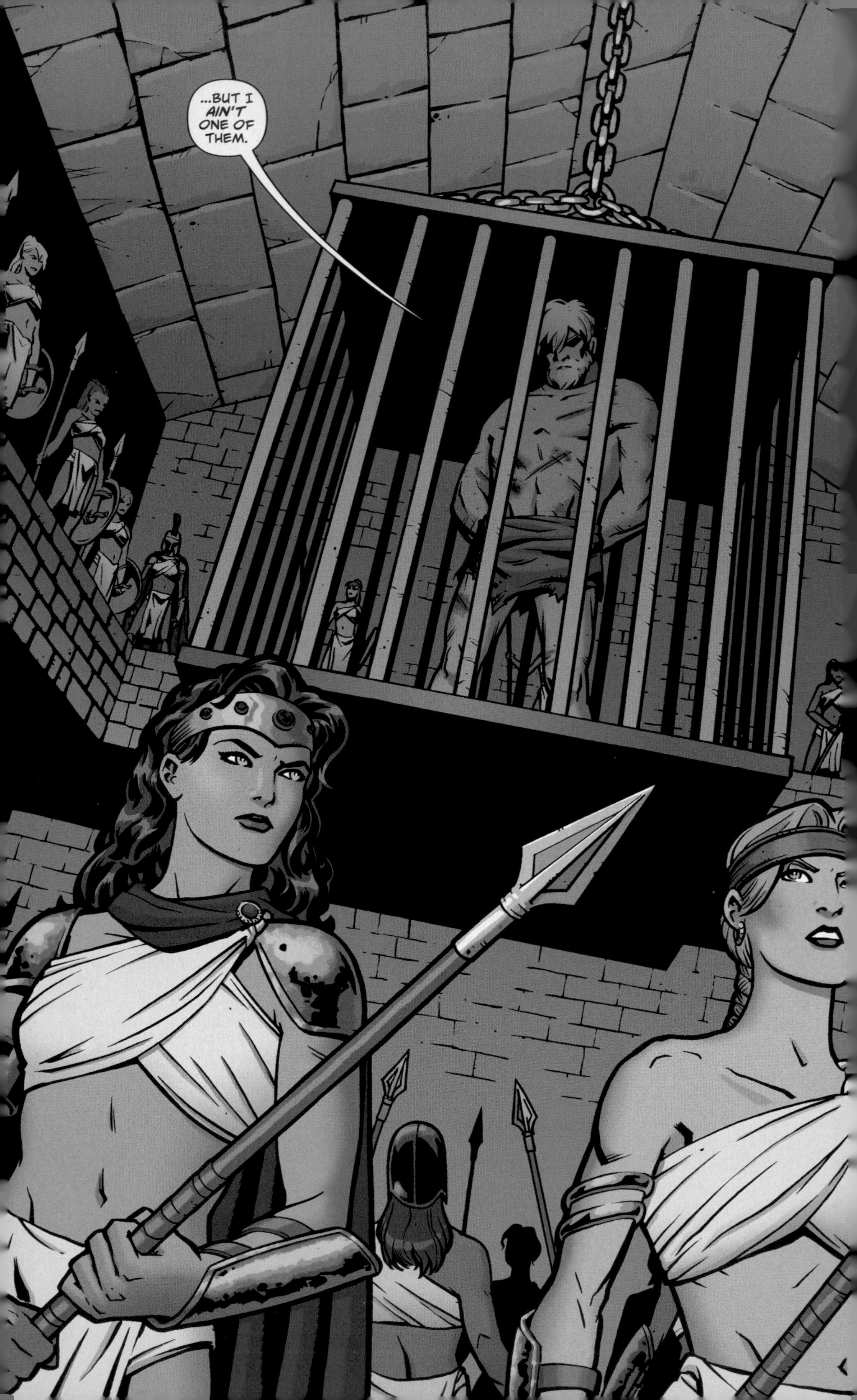
...BUT I AIN'T ONE OF THEM.

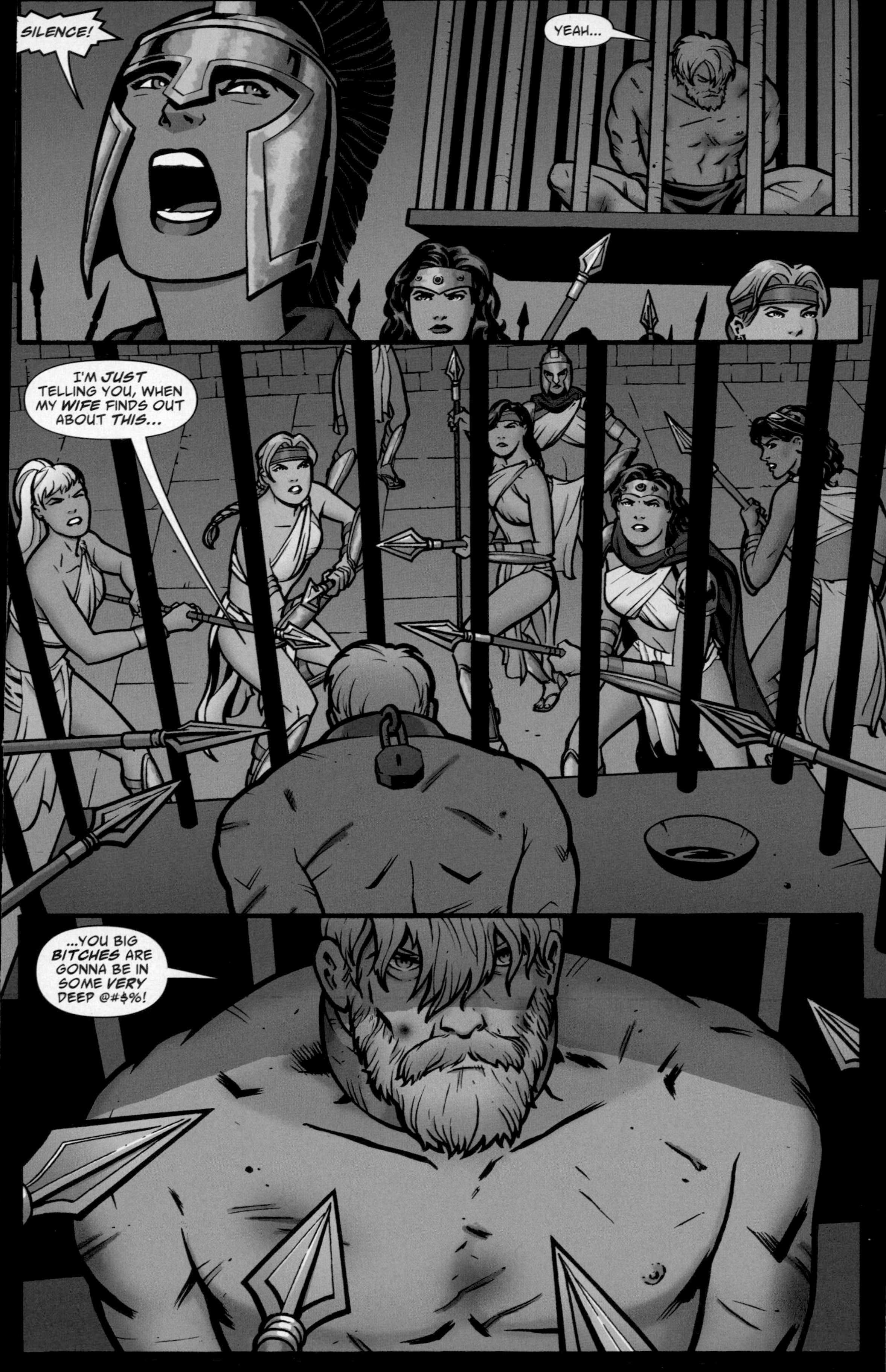
SILENCE!
YEAH...
I'M JUST TELLING YOU, WHEN MY WIFE FINDS OUT ABOUT THIS...
...YOU BIG BITCHES ARE GONNA BE IN SOME VERY DEEP @#$%!

GREEN ARROW AND BLACK CANARY #2 *Cliff Ch[redacted]g*

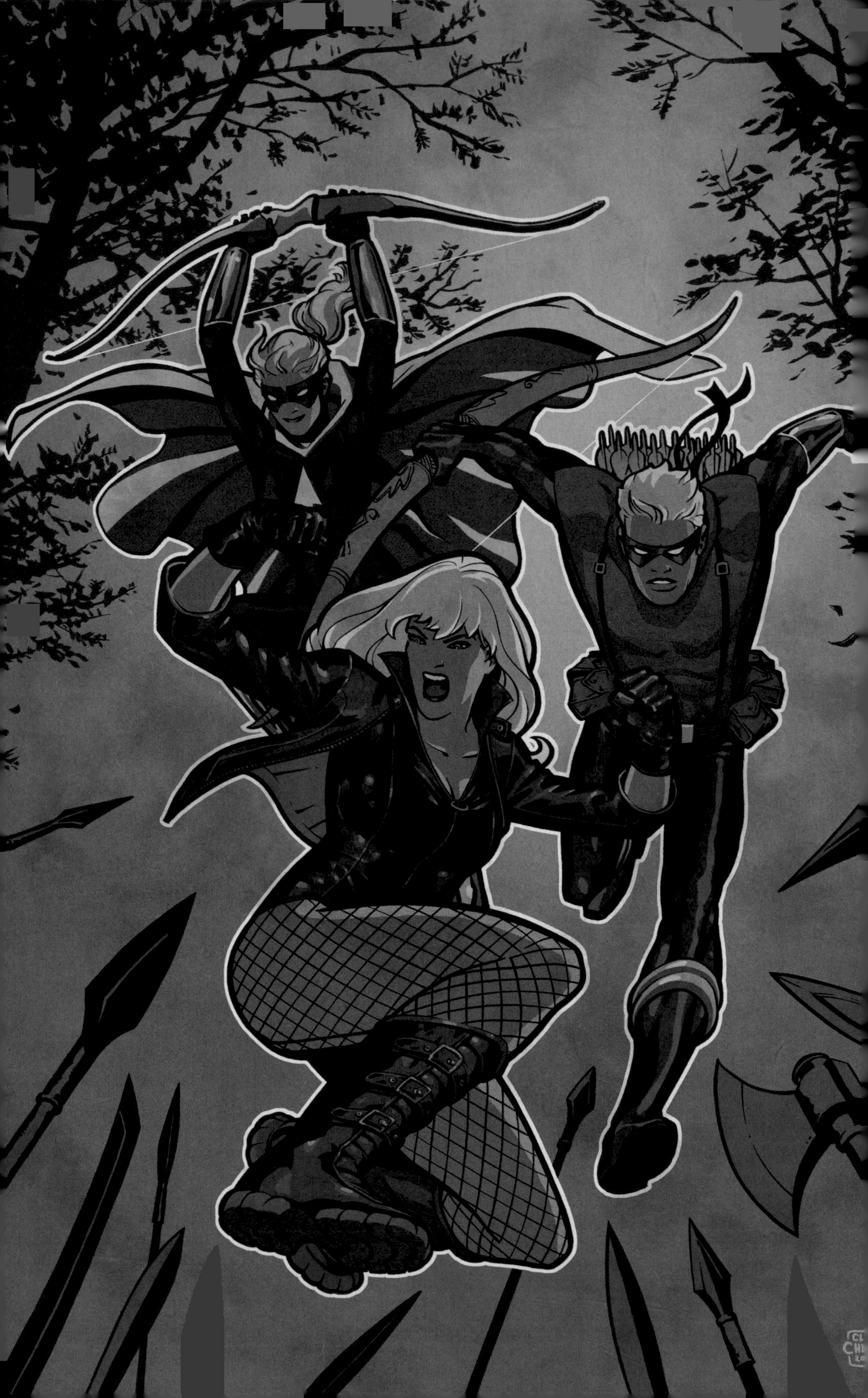

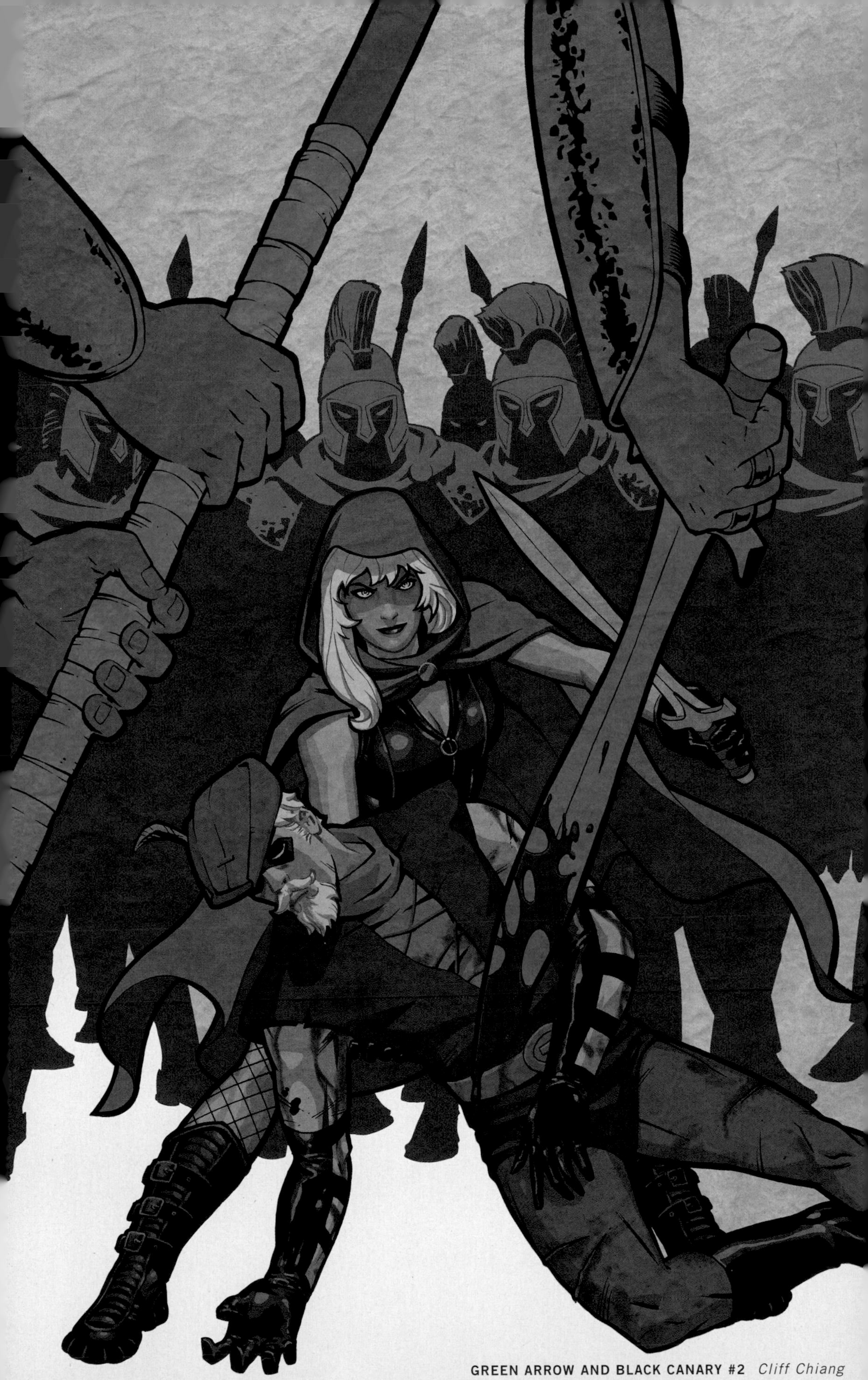

GREEN ARROW AND BLACK CANARY #2 *Cliff Chiang*

DEAD AGAIN PART TWO: THE NAKED AND THE *NOT-QUITE-SO*-DEAD

Story: **Judd Winick**   *Art:* **Cliff Chiang**   *Color:* **Trish Mulvihill**

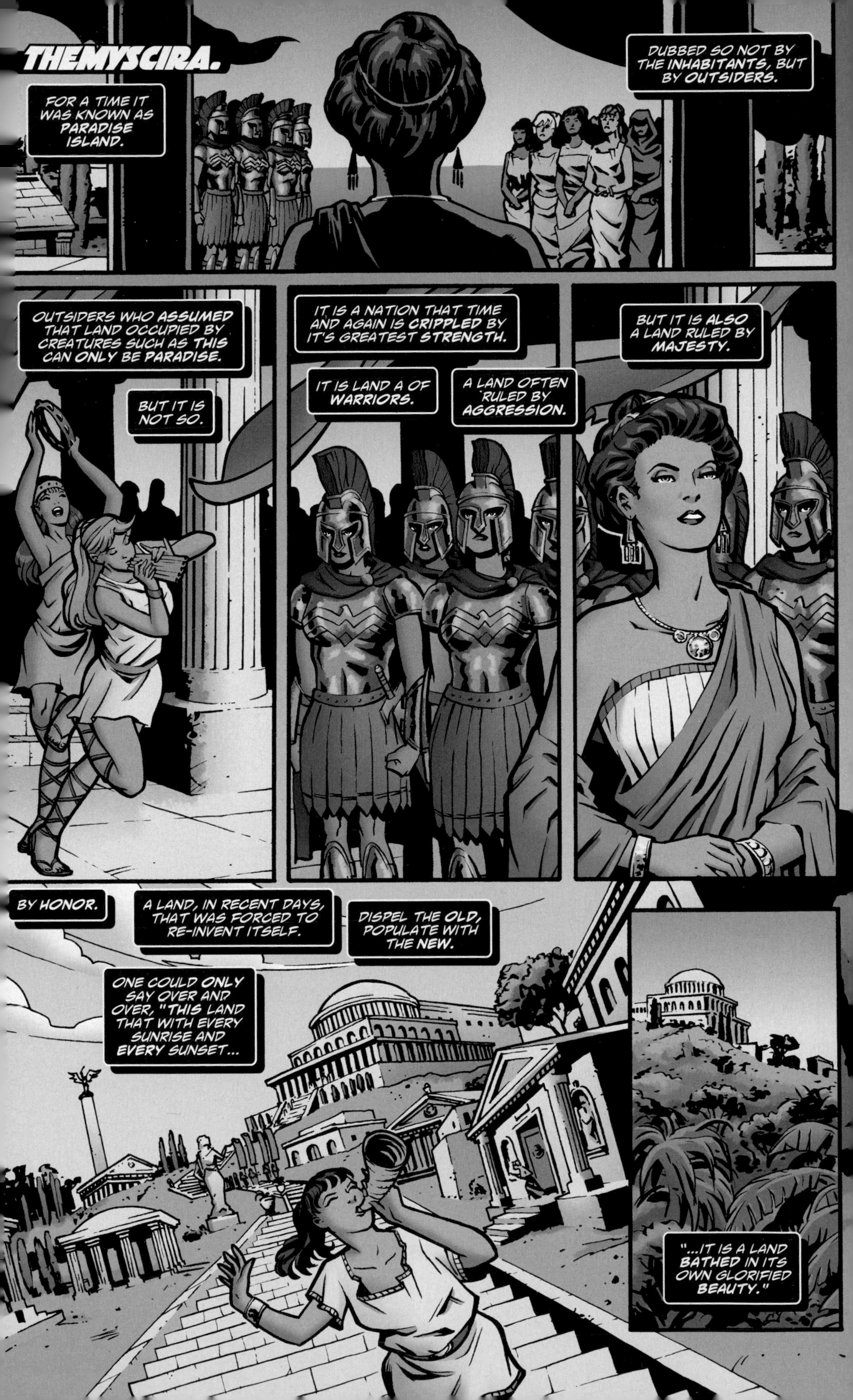
THEMYSCIRA.
FOR A TIME IT WAS KNOWN AS PARADISE ISLAND.
DUBBED SO NOT BY THE INHABITANTS, BUT BY OUTSIDERS.
OUTSIDERS WHO ASSUMED THAT LAND OCCUPIED BY CREATURES SUCH AS THIS CAN ONLY BE PARADISE.
BUT IT IS NOT SO.
IT IS A NATION THAT TIME AND AGAIN IS CRIPPLED BY IT'S GREATEST STRENGTH.
IT IS LAND A OF WARRIORS.
A LAND OFTEN RULED BY AGGRESSION.
BUT IT IS ALSO A LAND RULED BY MAJESTY.
BY HONOR.
A LAND, IN RECENT DAYS, THAT WAS FORCED TO RE-INVENT ITSELF.
DISPEL THE OLD, POPULATE WITH THE NEW.
ONE COULD ONLY SAY OVER AND OVER, "THIS LAND THAT WITH EVERY SUNRISE AND EVERY SUNSET...
"...IT IS A LAND BATHED IN ITS OWN GLORIFIED BEAUTY."

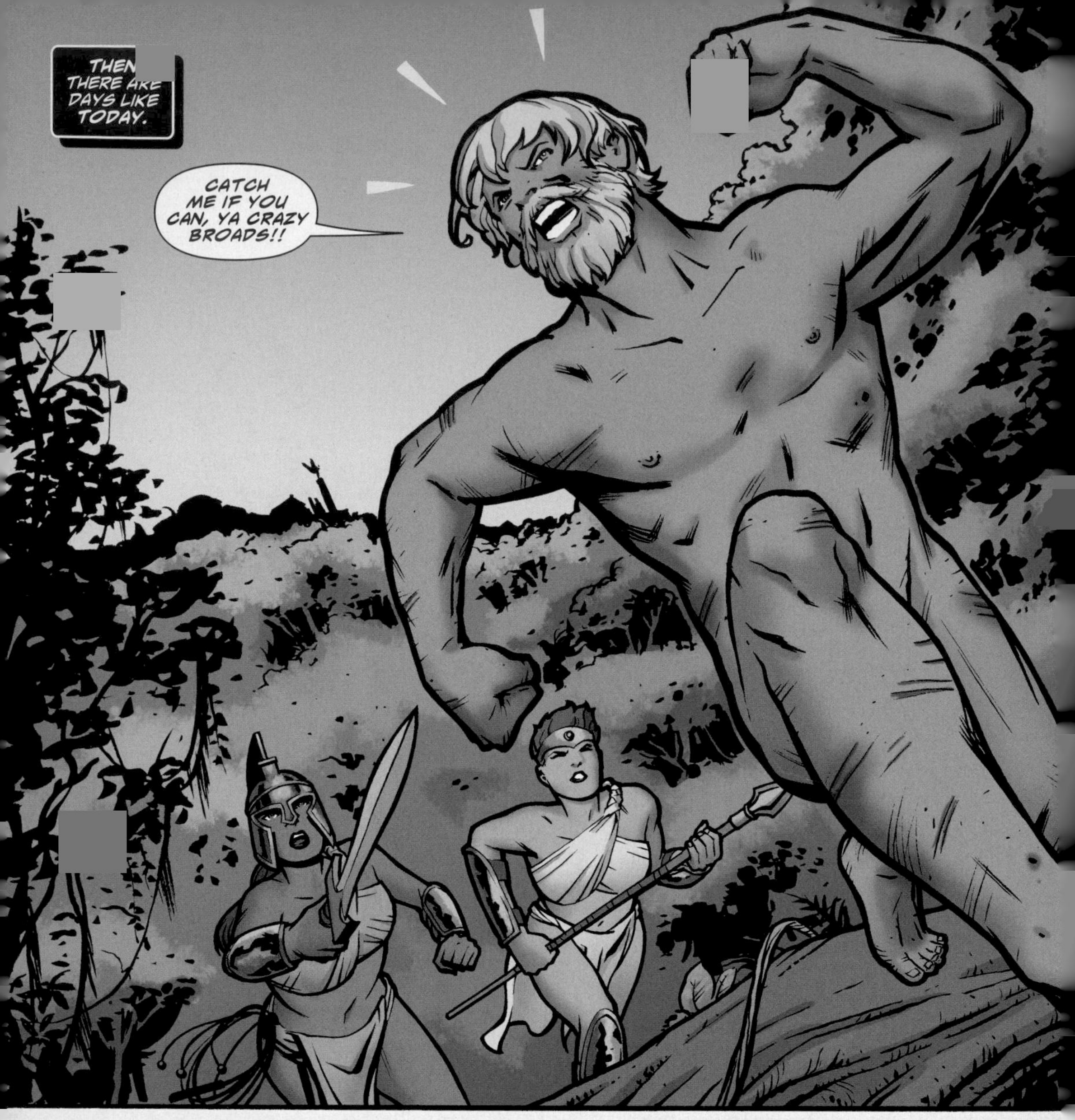
THEN THERE ARE DAYS LIKE TODAY.
CATCH ME IF YOU CAN, YA CRAZY BROADS!!

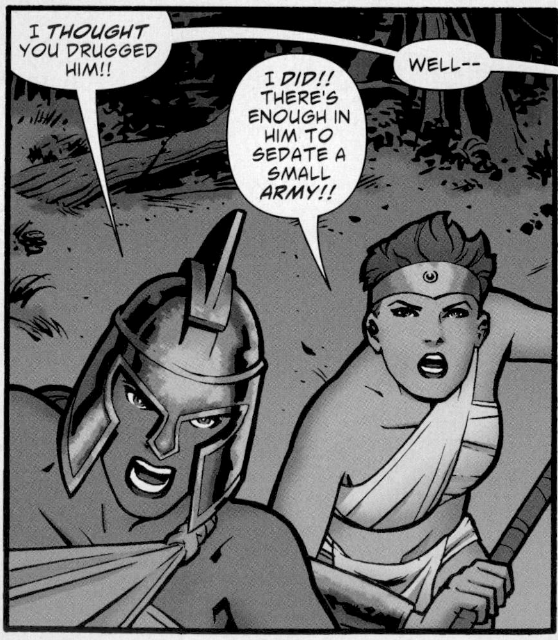
I *THOUGHT* YOU DRUGGED HIM!!
I *DID!!* THERE'S ENOUGH IN HIM TO SEDATE A SMALL *ARMY!!*
WELL--

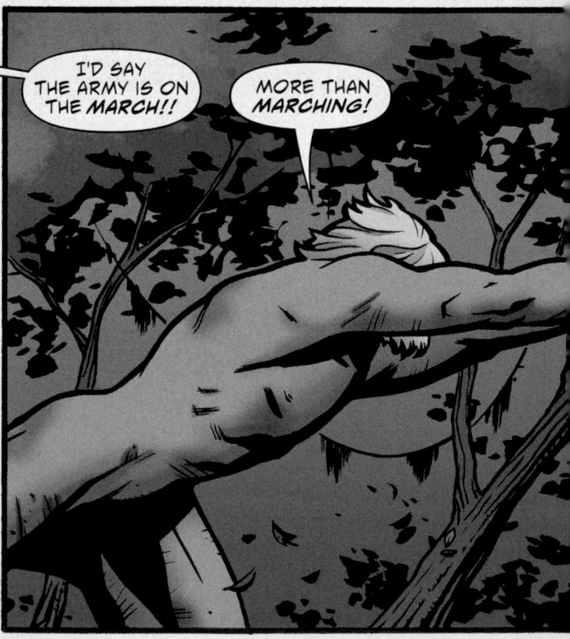
I'D SAY THE ARMY IS ON THE *MARCH!!*
MORE THAN *MARCHING!*

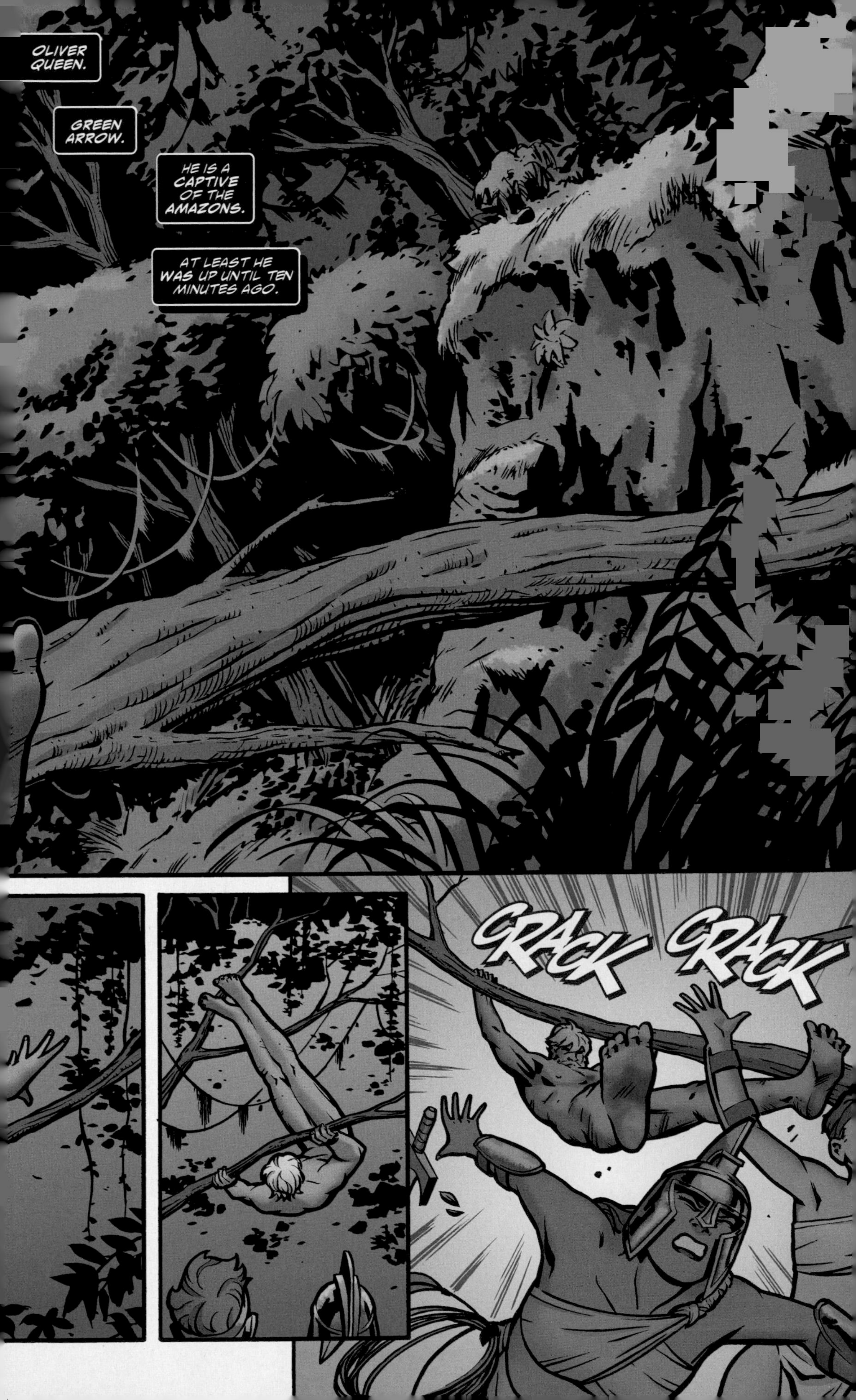
OLIVER QUEEN.
GREEN ARROW.
HE IS A CAPTIVE OF THE AMAZONS.
AT LEAST HE WAS UP UNTIL TEN MINUTES AGO.
CRACK CRACK

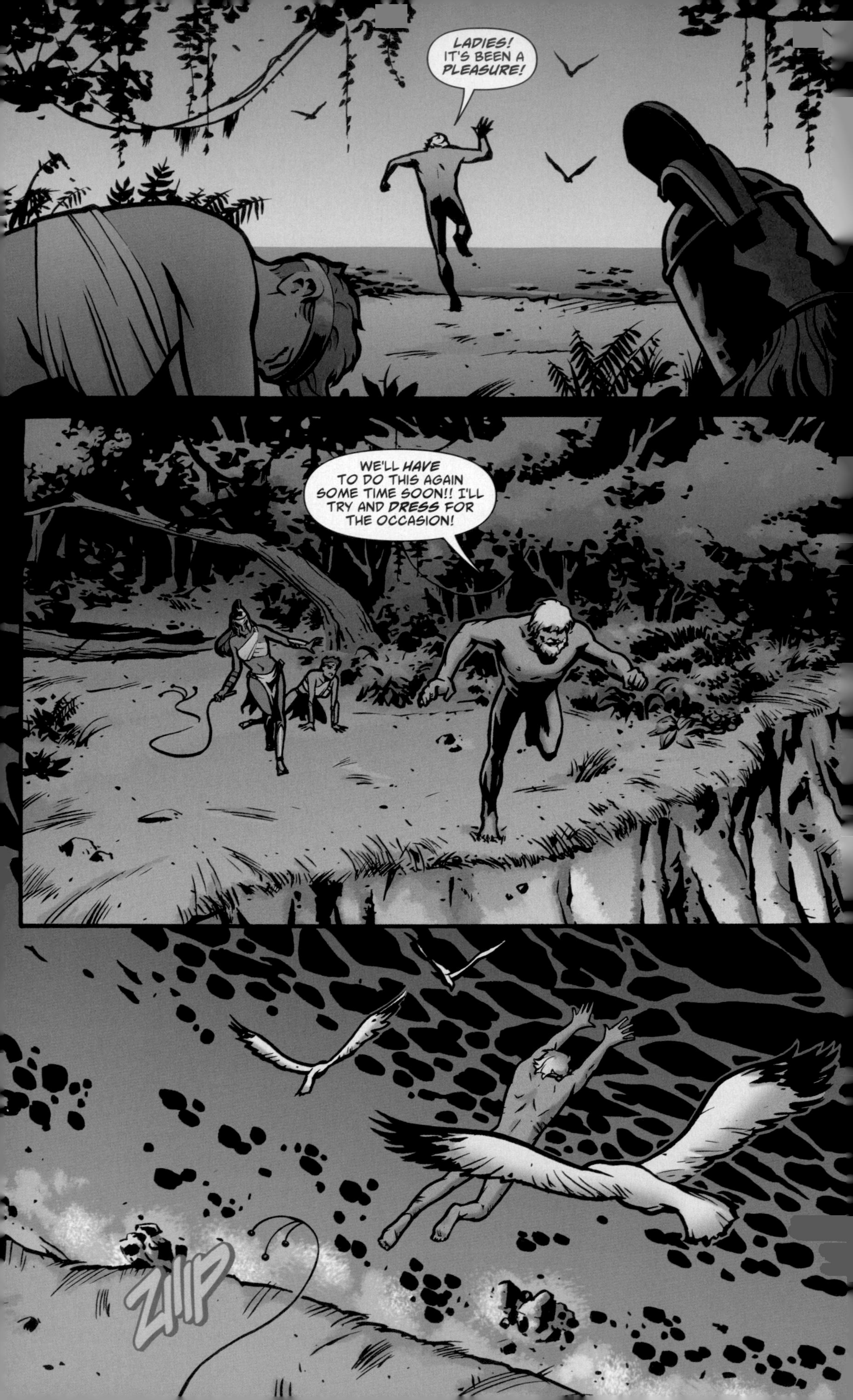
LADIES! IT'S BEEN A PLEASURE!
WE'LL HAVE TO DO THIS AGAIN SOME TIME SOON!! I'LL TRY AND DRESS FOR THE OCCASION!
ZIIIP

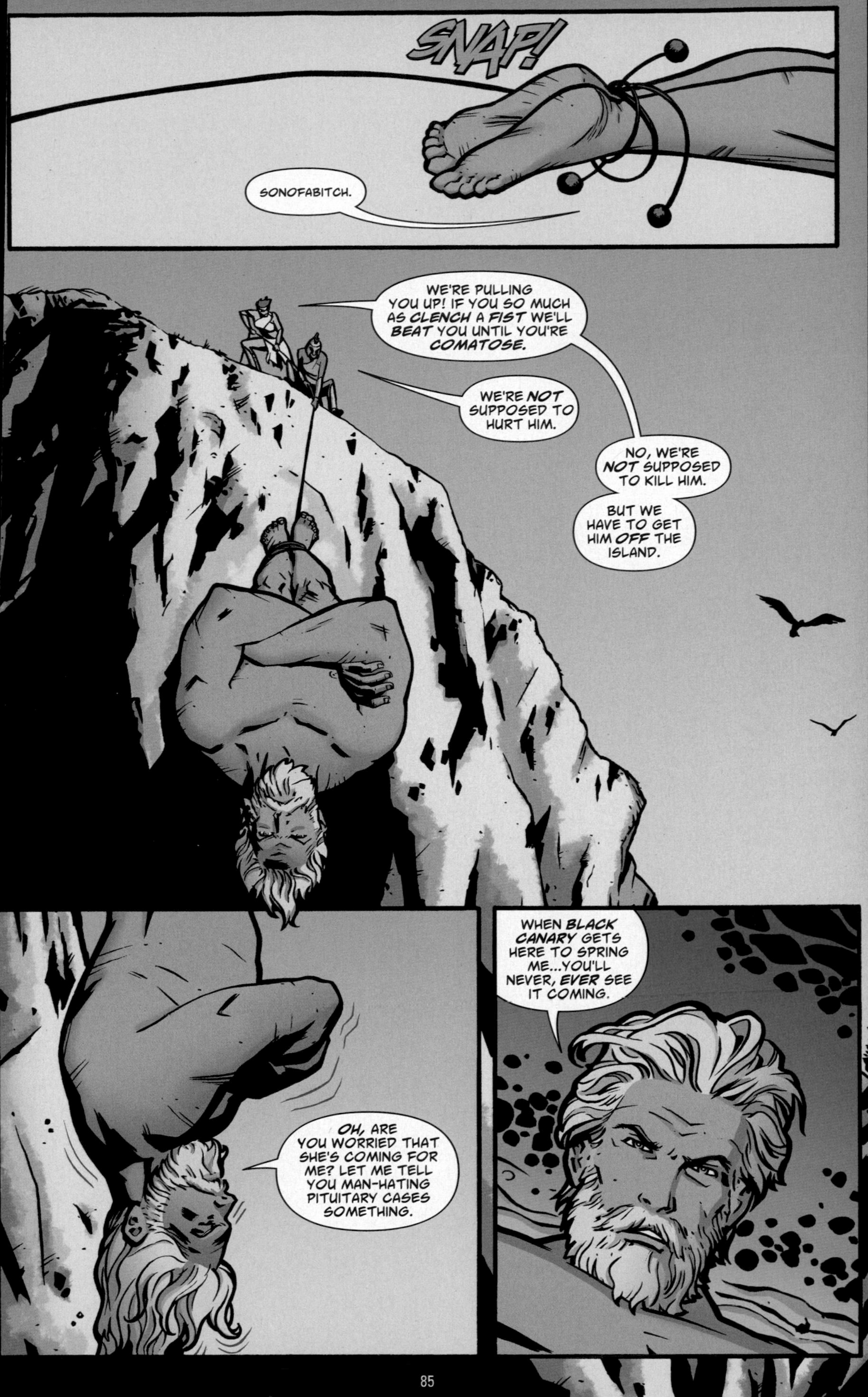
SNAP!
SONOFABITCH.
WE'RE PULLING YOU UP! IF YOU SO MUCH AS CLENCH A FIST WE'LL BEAT YOU UNTIL YOU'RE COMATOSE.
WE'RE NOT SUPPOSED TO HURT HIM.
NO, WE'RE NOT SUPPOSED TO KILL HIM.
BUT WE HAVE TO GET HIM OFF THE ISLAND.
OH, ARE YOU WORRIED THAT SHE'S COMING FOR ME? LET ME TELL YOU MAN-HATING PITUITARY CASES SOMETHING.
WHEN BLACK CANARY GETS HERE TO SPRING ME...YOU'LL NEVER, EVER SEE IT COMING.

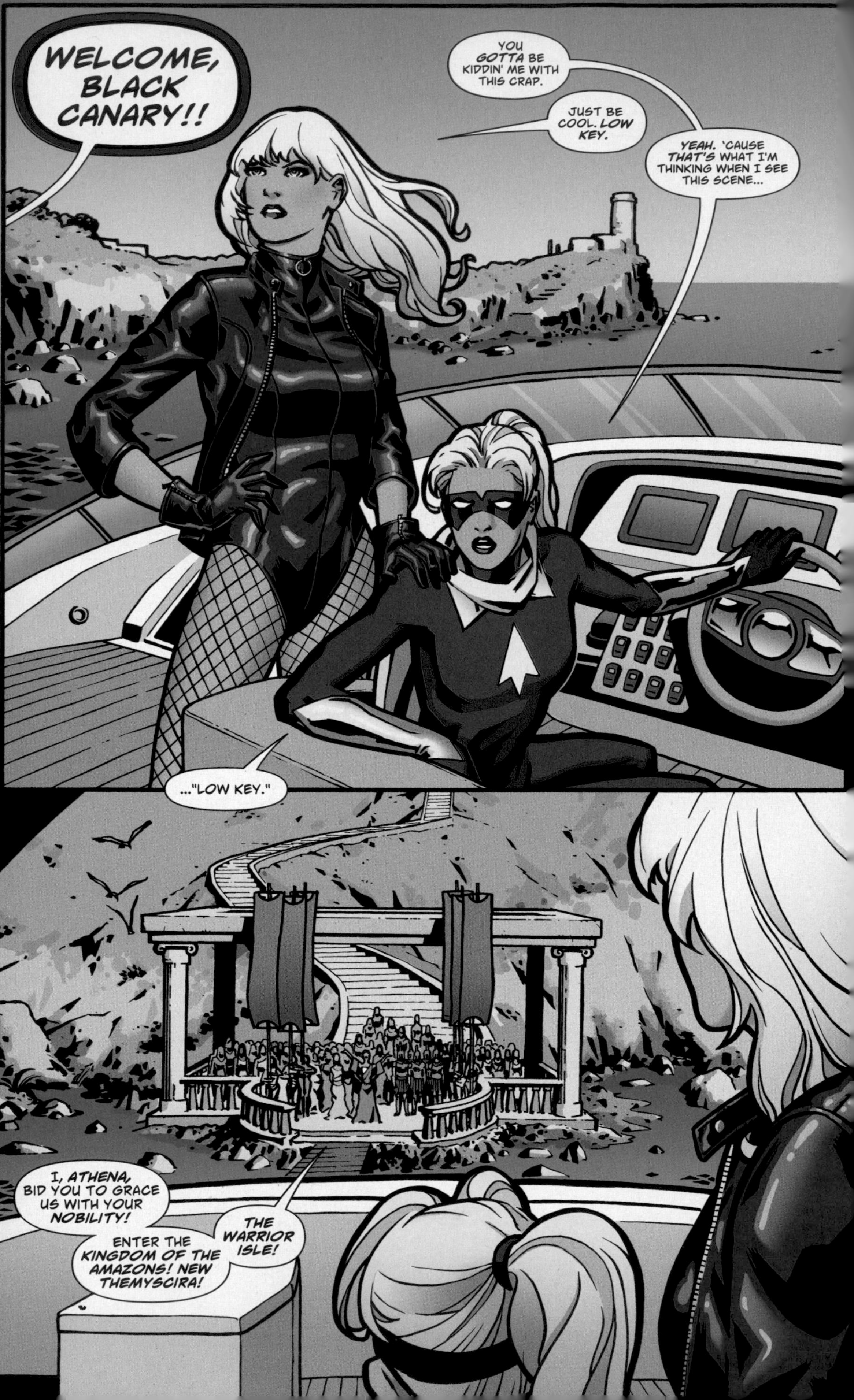

WELCOME, BLACK CANARY!!
YOU GOTTA BE KIDDIN' ME WITH THIS CRAP.
JUST BE COOL. LOW KEY.
YEAH. 'CAUSE THAT'S WHAT I'M THINKING WHEN I SEE THIS SCENE...
..."LOW KEY."
I, ATHENA, BID YOU TO GRACE US WITH YOUR NOBILITY!
THE WARRIOR ISLE!
ENTER THE KINGDOM OF THE AMAZONS! NEW THEMYSCIRA!

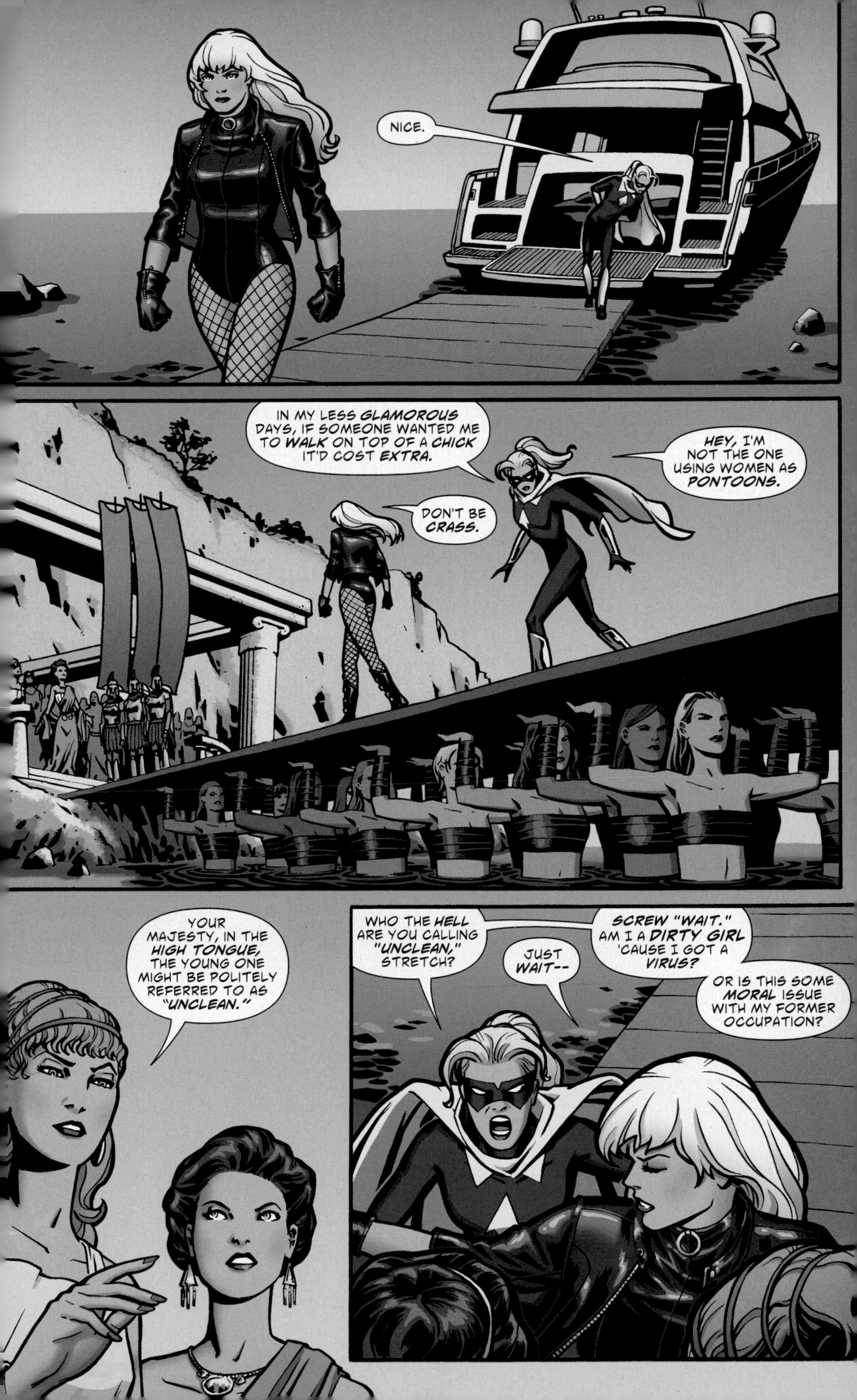
NICE.
IN MY LESS GLAMOROUS DAYS, IF SOMEONE WANTED ME TO WALK ON TOP OF A CHICK IT'D COST EXTRA.
HEY, I'M NOT THE ONE USING WOMEN AS PONTOONS.
DON'T BE CRASS.
YOUR MAJESTY, IN THE HIGH TONGUE, THE YOUNG ONE MIGHT BE POLITELY REFERRED TO AS "UNCLEAN."
WHO THE HELL ARE YOU CALLING "UNCLEAN," STRETCH?
JUST WAIT--
SCREW "WAIT." AM I A DIRTY GIRL 'CAUSE I GOT A VIRUS?
OR IS THIS SOME MORAL ISSUE WITH MY FORMER OCCUPATION?

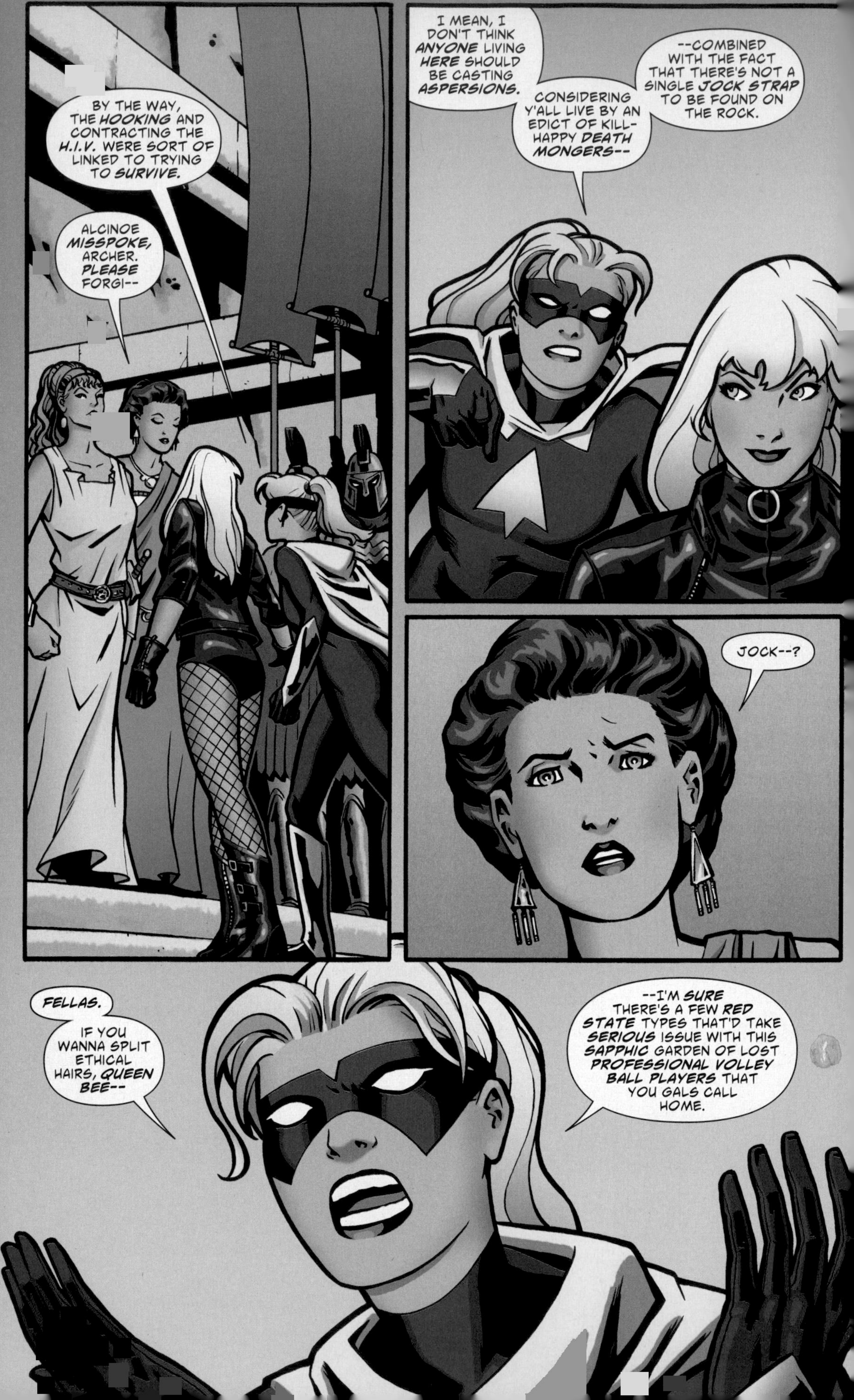
BY THE WAY, THE HOOKING AND CONTRACTING THE H.I.V. WERE SORT OF LINKED TO TRYING TO SURVIVE.
ALCINOE MISSPOKE, ARCHER. PLEASE FORGI--
I MEAN, I DON'T THINK ANYONE LIVING HERE SHOULD BE CASTING ASPERSIONS.
CONSIDERING Y'ALL LIVE BY AN EDICT OF KILL-HAPPY DEATH MONGERS--
--COMBINED WITH THE FACT THAT THERE'S NOT A SINGLE JOCK STRAP TO BE FOUND ON THE ROCK.
JOCK--?
FELLAS.
IF YOU WANNA SPLIT ETHICAL HAIRS, QUEEN BEE--
--I'M SURE THERE'S A FEW RED STATE TYPES THAT'D TAKE SERIOUS ISSUE WITH THIS SAPPHIC GARDEN OF LOST PROFESSIONAL VOLLEY BALL PLAYERS THAT YOU GALS CALL HOME.

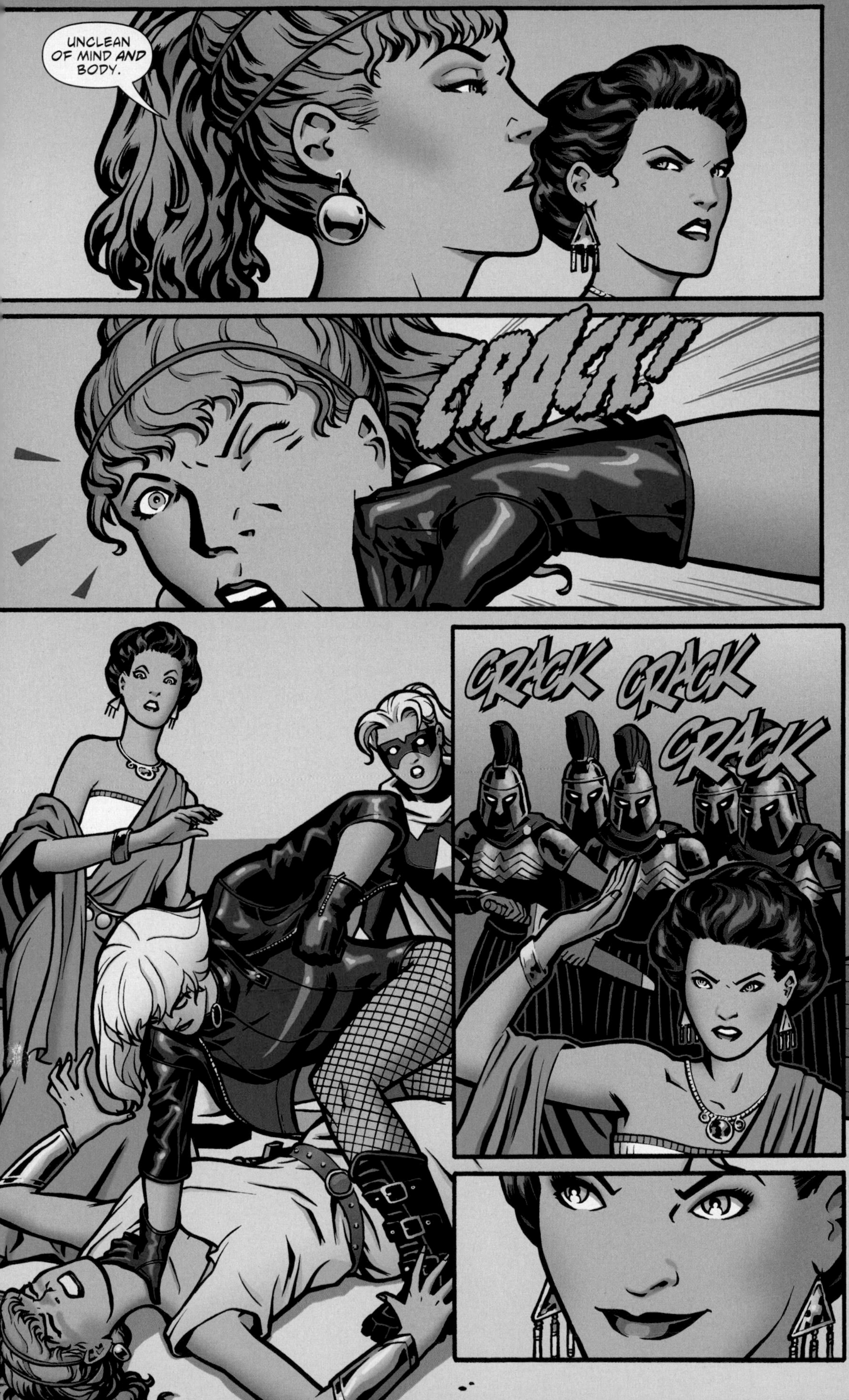
UNCLEAN OF MIND AND BODY.
CRACK!
CRACK CRACK
CRACK

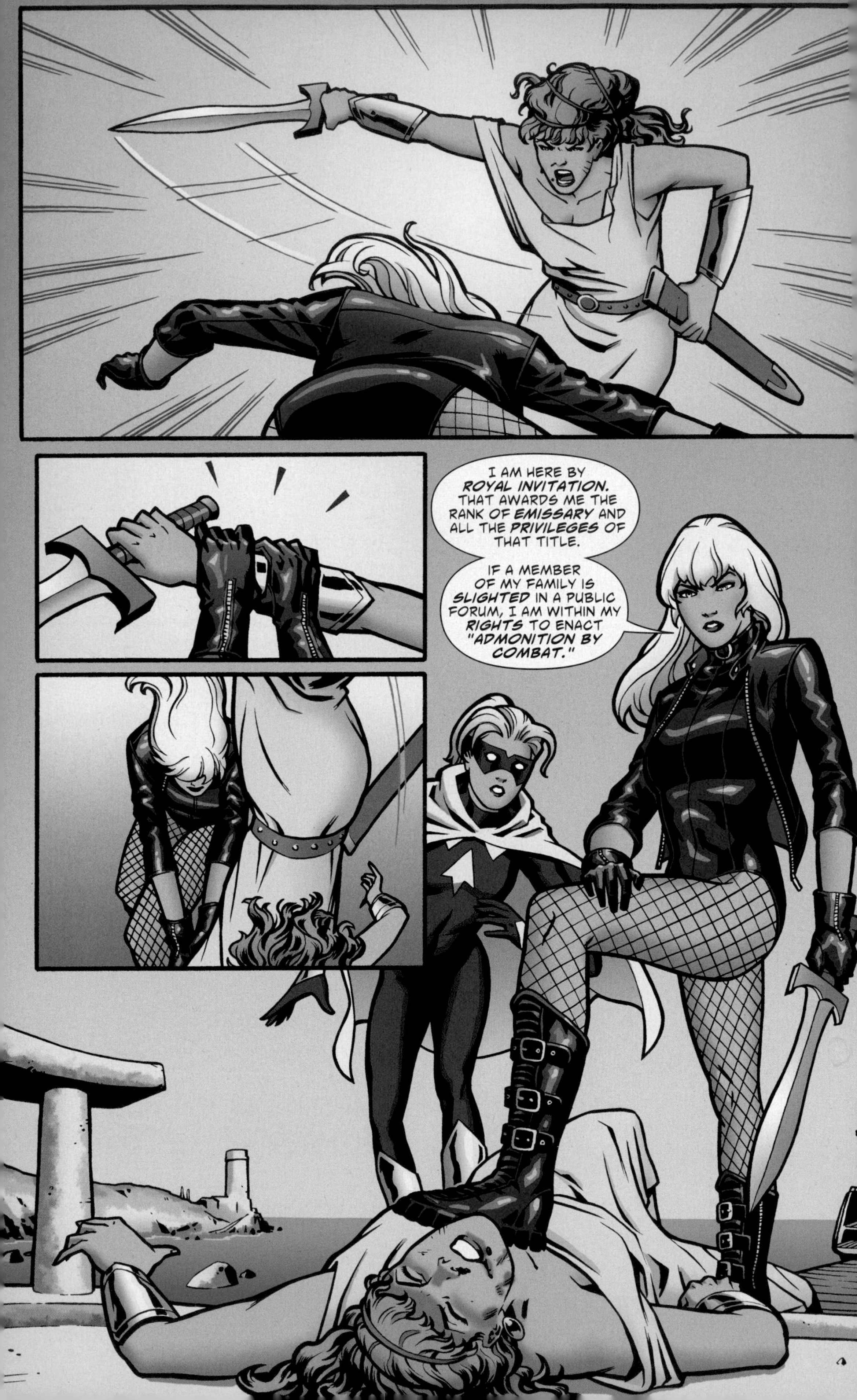
I AM HERE BY ROYAL INVITATION. THAT AWARDS ME THE RANK OF EMISSARY AND ALL THE PRIVILEGES OF THAT TITLE.
IF A MEMBER OF MY FAMILY IS SLIGHTED IN A PUBLIC FORUM, I AM WITHIN MY RIGHTS TO ENACT "ADMONITION BY COMBAT."

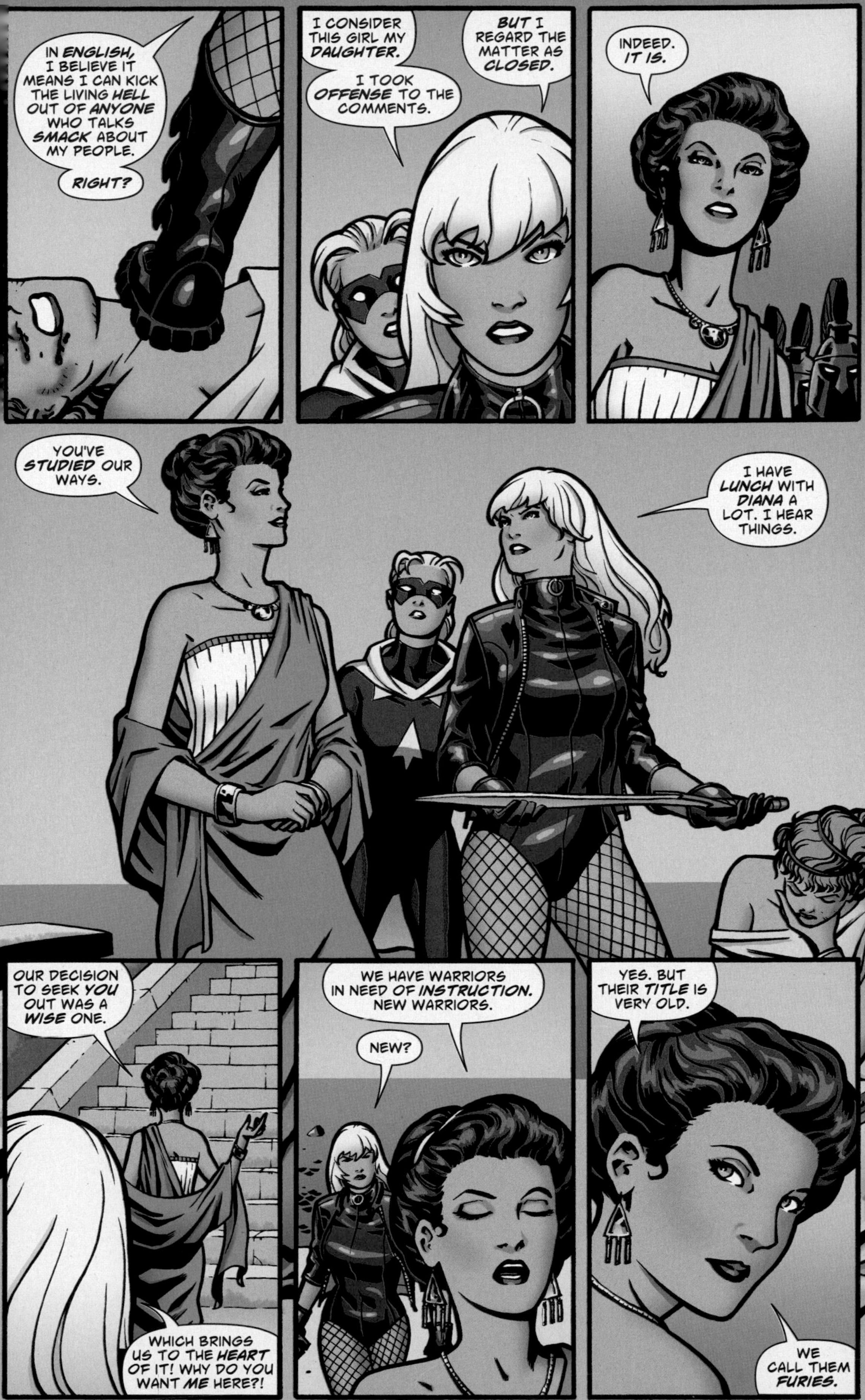
IN ENGLISH, I BELIEVE IT MEANS I CAN KICK THE LIVING HELL OUT OF ANYONE WHO TALKS SMACK ABOUT MY PEOPLE.
RIGHT?
I CONSIDER THIS GIRL MY DAUGHTER.
I TOOK OFFENSE TO THE COMMENTS.
BUT I REGARD THE MATTER AS CLOSED.
INDEED. IT IS.
YOU'VE STUDIED OUR WAYS.
I HAVE LUNCH WITH DIANA A LOT. I HEAR THINGS.
OUR DECISION TO SEEK YOU OUT WAS A WISE ONE.
WHICH BRINGS US TO THE HEART OF IT! WHY DO YOU WANT ME HERE?!
WE HAVE WARRIORS IN NEED OF INSTRUCTION. NEW WARRIORS.
NEW?
YES. BUT THEIR TITLE IS VERY OLD.
WE CALL THEM FURIES.

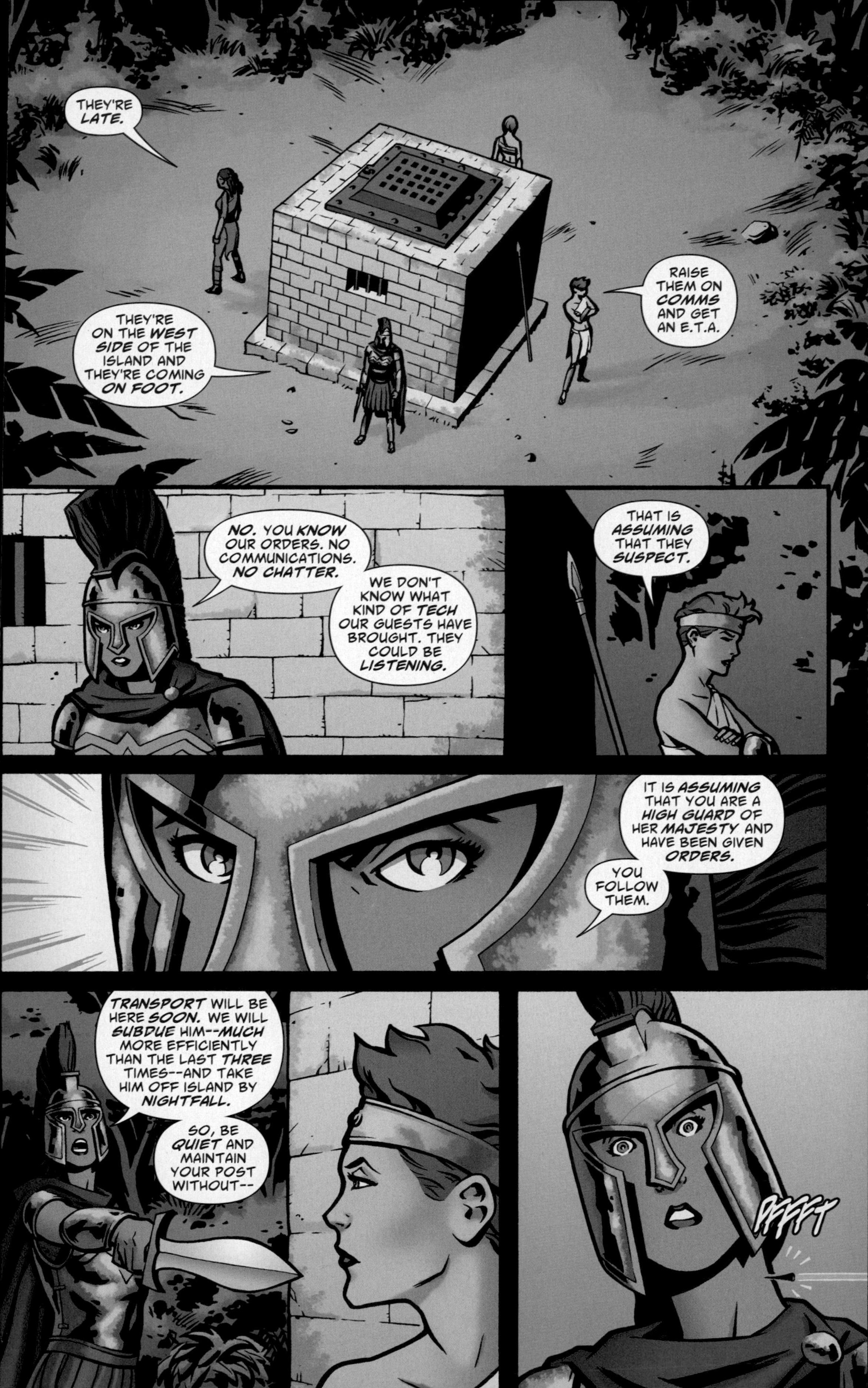
THEY'RE LATE.
THEY'RE ON THE WEST SIDE OF THE ISLAND AND THEY'RE COMING ON FOOT.
RAISE THEM ON COMMS AND GET AN E.T.A.
NO. YOU KNOW OUR ORDERS. NO COMMUNICATIONS. NO CHATTER.
WE DON'T KNOW WHAT KIND OF TECH OUR GUESTS HAVE BROUGHT. THEY COULD BE LISTENING.
THAT IS ASSUMING THAT THEY SUSPECT.
IT IS ASSUMING THAT YOU ARE A HIGH GUARD OF HER MAJESTY AND HAVE BEEN GIVEN ORDERS.
YOU FOLLOW THEM.
TRANSPORT WILL BE HERE SOON. WE WILL SUBDUE HIM--MUCH MORE EFFICIENTLY THAN THE LAST THREE TIMES--AND TAKE HIM OFF ISLAND BY NIGHTFALL.
SO, BE QUIET AND MAINTAIN YOUR POST WITHOUT--

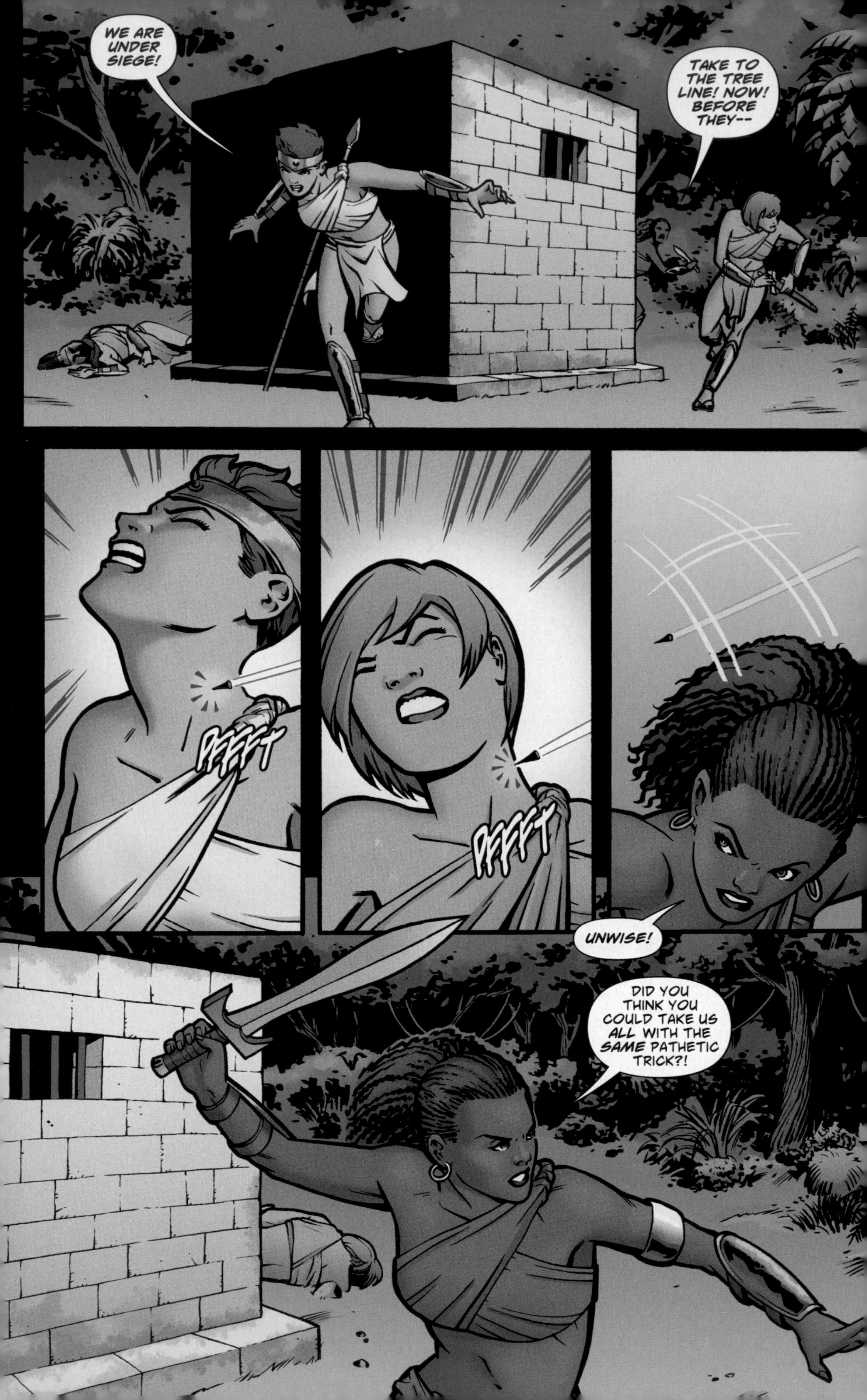
WE ARE UNDER SIEGE!
TAKE TO THE TREE LINE! NOW! BEFORE THEY--
PFFFT
PFFFT
UNWISE!
DID YOU THINK YOU COULD TAKE US ALL WITH THE SAME PATHETIC TRICK?!

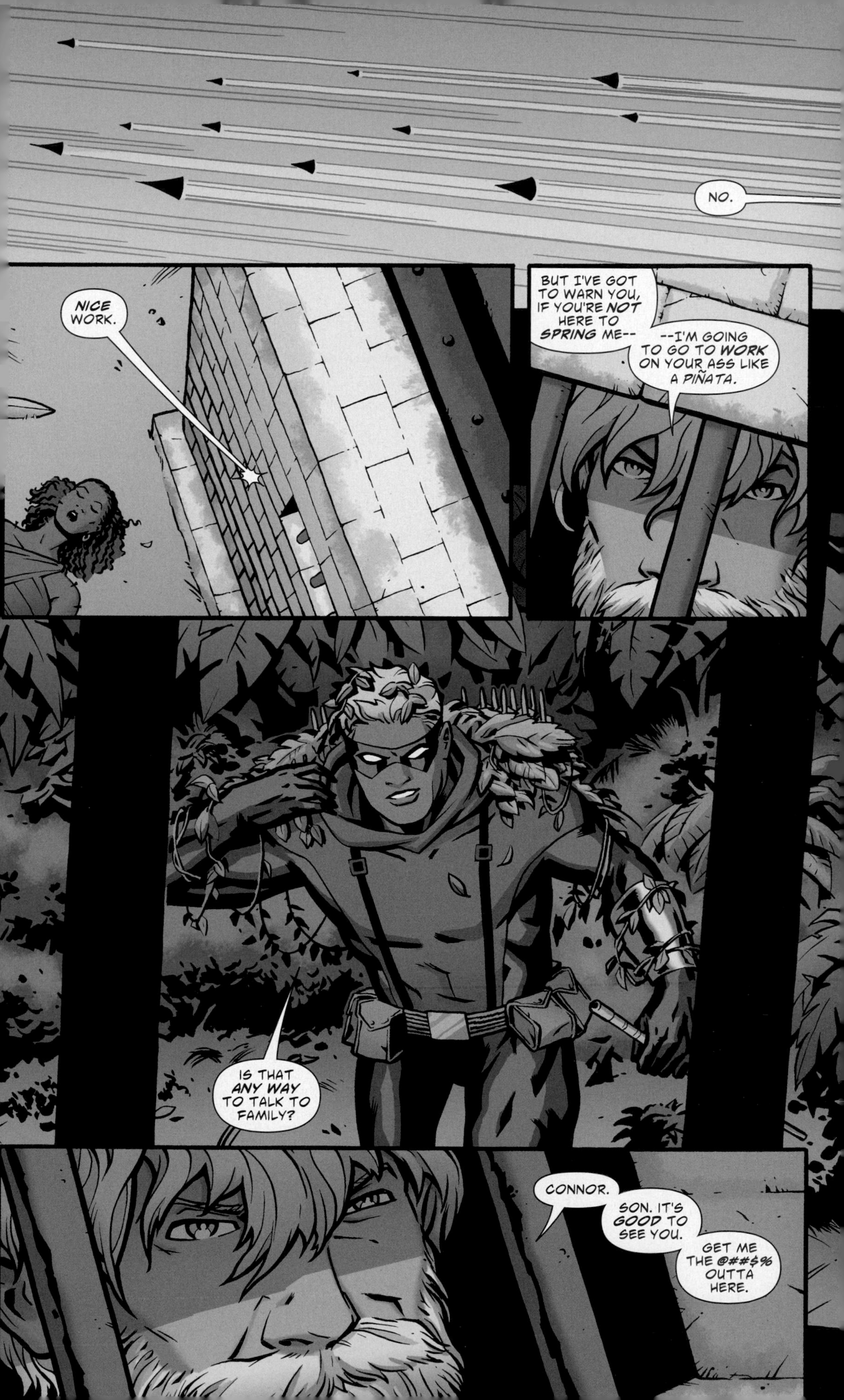
NO.
NICE WORK.
BUT I'VE GOT TO WARN YOU, IF YOU'RE NOT HERE TO SPRING ME--
--I'M GOING TO GO TO WORK ON YOUR ASS LIKE A PIÑATA.
IS THAT ANY WAY TO TALK TO FAMILY?
CONNOR.
SON. IT'S GOOD TO SEE YOU.
GET ME THE @#$% OUTTA HERE.

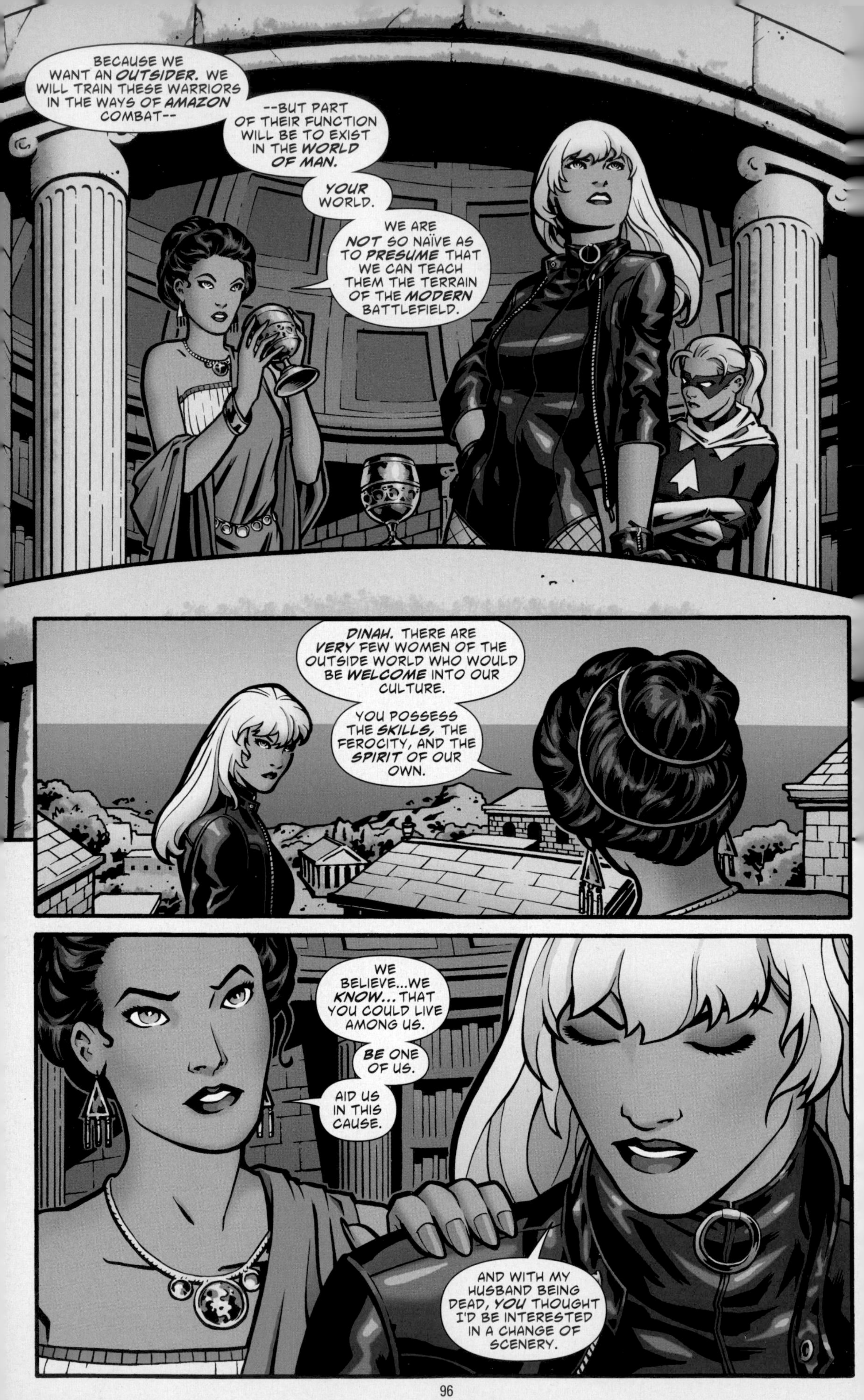
BECAUSE WE WANT AN OUTSIDER. WE WILL TRAIN THESE WARRIORS IN THE WAYS OF AMAZON COMBAT--
--BUT PART OF THEIR FUNCTION WILL BE TO EXIST IN THE WORLD OF MAN.
YOUR WORLD.
WE ARE NOT SO NAÏVE AS TO PRESUME THAT WE CAN TEACH THEM THE TERRAIN OF THE MODERN BATTLEFIELD.
DINAH. THERE ARE VERY FEW WOMEN OF THE OUTSIDE WORLD WHO WOULD BE WELCOME INTO OUR CULTURE.
YOU POSSESS THE SKILLS, THE FEROCITY, AND THE SPIRIT OF OUR OWN.
WE BELIEVE...WE KNOW... THAT YOU COULD LIVE AMONG US.
BE ONE OF US.
AID US IN THIS CAUSE.
AND WITH MY HUSBAND BEING DEAD, YOU THOUGHT I'D BE INTERESTED IN A CHANGE OF SCENERY.

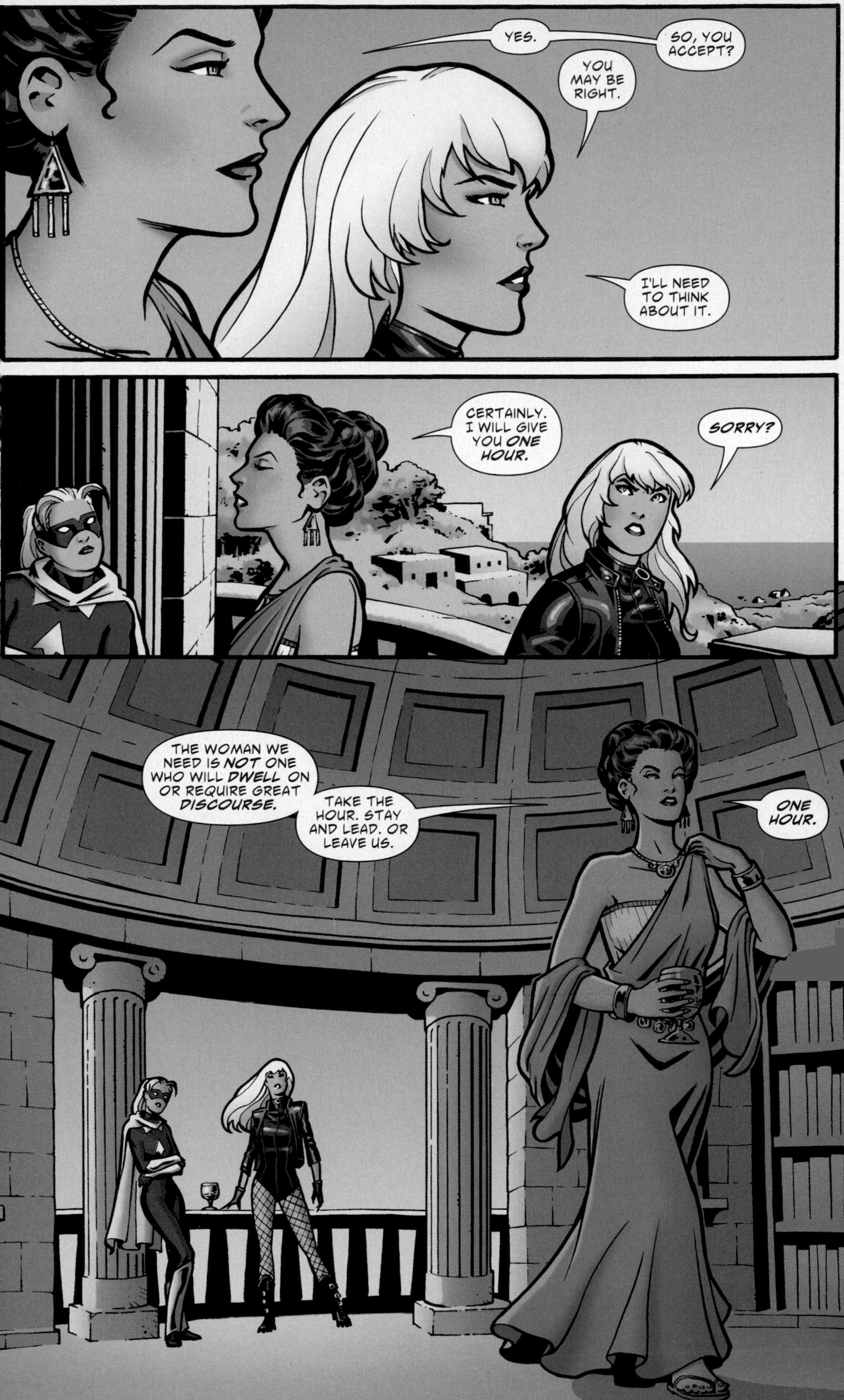

YES.
SO, YOU ACCEPT?
YOU MAY BE RIGHT.
I'LL NEED TO THINK ABOUT IT.
CERTAINLY. I WILL GIVE YOU *ONE HOUR.*
SORRY?
THE WOMAN WE NEED IS *NOT* ONE WHO WILL *DWELL* ON OR REQUIRE GREAT *DISCOURSE.*
TAKE THE HOUR. STAY AND LEAD. OR LEAVE US.
ONE HOUR.

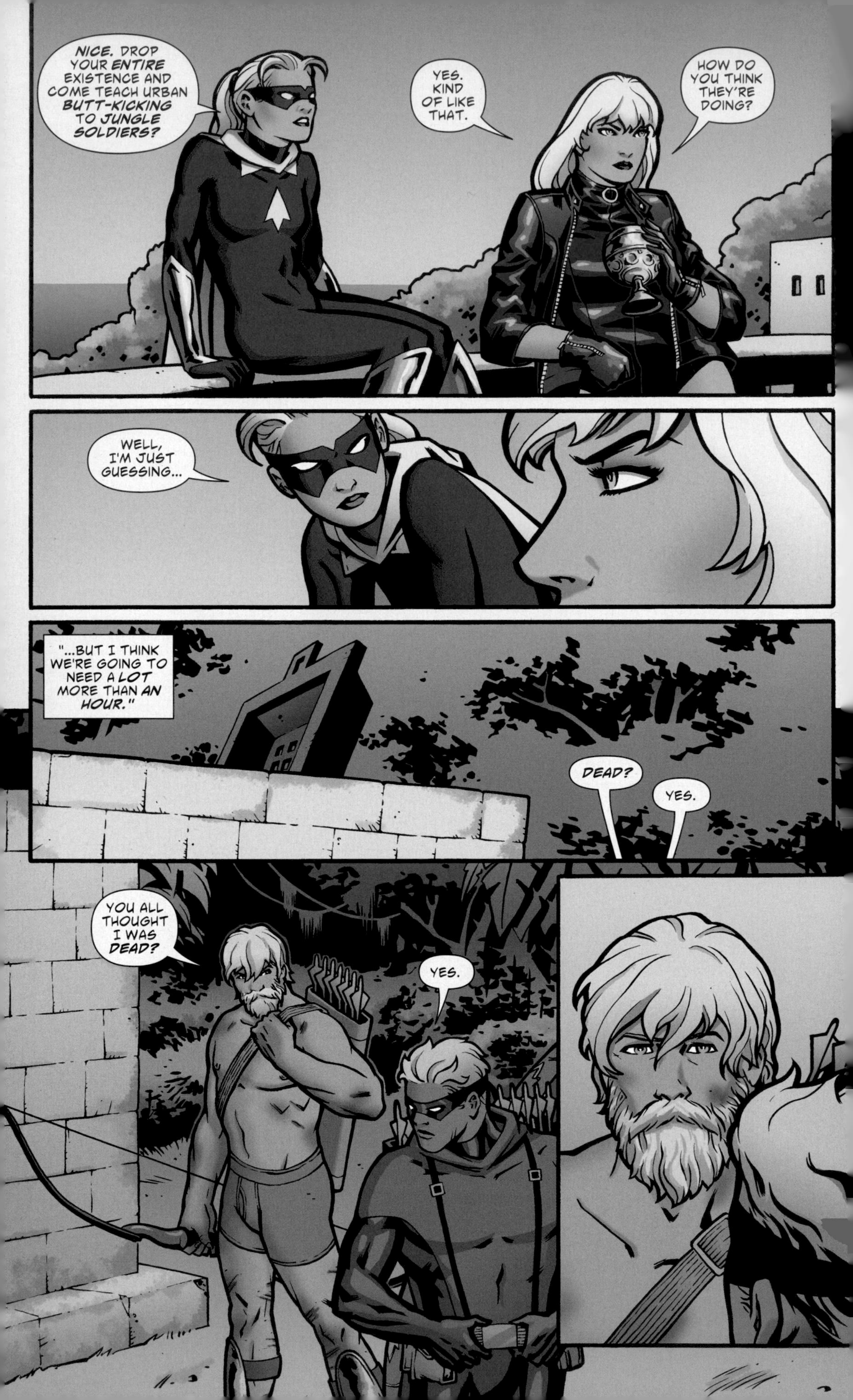
NICE. DROP YOUR ENTIRE EXISTENCE AND COME TEACH URBAN BUTT-KICKING TO JUNGLE SOLDIERS?
YES. KIND OF LIKE THAT.
HOW DO YOU THINK THEY'RE DOING?
WELL, I'M JUST GUESSING...
"...BUT I THINK WE'RE GOING TO NEED A LOT MORE THAN AN HOUR."
DEAD?
YES.
YOU ALL THOUGHT I WAS DEAD?
YES.

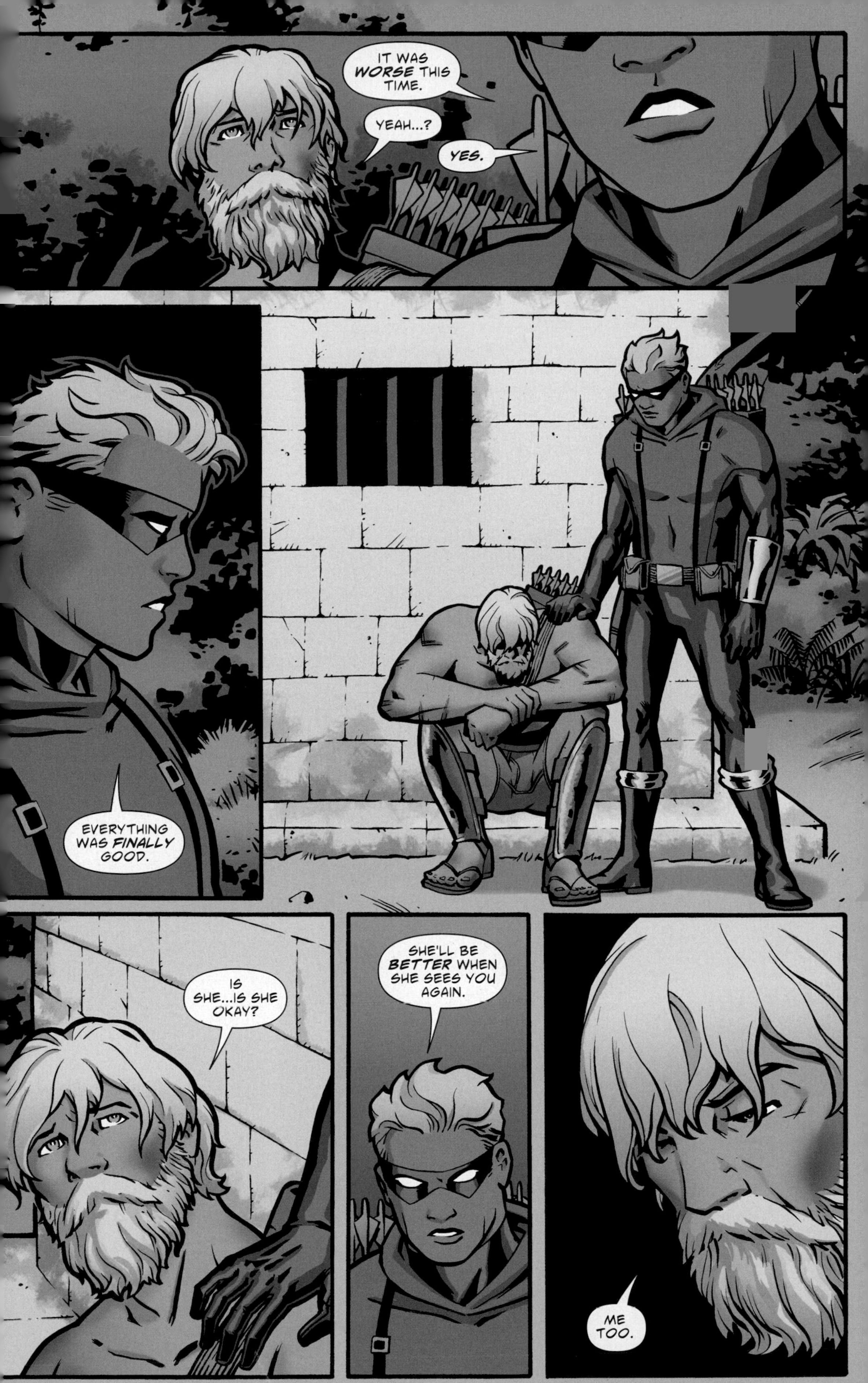
IT WAS WORSE THIS TIME.
YEAH...?
YES.
EVERYTHING WAS FINALLY GOOD.
IS SHE...IS SHE OKAY?
SHE'LL BE BETTER WHEN SHE SEES YOU AGAIN.
ME TOO.

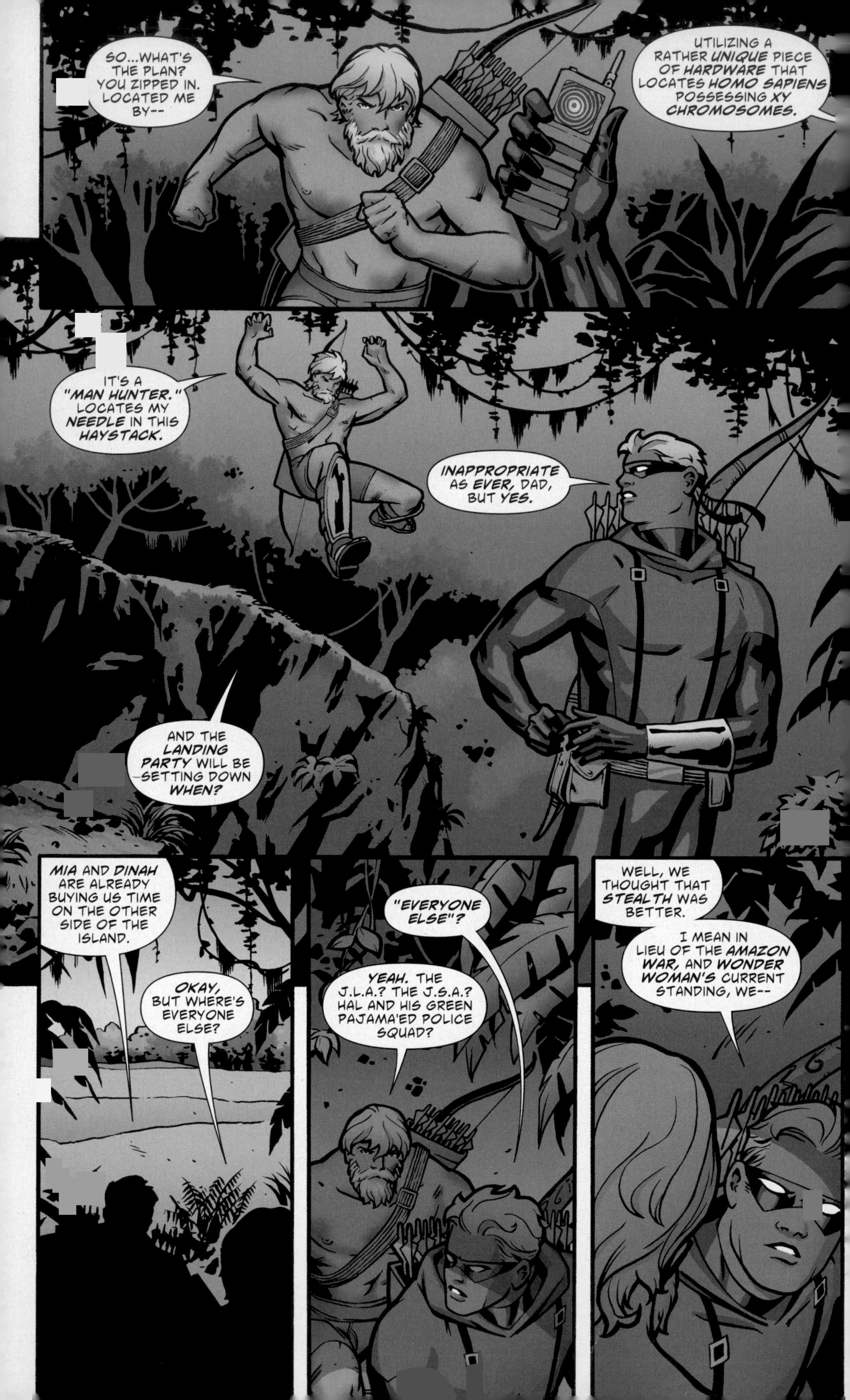
SO...WHAT'S THE PLAN? YOU ZIPPED IN. LOCATED ME BY--
UTILIZING A RATHER UNIQUE PIECE OF HARDWARE THAT LOCATES HOMO SAPIENS POSSESSING XY CHROMOSOMES.
IT'S A "MAN HUNTER." LOCATES MY NEEDLE IN THIS HAYSTACK.
INAPPROPRIATE AS EVER, DAD, BUT YES.
AND THE LANDING PARTY WILL BE SETTING DOWN WHEN?
MIA AND DINAH ARE ALREADY BUYING US TIME ON THE OTHER SIDE OF THE ISLAND.
OKAY, BUT WHERE'S EVERYONE ELSE?
"EVERYONE ELSE"?
YEAH. THE J.L.A.? THE J.S.A.? HAL AND HIS GREEN PAJAMA'ED POLICE SQUAD?
WELL, WE THOUGHT THAT STEALTH WAS BETTER.
I MEAN IN LIEU OF THE AMAZON WAR, AND WONDER WOMAN'S CURRENT STANDING, WE--

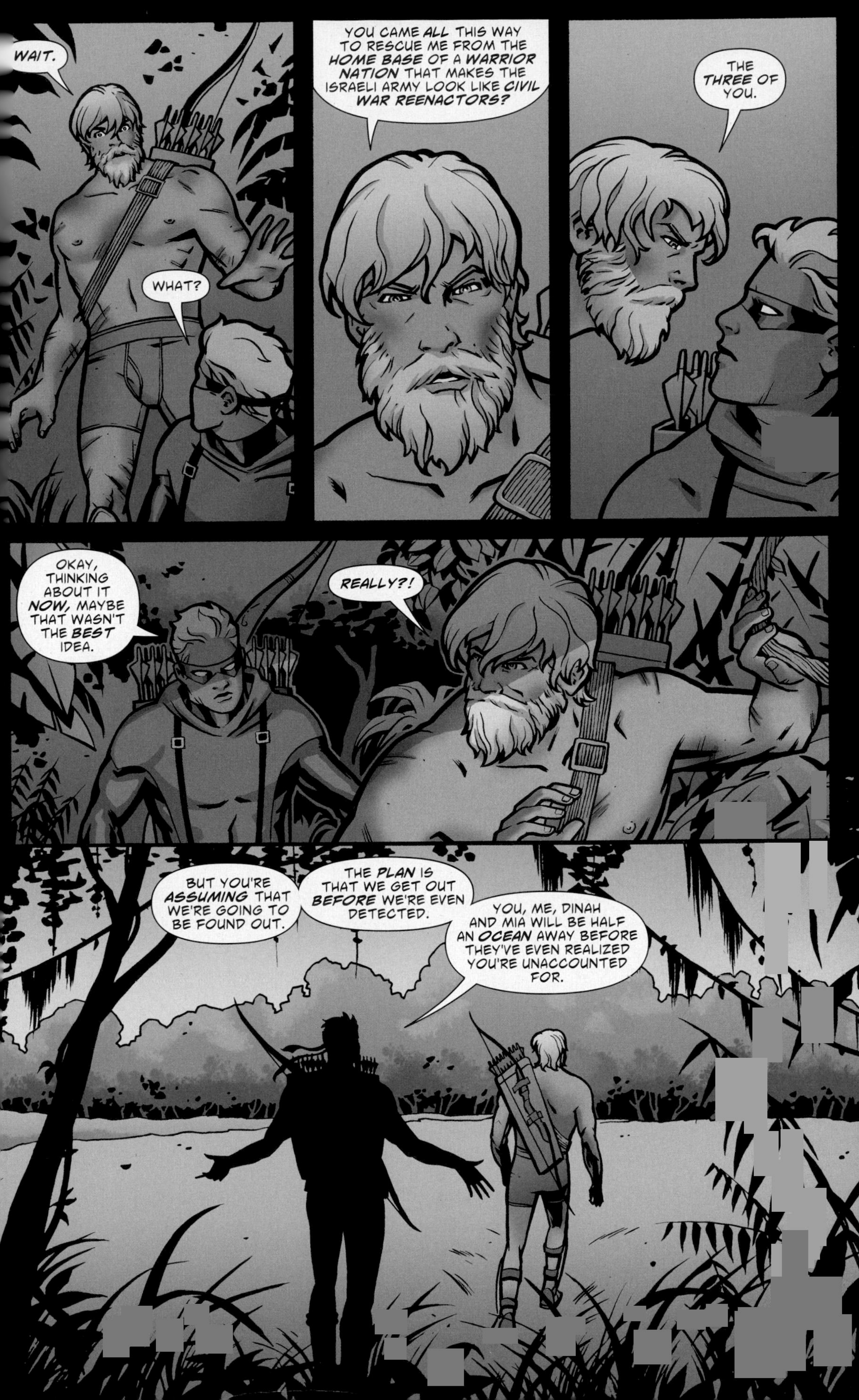
WAIT.
WHAT?
YOU CAME ALL THIS WAY TO RESCUE ME FROM THE HOME BASE OF A WARRIOR NATION THAT MAKES THE ISRAELI ARMY LOOK LIKE CIVIL WAR REENACTORS?
THE THREE OF YOU.
OKAY, THINKING ABOUT IT NOW, MAYBE THAT WASN'T THE BEST IDEA.
REALLY?!
BUT YOU'RE ASSUMING THAT WE'RE GOING TO BE FOUND OUT.
THE PLAN IS THAT WE GET OUT BEFORE WE'RE EVEN DETECTED.
YOU, ME, DINAH AND MIA WILL BE HALF AN OCEAN AWAY BEFORE THEY'VE EVEN REALIZED YOU'RE UNACCOUNTED FOR.

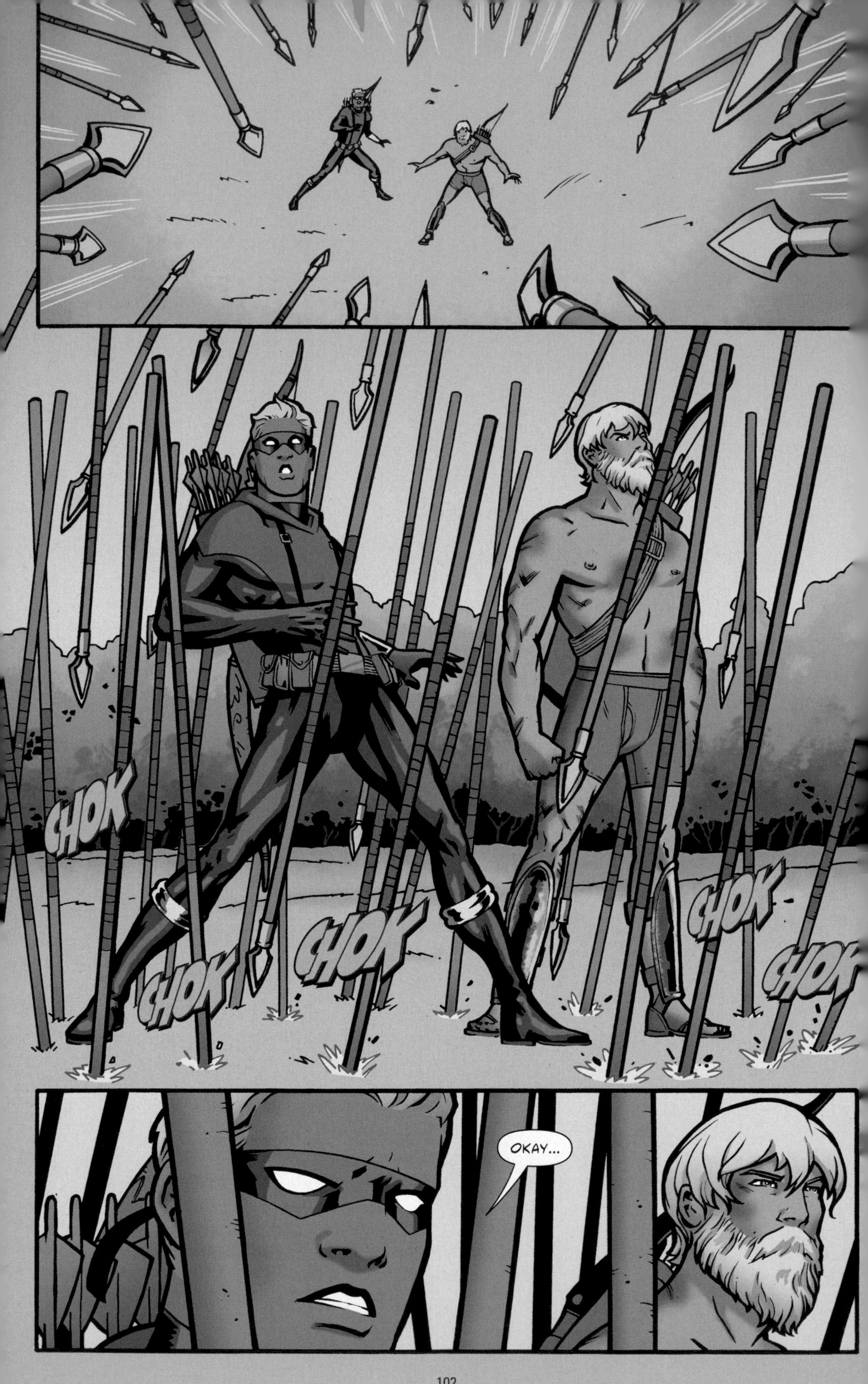
CHOK
CHOK
CHOK
CHOK
CHOK
OKAY...

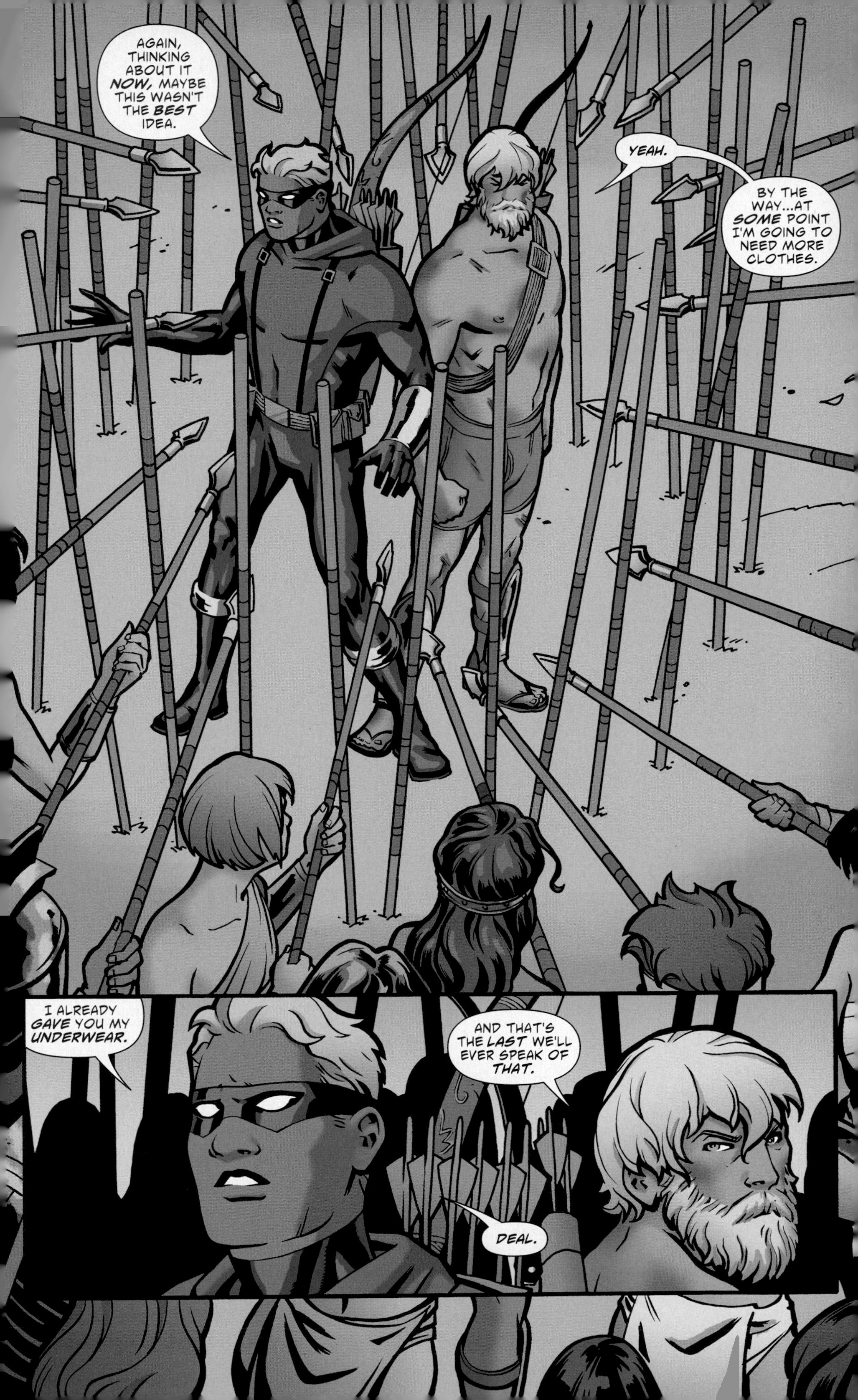
AGAIN, THINKING ABOUT IT NOW, MAYBE THIS WASN'T THE BEST IDEA.
YEAH.
BY THE WAY...AT SOME POINT I'M GOING TO NEED MORE CLOTHES.
I ALREADY GAVE YOU MY UNDERWEAR.
AND THAT'S THE LAST WE'LL EVER SPEAK OF THAT.
DEAL.

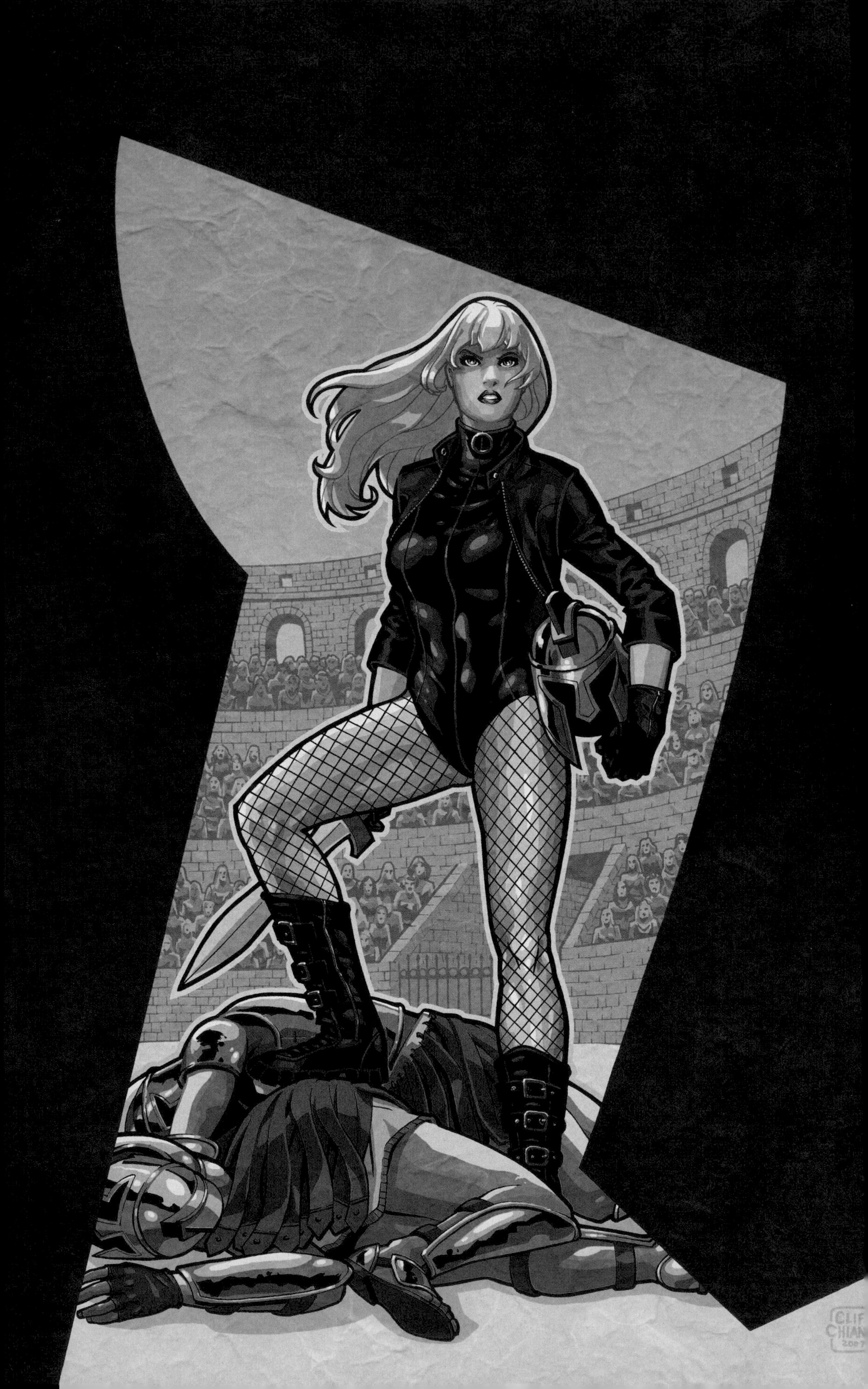
CLIF
CHIANG
2007

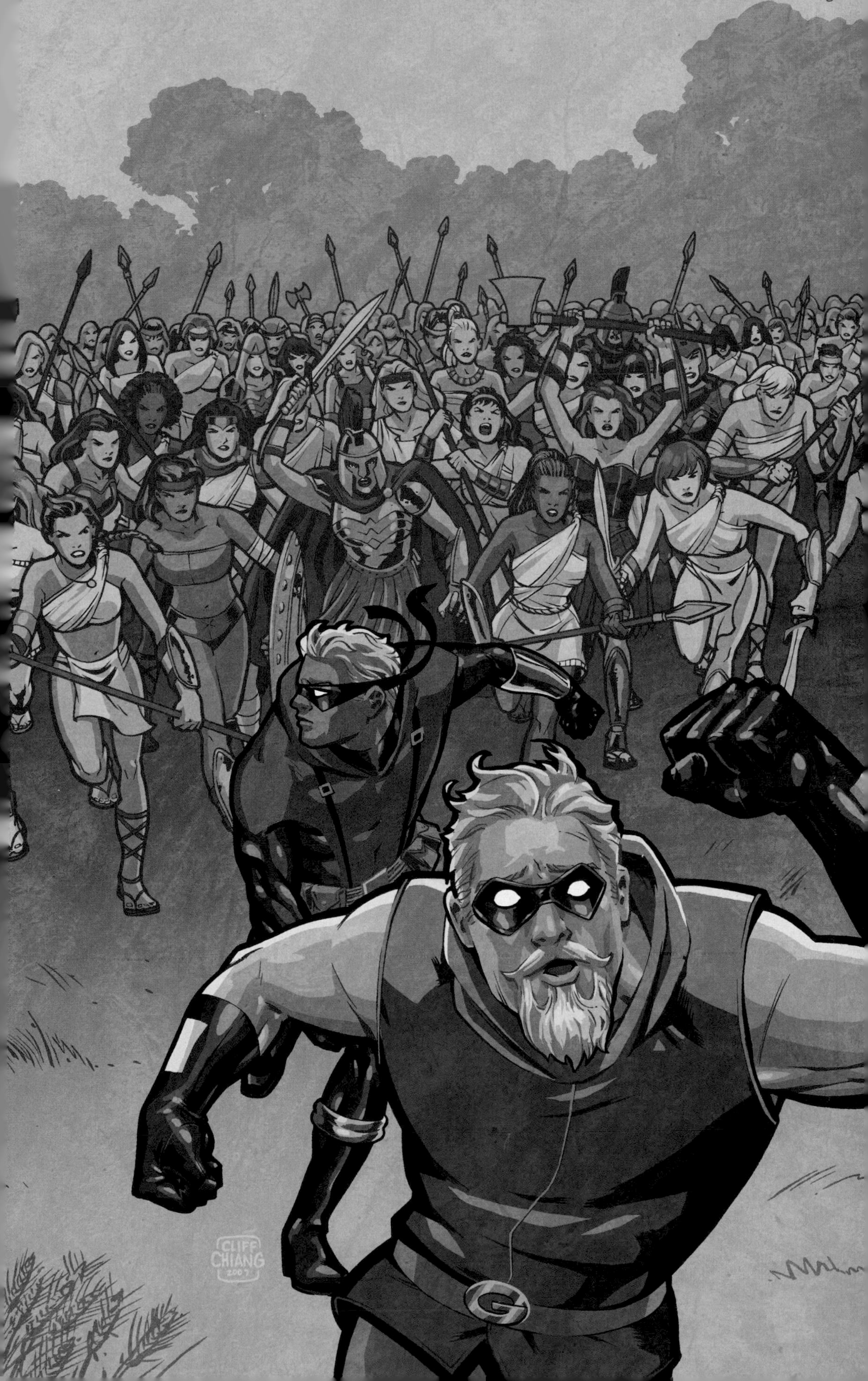
CLIFF
CHIANG
2007

DEAD AGAIN PART THREE: HIT AND RUN, RUN, RUN!

Story: **Judd Winick**   *Art:* **Cliff Chiang**   *Color:* **Trish Mulvihill**

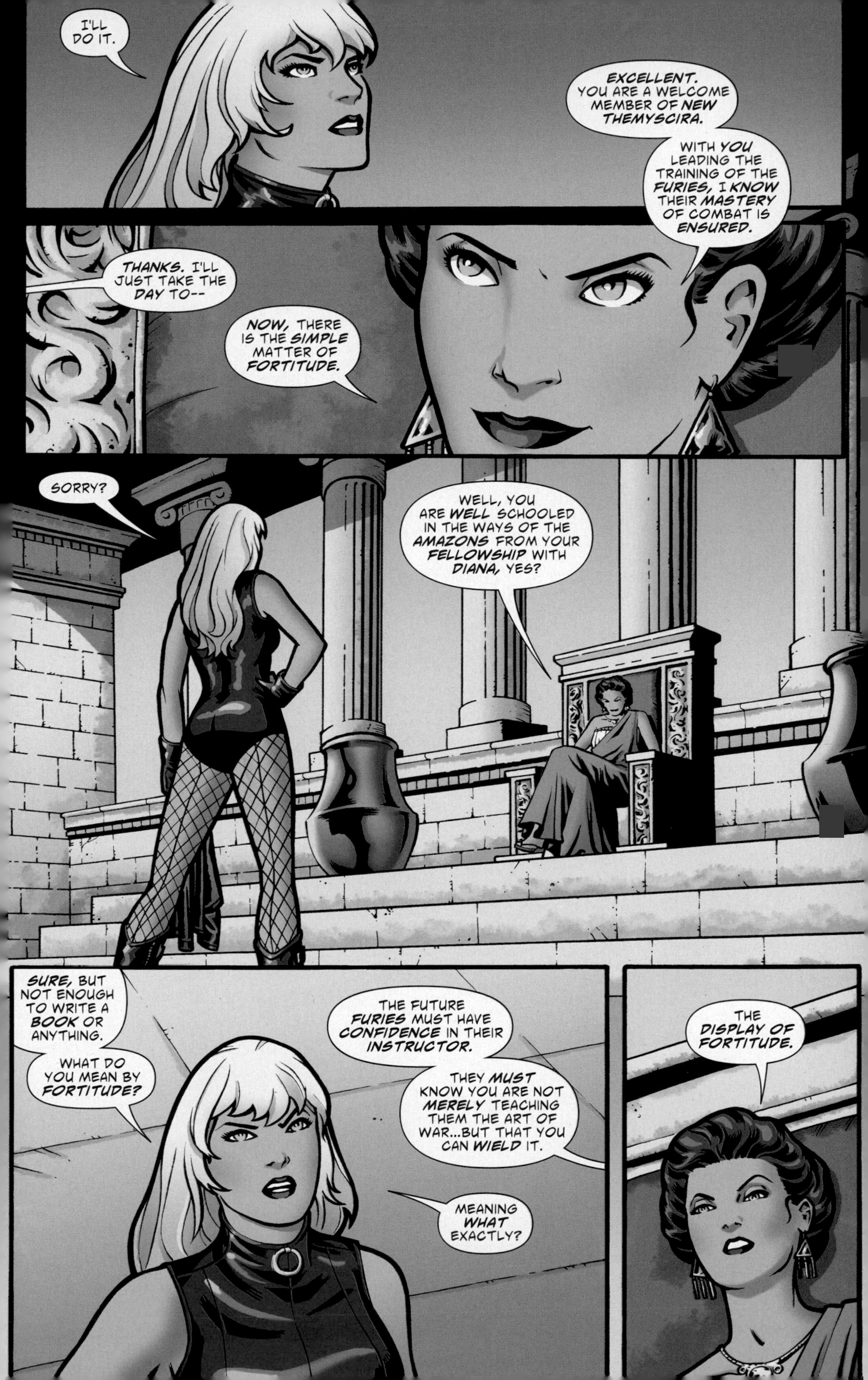
I'LL DO IT.
EXCELLENT. YOU ARE A WELCOME MEMBER OF NEW THEMYSCIRA.
WITH YOU LEADING THE TRAINING OF THE FURIES, I KNOW THEIR MASTERY OF COMBAT IS ENSURED.
THANKS. I'LL JUST TAKE THE DAY TO--
NOW, THERE IS THE SIMPLE MATTER OF FORTITUDE.
SORRY?
WELL, YOU ARE WELL SCHOOLED IN THE WAYS OF THE AMAZONS FROM YOUR FELLOWSHIP WITH DIANA, YES?
SURE, BUT NOT ENOUGH TO WRITE A BOOK OR ANYTHING.
WHAT DO YOU MEAN BY FORTITUDE?
THE FUTURE FURIES MUST HAVE CONFIDENCE IN THEIR INSTRUCTOR.
THEY MUST KNOW YOU ARE NOT MERELY TEACHING THEM THE ART OF WAR...BUT THAT YOU CAN WIELD IT.
MEANING WHAT EXACTLY?
THE DISPLAY OF FORTITUDE.

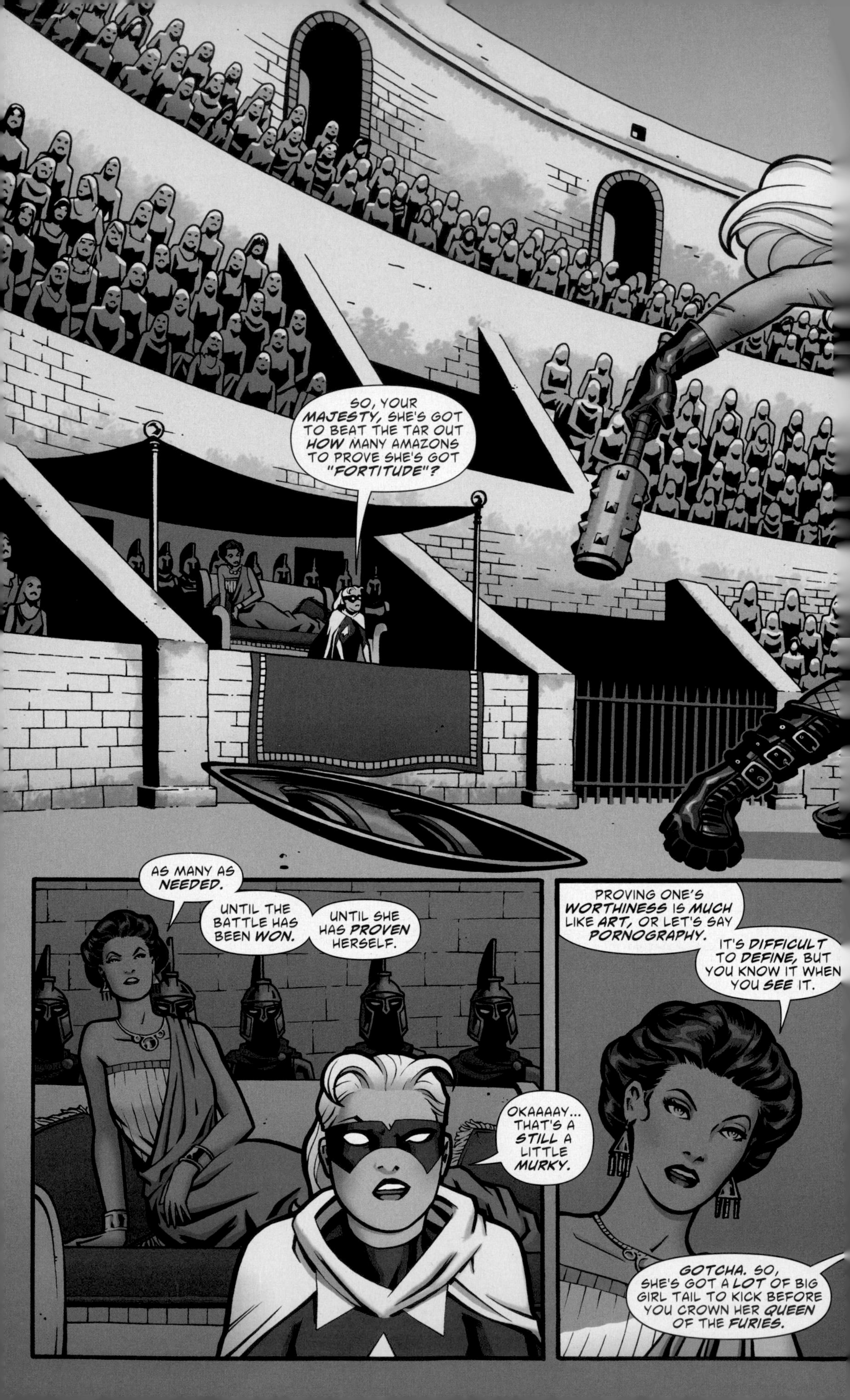
SO, YOUR MAJESTY, SHE'S GOT TO BEAT THE TAR OUT HOW MANY AMAZONS TO PROVE SHE'S GOT "FORTITUDE"?
AS MANY AS NEEDED.
UNTIL THE BATTLE HAS BEEN WON.
UNTIL SHE HAS PROVEN HERSELF.
OKAAAAY... THAT'S A STILL A LITTLE MURKY.
PROVING ONE'S WORTHINESS IS MUCH LIKE ART, OR LET'S SAY PORNOGRAPHY.
IT'S DIFFICULT TO DEFINE, BUT YOU KNOW IT WHEN YOU SEE IT.
GOTCHA. SO, SHE'S GOT A LOT OF BIG GIRL TAIL TO KICK BEFORE YOU CROWN HER QUEEN OF THE FURIES.

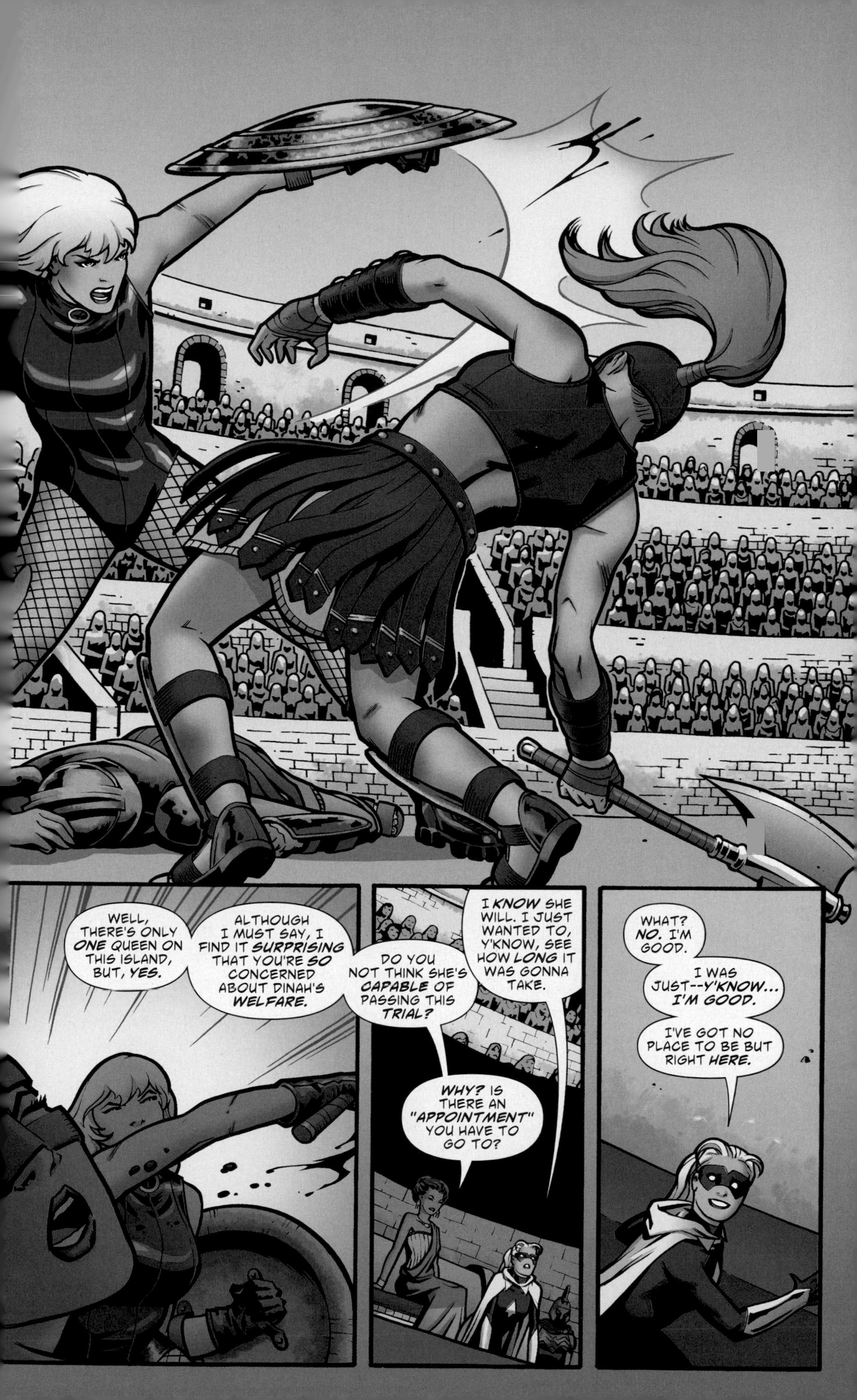
WELL, THERE'S ONLY ONE QUEEN ON THIS ISLAND, BUT, YES.
ALTHOUGH I MUST SAY, I FIND IT SURPRISING THAT YOU'RE SO CONCERNED ABOUT DINAH'S WELFARE.
DO YOU NOT THINK SHE'S CAPABLE OF PASSING THIS TRIAL?
I KNOW SHE WILL. I JUST WANTED TO, Y'KNOW, SEE HOW LONG IT WAS GONNA TAKE.
WHY? IS THERE AN "APPOINTMENT" YOU HAVE TO GO TO?
WHAT? NO. I'M GOOD.
I WAS JUST--Y'KNOW... I'M GOOD.
I'VE GOT NO PLACE TO BE BUT RIGHT HERE.

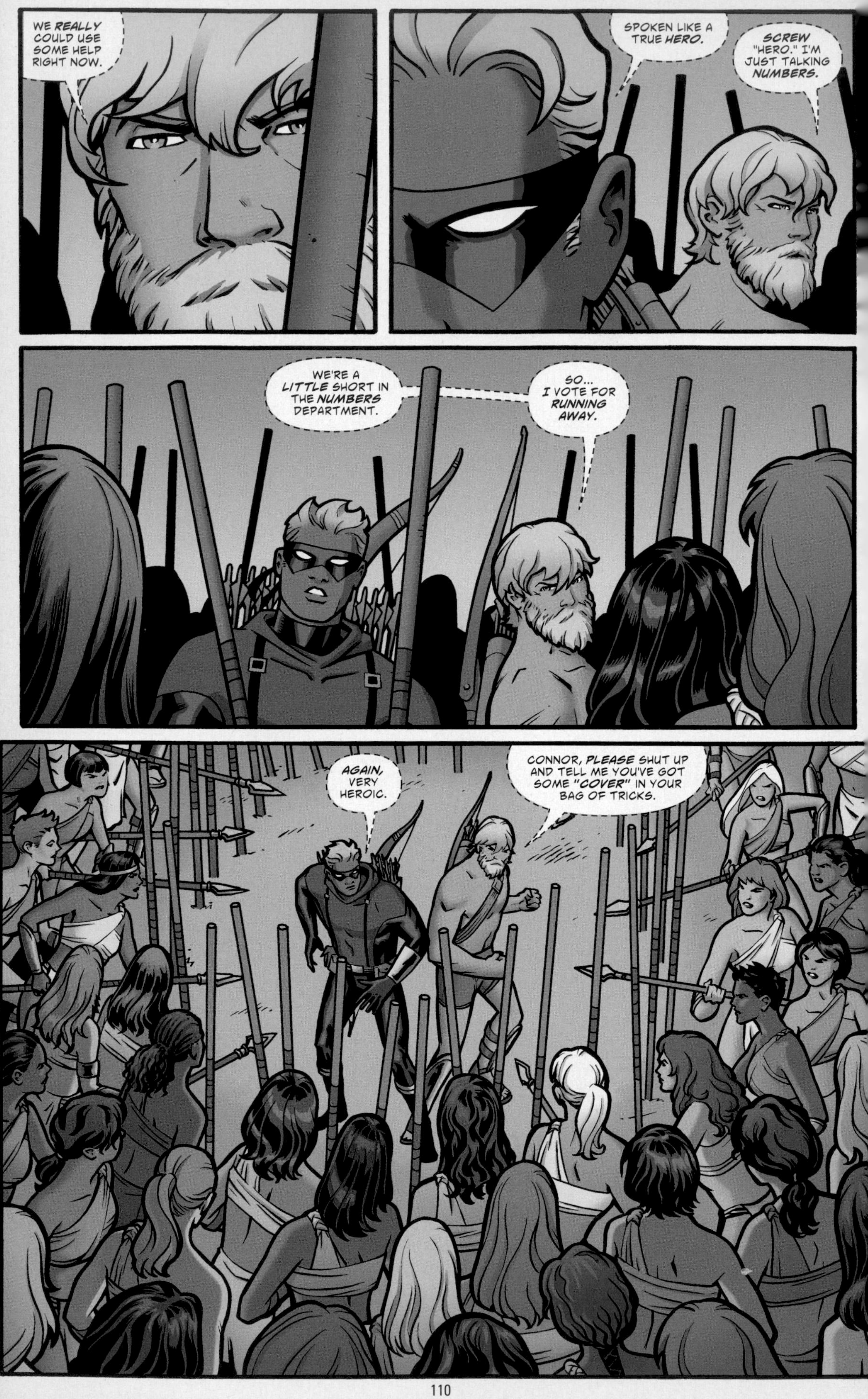
WE REALLY COULD USE SOME HELP RIGHT NOW.
SPOKEN LIKE A TRUE HERO.
SCREW "HERO." I'M JUST TALKING NUMBERS.
WE'RE A LITTLE SHORT IN THE NUMBERS DEPARTMENT.
SO... I VOTE FOR RUNNING AWAY.
AGAIN, VERY HEROIC.
CONNOR, PLEASE SHUT UP AND TELL ME YOU'VE GOT SOME "COVER" IN YOUR BAG OF TRICKS.

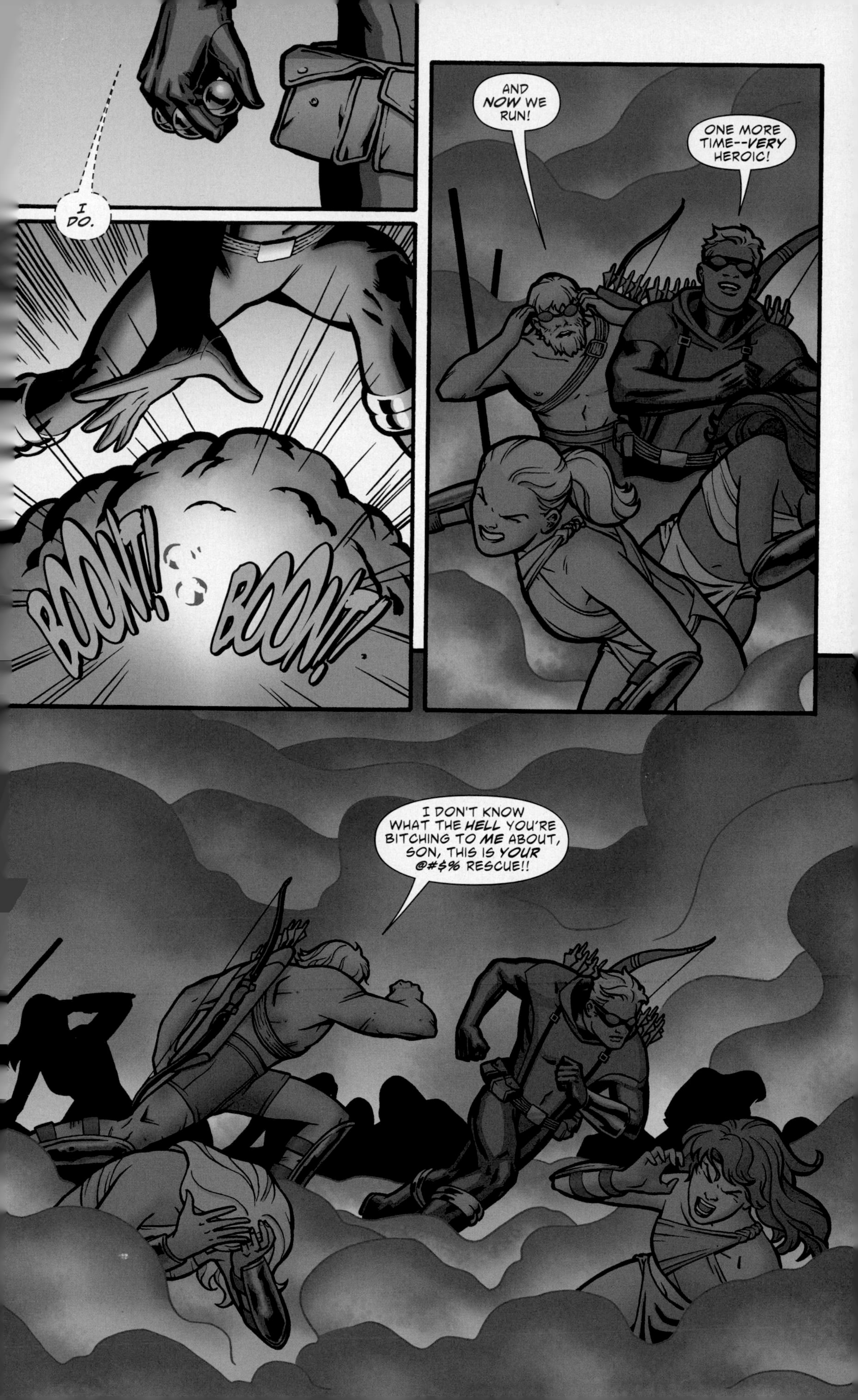
I DO.
BOOM!! BOOM!!
AND NOW WE RUN!
ONE MORE TIME--VERY HEROIC!
I DON'T KNOW WHAT THE HELL YOU'RE BITCHING TO ME ABOUT, SON, THIS IS YOUR @#$% RESCUE!!

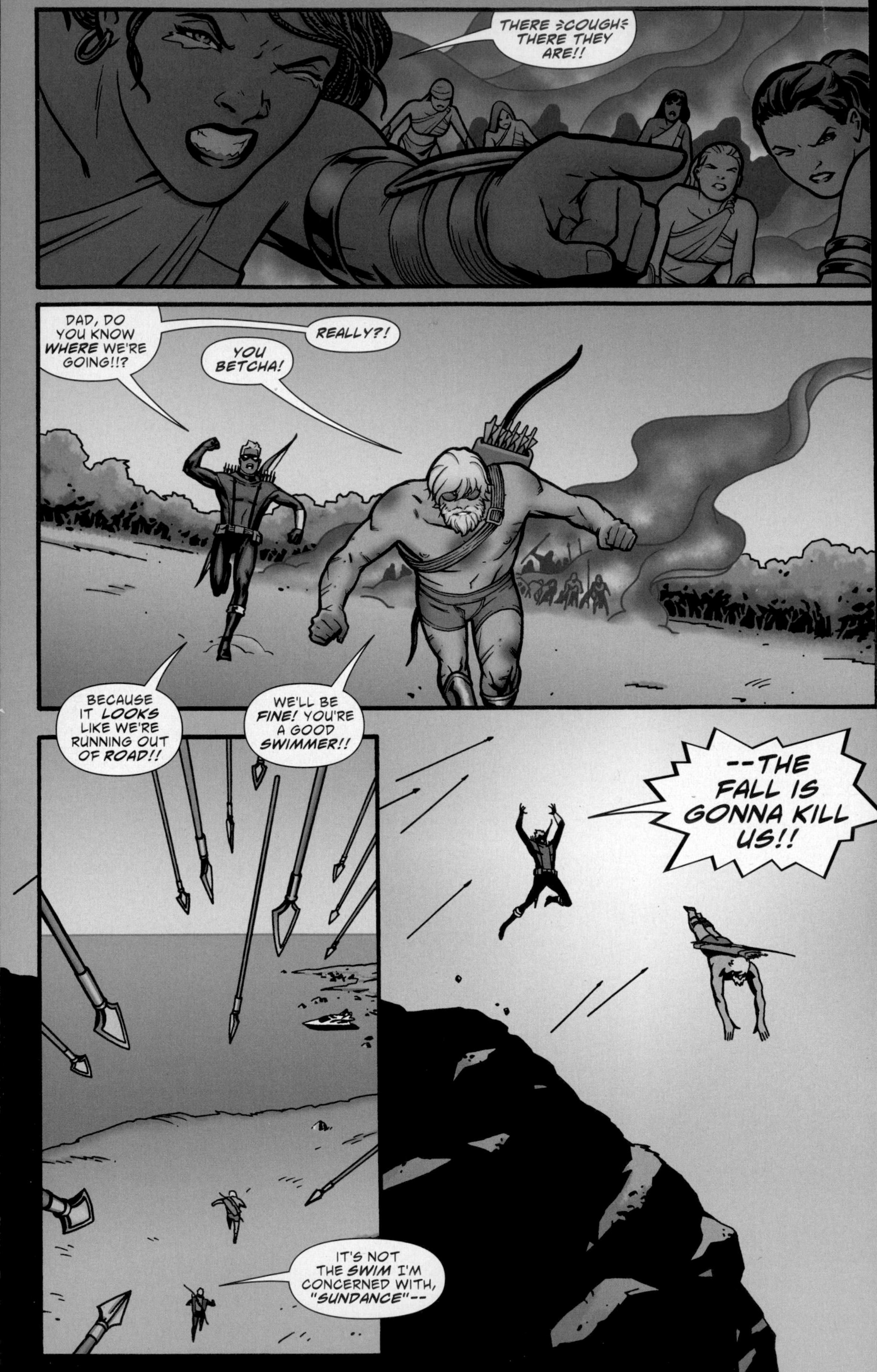
THERE ≶COUGH≶ THERE THEY ARE!!
DAD, DO YOU KNOW WHERE WE'RE GOING!!?
YOU BETCHA!
REALLY?!
BECAUSE IT LOOKS LIKE WE'RE RUNNING OUT OF ROAD!!
WE'LL BE FINE! YOU'RE A GOOD SWIMMER!!
IT'S NOT THE SWIM I'M CONCERNED WITH, "SUNDANCE"--
--THE FALL IS GONNA KILL US!!

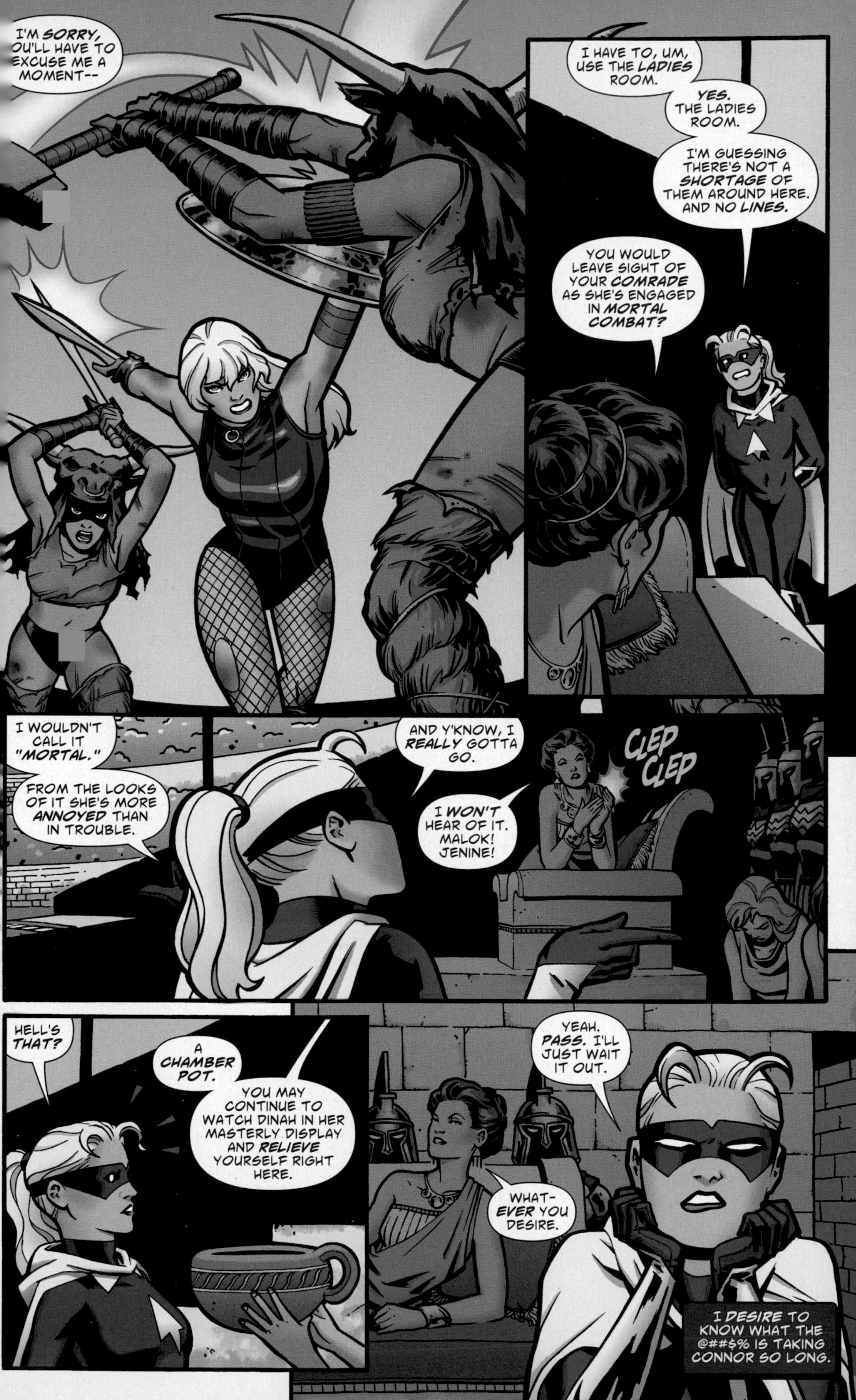
I'M SORRY, YOU'LL HAVE TO EXCUSE ME A MOMENT--
I HAVE TO, UM, USE THE LADIES ROOM.
YES. THE LADIES ROOM.
I'M GUESSING THERE'S NOT A SHORTAGE OF THEM AROUND HERE. AND NO LINES.
YOU WOULD LEAVE SIGHT OF YOUR COMRADE AS SHE'S ENGAGED IN MORTAL COMBAT?
I WOULDN'T CALL IT "MORTAL."
FROM THE LOOKS OF IT SHE'S MORE ANNOYED THAN IN TROUBLE.
AND Y'KNOW, I REALLY GOTTA GO.
I WON'T HEAR OF IT. MALOK! JENINE!
CLEP CLEP
HELL'S THAT?
A CHAMBER POT.
YOU MAY CONTINUE TO WATCH DINAH IN HER MASTERLY DISPLAY AND RELIEVE YOURSELF RIGHT HERE.
YEAH. PASS. I'LL JUST WAIT IT OUT.
WHAT-EVER YOU DESIRE.
I DESIRE TO KNOW WHAT THE @##$% IS TAKING CONNOR SO LONG.

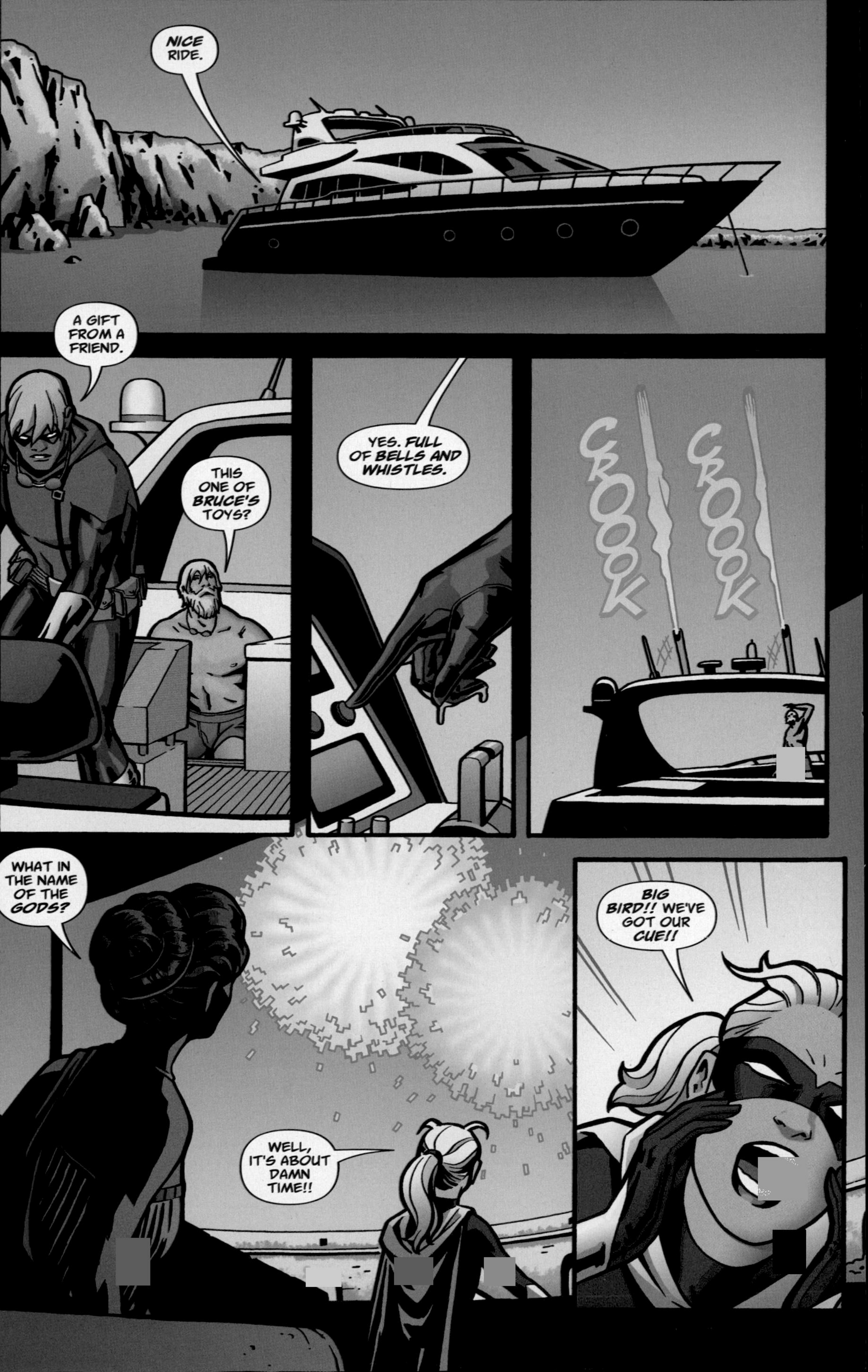
NICE RIDE.
A GIFT FROM A FRIEND.
THIS ONE OF BRUCE'S TOYS?
YES. FULL OF BELLS AND WHISTLES.
CROOOK
CROOOK
WHAT IN THE NAME OF THE GODS?
WELL, IT'S ABOUT DAMN TIME!!
BIG BIRD!! WE'VE GOT OUR CUE!!

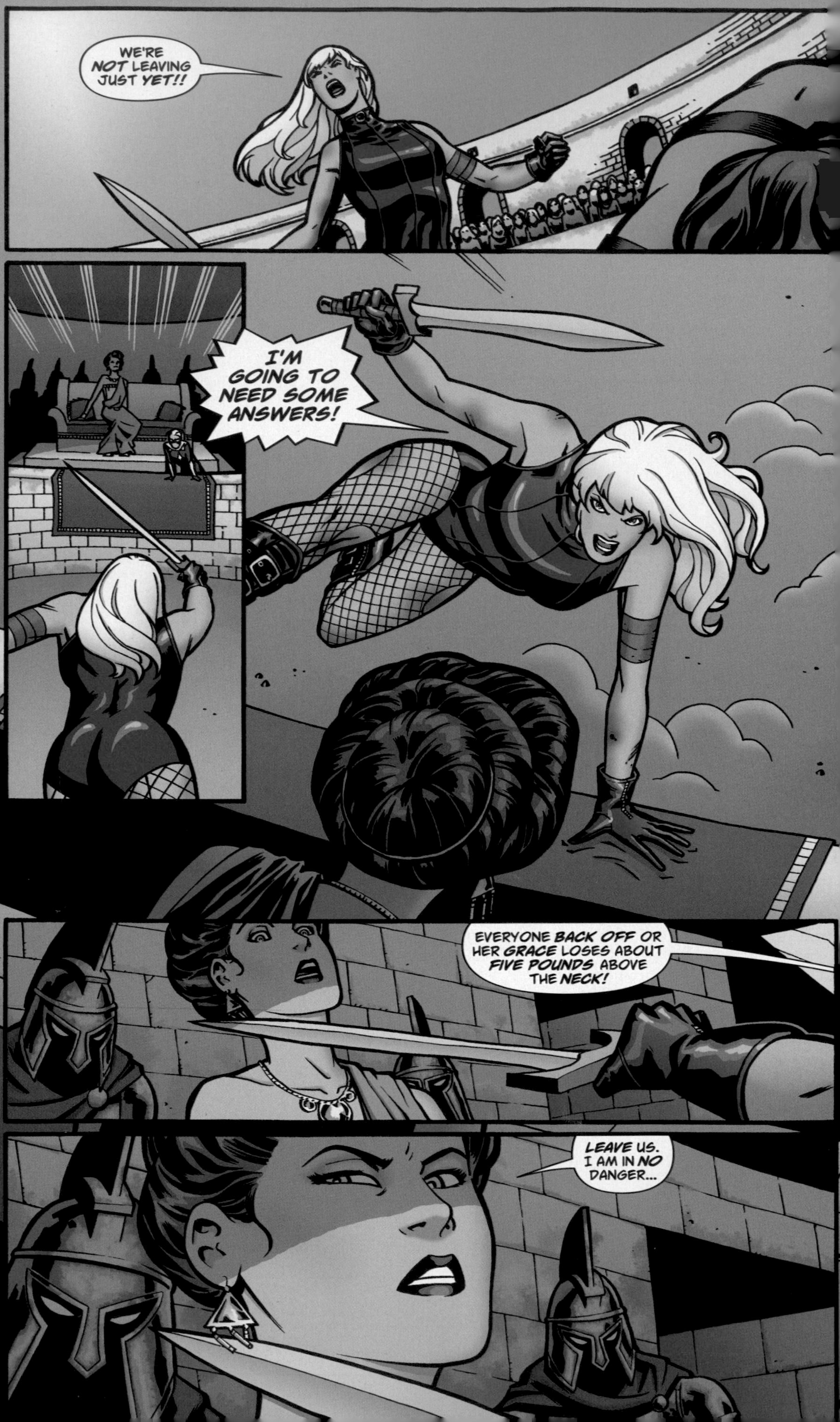
WE'RE NOT LEAVING JUST YET!!
I'M GOING TO NEED SOME ANSWERS!
EVERYONE BACK OFF OR HER GRACE LOSES ABOUT FIVE POUNDS ABOVE THE NECK!
LEAVE US. I AM IN NO DANGER...

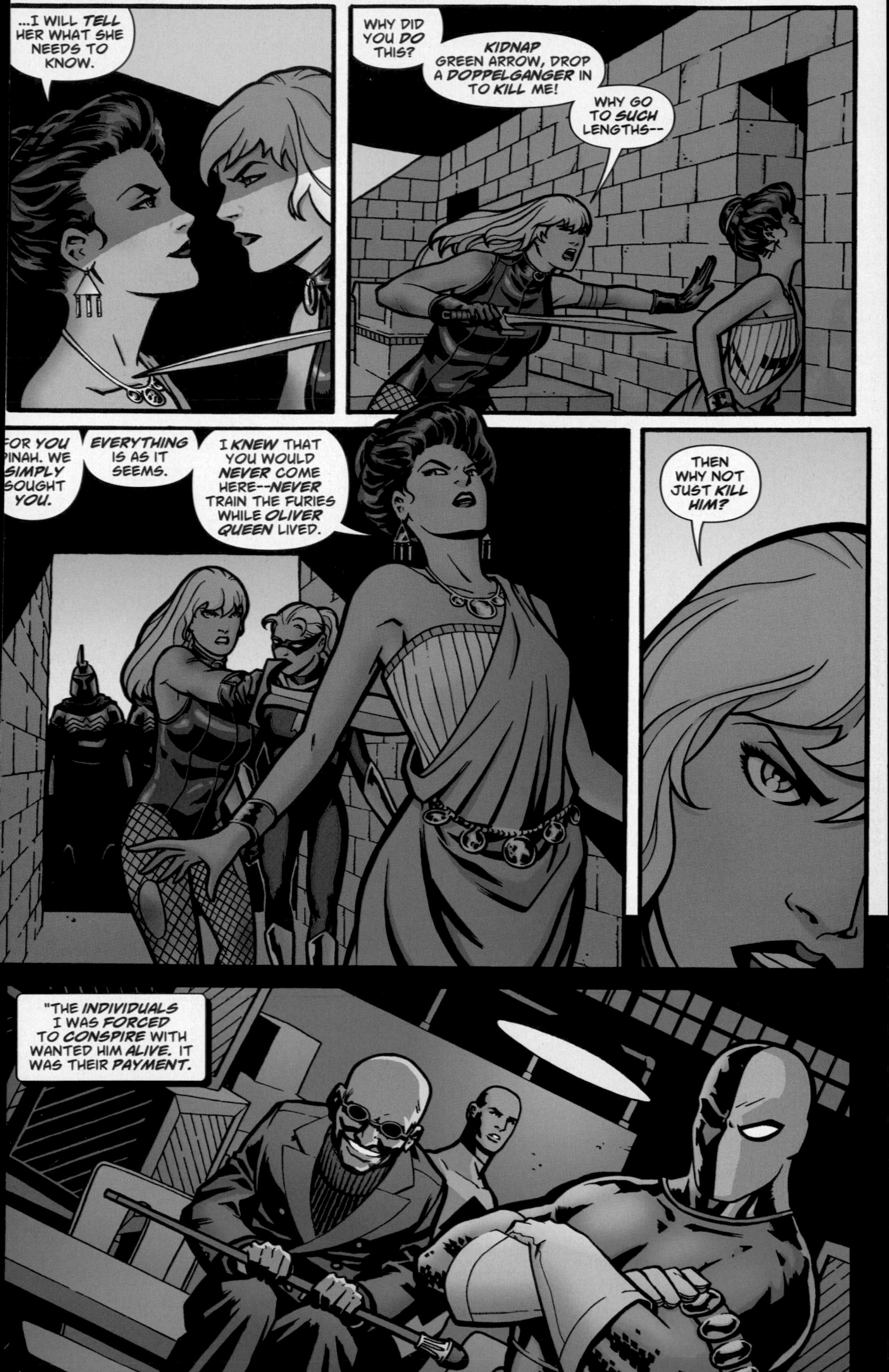
...I WILL TELL HER WHAT SHE NEEDS TO KNOW.
WHY DID YOU DO THIS?
KIDNAP GREEN ARROW, DROP A DOPPELGANGER IN TO KILL ME!
WHY GO TO SUCH LENGTHS--
FOR YOU DINAH. WE SIMPLY SOUGHT YOU.
EVERYTHING IS AS IT SEEMS.
I KNEW THAT YOU WOULD NEVER COME HERE--NEVER TRAIN THE FURIES WHILE OLIVER QUEEN LIVED.
THEN WHY NOT JUST KILL HIM?
"THE INDIVIDUALS I WAS FORCED TO CONSPIRE WITH WANTED HIM ALIVE. IT WAS THEIR PAYMENT.

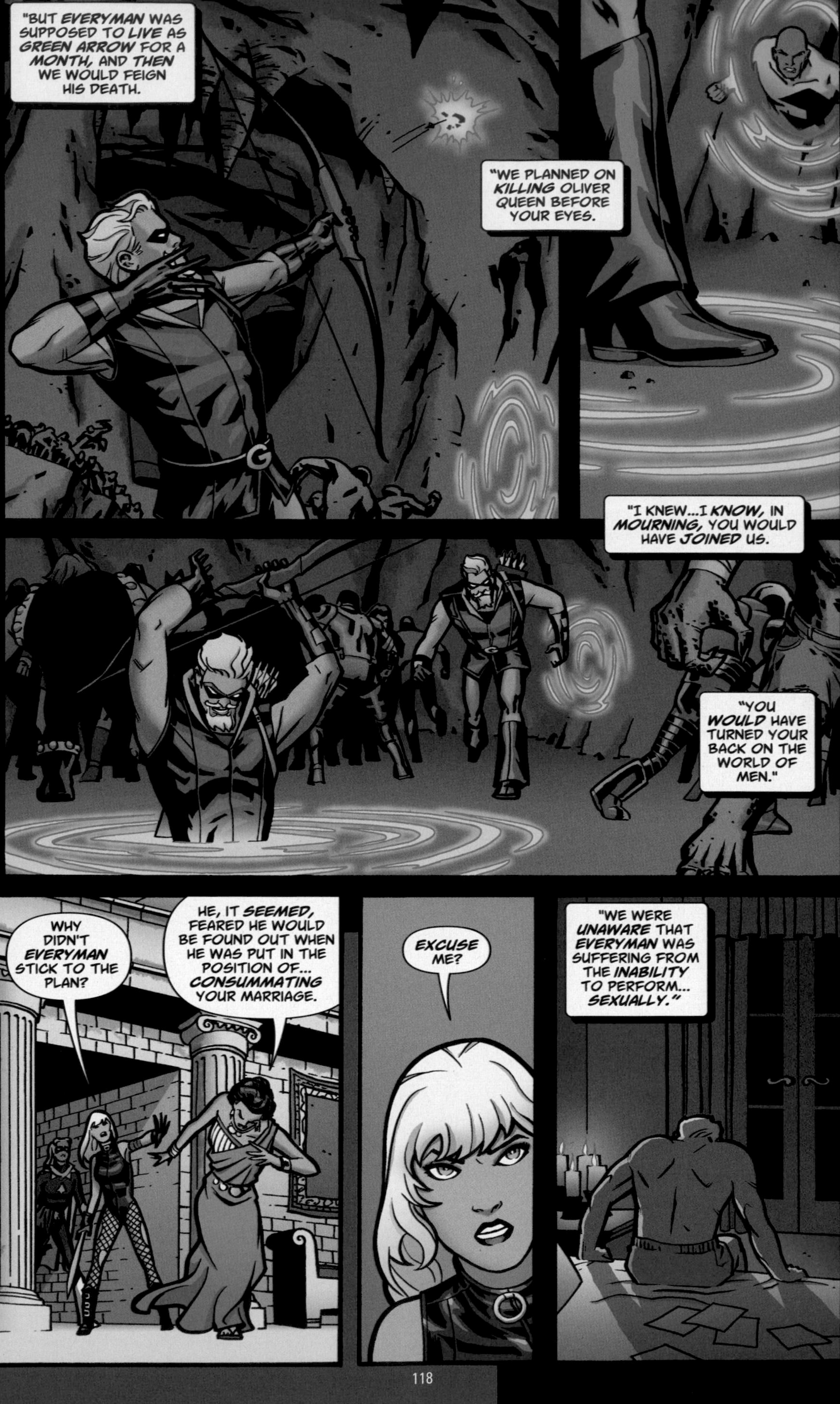
"BUT EVERYMAN WAS SUPPOSED TO LIVE AS GREEN ARROW FOR A MONTH, AND THEN WE WOULD FEIGN HIS DEATH.
"WE PLANNED ON KILLING OLIVER QUEEN BEFORE YOUR EYES.
"I KNEW...I KNOW, IN MOURNING, YOU WOULD HAVE JOINED US.
"YOU WOULD HAVE TURNED YOUR BACK ON THE WORLD OF MEN."
WHY DIDN'T EVERYMAN STICK TO THE PLAN?
HE, IT SEEMED, FEARED HE WOULD BE FOUND OUT WHEN HE WAS PUT IN THE POSITION OF... CONSUMMATING YOUR MARRIAGE.
EXCUSE ME?
"WE WERE UNAWARE THAT EVERYMAN WAS SUFFERING FROM THE INABILITY TO PERFORM... SEXUALLY."

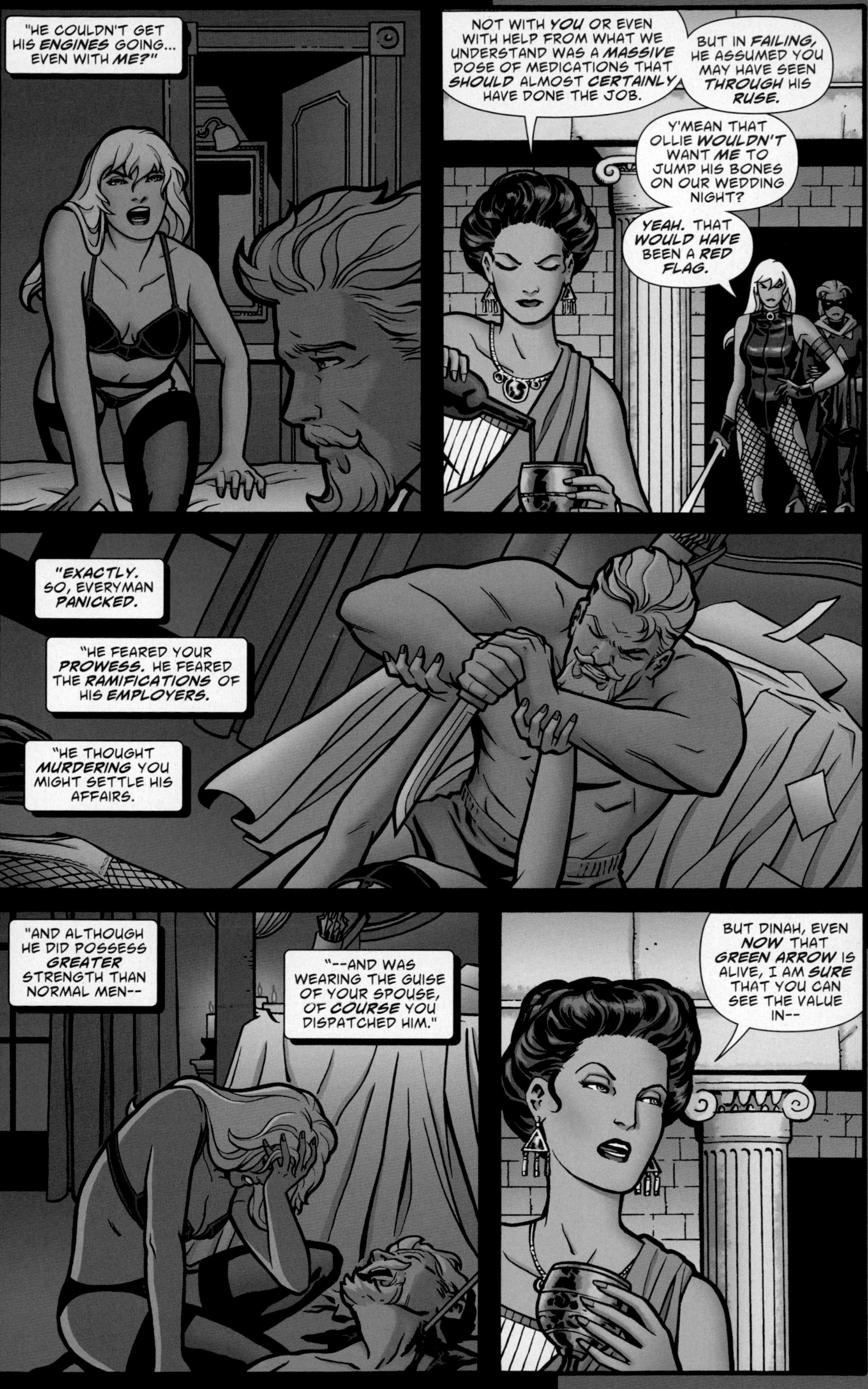
"HE COULDN'T GET HIS ENGINES GOING... EVEN WITH ME?"
NOT WITH YOU OR EVEN WITH HELP FROM WHAT WE UNDERSTAND WAS A MASSIVE DOSE OF MEDICATIONS THAT SHOULD ALMOST CERTAINLY HAVE DONE THE JOB.
BUT IN FAILING, HE ASSUMED YOU MAY HAVE SEEN THROUGH HIS RUSE.
Y'MEAN THAT OLLIE WOULDN'T WANT ME TO JUMP HIS BONES ON OUR WEDDING NIGHT?
YEAH. THAT WOULD HAVE BEEN A RED FLAG.
"EXACTLY. SO, EVERYMAN PANICKED.
"HE FEARED YOUR PROWESS. HE FEARED THE RAMIFICATIONS OF HIS EMPLOYERS.
"HE THOUGHT MURDERING YOU MIGHT SETTLE HIS AFFAIRS.
"AND ALTHOUGH HE DID POSSESS GREATER STRENGTH THAN NORMAL MEN--
"--AND WAS WEARING THE GUISE OF YOUR SPOUSE, OF COURSE YOU DISPATCHED HIM."
BUT DINAH, EVEN NOW THAT GREEN ARROW IS ALIVE, I AM SURE THAT YOU CAN SEE THE VALUE IN--

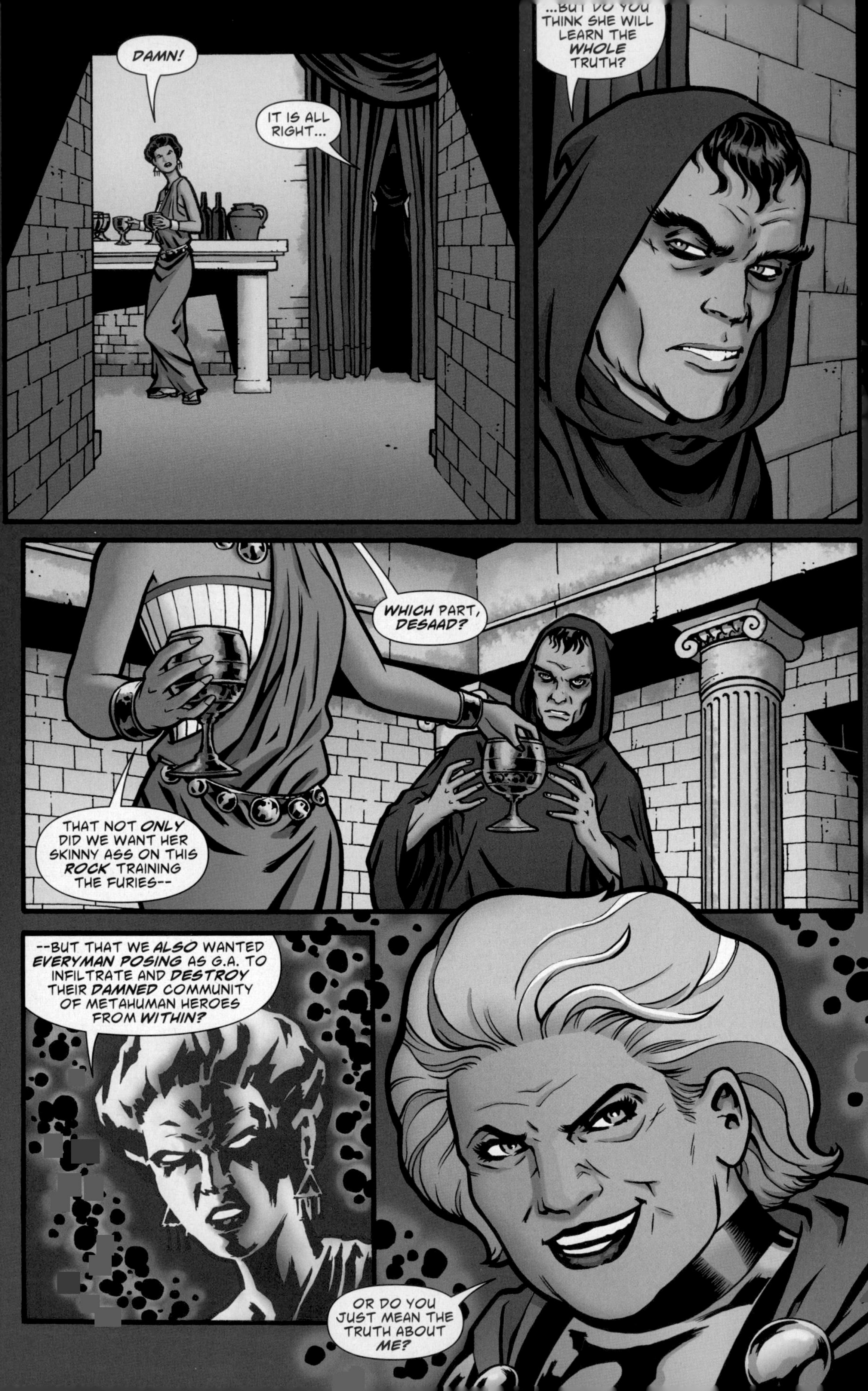
DAMN!
IT IS ALL RIGHT...
...BUT DO YOU THINK SHE WILL LEARN THE WHOLE TRUTH?
WHICH PART, DESAAD?
THAT NOT ONLY DID WE WANT HER SKINNY ASS ON THIS ROCK TRAINING THE FURIES--
--BUT THAT WE ALSO WANTED EVERYMAN POSING AS G.A. TO INFILTRATE AND DESTROY THEIR DAMNED COMMUNITY OF METAHUMAN HEROES FROM WITHIN?
OR DO YOU JUST MEAN THE TRUTH ABOUT ME?

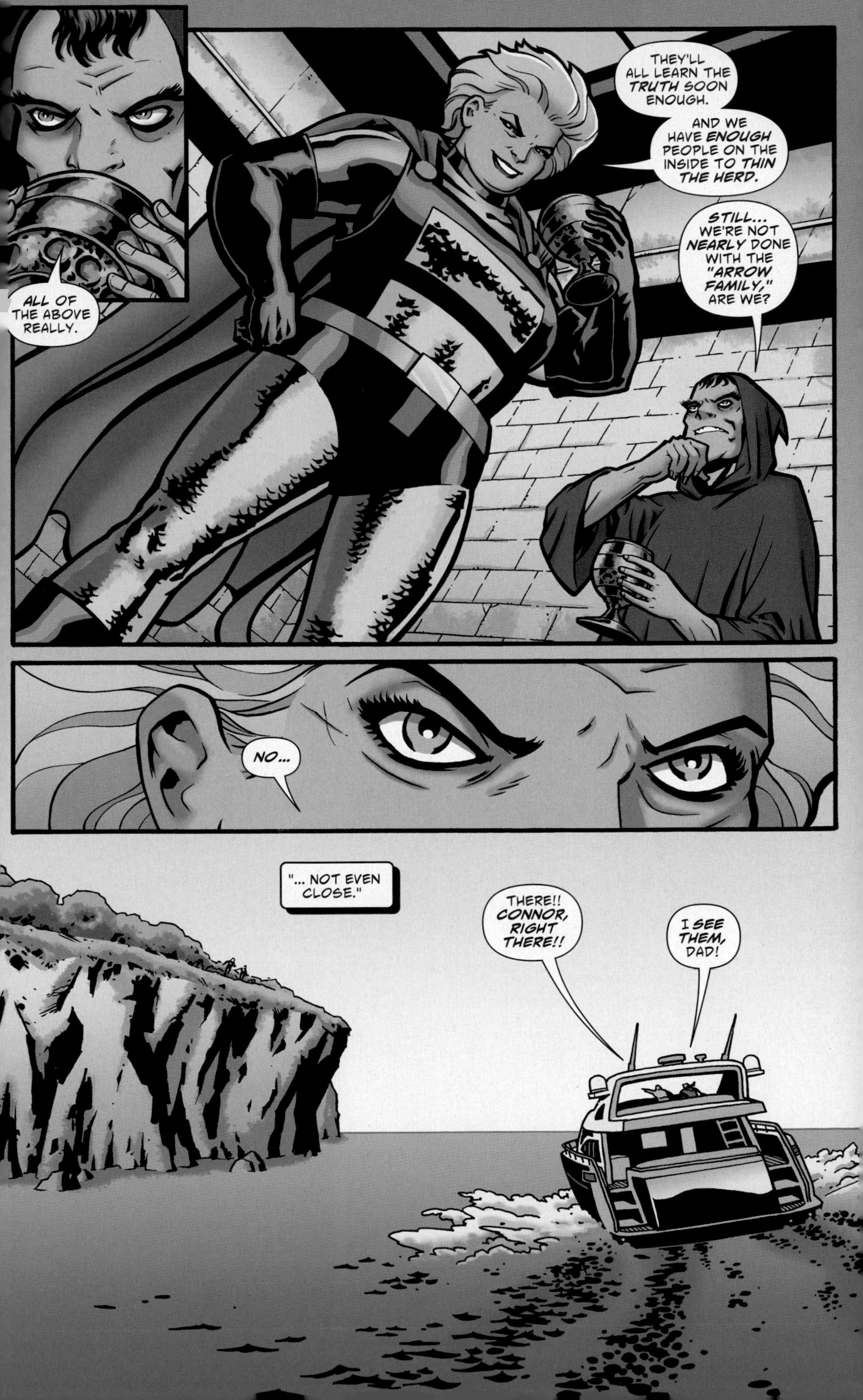
ALL OF THE ABOVE REALLY.
THEY'LL ALL LEARN THE TRUTH SOON ENOUGH.
AND WE HAVE ENOUGH PEOPLE ON THE INSIDE TO THIN THE HERD.
STILL... WE'RE NOT NEARLY DONE WITH THE "ARROW FAMILY," ARE WE?
NO...
"... NOT EVEN CLOSE."
THERE!! CONNOR, RIGHT THERE!!
I SEE THEM, DAD!

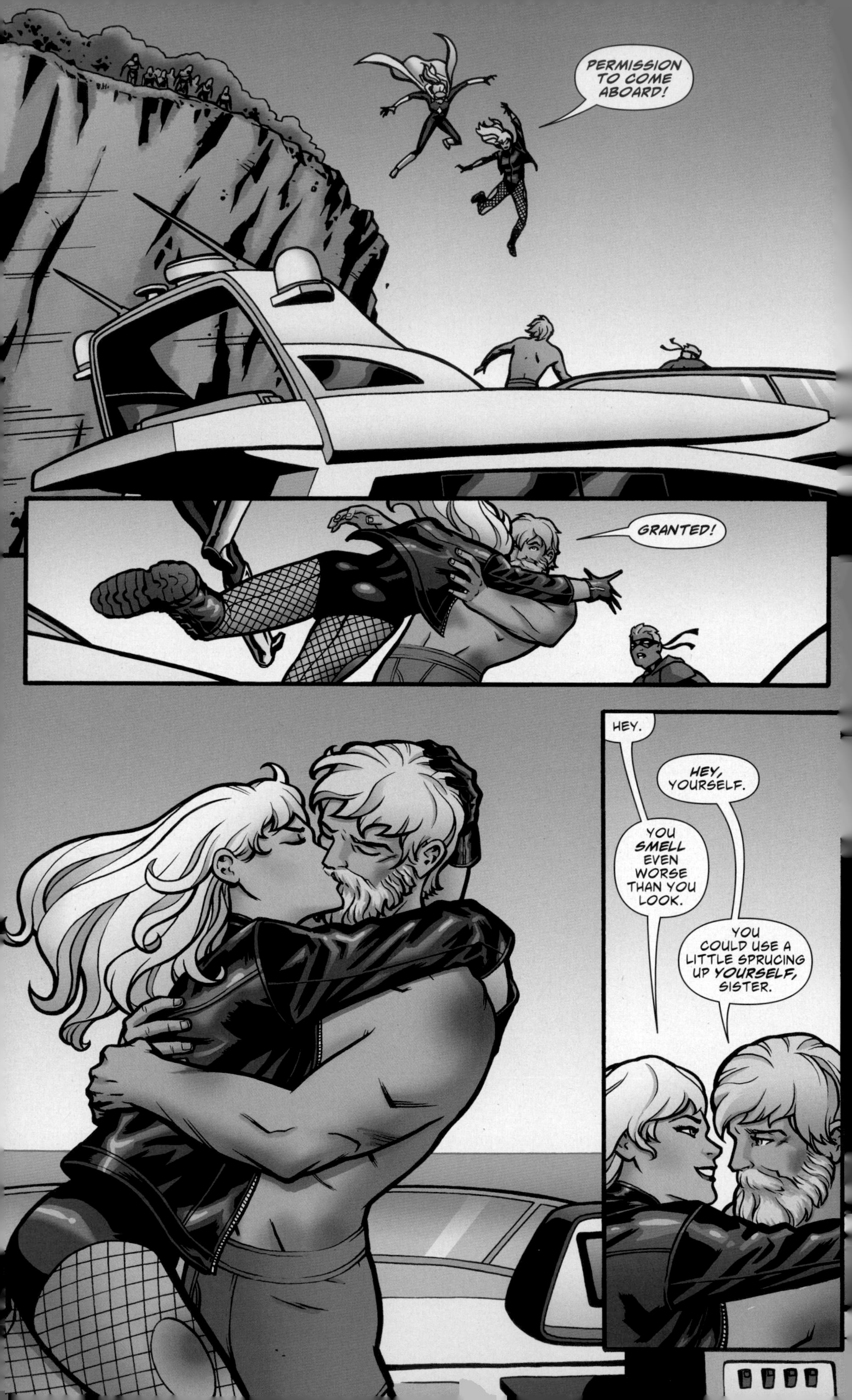
PERMISSION TO COME ABOARD!
GRANTED!
HEY.
HEY, YOURSELF.
YOU SMELL EVEN WORSE THAN YOU LOOK.
YOU COULD USE A LITTLE SPRUCING UP YOURSELF, SISTER.

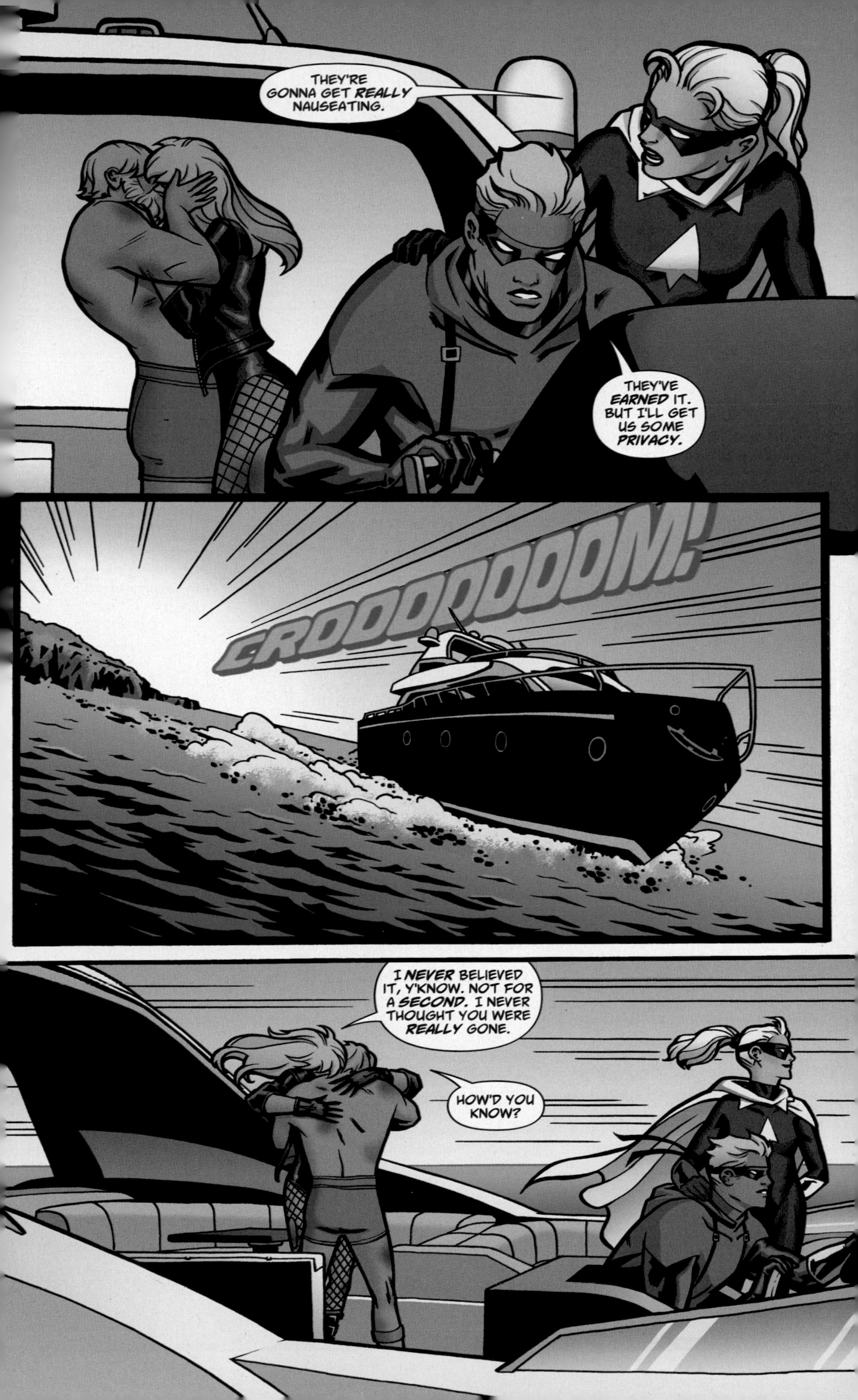
THEY'RE GONNA GET REALLY NAUSEATING.
THEY'VE EARNED IT. BUT I'LL GET US SOME PRIVACY.
CRODDDDDOM!
I NEVER BELIEVED IT, Y'KNOW. NOT FOR A SECOND. I NEVER THOUGHT YOU WERE REALLY GONE.
HOW'D YOU KNOW?

THE *LAST TIME...* THE *LAST TIME* I *LOST* YOU, A PART OF ME WAS *GONE.* I COULD FEEL IT.

NOT THIS TIME.

LAST TIME I CAME BACK TOO.

YOU'RE JUST A *BAD PENNY.*

I AM SUCH A *BAD PENNY.*

SO... Y'WANNA GO *BELOW DECK* AND SHINE THIS *PENNY* UP?

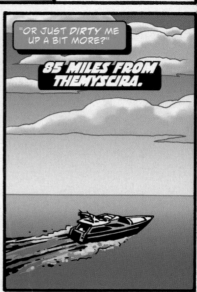

"OR JUST *DIRTY* ME UP A BIT MORE?"

85 MILES FROM THEMYSCIRA.

I LIKE IT.

ME TOO, IT'S GOT STYLE.

I JUST LIKE THAT HE'S NOT RUNNING AROUND IN MY *UNDERWEAR* ANYMORE.

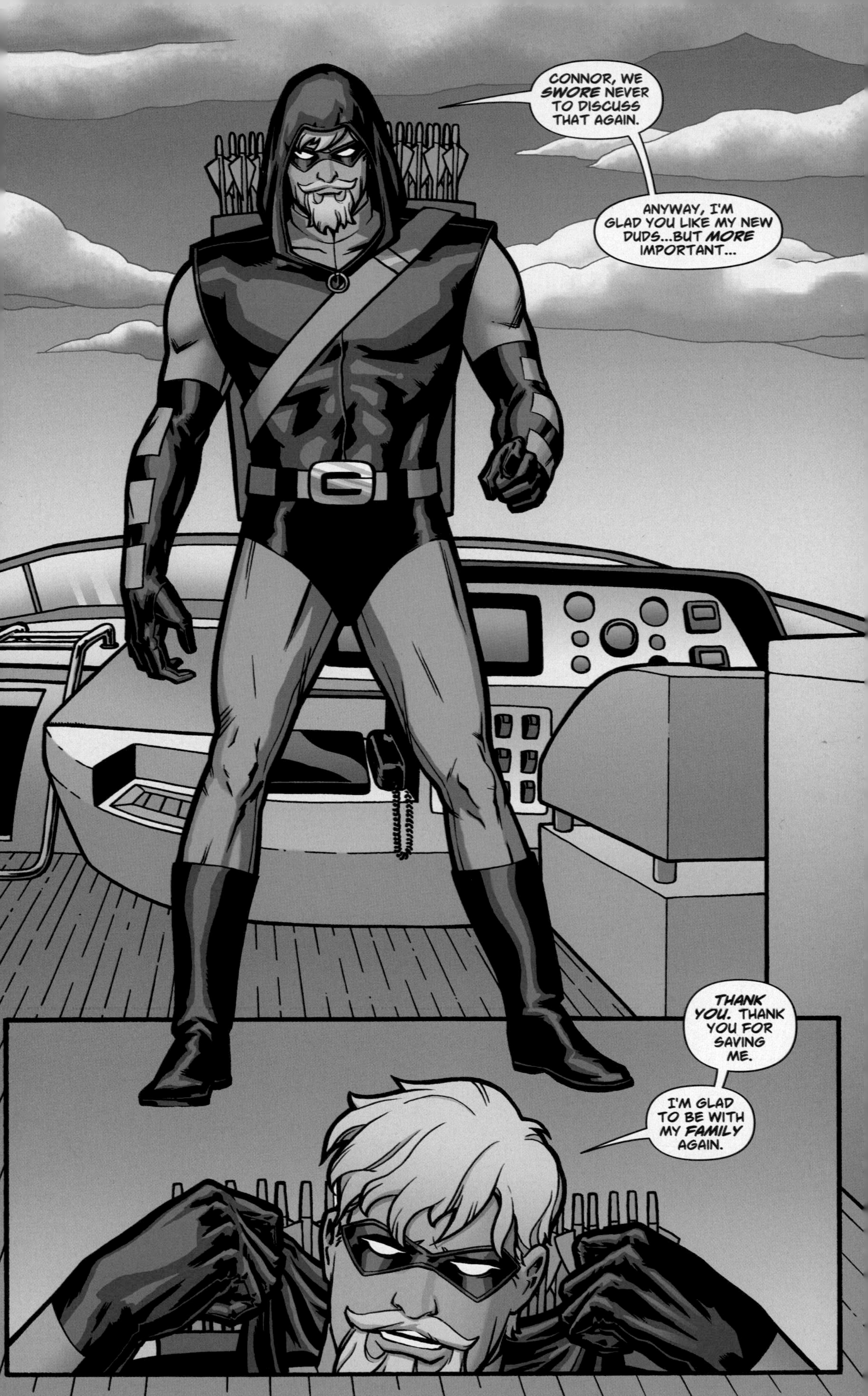
CONNOR, WE SWORE NEVER TO DISCUSS THAT AGAIN.
ANYWAY, I'M GLAD YOU LIKE MY NEW DUDS...BUT MORE IMPORTANT...
THANK YOU. THANK YOU FOR SAVING ME.
I'M GLAD TO BE WITH MY FAMILY AGAIN.

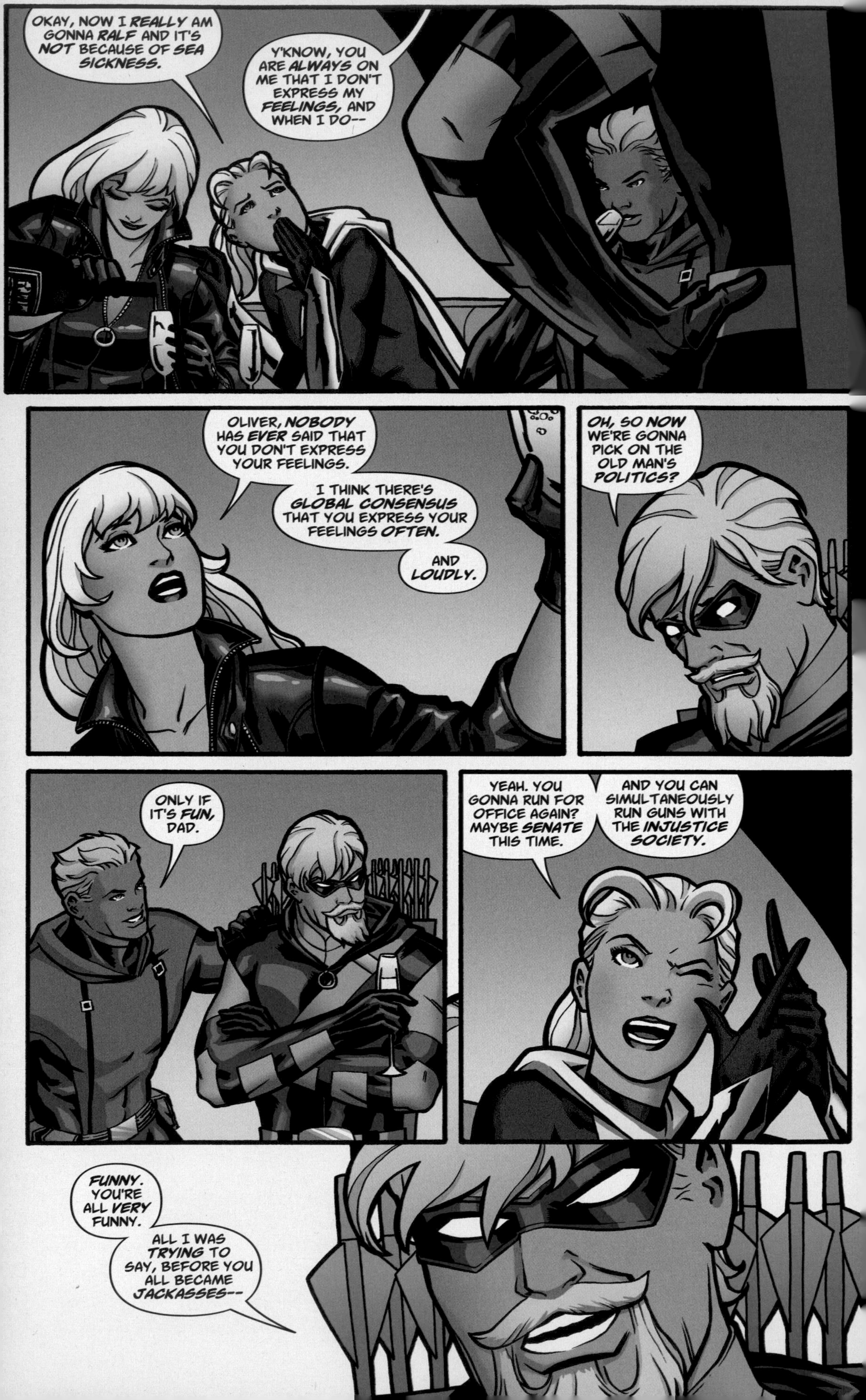
OKAY, NOW I REALLY AM GONNA RALF AND IT'S NOT BECAUSE OF SEA SICKNESS.
Y'KNOW, YOU ARE ALWAYS ON ME THAT I DON'T EXPRESS MY FEELINGS, AND WHEN I DO--
OLIVER, NOBODY HAS EVER SAID THAT YOU DON'T EXPRESS YOUR FEELINGS.
I THINK THERE'S GLOBAL CONSENSUS THAT YOU EXPRESS YOUR FEELINGS OFTEN.
AND LOUDLY.
OH, SO NOW WE'RE GONNA PICK ON THE OLD MAN'S POLITICS?
ONLY IF IT'S FUN, DAD.
YEAH. YOU GONNA RUN FOR OFFICE AGAIN? MAYBE SENATE THIS TIME.
AND YOU CAN SIMULTANEOUSLY RUN GUNS WITH THE INJUSTICE SOCIETY.
FUNNY. YOU'RE ALL VERY FUNNY.
ALL I WAS TRYING TO SAY, BEFORE YOU ALL BECAME JACKASSES--

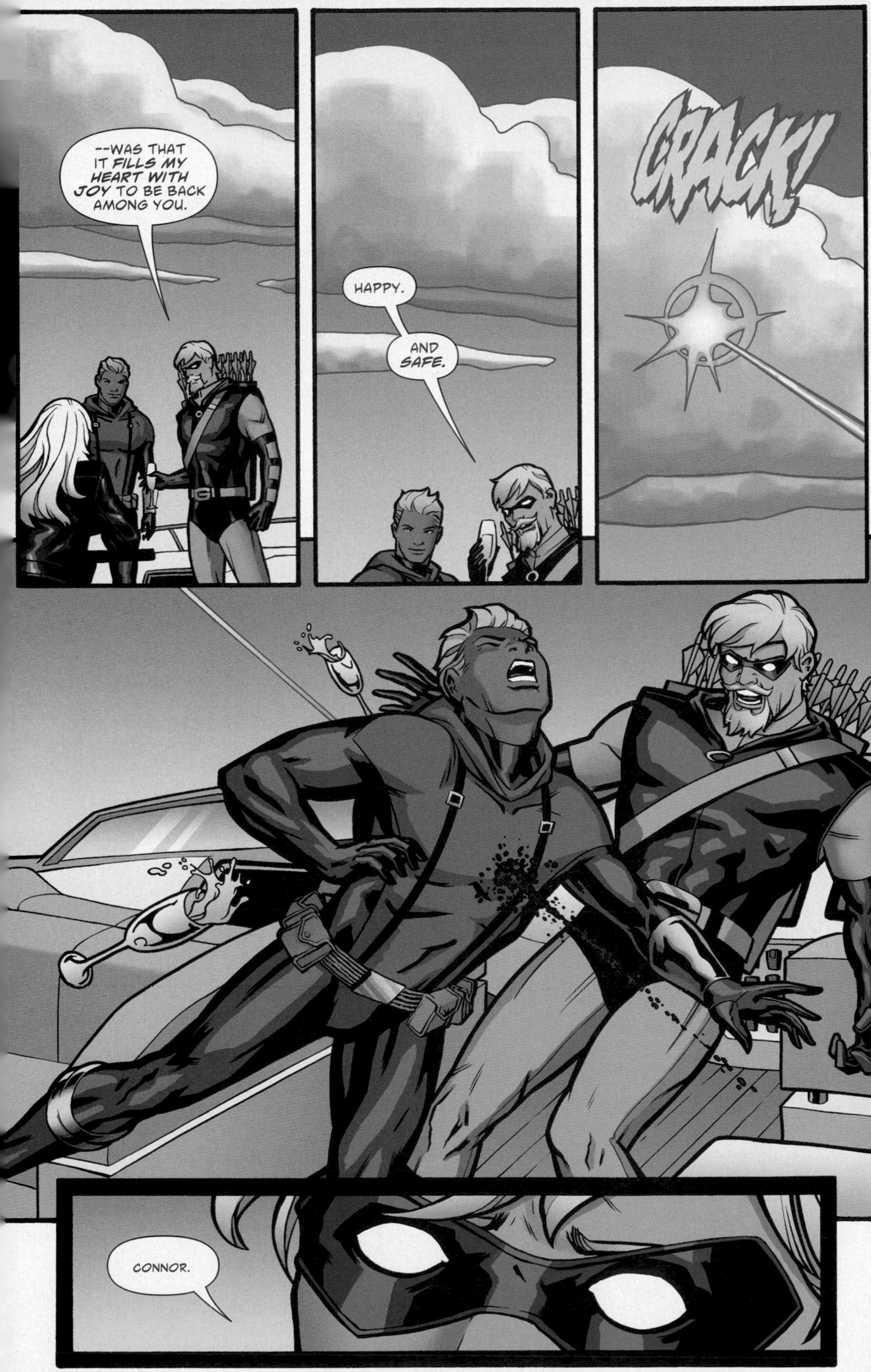
--WAS THAT IT FILLS MY HEART WITH JOY TO BE BACK AMONG YOU.
HAPPY.
AND SAFE.
CRACK!
CONNOR.

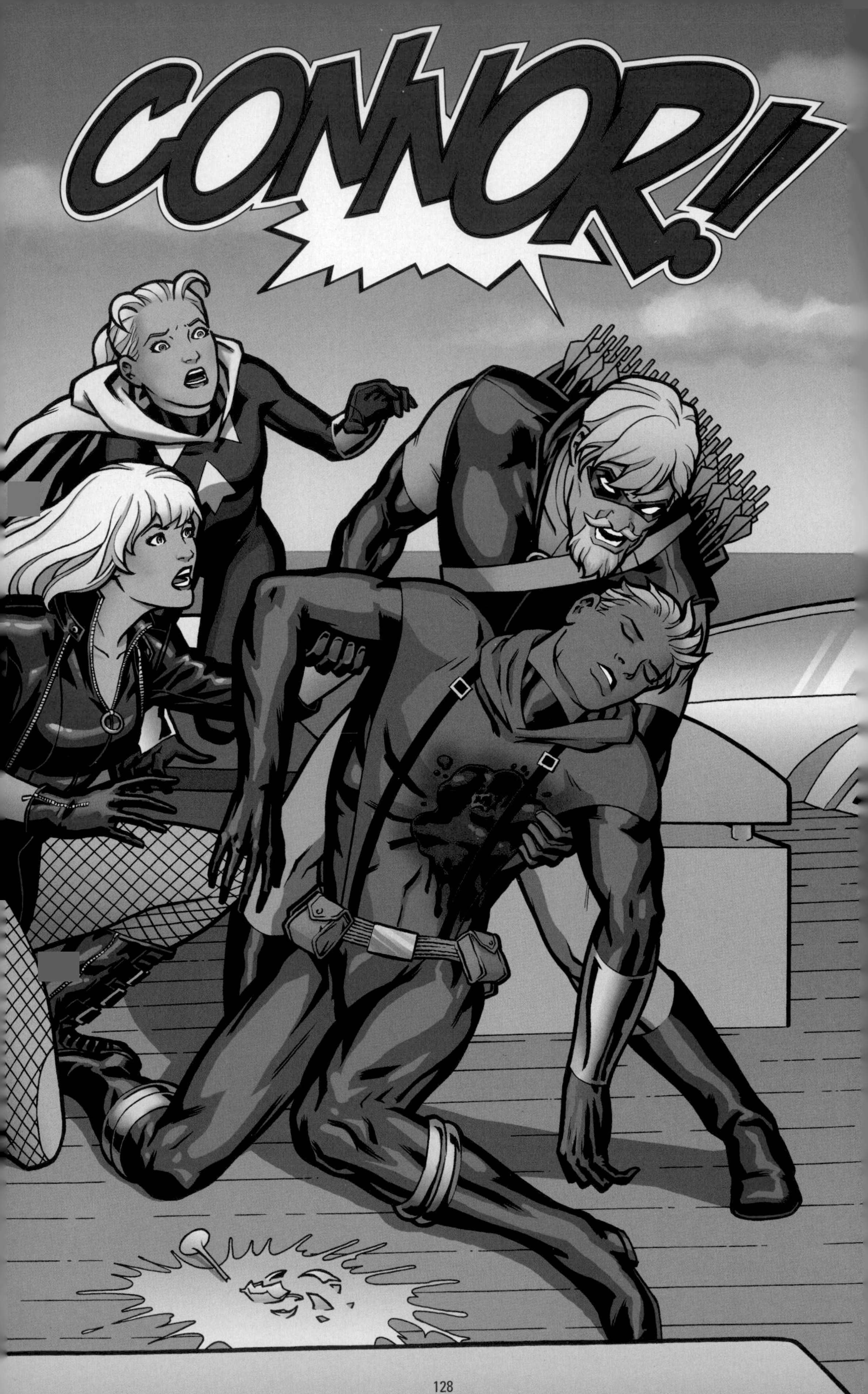
CONNOR!!

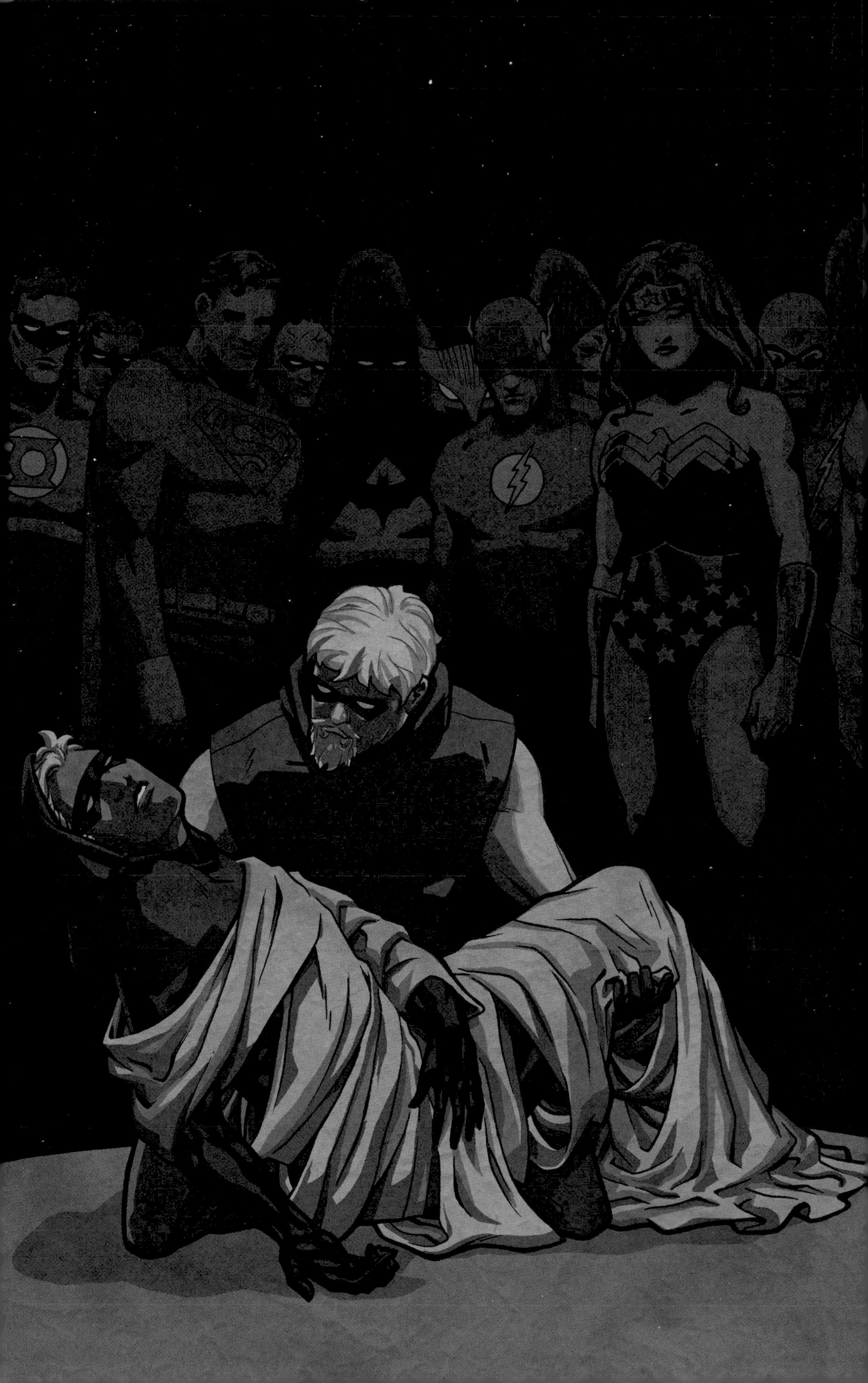

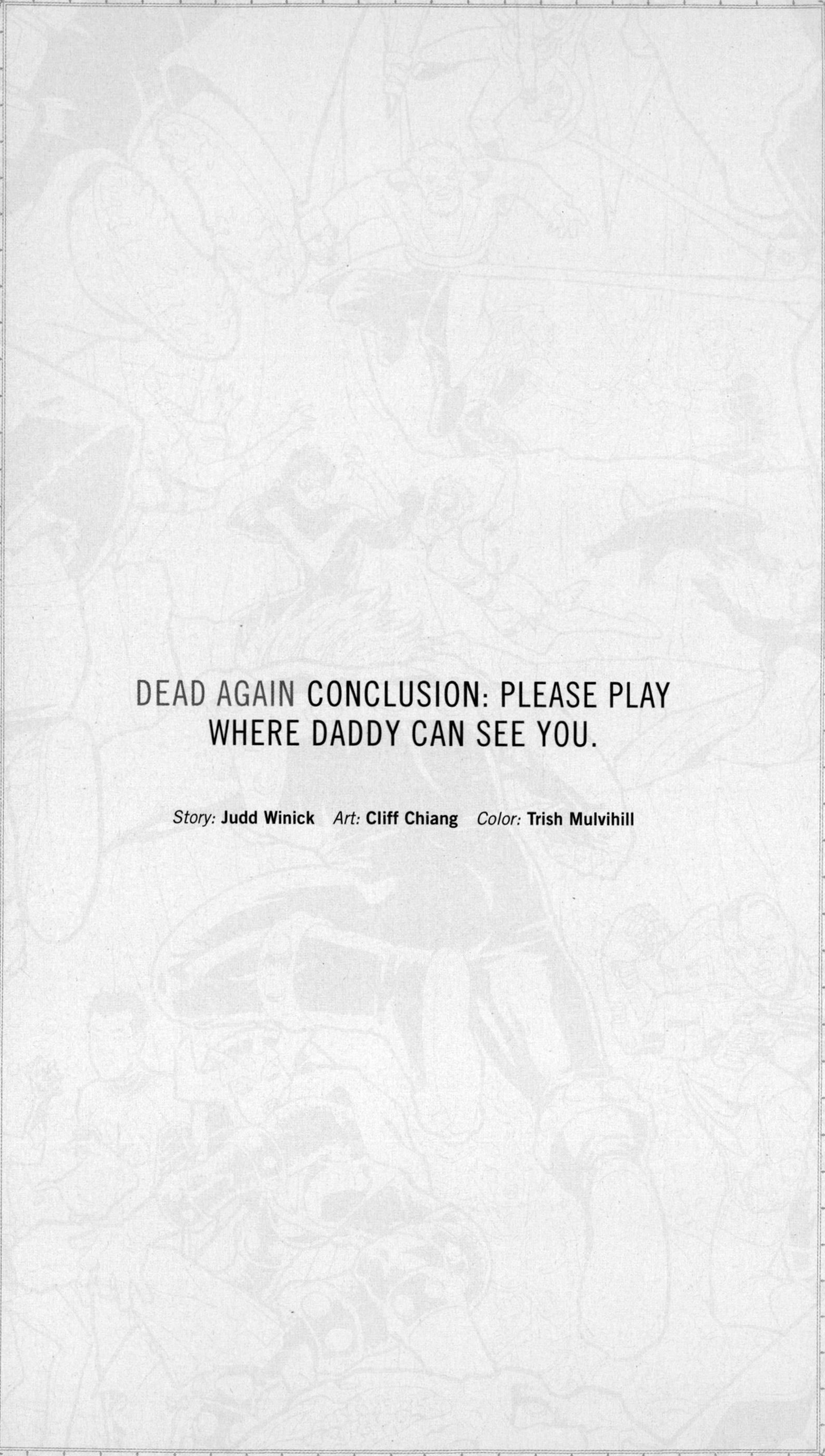

DEAD AGAIN CONCLUSION: PLEASE PLAY WHERE DADDY CAN SEE YOU.

Story: **Judd Winick** *Art:* **Cliff Chiang** *Color:* **Trish Mulvihill**

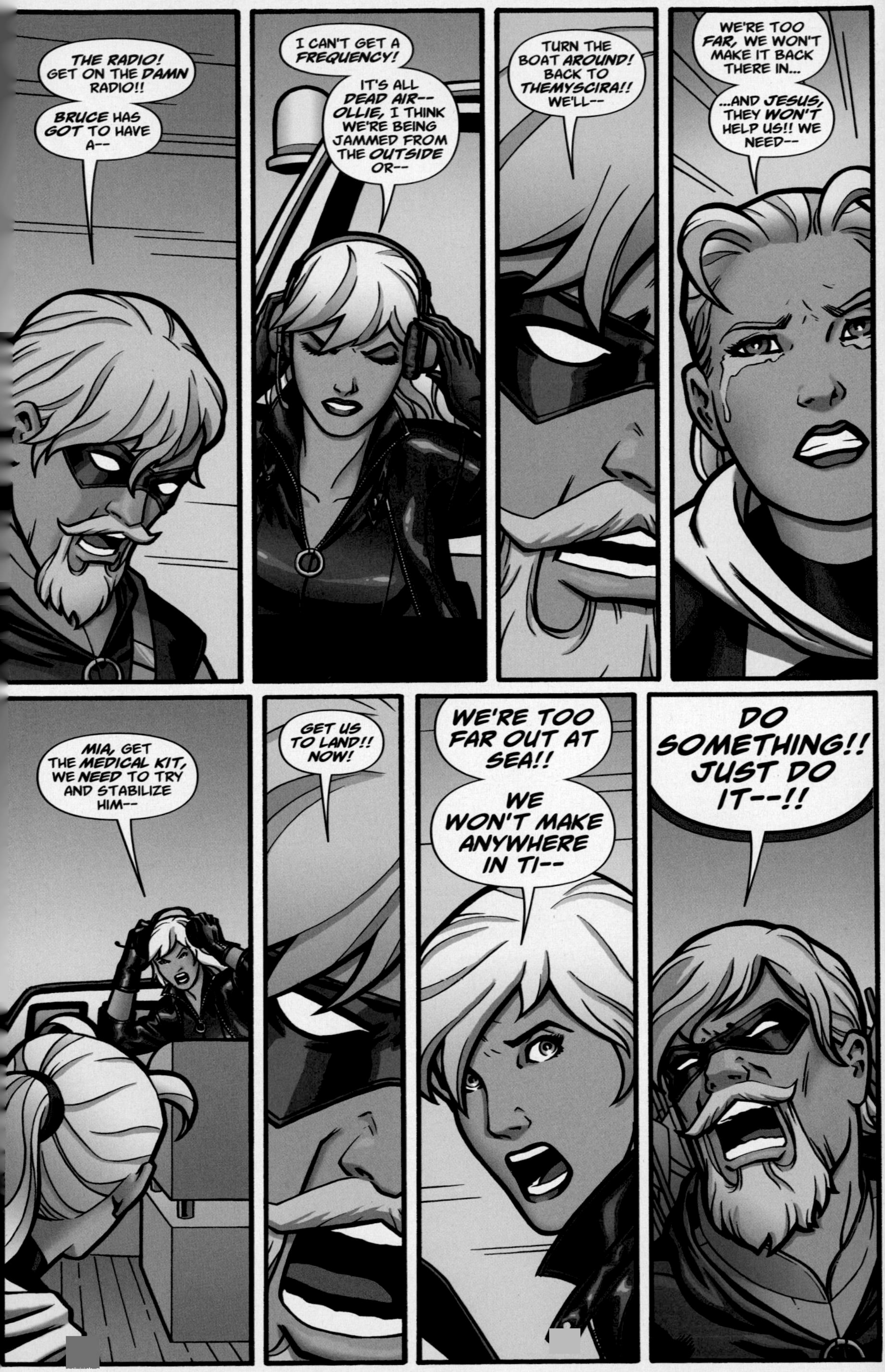
THE RADIO! GET ON THE DAMN RADIO!!
BRUCE HAS GOT TO HAVE A--
I CAN'T GET A FREQUENCY!
IT'S ALL DEAD AIR-- OLLIE, I THINK WE'RE BEING JAMMED FROM THE OUTSIDE OR--
TURN THE BOAT AROUND! BACK TO THEMYSCIRA!! WE'LL--
WE'RE TOO FAR, WE WON'T MAKE IT BACK THERE IN...
...AND JESUS, THEY WON'T HELP US!! WE NEED--
MIA, GET THE MEDICAL KIT, WE NEED TO TRY AND STABILIZE HIM--
GET US TO LAND!! NOW!
WE'RE TOO FAR OUT AT SEA!!
WE WON'T MAKE ANYWHERE IN TI--
DO SOMETHING!! JUST DO IT--!!

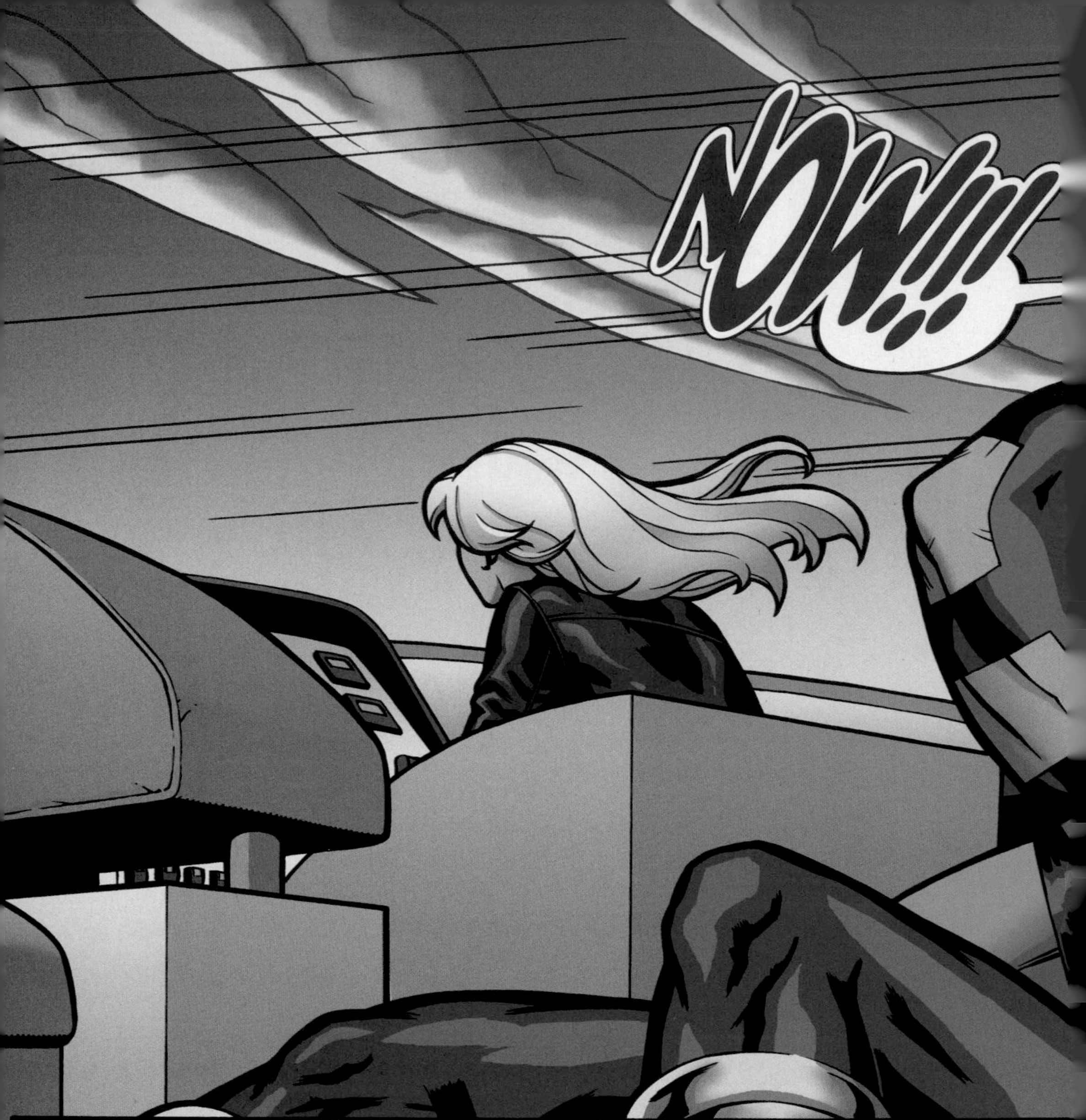
NOW!!!

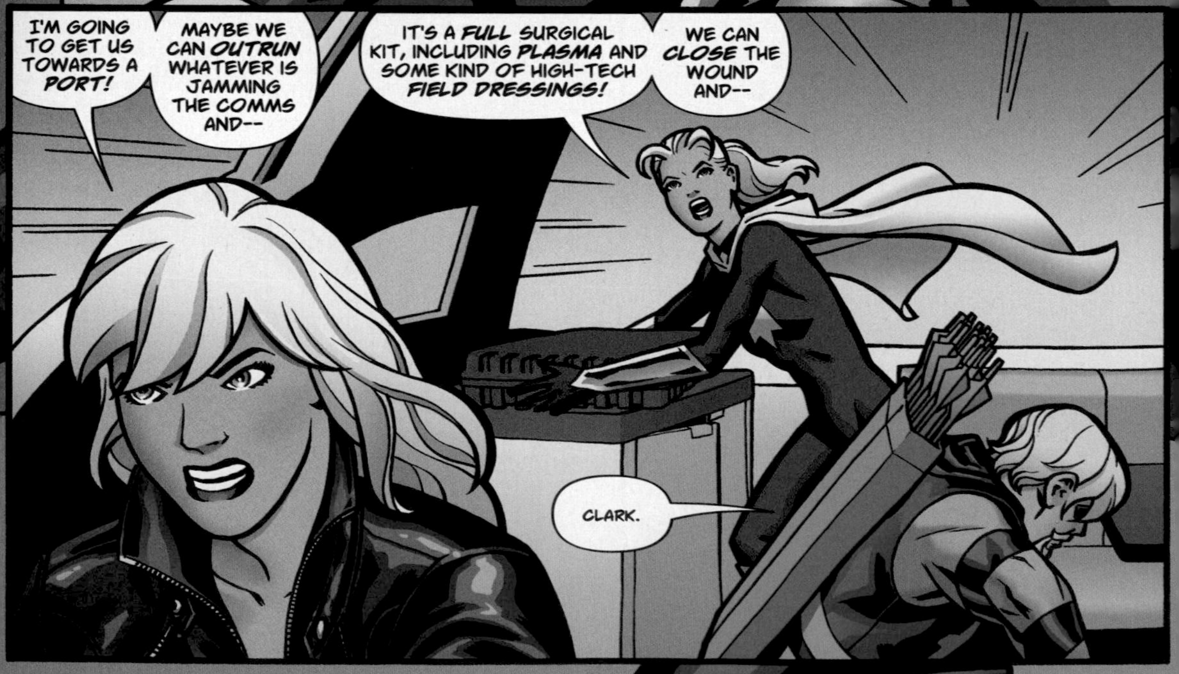
I'M GOING TO GET US TOWARDS A PORT!
MAYBE WE CAN OUTRUN WHATEVER IS JAMMING THE COMMS AND--
IT'S A FULL SURGICAL KIT, INCLUDING PLASMA AND SOME KIND OF HIGH-TECH FIELD DRESSINGS!
WE CAN CLOSE THE WOUND AND--
CLARK.

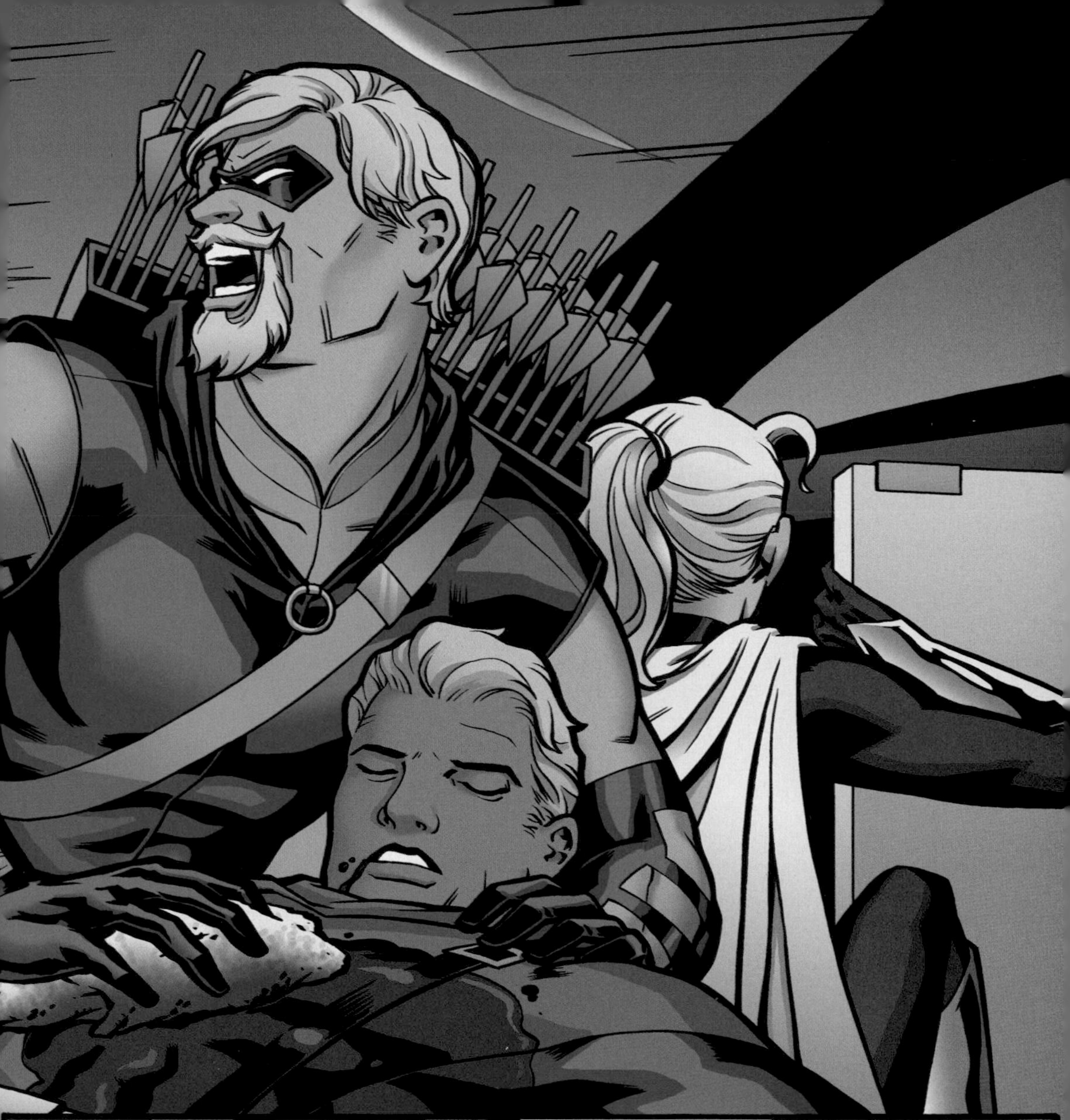

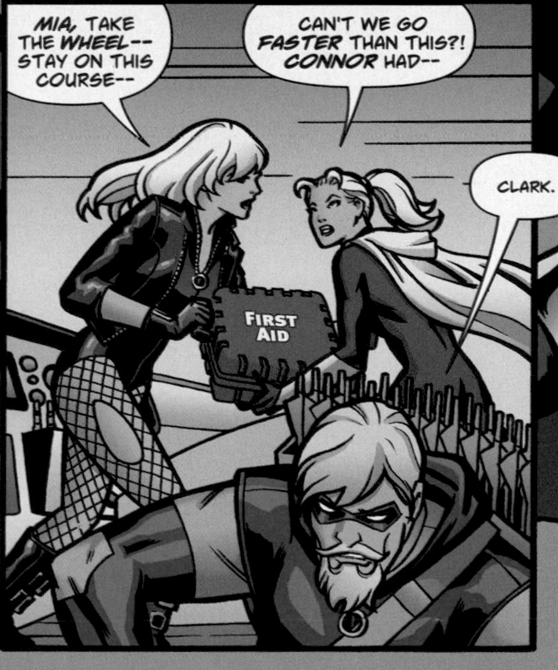

MIA, TAKE THE WHEEL-- STAY ON THIS COURSE--
CAN'T WE GO FASTER THAN THIS?! CONNOR HAD--
CLARK.
FIRST AID

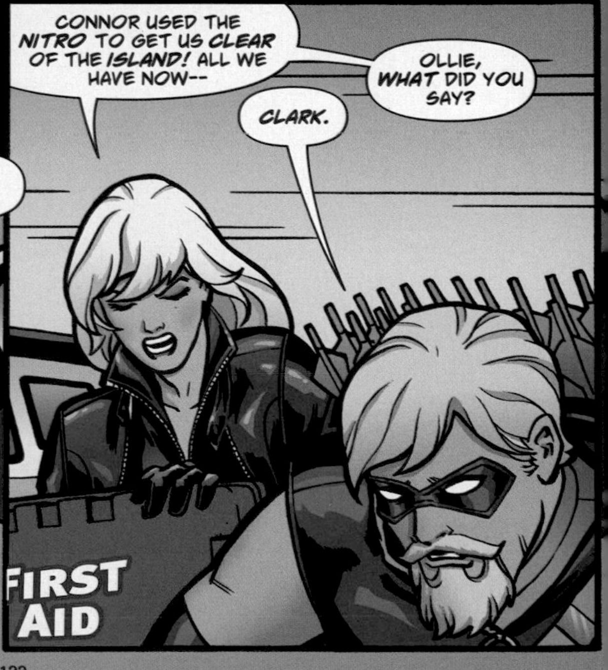

CONNOR USED THE NITRO TO GET US CLEAR OF THE ISLAND! ALL WE HAVE NOW--
CLARK.
OLLIE, WHAT DID YOU SAY?
FIRST AID

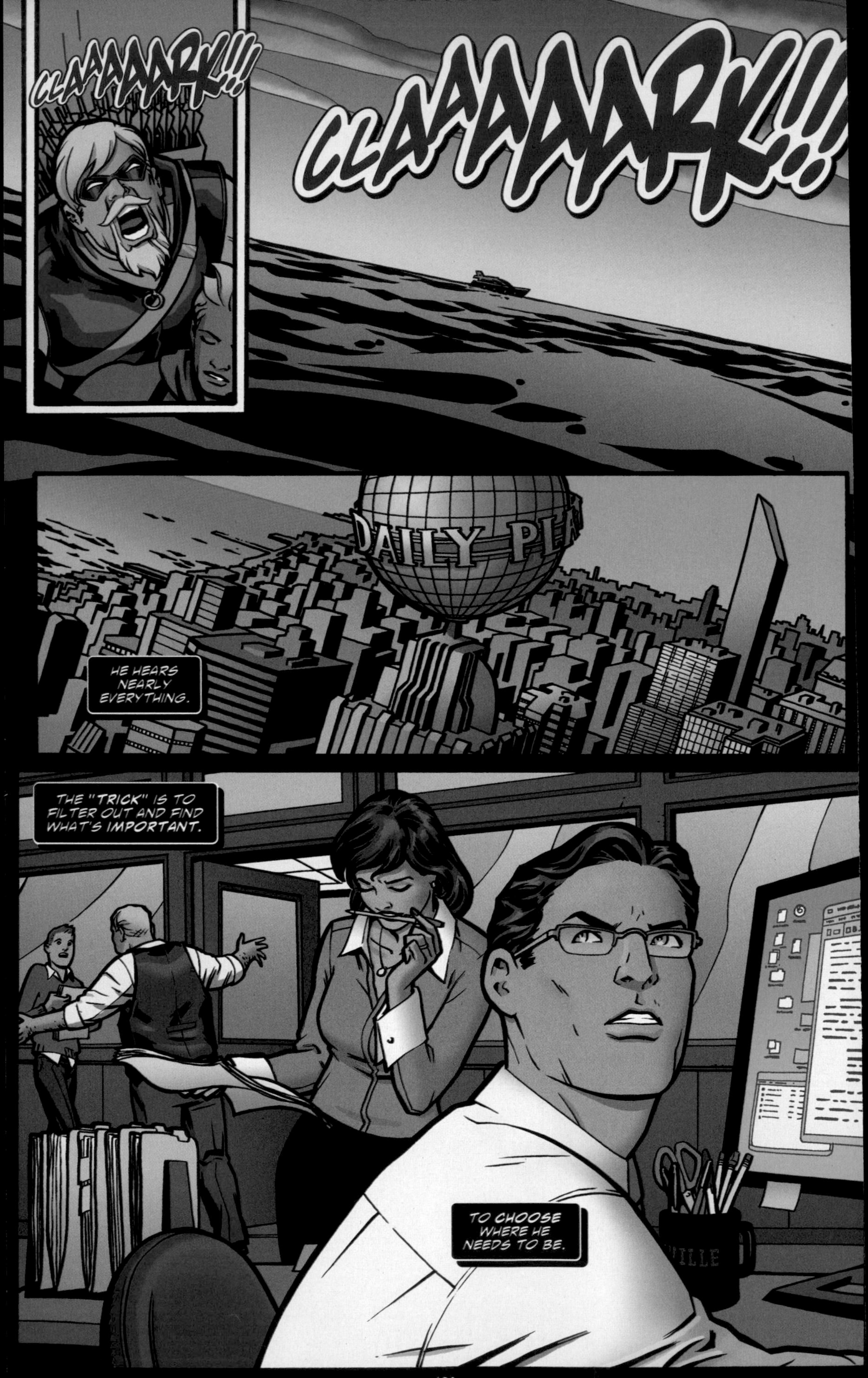
CLAAAARK!!!
CLAAAAARK!!!
DAILY PL
HE HEARS NEARLY EVERYTHING.
THE "TRICK" IS TO FILTER OUT AND FIND WHAT'S IMPORTANT.
TO CHOOSE WHERE HE NEEDS TO BE.

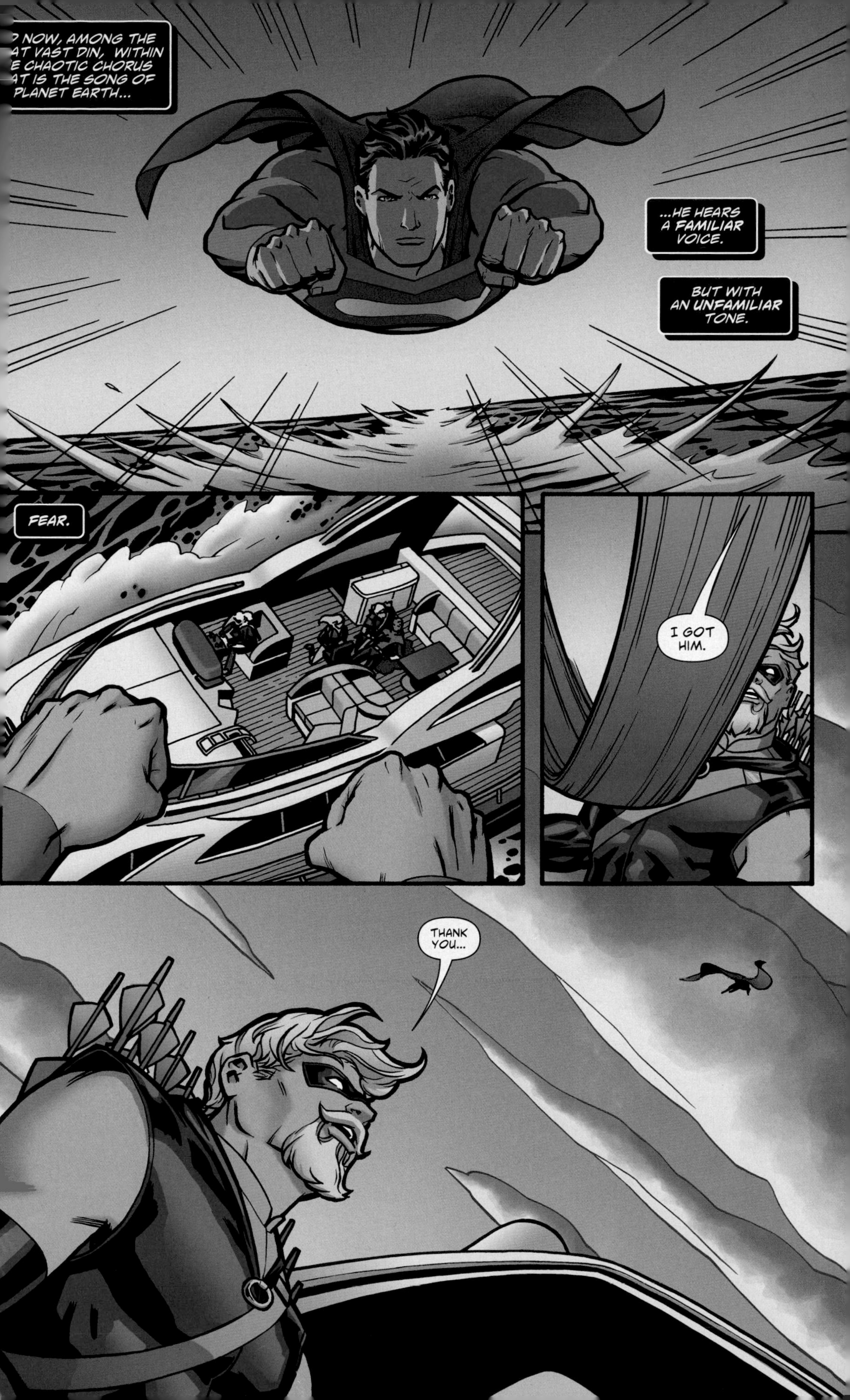
NOW, AMONG THE VAST DIN, WITHIN CHAOTIC CHORUS IS THE SONG OF PLANET EARTH...
...HE HEARS A FAMILIAR VOICE.
BUT WITH AN UNFAMILIAR TONE.
FEAR.
I GOT HIM.
THANK YOU...

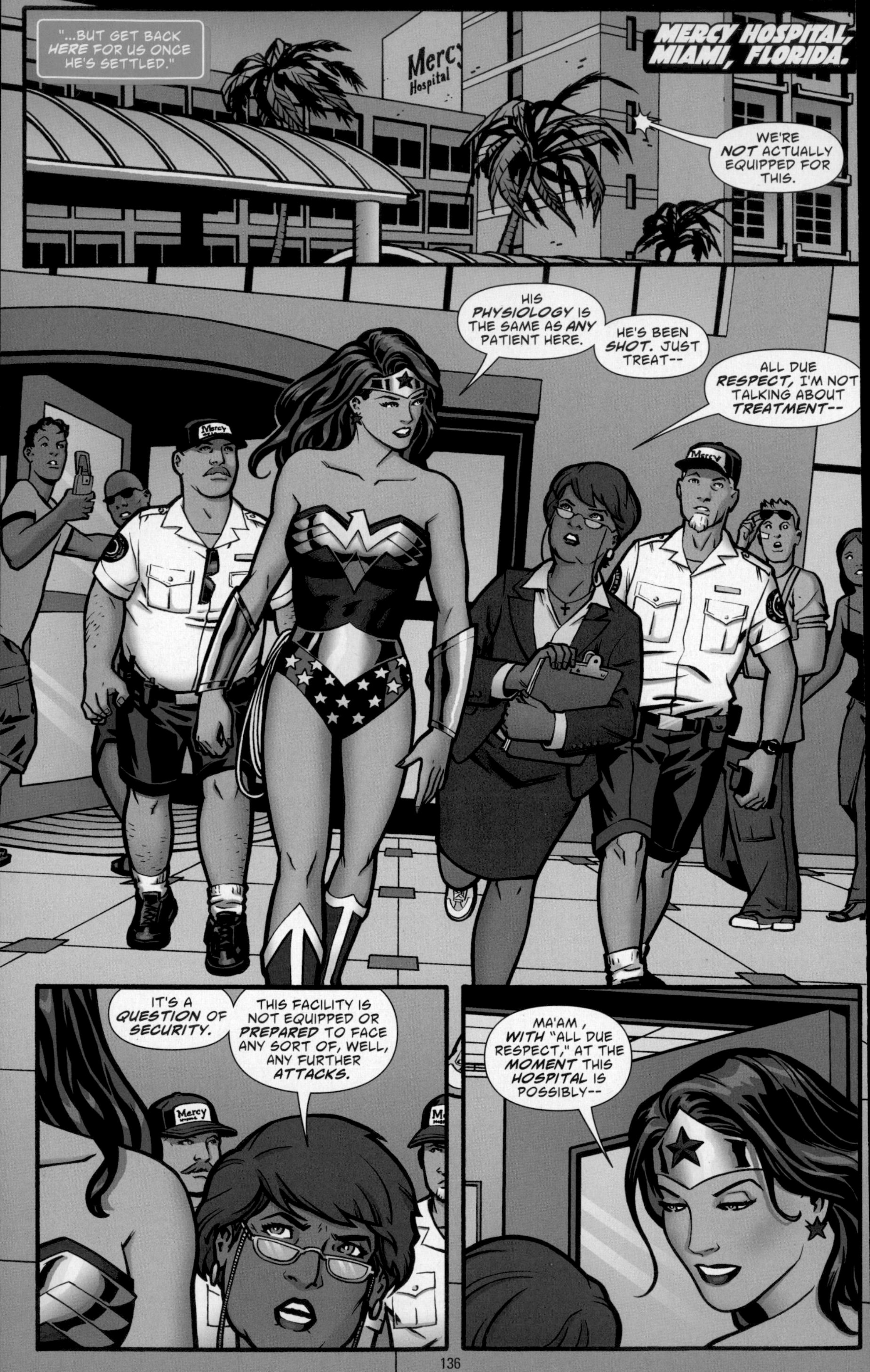
"...BUT GET BACK HERE FOR US ONCE HE'S SETTLED."
MERCY HOSPITAL, MIAMI, FLORIDA.
Mercy Hospital
WE'RE NOT ACTUALLY EQUIPPED FOR THIS.
HIS PHYSIOLOGY IS THE SAME AS ANY PATIENT HERE.
HE'S BEEN SHOT. JUST TREAT--
ALL DUE RESPECT, I'M NOT TALKING ABOUT TREATMENT--
IT'S A QUESTION OF SECURITY.
THIS FACILITY IS NOT EQUIPPED OR PREPARED TO FACE ANY SORT OF, WELL, ANY FURTHER ATTACKS.
MA'AM, WITH "ALL DUE RESPECT," AT THE MOMENT THIS HOSPITAL IS POSSIBLY--

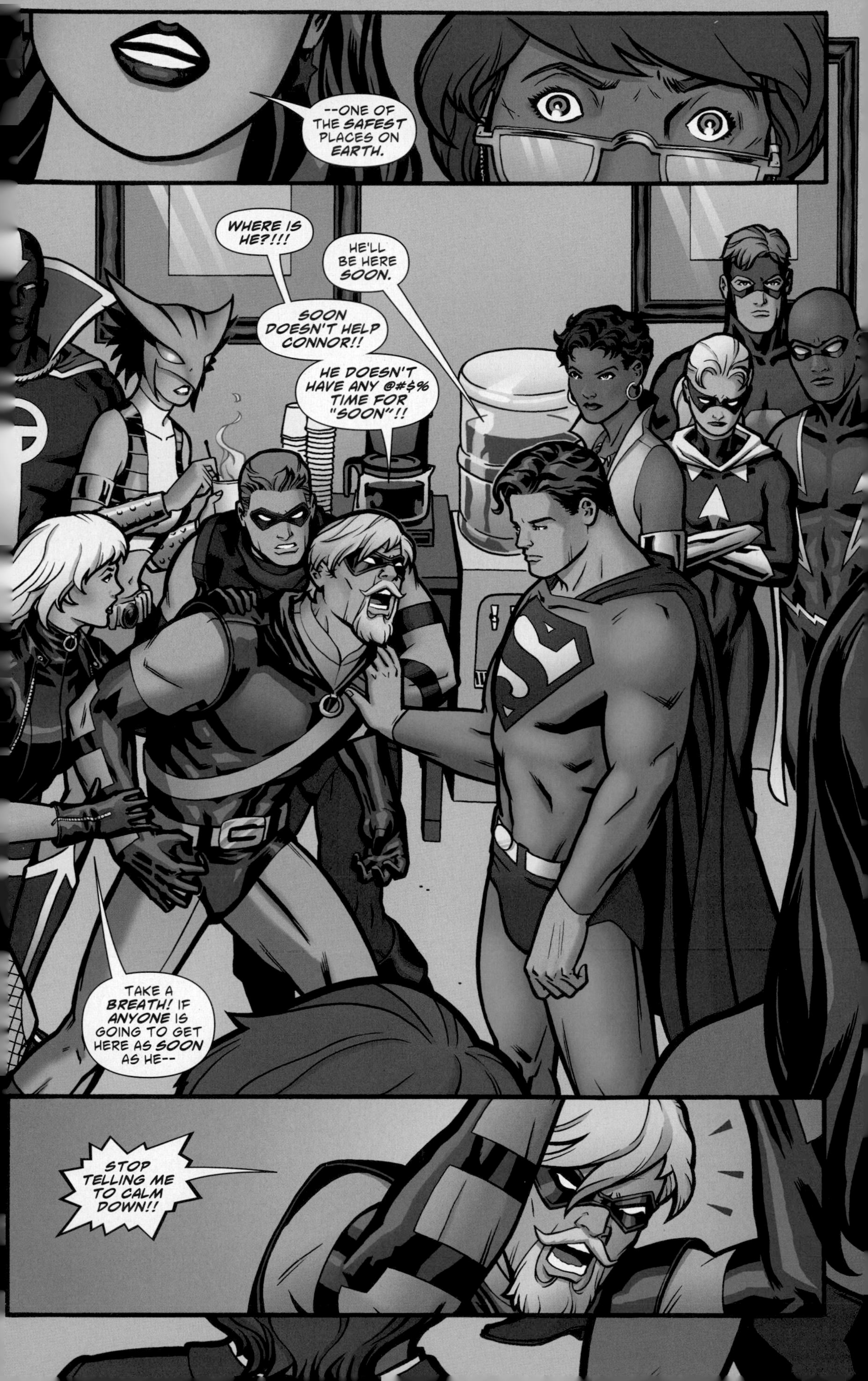
--ONE OF THE SAFEST PLACES ON EARTH.
WHERE IS HE?!!!
HE'LL BE HERE SOON.
SOON DOESN'T HELP CONNOR!!
HE DOESN'T HAVE ANY @#$% TIME FOR "SOON"!!
TAKE A BREATH! IF ANYONE IS GOING TO GET HERE AS SOON AS HE--
STOP TELLING ME TO CALM DOWN!!

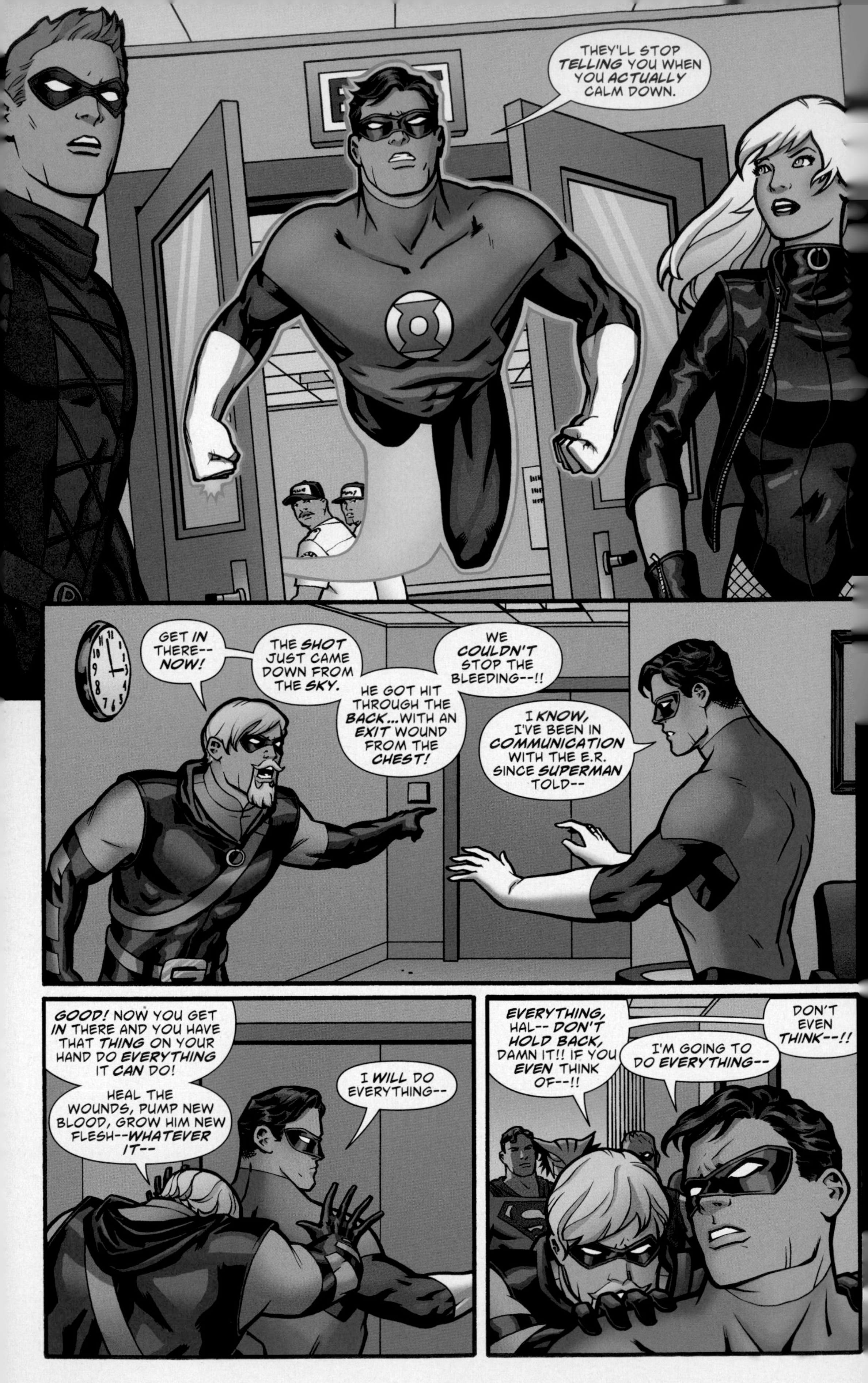
THEY'LL STOP TELLING YOU WHEN YOU ACTUALLY CALM DOWN.
GET IN THERE-- NOW!
THE SHOT JUST CAME DOWN FROM THE SKY.
WE COULDN'T STOP THE BLEEDING--!!
HE GOT HIT THROUGH THE BACK...WITH AN EXIT WOUND FROM THE CHEST!
I KNOW, I'VE BEEN IN COMMUNICATION WITH THE E.R. SINCE SUPERMAN TOLD--
GOOD! NOW YOU GET IN THERE AND YOU HAVE THAT THING ON YOUR HAND DO EVERYTHING IT CAN DO!
HEAL THE WOUNDS, PUMP NEW BLOOD, GROW HIM NEW FLESH--WHATEVER IT--
I WILL DO EVERYTHING--
EVERYTHING, HAL-- DON'T HOLD BACK, DAMN IT!! IF YOU EVEN THINK OF--!!
I'M GOING TO DO EVERYTHING--
DON'T EVEN THINK--!!

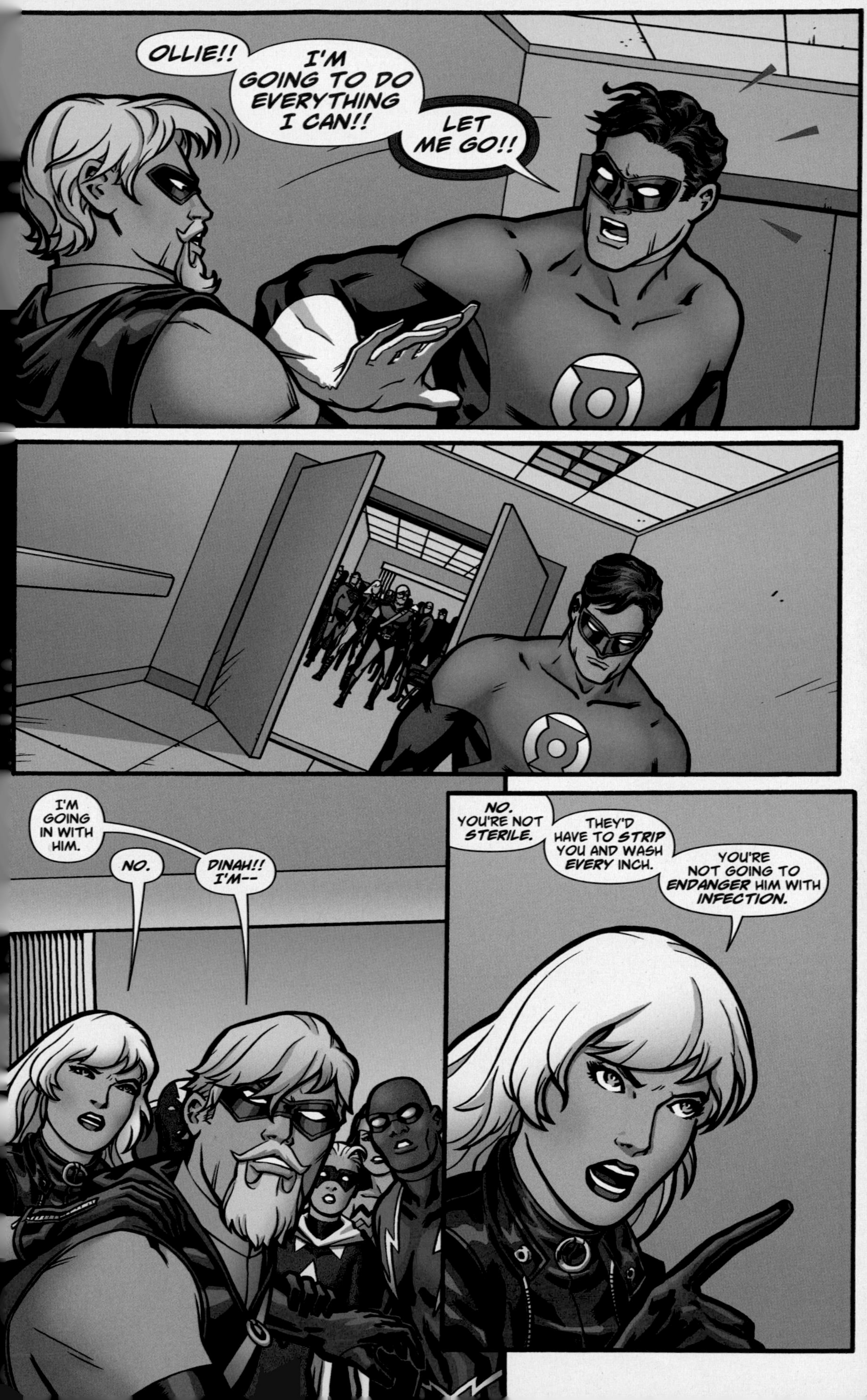
OLLIE!!
I'M GOING TO DO EVERYTHING I CAN!!
LET ME GO!!
I'M GOING IN WITH HIM.
NO.
DINAH!! I'M--
NO. YOU'RE NOT STERILE.
THEY'D HAVE TO STRIP YOU AND WASH EVERY INCH.
YOU'RE NOT GOING TO ENDANGER HIM WITH INFECTION.

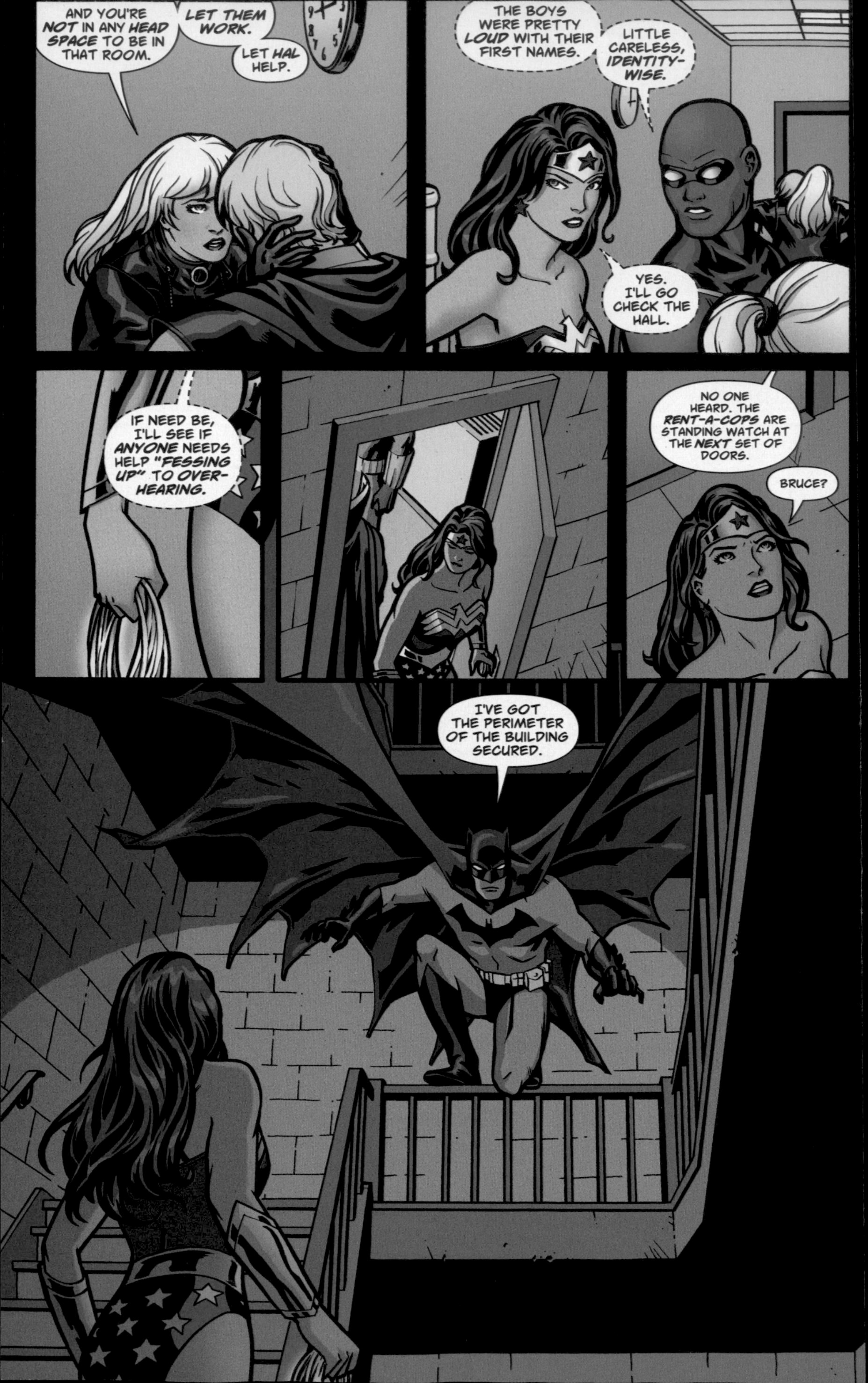
AND YOU'RE NOT IN ANY HEAD SPACE TO BE IN THAT ROOM.
LET THEM WORK.
LET HAL HELP.
THE BOYS WERE PRETTY LOUD WITH THEIR FIRST NAMES.
LITTLE CARELESS, IDENTITY-WISE.
YES. I'LL GO CHECK THE HALL.
IF NEED BE, I'LL SEE IF ANYONE NEEDS HELP "FESSING UP" TO OVER-HEARING.
NO ONE HEARD. THE RENT-A-COPS ARE STANDING WATCH AT THE NEXT SET OF DOORS.
BRUCE?
I'VE GOT THE PERIMETER OF THE BUILDING SECURED.

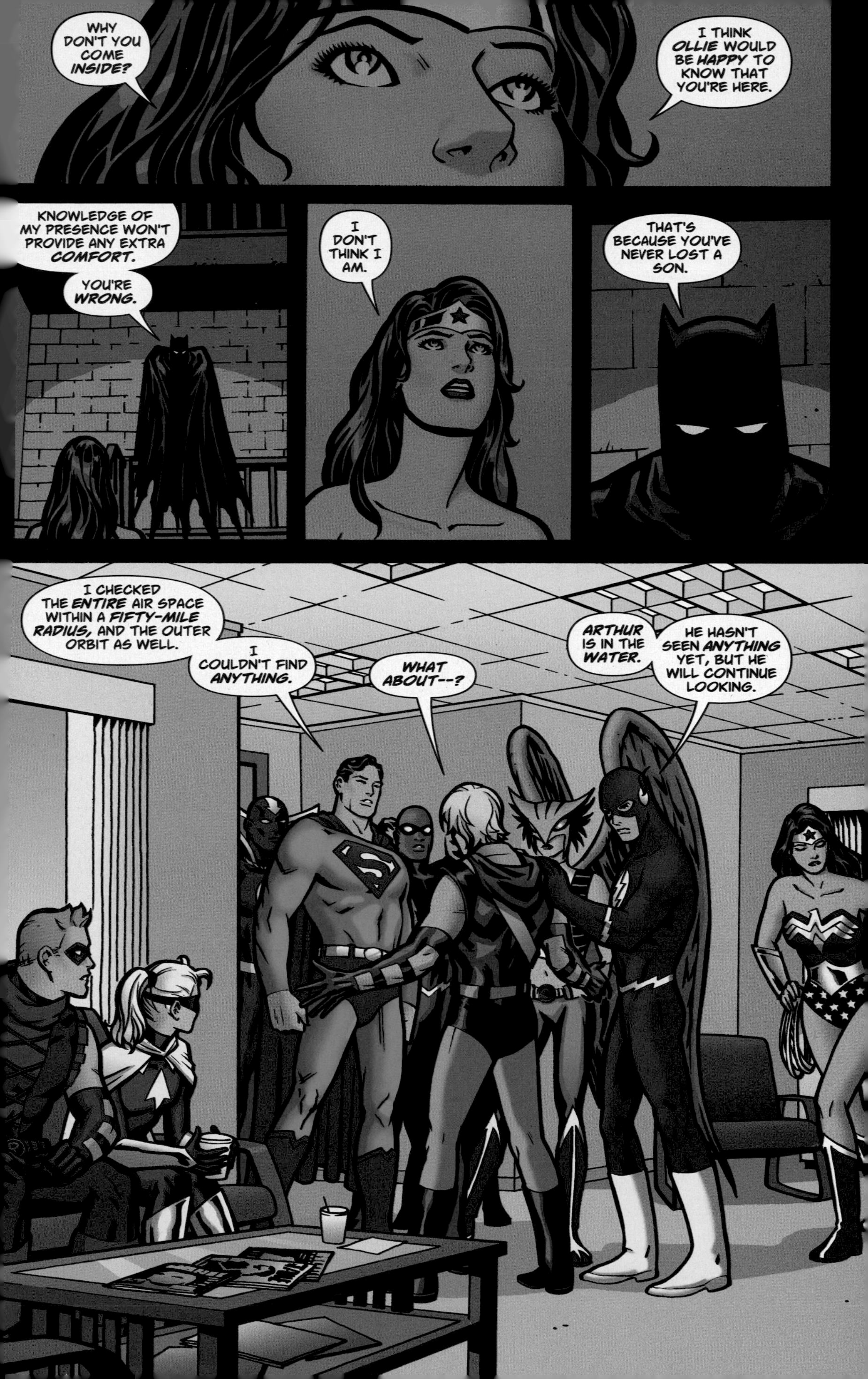
WHY DON'T YOU COME INSIDE?
I THINK OLLIE WOULD BE HAPPY TO KNOW THAT YOU'RE HERE.
KNOWLEDGE OF MY PRESENCE WON'T PROVIDE ANY EXTRA COMFORT.
YOU'RE WRONG.
I DON'T THINK I AM.
THAT'S BECAUSE YOU'VE NEVER LOST A SON.
I CHECKED THE ENTIRE AIR SPACE WITHIN A FIFTY-MILE RADIUS, AND THE OUTER ORBIT AS WELL.
I COULDN'T FIND ANYTHING.
WHAT ABOUT--?
ARTHUR IS IN THE WATER.
HE HASN'T SEEN ANYTHING YET, BUT HE WILL CONTINUE LOOKING.

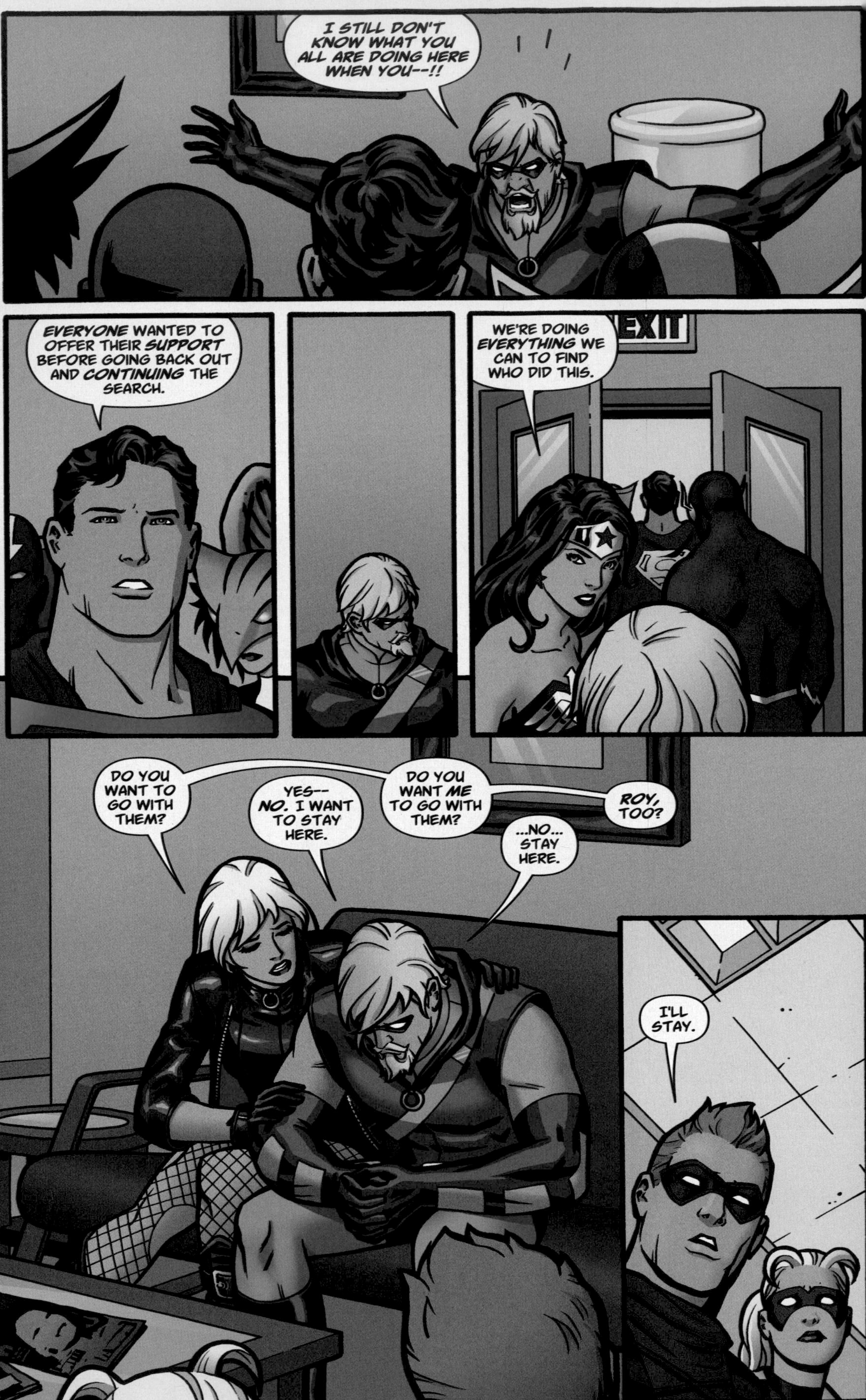
I STILL DON'T KNOW WHAT YOU ALL ARE DOING HERE WHEN YOU--!!
EVERYONE WANTED TO OFFER THEIR SUPPORT BEFORE GOING BACK OUT AND CONTINUING THE SEARCH.
EXIT
WE'RE DOING EVERYTHING WE CAN TO FIND WHO DID THIS.
DO YOU WANT TO GO WITH THEM?
YES-- NO. I WANT TO STAY HERE.
DO YOU WANT ME TO GO WITH THEM?
ROY, TOO?
...NO... STAY HERE.
I'LL STAY.

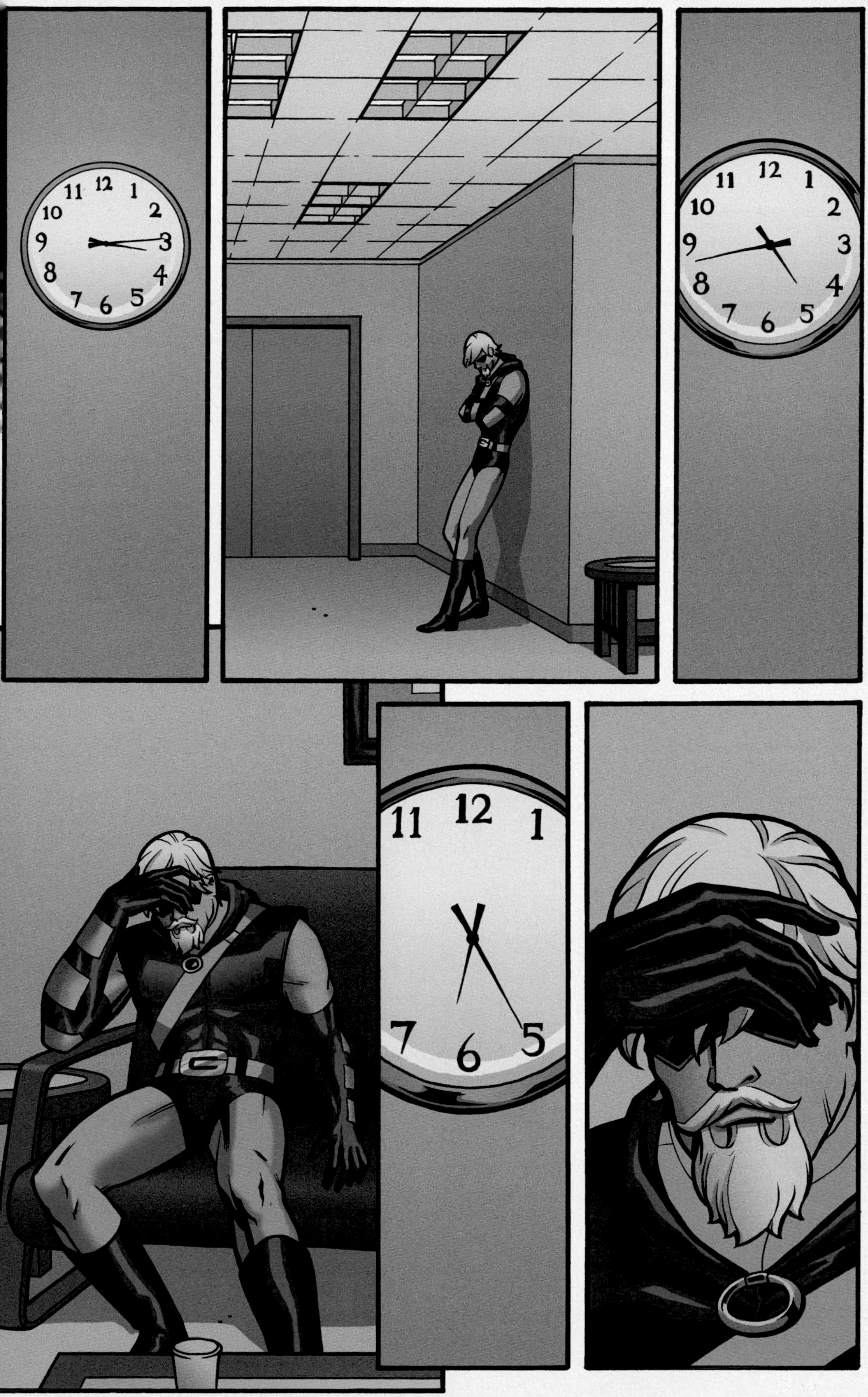

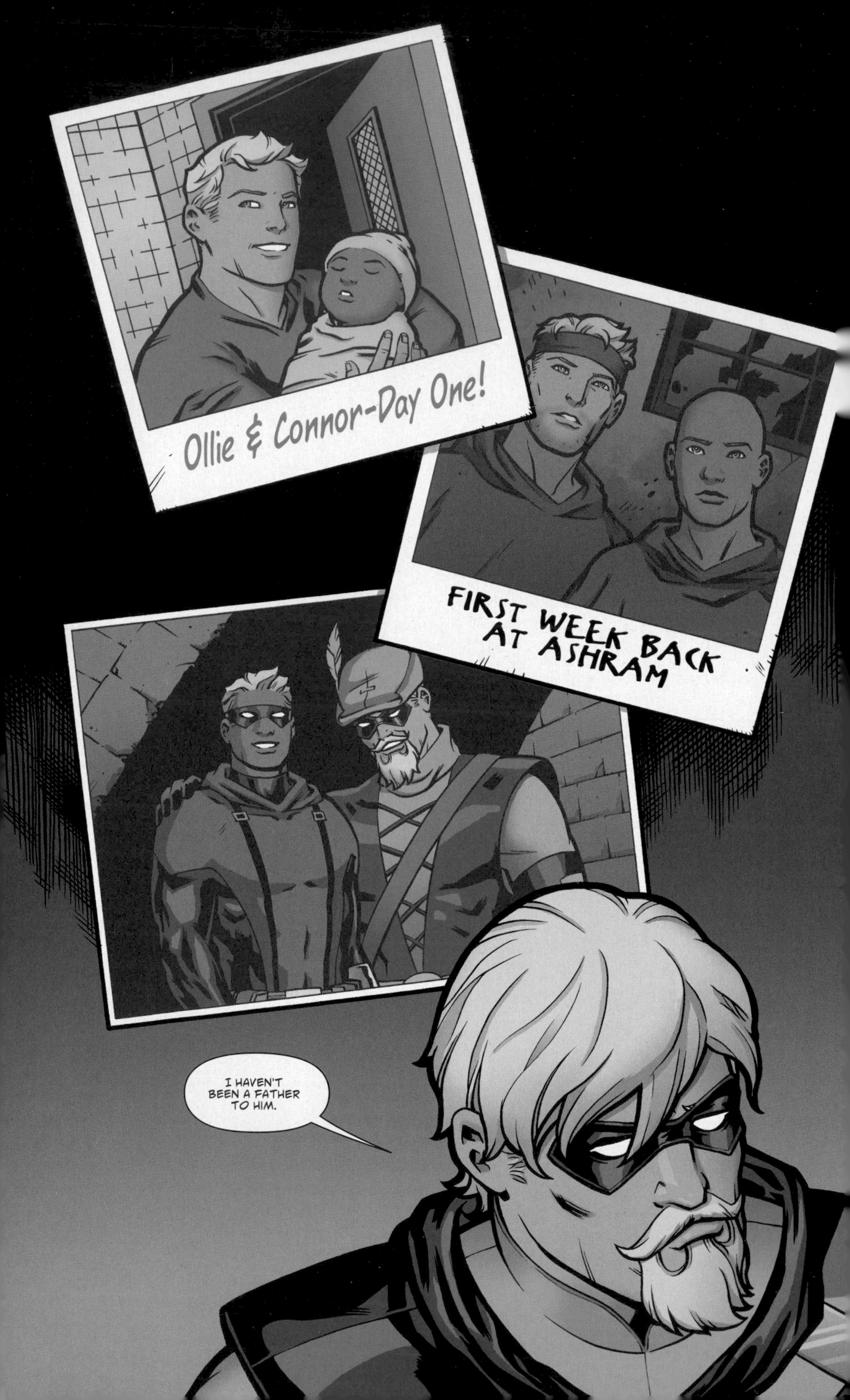
Ollie & Connor-Day One!
FIRST WEEK BACK AT ASHRAM
I HAVEN'T BEEN A FATHER TO HIM.

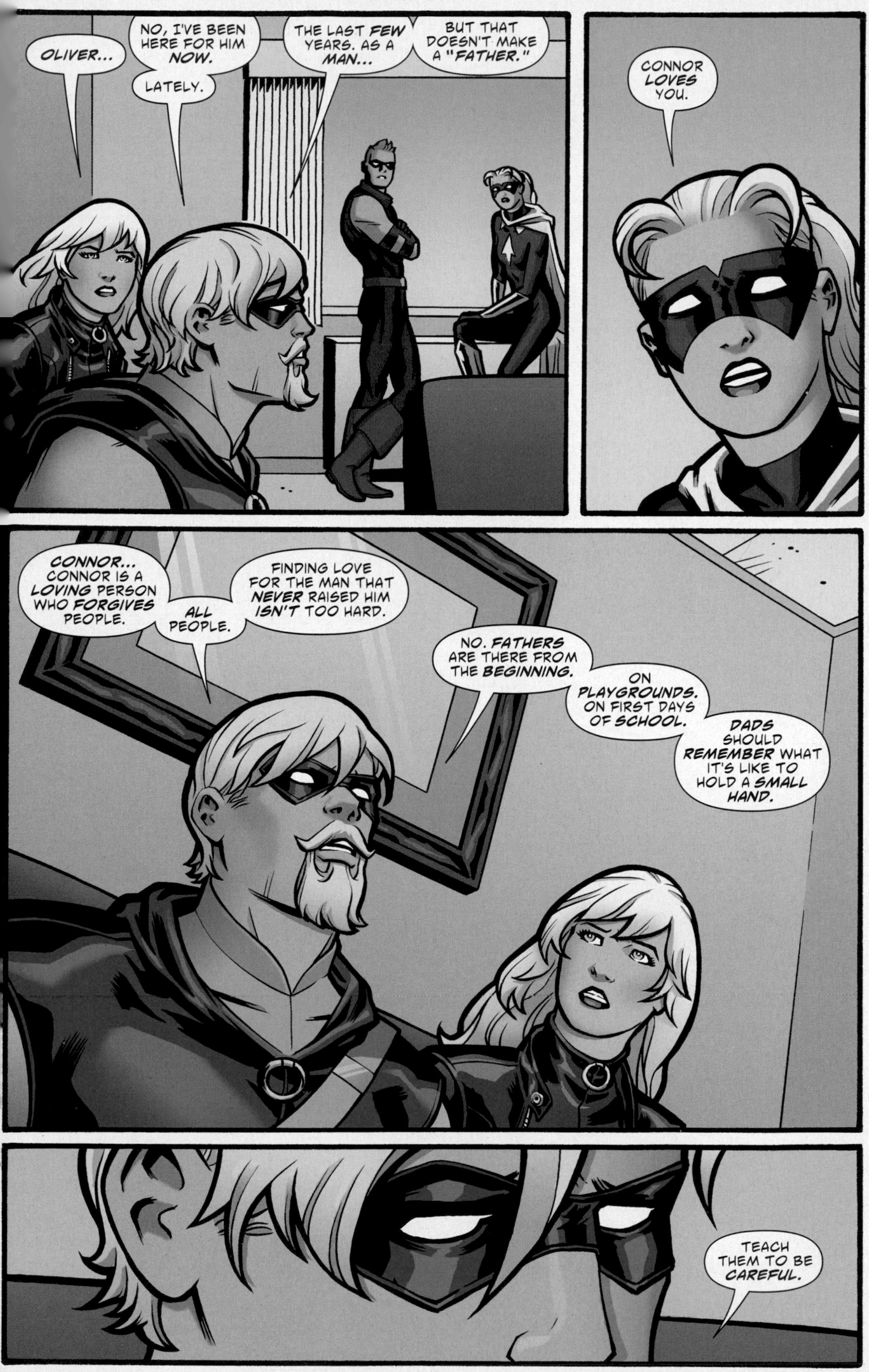
OLIVER...
NO, I'VE BEEN HERE FOR HIM NOW.
LATELY.
THE LAST FEW YEARS. AS A MAN...
BUT THAT DOESN'T MAKE A "FATHER."
CONNOR LOVES YOU.
CONNOR... CONNOR IS A LOVING PERSON WHO FORGIVES PEOPLE.
ALL PEOPLE.
FINDING LOVE FOR THE MAN THAT NEVER RAISED HIM ISN'T TOO HARD.
NO. FATHERS ARE THERE FROM THE BEGINNING.
ON PLAYGROUNDS. ON FIRST DAYS OF SCHOOL.
DADS SHOULD REMEMBER WHAT IT'S LIKE TO HOLD A SMALL HAND.
TEACH THEM TO BE CAREFUL.

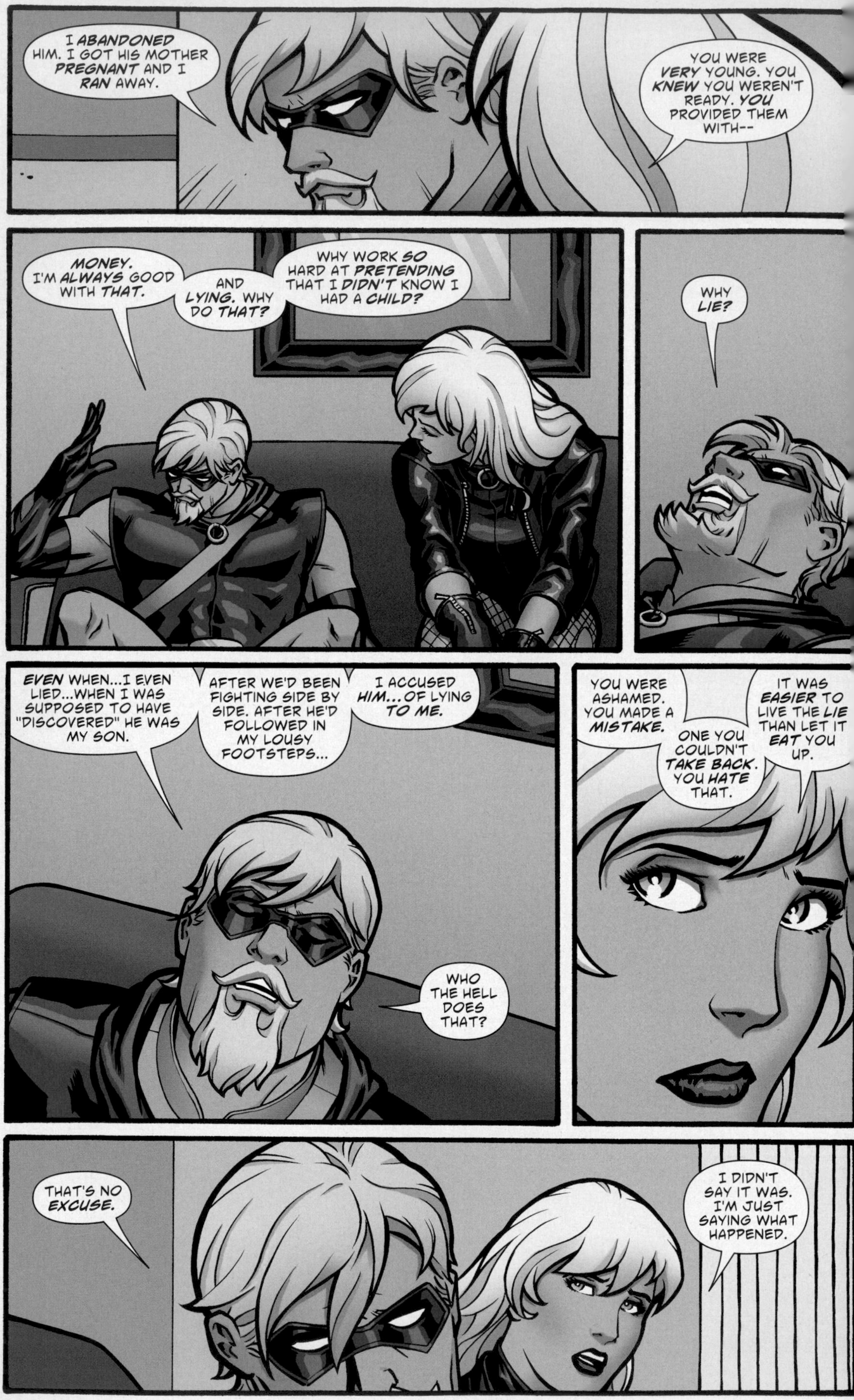

I ABANDONED HIM. I GOT HIS MOTHER PREGNANT AND I RAN AWAY.
YOU WERE VERY YOUNG. YOU KNEW YOU WEREN'T READY. YOU PROVIDED THEM WITH--
MONEY. I'M ALWAYS GOOD WITH THAT.
AND LYING. WHY DO THAT?
WHY WORK SO HARD AT PRETENDING THAT I DIDN'T KNOW I HAD A CHILD?
WHY LIE?
EVEN WHEN...I EVEN LIED...WHEN I WAS SUPPOSED TO HAVE "DISCOVERED" HE WAS MY SON.
AFTER WE'D BEEN FIGHTING SIDE BY SIDE. AFTER HE'D FOLLOWED IN MY LOUSY FOOTSTEPS...
I ACCUSED HIM...OF LYING TO ME.
WHO THE HELL DOES THAT?
YOU WERE ASHAMED. YOU MADE A MISTAKE.
ONE YOU COULDN'T TAKE BACK. YOU HATE THAT.
IT WAS EASIER TO LIVE THE LIE THAN LET IT EAT YOU UP.
THAT'S NO EXCUSE.
I DIDN'T SAY IT WAS. I'M JUST SAYING WHAT HAPPENED.

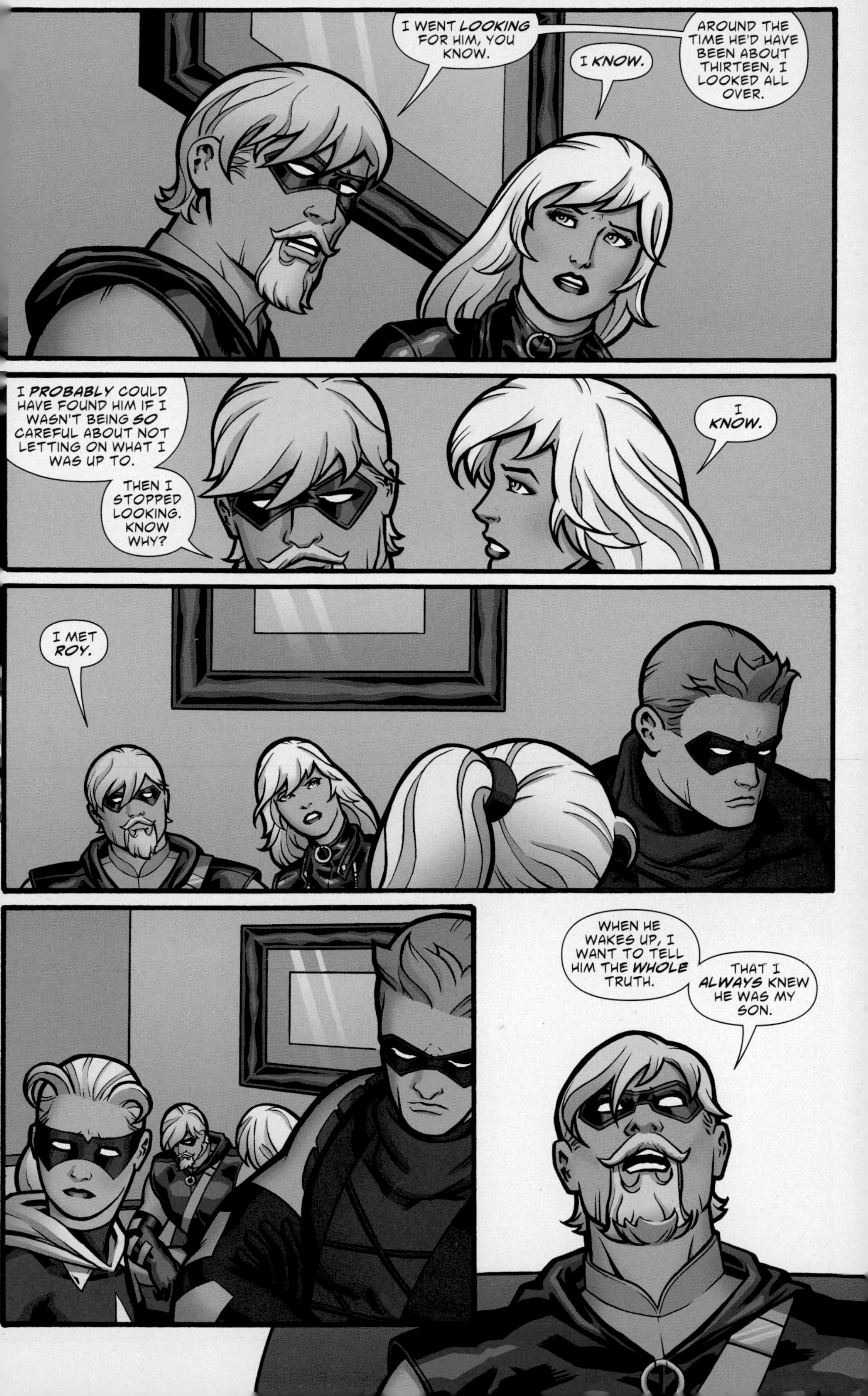
I WENT *LOOKING* FOR HIM, YOU KNOW.
I *KNOW.*
AROUND THE TIME HE'D HAVE BEEN ABOUT THIRTEEN, I LOOKED ALL OVER.
I *PROBABLY* COULD HAVE FOUND HIM IF I WASN'T BEING *SO* CAREFUL ABOUT NOT LETTING ON WHAT I WAS UP TO.
THEN I STOPPED LOOKING. KNOW WHY?
I *KNOW.*
I MET *ROY.*
WHEN HE WAKES UP, I WANT TO TELL HIM THE *WHOLE* TRUTH.
THAT I *ALWAYS* KNEW HE WAS MY SON.

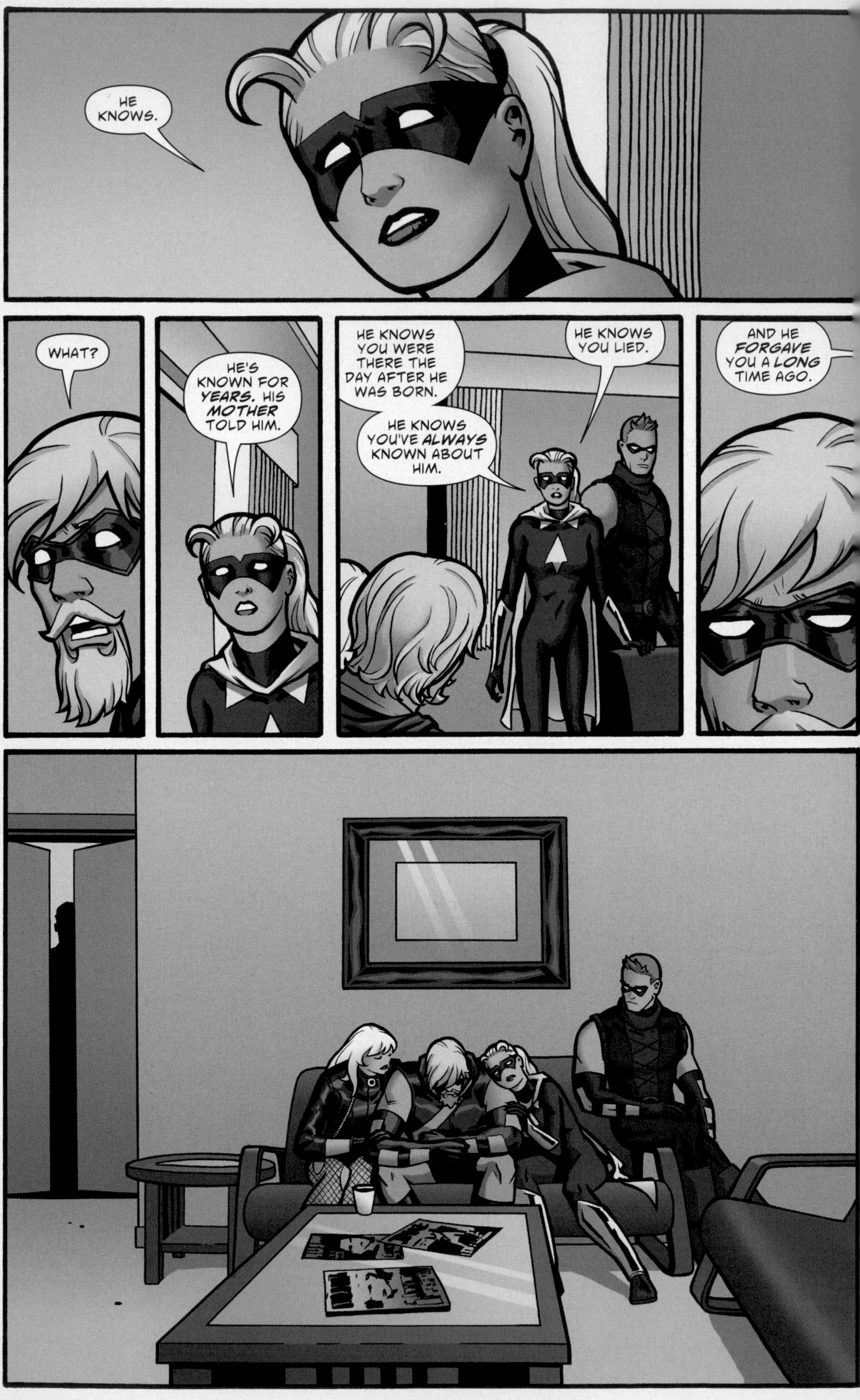
HE KNOWS.
WHAT?
HE'S KNOWN FOR *YEARS*. HIS *MOTHER* TOLD HIM.
HE KNOWS YOU WERE THERE THE DAY AFTER HE WAS BORN.
HE KNOWS YOU'VE *ALWAYS* KNOWN ABOUT HIM.
HE KNOWS YOU LIED.
AND HE *FORGAVE* YOU A *LONG* TIME AGO.

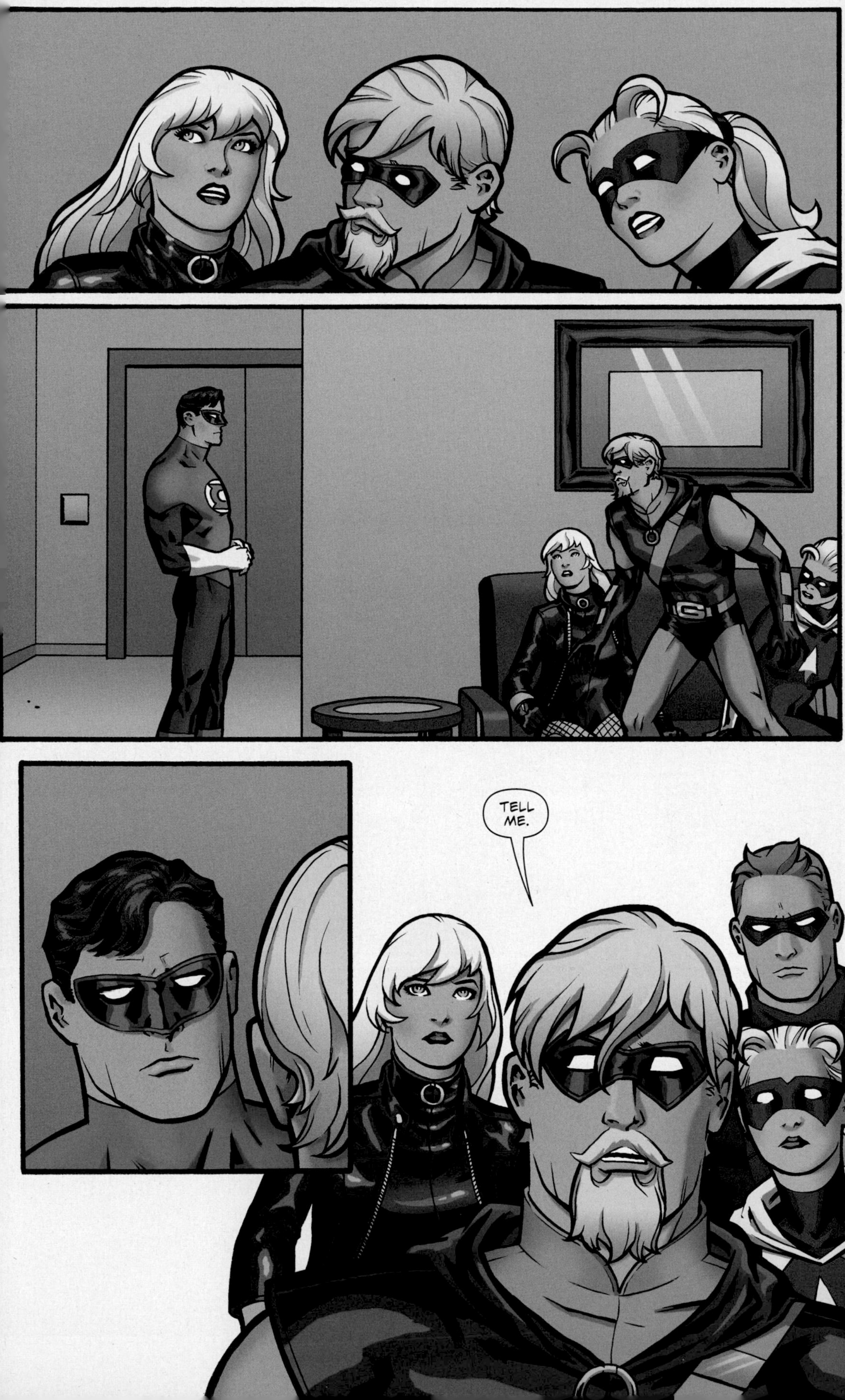
TELL ME.

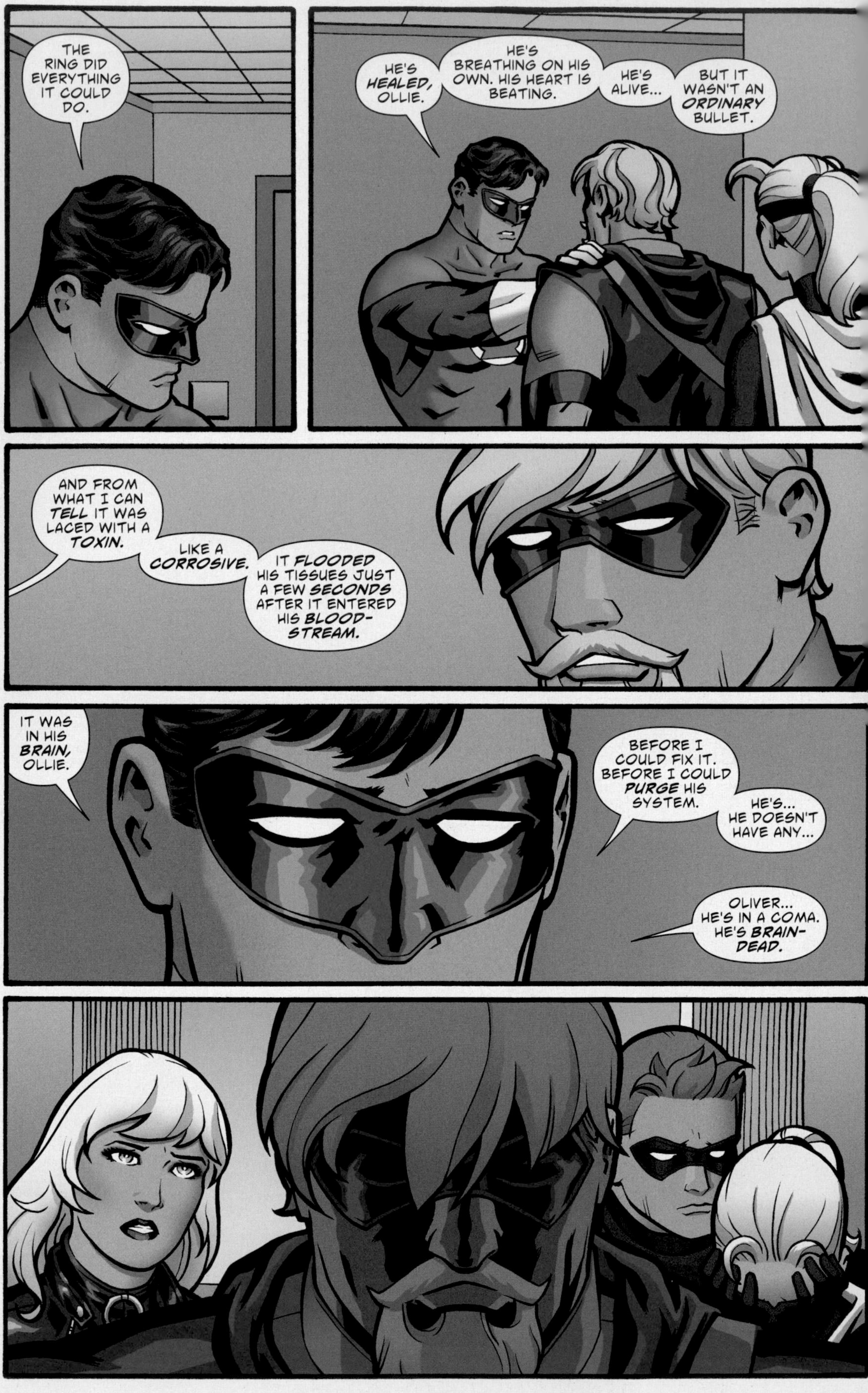

THE RING DID EVERYTHING IT COULD DO.
HE'S HEALED, OLLIE.
HE'S BREATHING ON HIS OWN. HIS HEART IS BEATING.
HE'S ALIVE...
BUT IT WASN'T AN ORDINARY BULLET.
AND FROM WHAT I CAN TELL IT WAS LACED WITH A TOXIN.
LIKE A CORROSIVE.
IT FLOODED HIS TISSUES JUST A FEW SECONDS AFTER IT ENTERED HIS BLOOD-STREAM.
IT WAS IN HIS BRAIN, OLLIE.
BEFORE I COULD FIX IT. BEFORE I COULD PURGE HIS SYSTEM.
HE'S... HE DOESN'T HAVE ANY...
OLIVER... HE'S IN A COMA. HE'S BRAIN-DEAD.

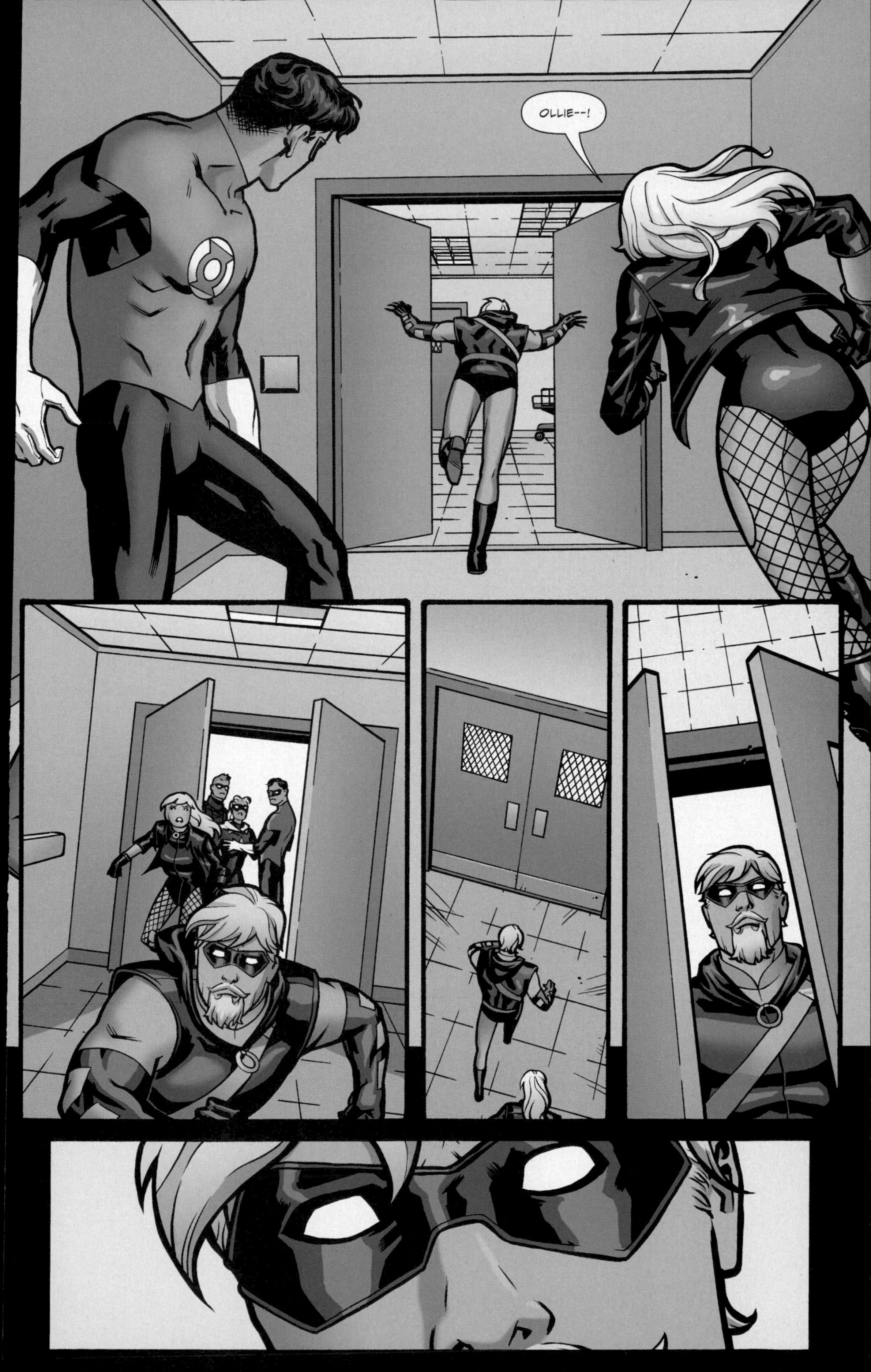
OLLIE--!

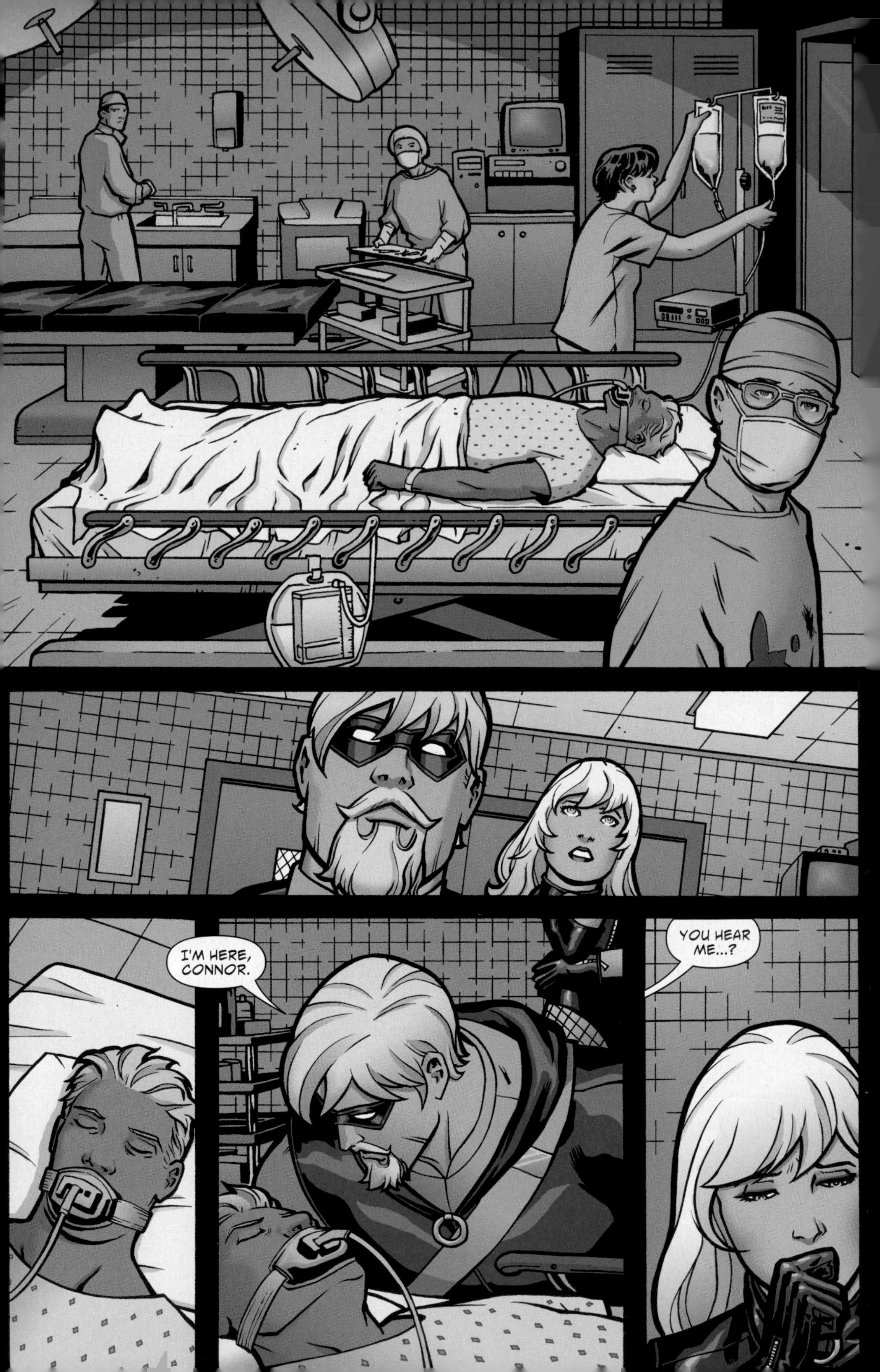
I'M HERE, CONNOR.
YOU HEAR ME...?

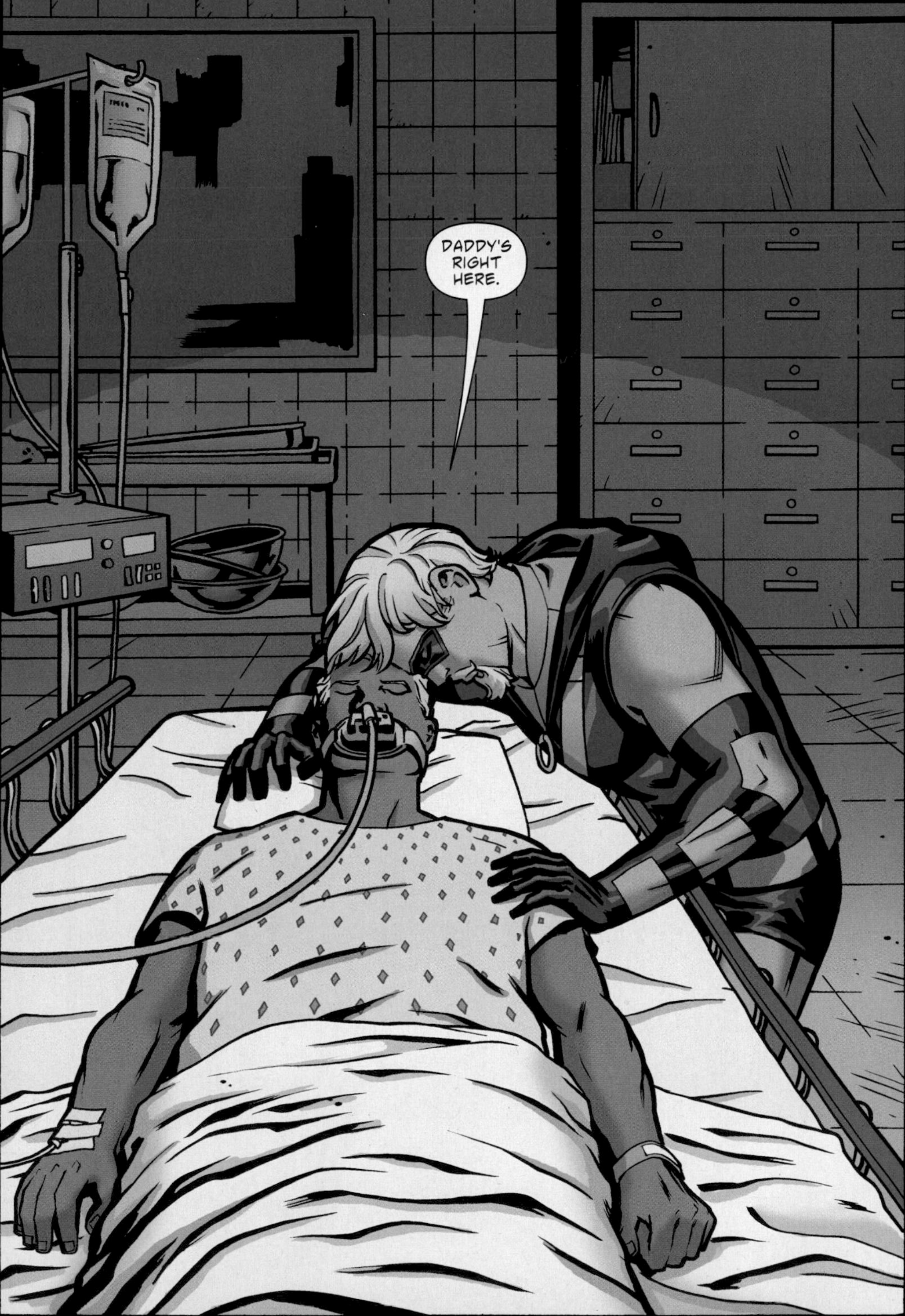
DADDY'S RIGHT HERE.

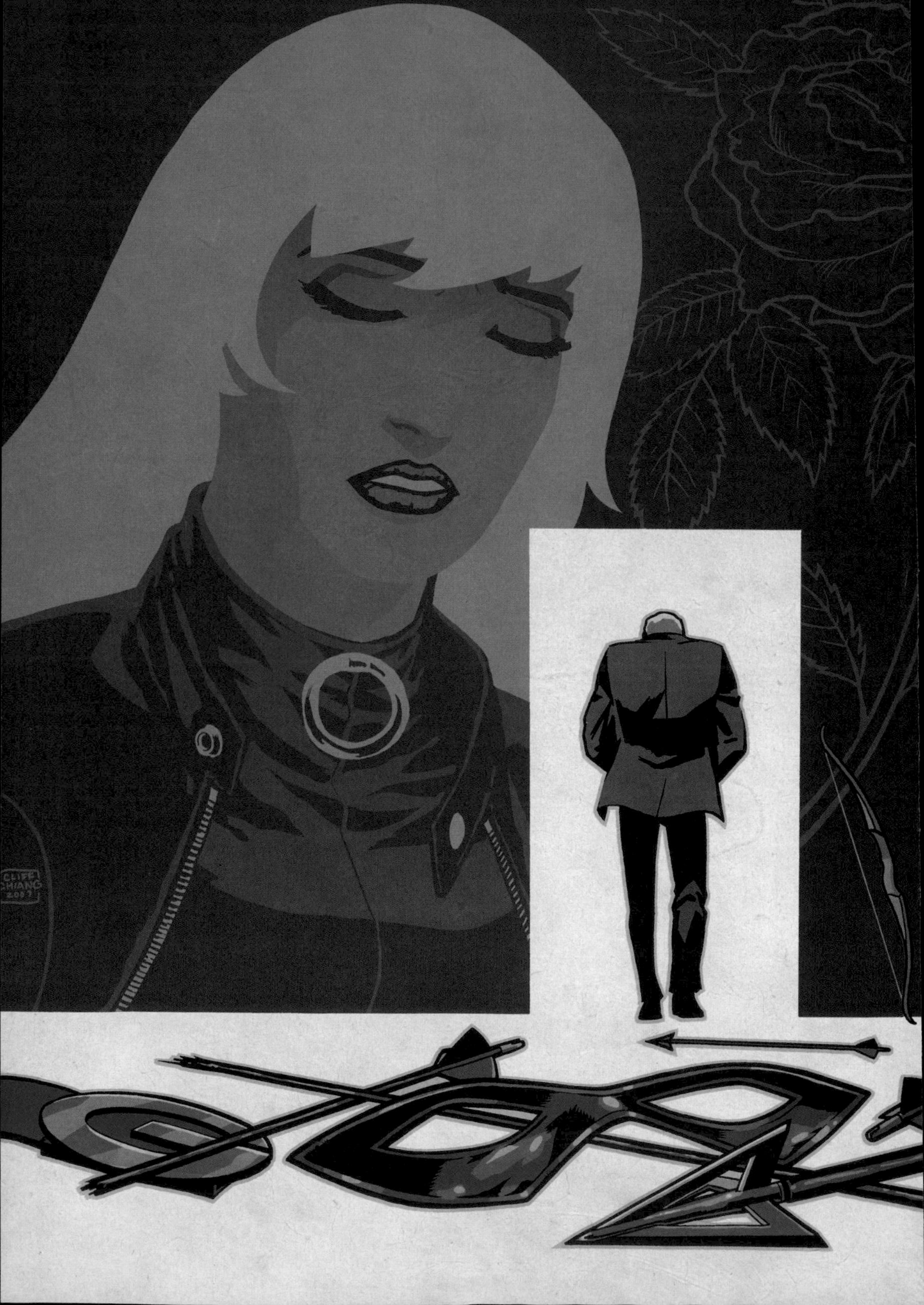
CLIFF CHIANG 2007

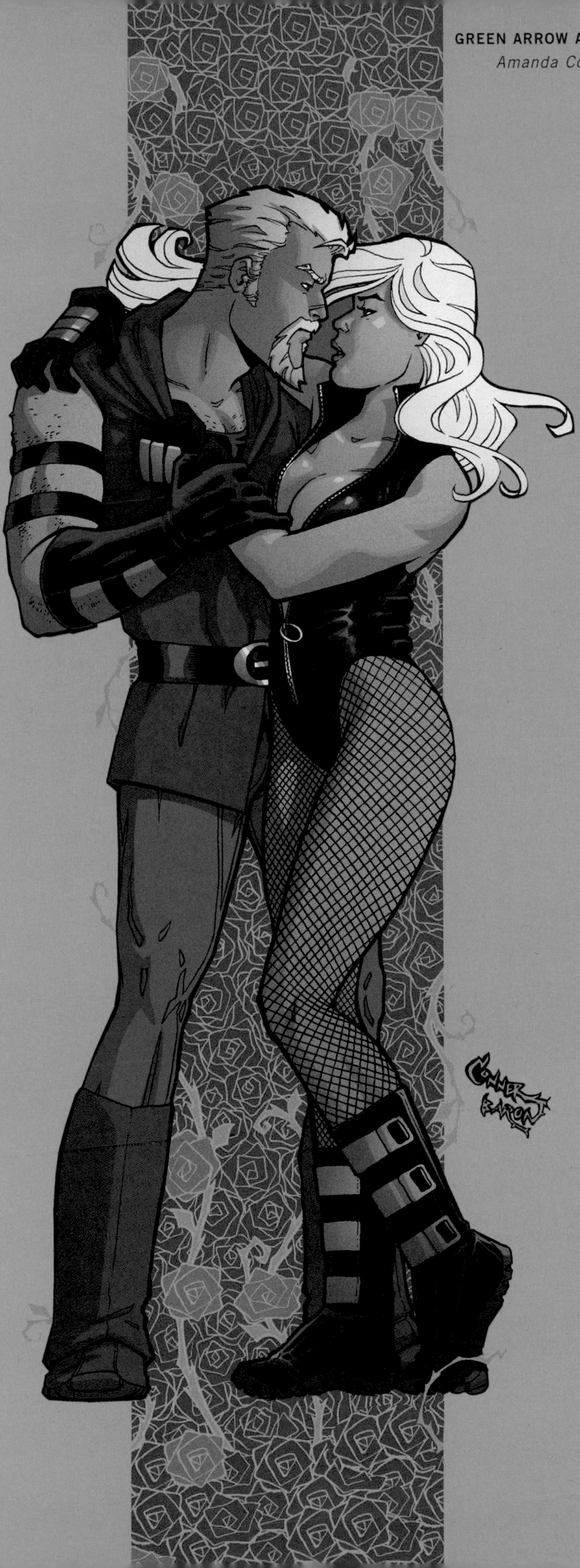
CONNER
BARON

GREEN ARROW AND BLACK CANARY #5

Amanda Conner and David Baron

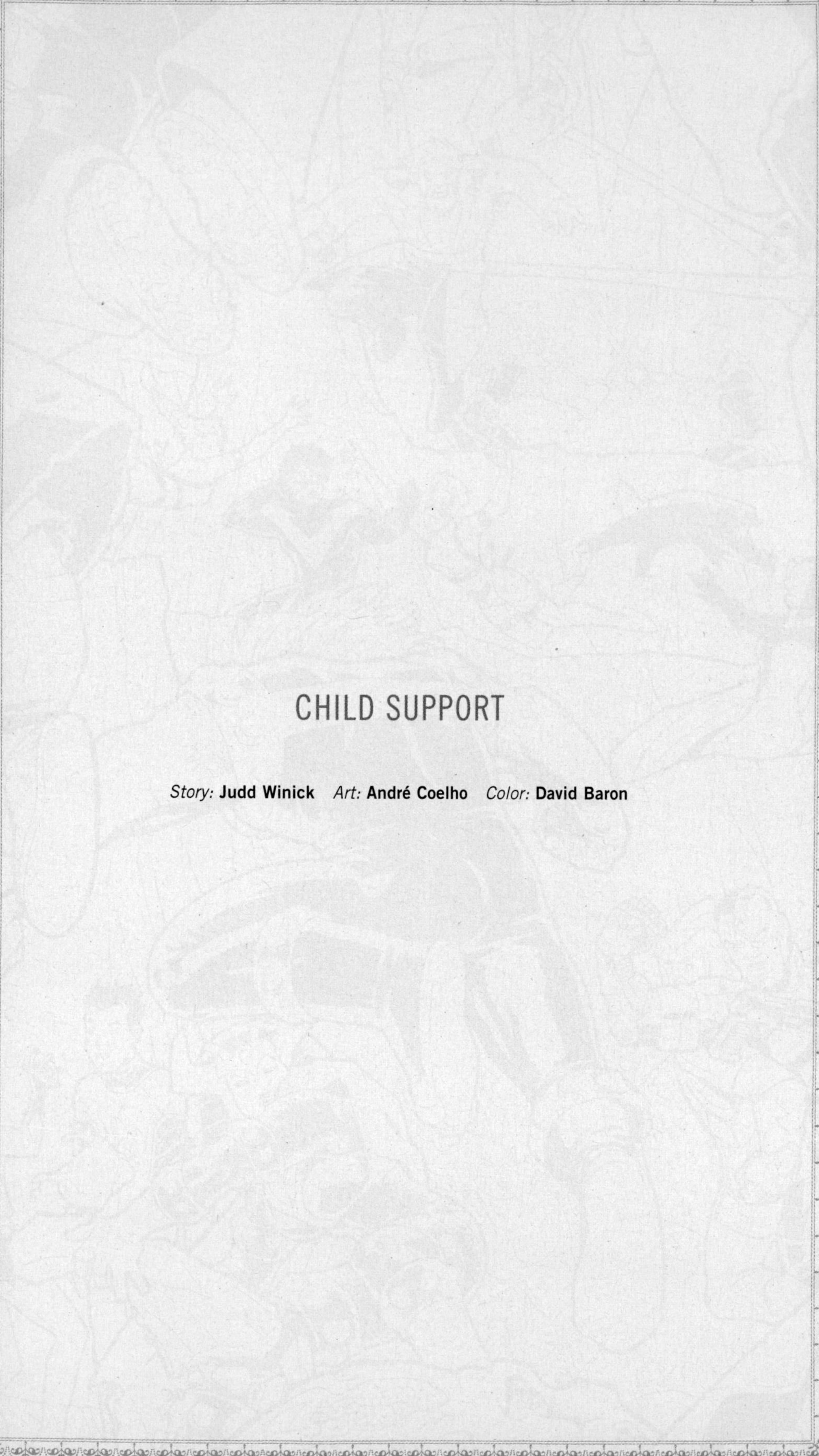

CHILD SUPPORT

Story: **Judd Winick** *Art:* **André Coelho** *Color:* **David Baron**

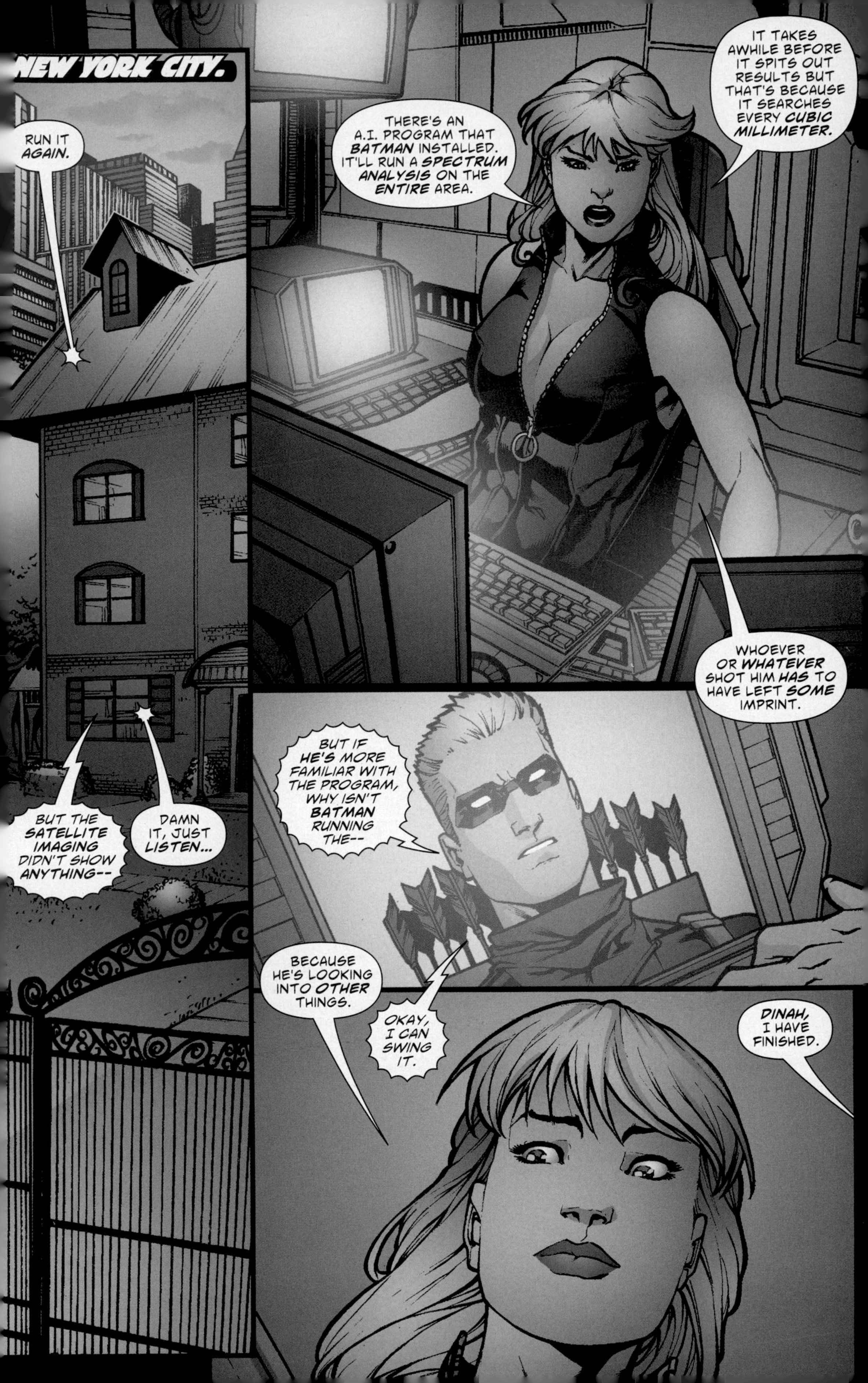
NEW YORK CITY.
RUN IT AGAIN.
THERE'S AN A.I. PROGRAM THAT BATMAN INSTALLED. IT'LL RUN A SPECTRUM ANALYSIS ON THE ENTIRE AREA.
IT TAKES AWHILE BEFORE IT SPITS OUT RESULTS BUT THAT'S BECAUSE IT SEARCHES EVERY CUBIC MILLIMETER.
BUT THE SATELLITE IMAGING DIDN'T SHOW ANYTHING--
DAMN IT, JUST LISTEN...
WHOEVER OR WHATEVER SHOT HIM HAS TO HAVE LEFT SOME IMPRINT.
BUT IF HE'S MORE FAMILIAR WITH THE PROGRAM, WHY ISN'T BATMAN RUNNING THE--
BECAUSE HE'S LOOKING INTO OTHER THINGS.
OKAY, I CAN SWING IT.
DINAH, I HAVE FINISHED.

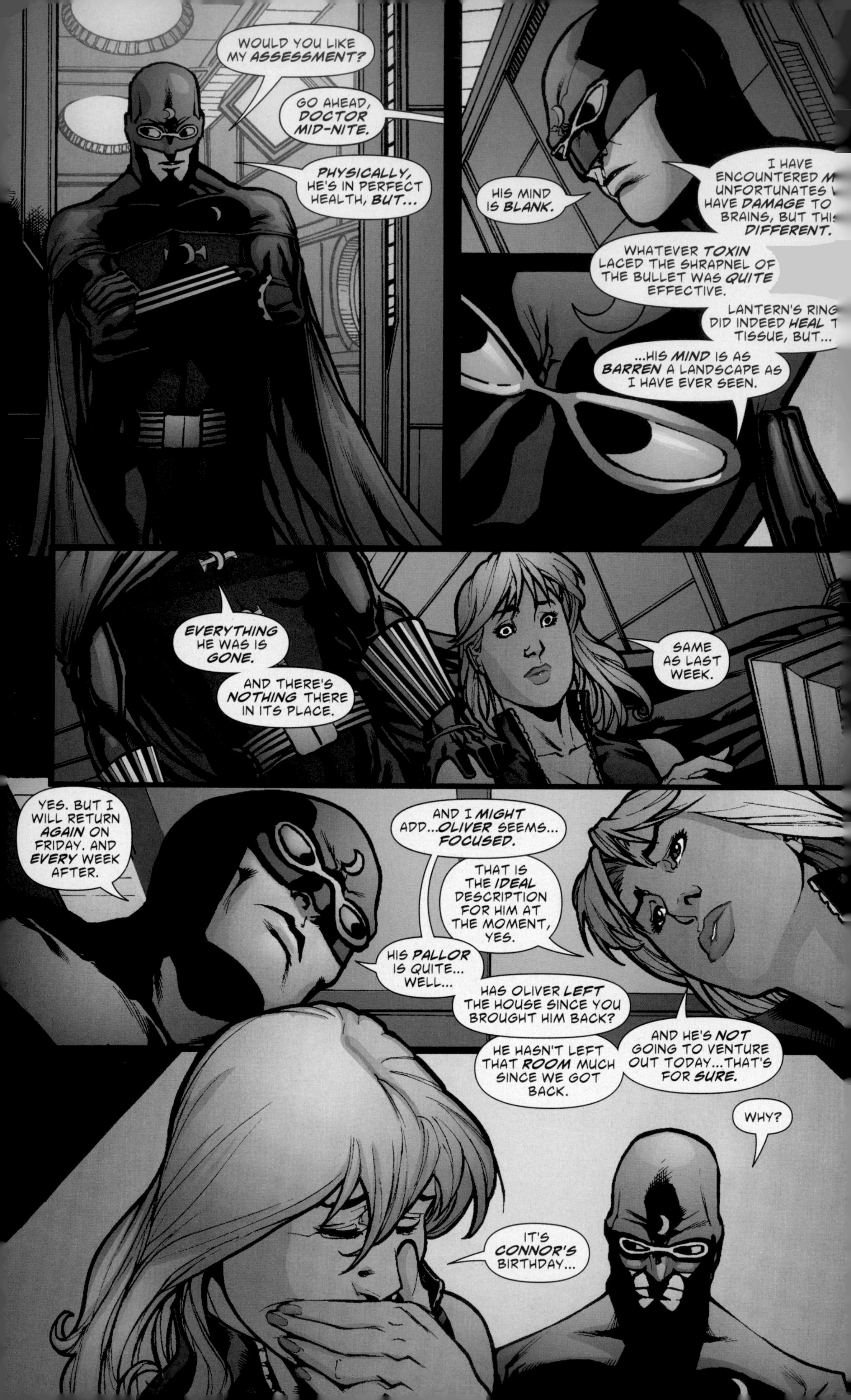
WOULD YOU LIKE MY ASSESSMENT?
GO AHEAD, DOCTOR MID-NITE.
PHYSICALLY, HE'S IN PERFECT HEALTH, BUT...
HIS MIND IS BLANK.
I HAVE ENCOUNTERED M UNFORTUNATES W HAVE DAMAGE TO BRAINS, BUT THIS DIFFERENT.
WHATEVER TOXIN LACED THE SHRAPNEL OF THE BULLET WAS QUITE EFFECTIVE.
LANTERN'S RING DID INDEED HEAL T TISSUE, BUT...
...HIS MIND IS AS BARREN A LANDSCAPE AS I HAVE EVER SEEN.
EVERYTHING HE WAS IS GONE.
AND THERE'S NOTHING THERE IN ITS PLACE.
SAME AS LAST WEEK.
YES. BUT I WILL RETURN AGAIN ON FRIDAY. AND EVERY WEEK AFTER.
AND I MIGHT ADD...OLIVER SEEMS... FOCUSED.
THAT IS THE IDEAL DESCRIPTION FOR HIM AT THE MOMENT, YES.
HIS PALLOR IS QUITE... WELL...
HAS OLIVER LEFT THE HOUSE SINCE YOU BROUGHT HIM BACK?
HE HASN'T LEFT THAT ROOM MUCH SINCE WE GOT BACK.
AND HE'S NOT GOING TO VENTURE OUT TODAY...THAT'S FOR SURE.
WHY?
IT'S CONNOR'S BIRTHDAY...

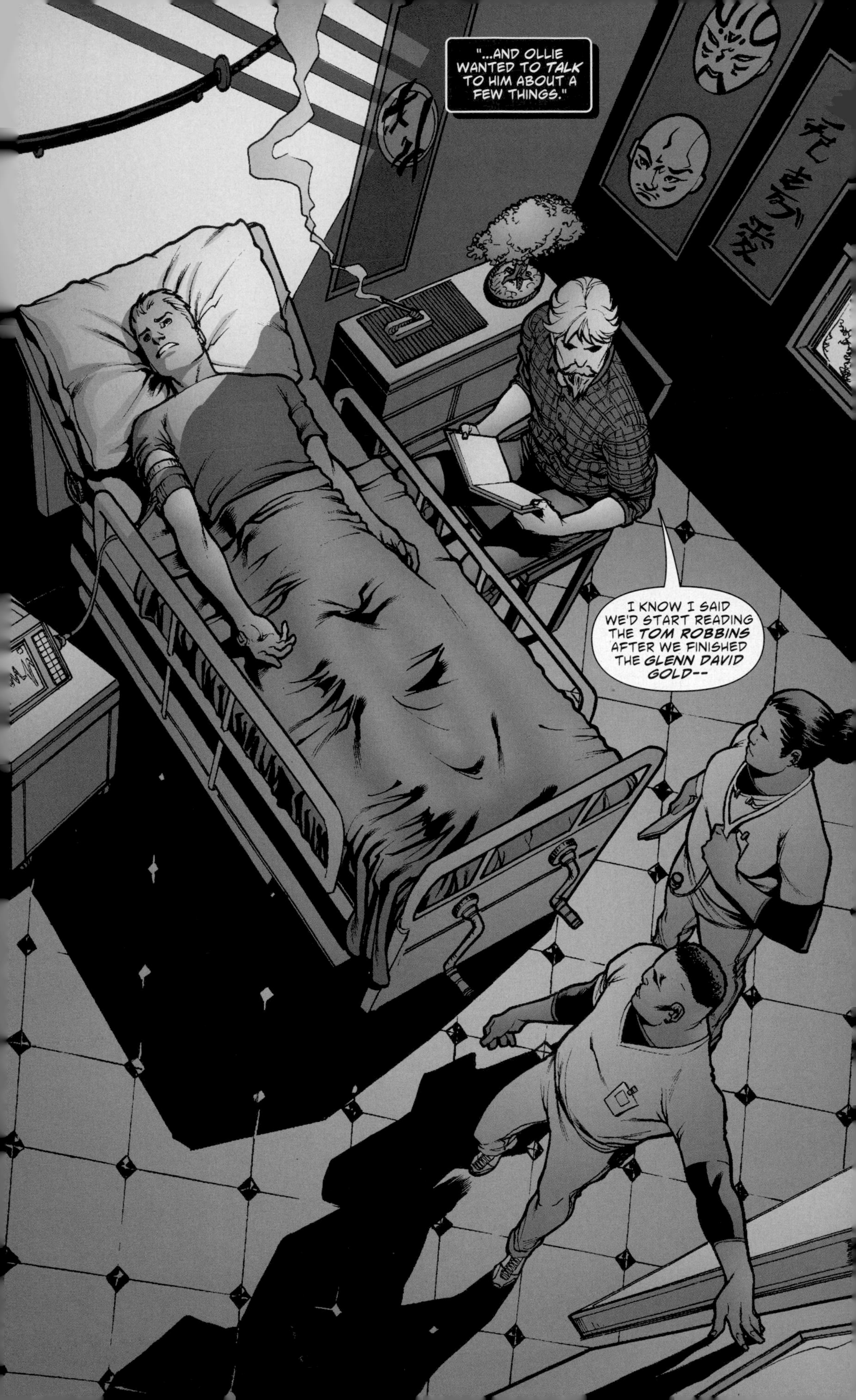
"...AND OLLIE WANTED TO TALK TO HIM ABOUT A FEW THINGS."
I KNOW I SAID WE'D START READING THE TOM ROBBINS AFTER WE FINISHED THE GLENN DAVID GOLD--

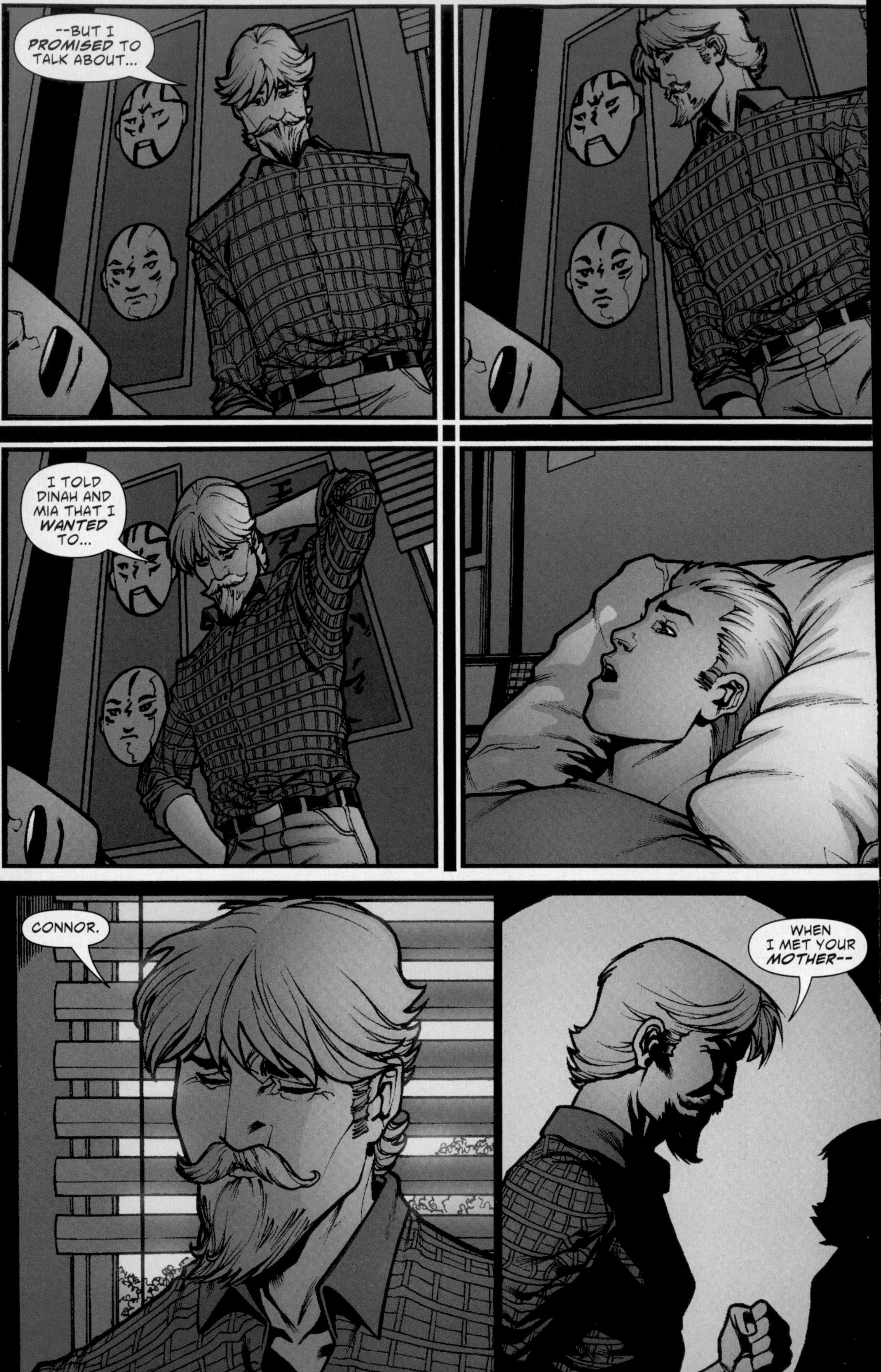
--BUT I PROMISED TO TALK ABOUT...
I TOLD DINAH AND MIA THAT I WANTED TO...
CONNOR.
WHEN I MET YOUR MOTHER--

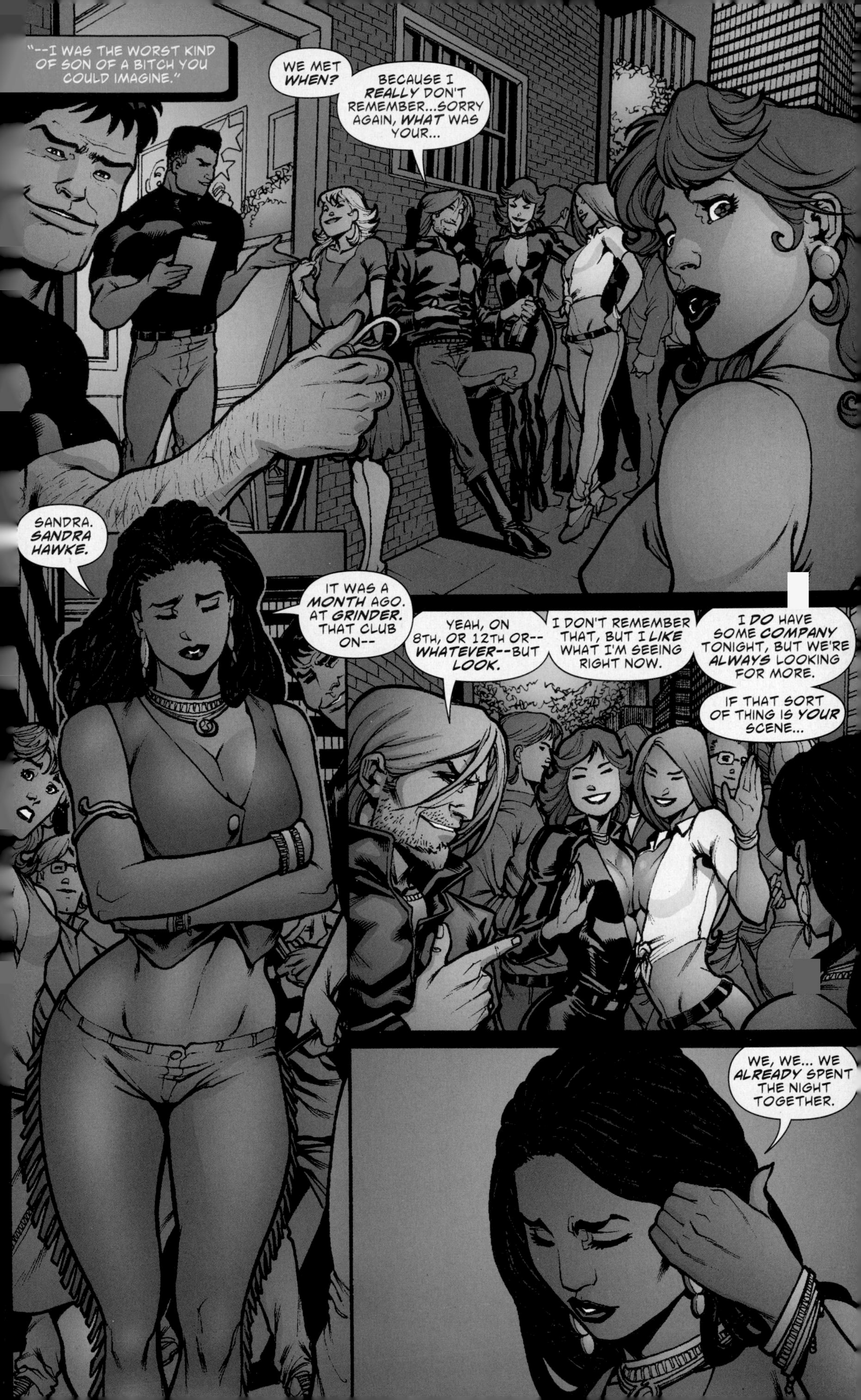
"--I WAS THE WORST KIND OF SON OF A BITCH YOU COULD IMAGINE."
WE MET WHEN?
BECAUSE I REALLY DON'T REMEMBER...SORRY AGAIN, WHAT WAS YOUR...
SANDRA. SANDRA HAWKE.
IT WAS A MONTH AGO. AT GRINDER. THAT CLUB ON--
YEAH, ON 8TH, OR 12TH OR--WHATEVER--BUT LOOK.
I DON'T REMEMBER THAT, BUT I LIKE WHAT I'M SEEING RIGHT NOW.
I DO HAVE SOME COMPANY TONIGHT, BUT WE'RE ALWAYS LOOKING FOR MORE.
IF THAT SORT OF THING IS YOUR SCENE...
WE, WE... WE ALREADY SPENT THE NIGHT TOGETHER.

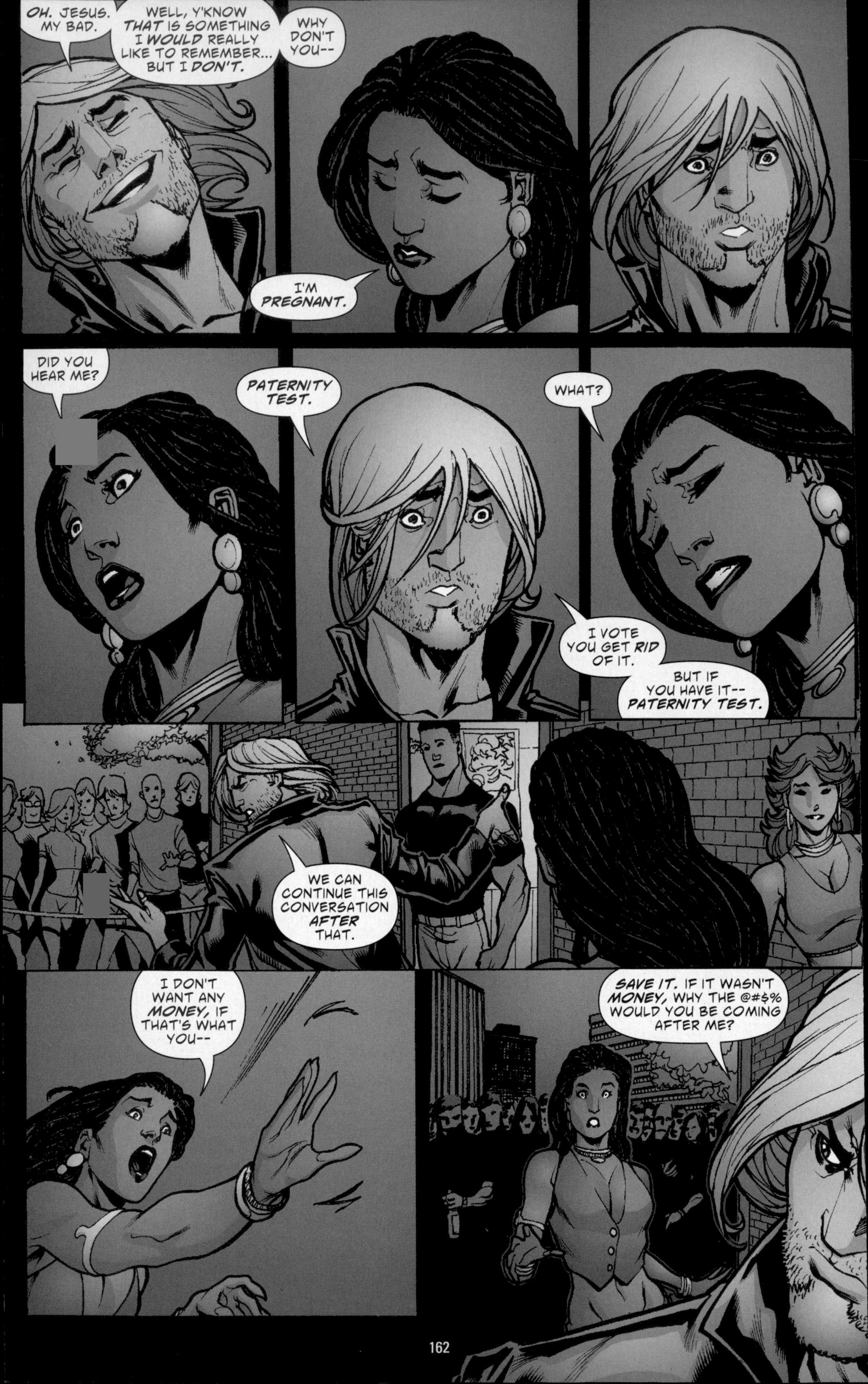
OH. JESUS. MY BAD.
WELL, Y'KNOW THAT IS SOMETHING I WOULD REALLY LIKE TO REMEMBER... BUT I DON'T.
WHY DON'T YOU--
I'M PREGNANT.
DID YOU HEAR ME?
PATERNITY TEST.
WHAT?
I VOTE YOU GET RID OF IT.
BUT IF YOU HAVE IT-- PATERNITY TEST.
WE CAN CONTINUE THIS CONVERSATION AFTER THAT.
I DON'T WANT ANY MONEY, IF THAT'S WHAT YOU--
SAVE IT. IF IT WASN'T MONEY, WHY THE @#$% WOULD YOU BE COMING AFTER ME?

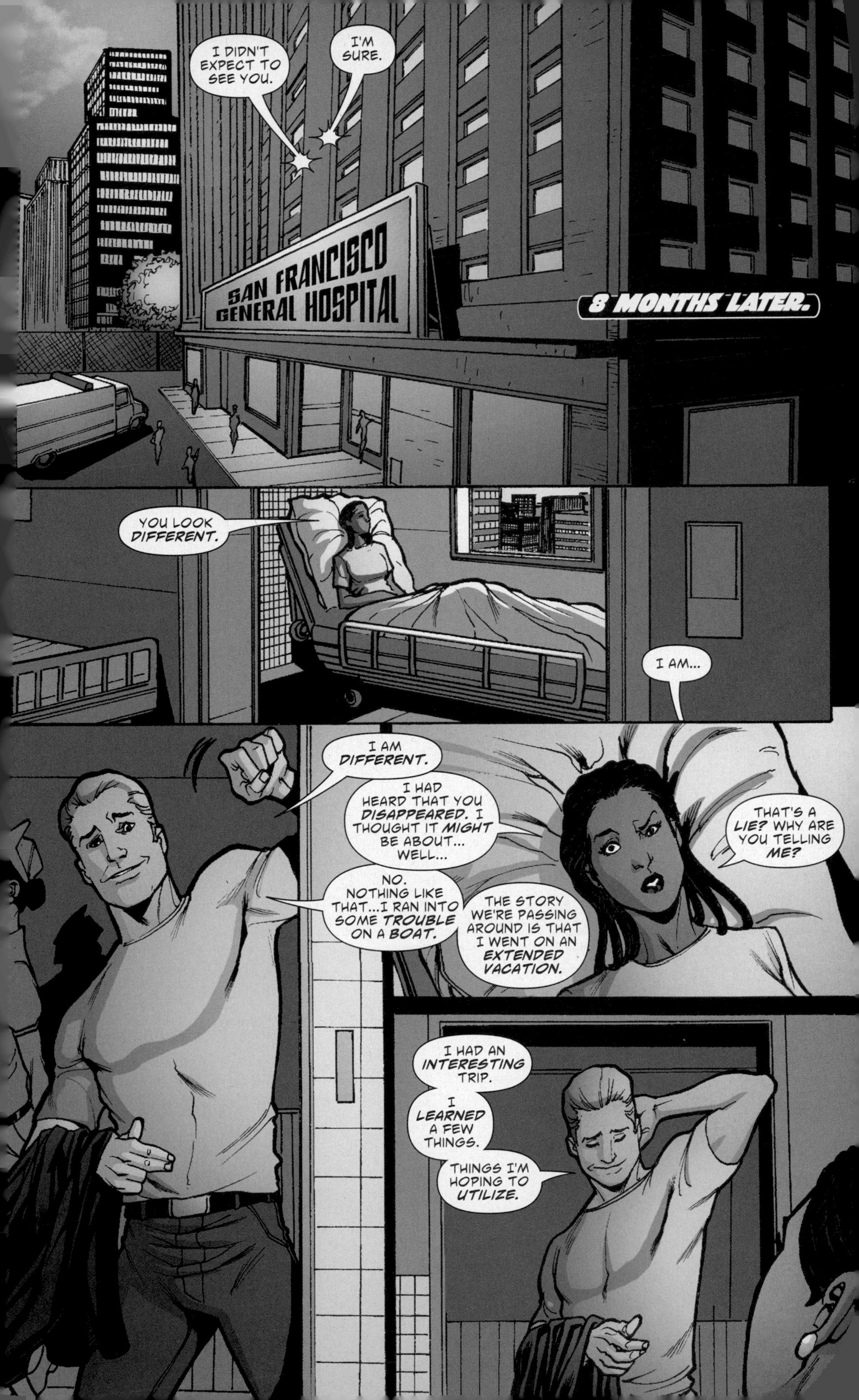
I DIDN'T EXPECT TO SEE YOU.
I'M SURE.
SAN FRANCISCO GENERAL HOSPITAL
8 MONTHS LATER.
YOU LOOK *DIFFERENT*.
I AM...
I AM *DIFFERENT*.
I HAD HEARD THAT YOU *DISAPPEARED*. I THOUGHT IT *MIGHT* BE ABOUT... WELL...
NO. NOTHING LIKE THAT...I RAN INTO SOME *TROUBLE* ON A *BOAT*.
THE STORY WE'RE PASSING AROUND IS THAT I WENT ON AN *EXTENDED VACATION*.
THAT'S A *LIE?* WHY ARE YOU TELLING *ME?*
I HAD AN *INTERESTING* TRIP.
I *LEARNED* A FEW THINGS.
THINGS I'M HOPING TO *UTILIZE*.

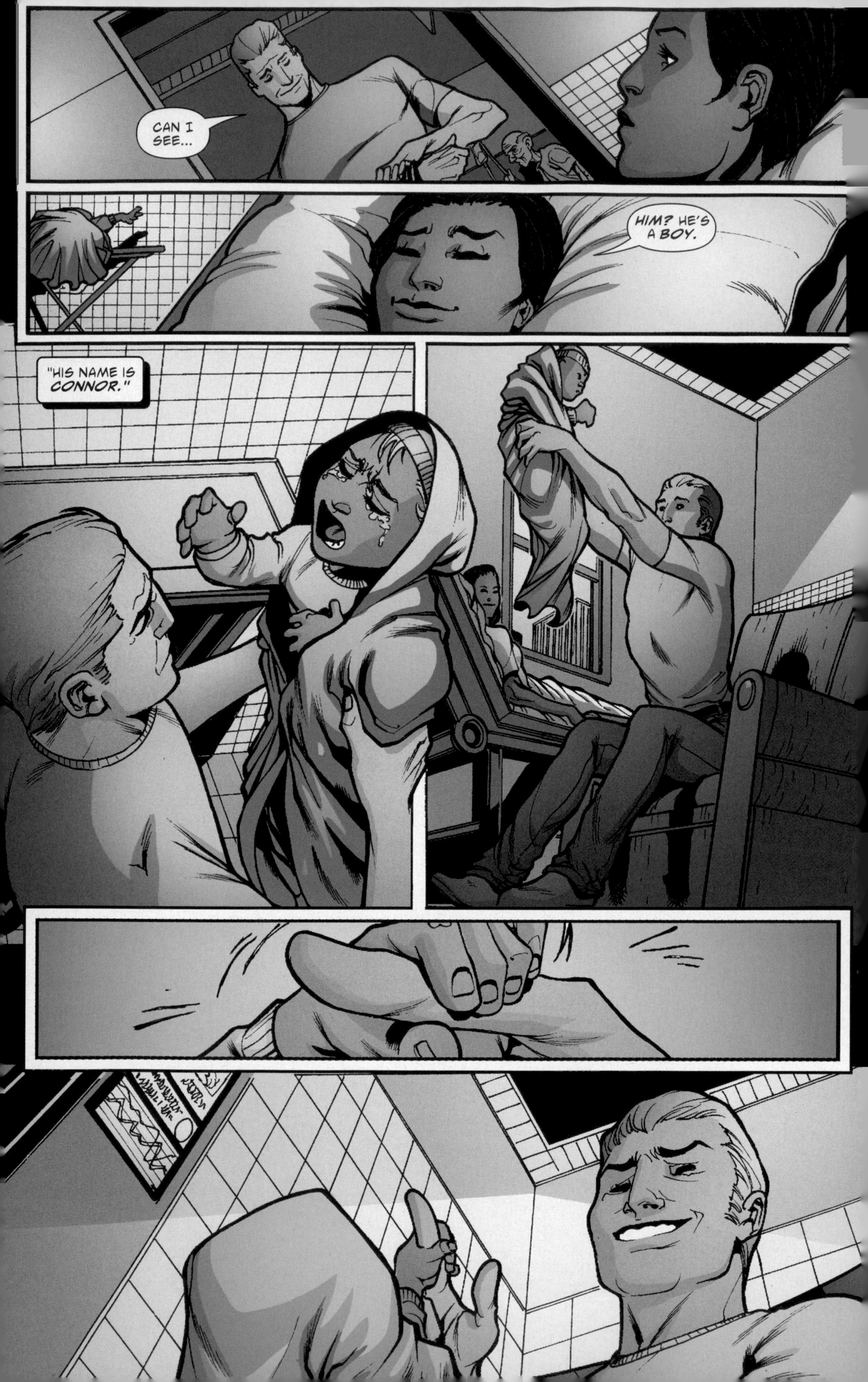
CAN I SEE...
HIM? HE'S A BOY.
"HIS NAME IS CONNOR."

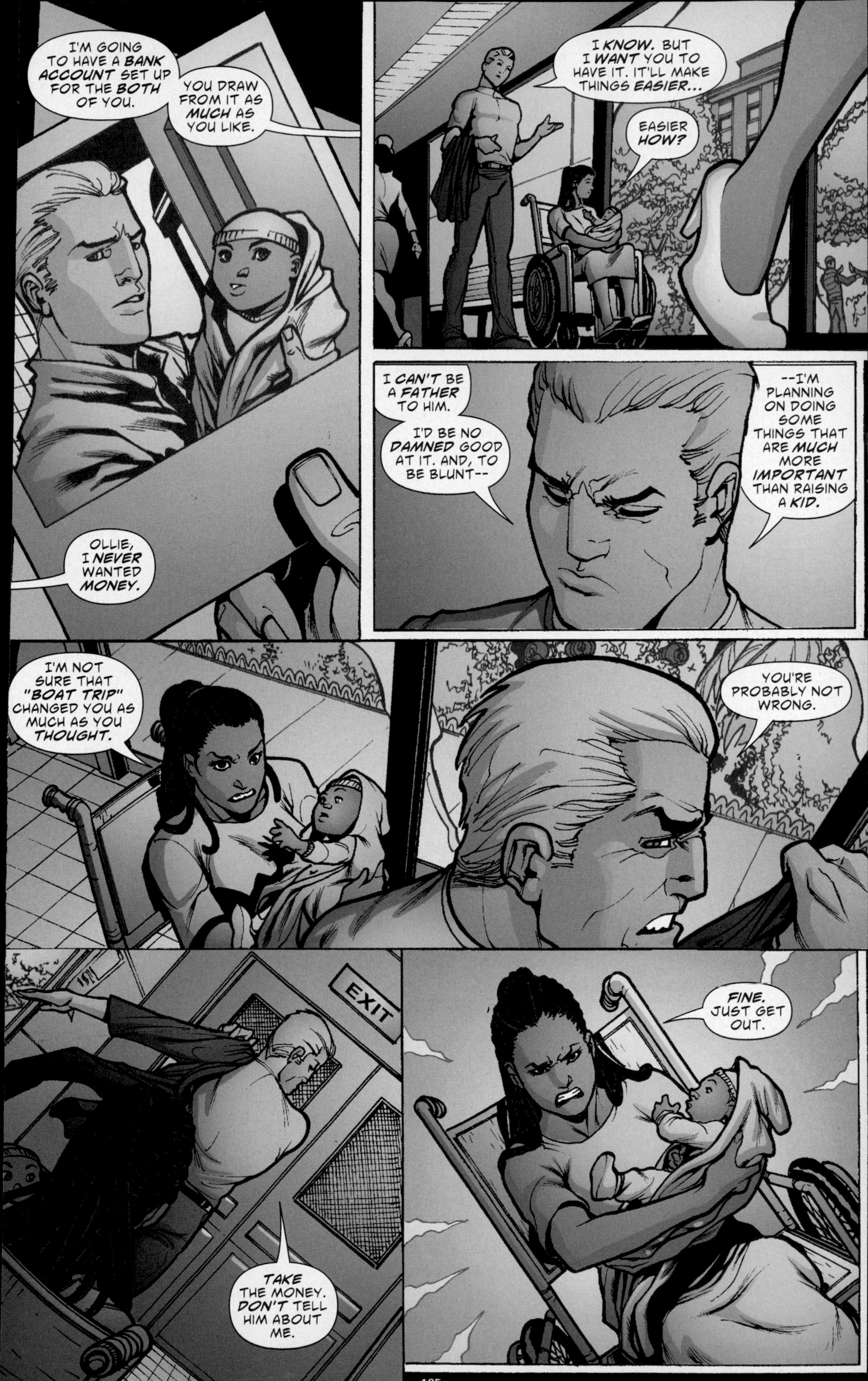
I'M GOING TO HAVE A BANK ACCOUNT SET UP FOR THE BOTH OF YOU.
YOU DRAW FROM IT AS MUCH AS YOU LIKE.
OLLIE, I NEVER WANTED MONEY.
I KNOW. BUT I WANT YOU TO HAVE IT. IT'LL MAKE THINGS EASIER...
EASIER HOW?
I CAN'T BE A FATHER TO HIM.
I'D BE NO DAMNED GOOD AT IT. AND, TO BE BLUNT--
--I'M PLANNING ON DOING SOME THINGS THAT ARE MUCH MORE IMPORTANT THAN RAISING A KID.
I'M NOT SURE THAT "BOAT TRIP" CHANGED YOU AS MUCH AS YOU THOUGHT.
YOU'RE PROBABLY NOT WRONG.
EXIT
TAKE THE MONEY. DON'T TELL HIM ABOUT ME.
FINE. JUST GET OUT.

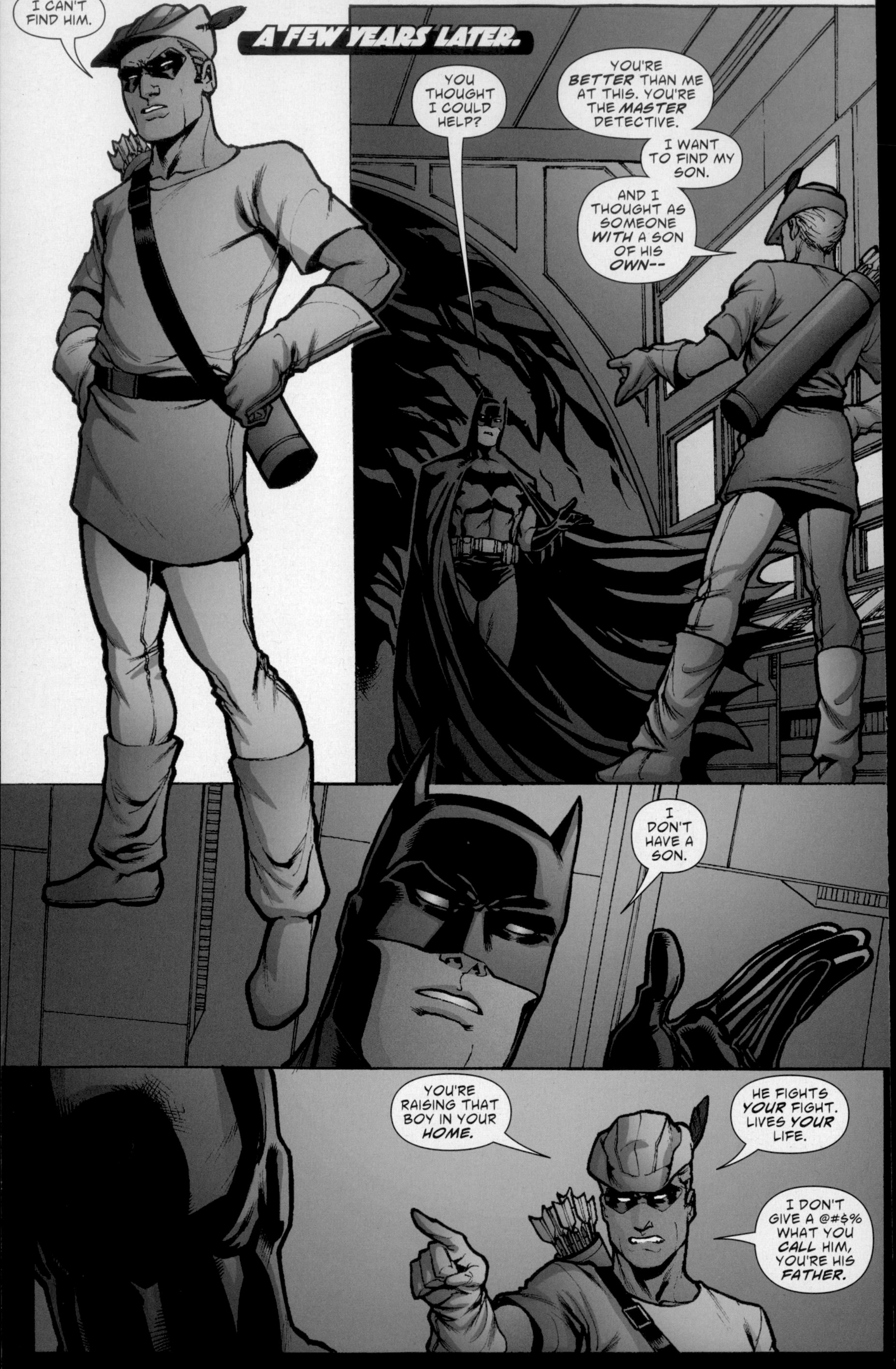
I CAN'T FIND HIM.
A FEW YEARS LATER.
YOU THOUGHT I COULD HELP?
YOU'RE BETTER THAN ME AT THIS. YOU'RE THE MASTER DETECTIVE.
I WANT TO FIND MY SON.
AND I THOUGHT AS SOMEONE WITH A SON OF HIS OWN--
I DON'T HAVE A SON.
YOU'RE RAISING THAT BOY IN YOUR HOME.
HE FIGHTS YOUR FIGHT. LIVES YOUR LIFE.
I DON'T GIVE A @#$% WHAT YOU CALL HIM, YOU'RE HIS FATHER.

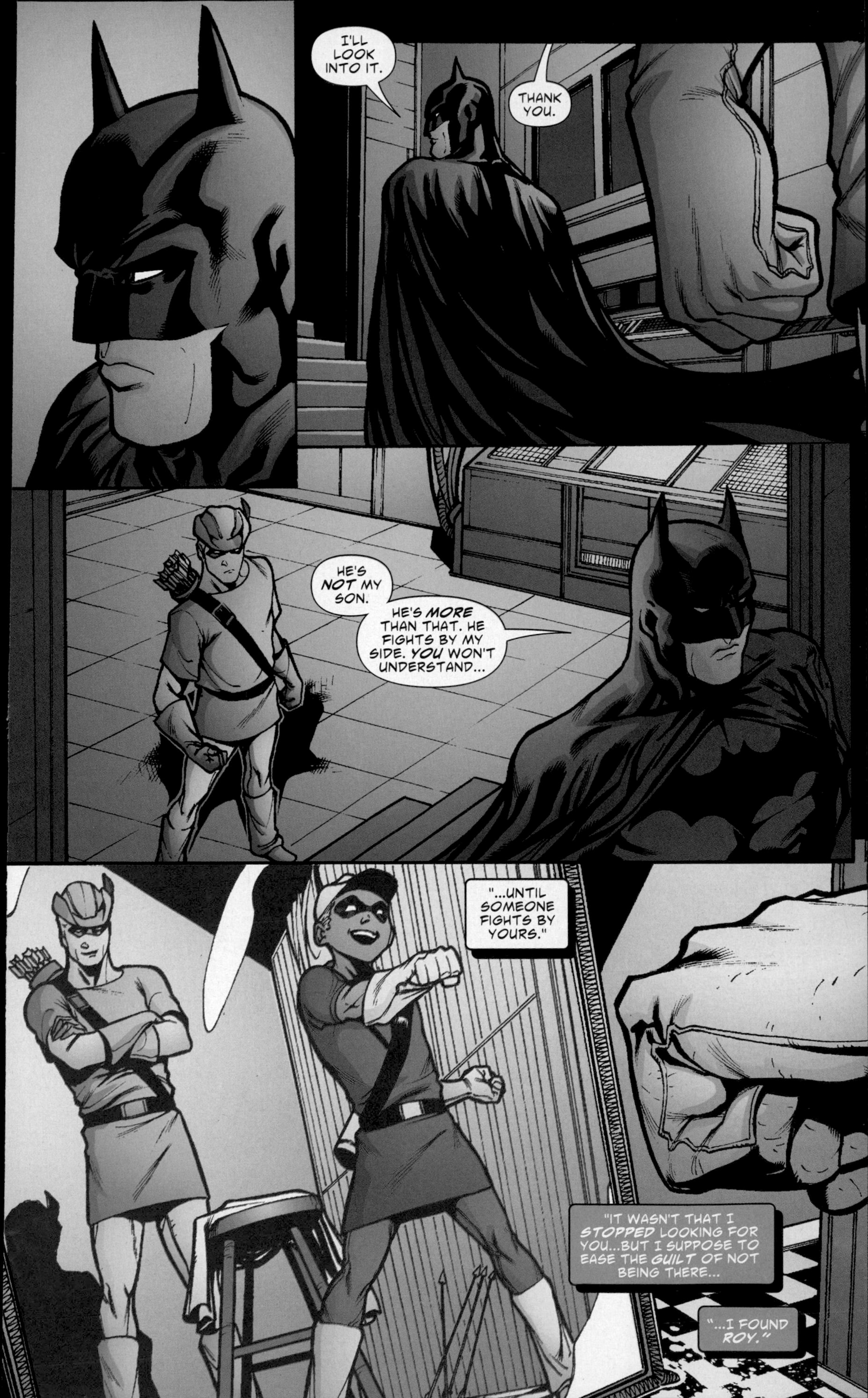
I'LL LOOK INTO IT.
THANK YOU.
HE'S NOT MY SON.
HE'S MORE THAN THAT. HE FIGHTS BY MY SIDE. YOU WON'T UNDERSTAND...
"...UNTIL SOMEONE FIGHTS BY YOURS."
"IT WASN'T THAT I STOPPED LOOKING FOR YOU...BUT I SUPPOSE TO EASE THE GUILT OF NOT BEING THERE...
"...I FOUND ROY."

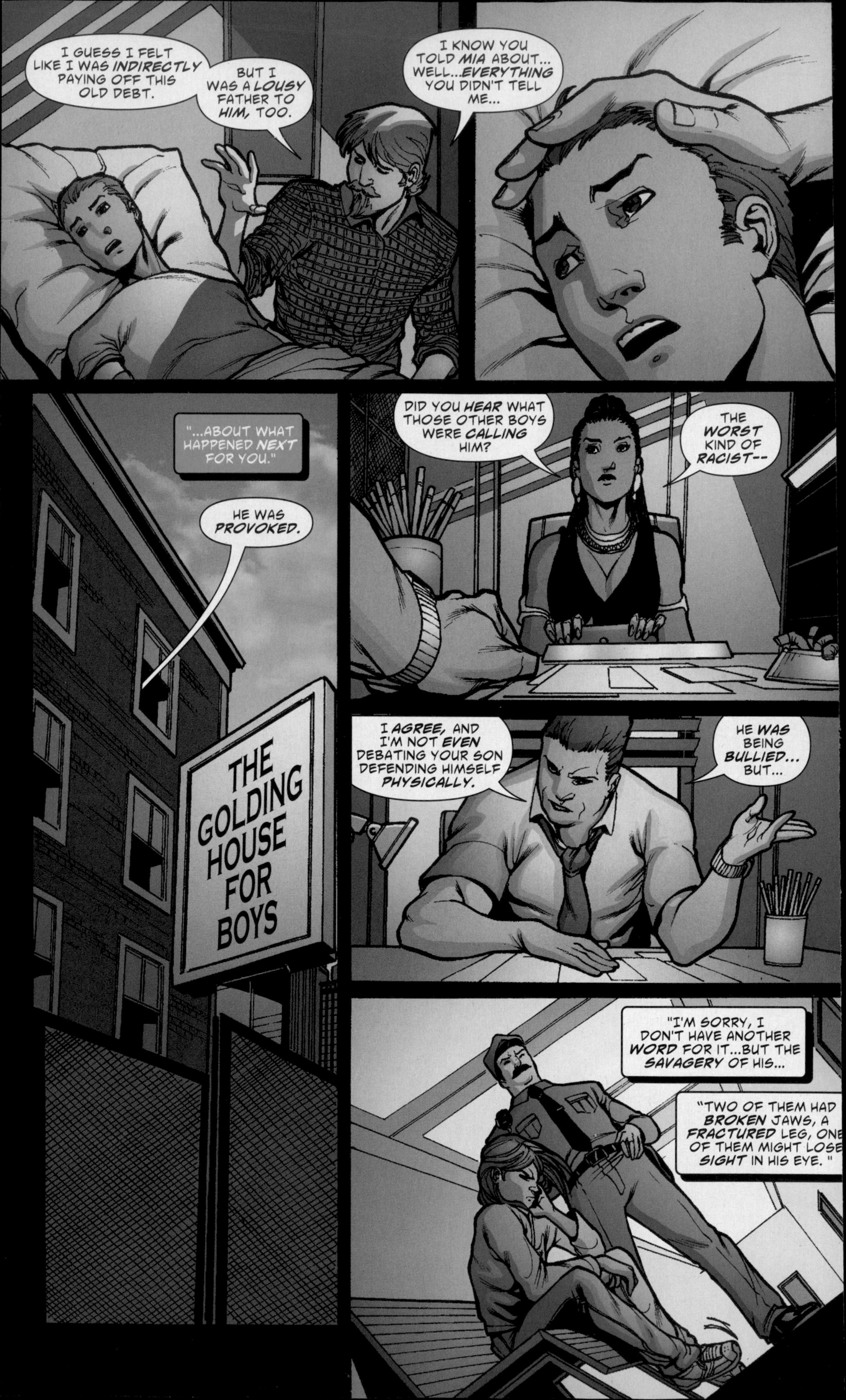
I GUESS I FELT LIKE I WAS INDIRECTLY PAYING OFF THIS OLD DEBT.
BUT I WAS A LOUSY FATHER TO HIM, TOO.
I KNOW YOU TOLD MIA ABOUT... WELL...EVERYTHING YOU DIDN'T TELL ME...
"...ABOUT WHAT HAPPENED NEXT FOR YOU."
HE WAS PROVOKED.
THE GOLDING HOUSE FOR BOYS
DID YOU HEAR WHAT THOSE OTHER BOYS WERE CALLING HIM?
THE WORST KIND OF RACIST--
I AGREE, AND I'M NOT EVEN DEBATING YOUR SON DEFENDING HIMSELF PHYSICALLY.
HE WAS BEING BULLIED... BUT...
"I'M SORRY, I DON'T HAVE ANOTHER WORD FOR IT...BUT THE SAVAGERY OF HIS...
"TWO OF THEM HAD BROKEN JAWS, A FRACTURED LEG, ONE OF THEM MIGHT LOSE SIGHT IN HIS EYE."

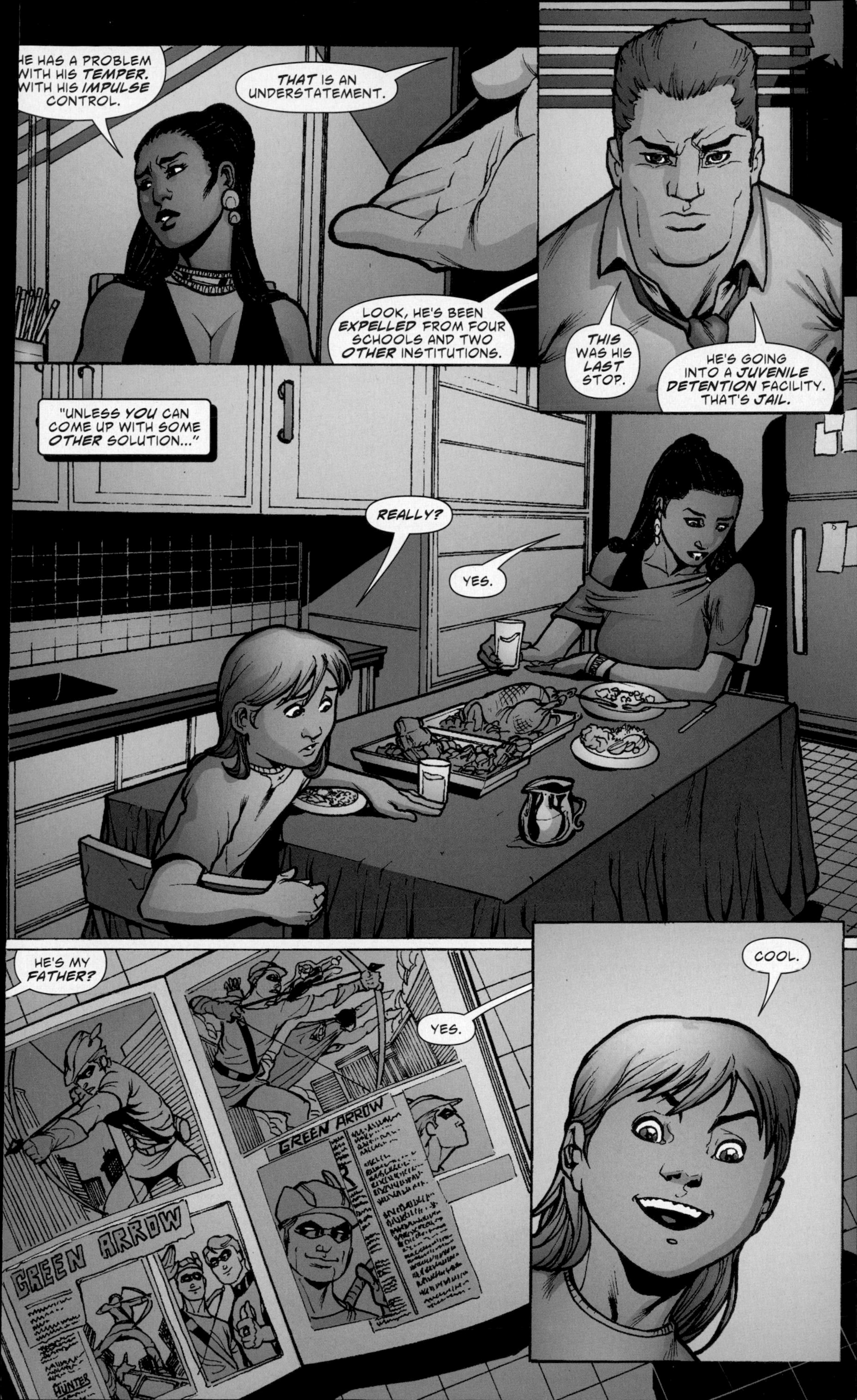
HE HAS A PROBLEM WITH HIS TEMPER. WITH HIS IMPULSE CONTROL.
THAT IS AN UNDERSTATEMENT.
LOOK, HE'S BEEN EXPELLED FROM FOUR SCHOOLS AND TWO OTHER INSTITUTIONS.
THIS WAS HIS LAST STOP.
HE'S GOING INTO A JUVENILE DETENTION FACILITY. THAT'S JAIL.
"UNLESS YOU CAN COME UP WITH SOME OTHER SOLUTION..."
REALLY?
YES.
HE'S MY FATHER?
YES.
COOL.
GREEN ARROW
GREEN ARROW
GREEN ARROW

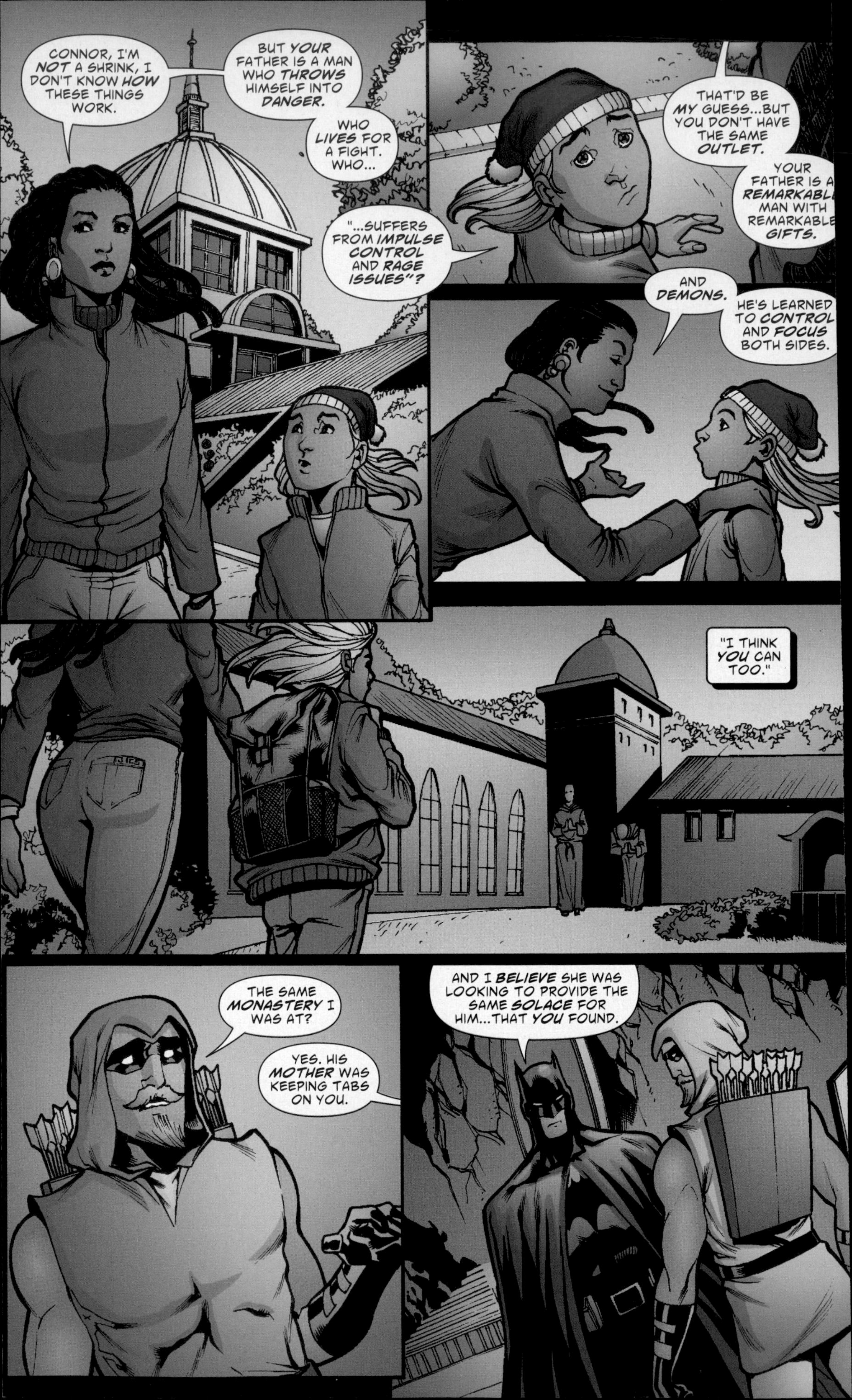
CONNOR, I'M NOT A SHRINK, I DON'T KNOW HOW THESE THINGS WORK.
BUT YOUR FATHER IS A MAN WHO THROWS HIMSELF INTO DANGER.
WHO LIVES FOR A FIGHT. WHO...
"...SUFFERS FROM IMPULSE CONTROL AND RAGE ISSUES"?
THAT'D BE MY GUESS...BUT YOU DON'T HAVE THE SAME OUTLET.
YOUR FATHER IS A REMARKABLE MAN WITH REMARKABLE GIFTS.
AND DEMONS.
HE'S LEARNED TO CONTROL AND FOCUS BOTH SIDES.
"I THINK YOU CAN TOO."
THE SAME MONASTERY I WAS AT?
YES. HIS MOTHER WAS KEEPING TABS ON YOU.
AND I BELIEVE SHE WAS LOOKING TO PROVIDE THE SAME SOLACE FOR HIM...THAT YOU FOUND.

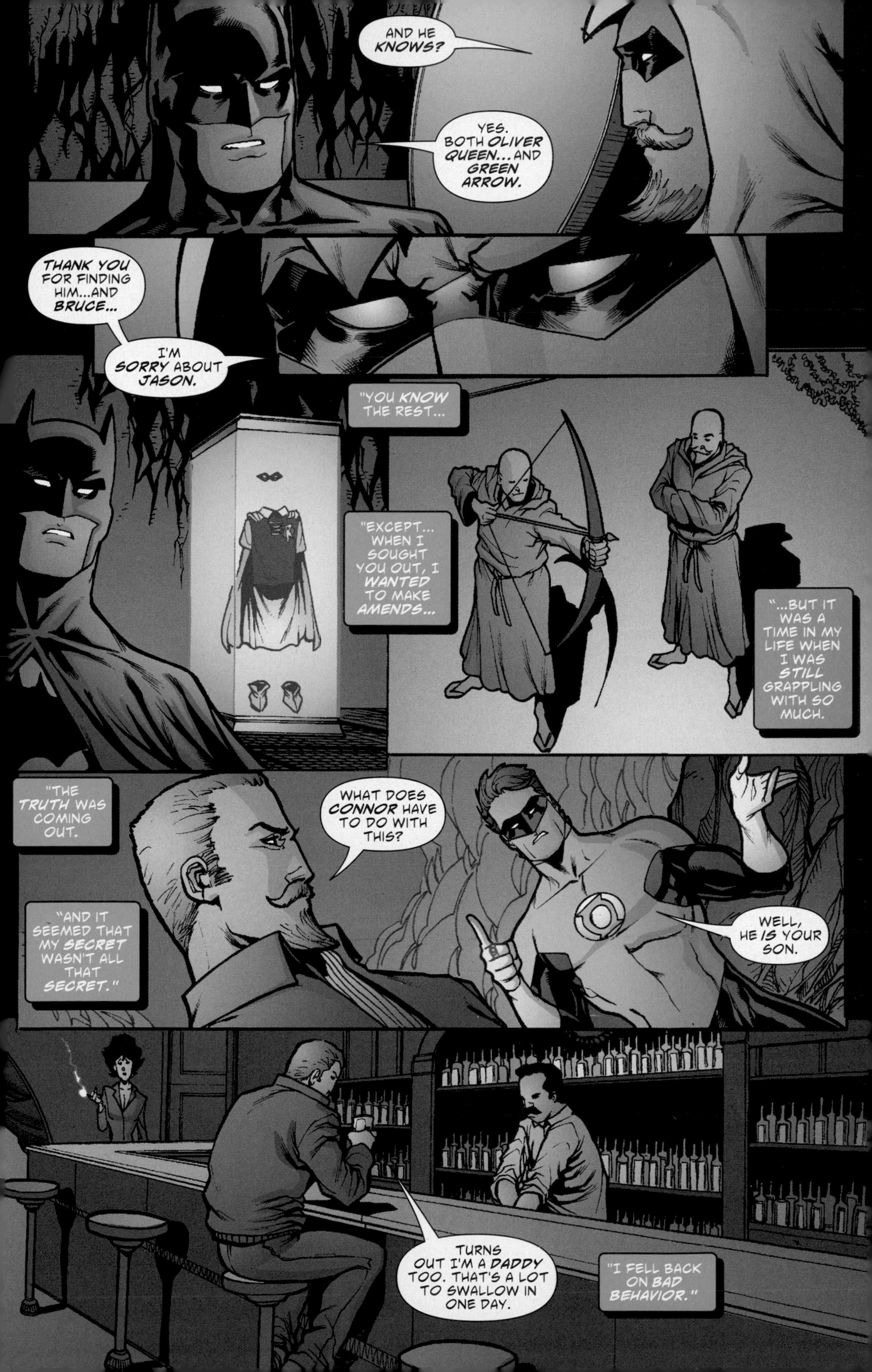
AND HE KNOWS?
YES. BOTH OLIVER QUEEN... AND GREEN ARROW.
THANK YOU FOR FINDING HIM...AND BRUCE...
I'M SORRY ABOUT JASON.
"YOU KNOW THE REST...
"EXCEPT... WHEN I SOUGHT YOU OUT, I WANTED TO MAKE AMENDS...
"...BUT IT WAS A TIME IN MY LIFE WHEN I WAS STILL GRAPPLING WITH SO MUCH.
"THE TRUTH WAS COMING OUT.
WHAT DOES CONNOR HAVE TO DO WITH THIS?
"AND IT SEEMED THAT MY SECRET WASN'T ALL THAT SECRET."
WELL, HE IS YOUR SON.
TURNS OUT I'M A DADDY TOO. THAT'S A LOT TO SWALLOW IN ONE DAY.
"I FELL BACK ON BAD BEHAVIOR."

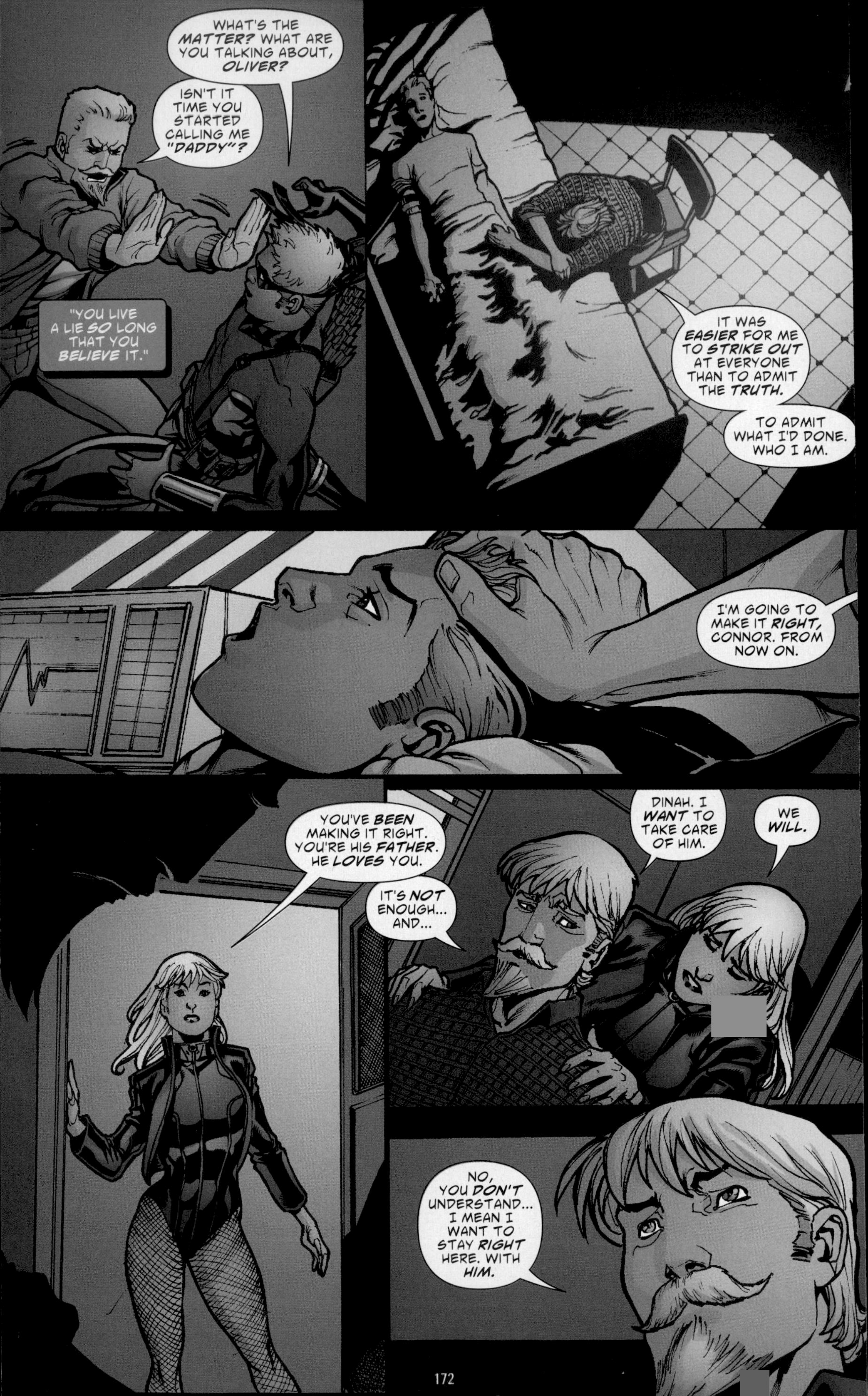
WHAT'S THE MATTER? WHAT ARE YOU TALKING ABOUT, OLIVER?
ISN'T IT TIME YOU STARTED CALLING ME "DADDY"?
"YOU LIVE A LIE SO LONG THAT YOU BELIEVE IT."
IT WAS EASIER FOR ME TO STRIKE OUT AT EVERYONE THAN TO ADMIT THE TRUTH.
TO ADMIT WHAT I'D DONE. WHO I AM.
I'M GOING TO MAKE IT RIGHT, CONNOR. FROM NOW ON.
YOU'VE BEEN MAKING IT RIGHT. YOU'RE HIS FATHER. HE LOVES YOU.
IT'S NOT ENOUGH... AND...
DINAH. I WANT TO TAKE CARE OF HIM.
WE WILL.
NO, YOU DON'T UNDERSTAND... I MEAN I WANT TO STAY RIGHT HERE. WITH HIM.

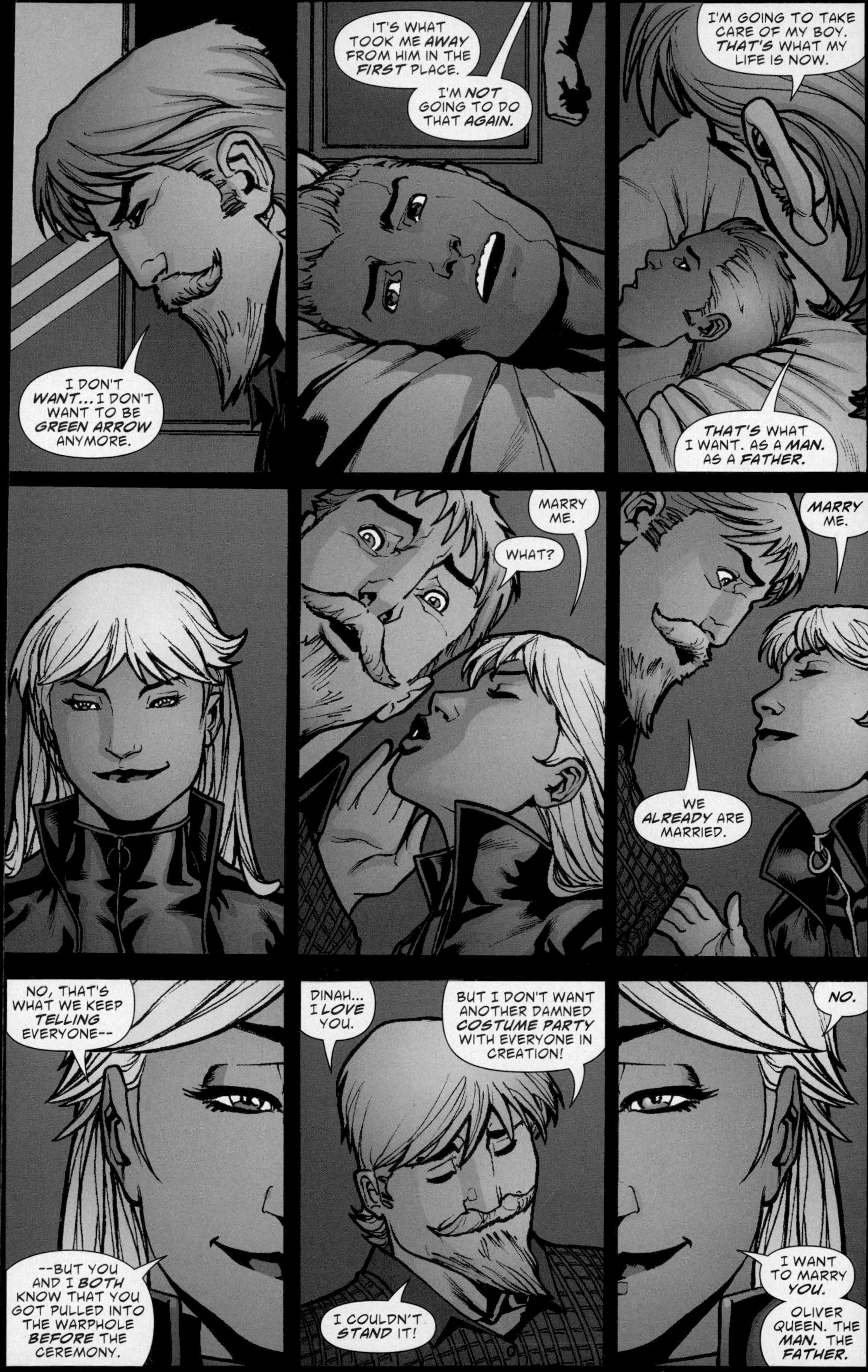
I DON'T WANT... I DON'T WANT TO BE GREEN ARROW ANYMORE.
IT'S WHAT TOOK ME AWAY FROM HIM IN THE FIRST PLACE.
I'M NOT GOING TO DO THAT AGAIN.
I'M GOING TO TAKE CARE OF MY BOY. THAT'S WHAT MY LIFE IS NOW.
THAT'S WHAT I WANT. AS A MAN. AS A FATHER.
MARRY ME.
WHAT?
MARRY ME.
WE ALREADY ARE MARRIED.
NO, THAT'S WHAT WE KEEP TELLING EVERYONE--
--BUT YOU AND I BOTH KNOW THAT YOU GOT PULLED INTO THE WARPHOLE BEFORE THE CEREMONY.
DINAH... I LOVE YOU.
BUT I DON'T WANT ANOTHER DAMNED COSTUME PARTY WITH EVERYONE IN CREATION!
I COULDN'T STAND IT!
NO.
I WANT TO MARRY YOU.
OLIVER QUEEN. THE MAN. THE FATHER.

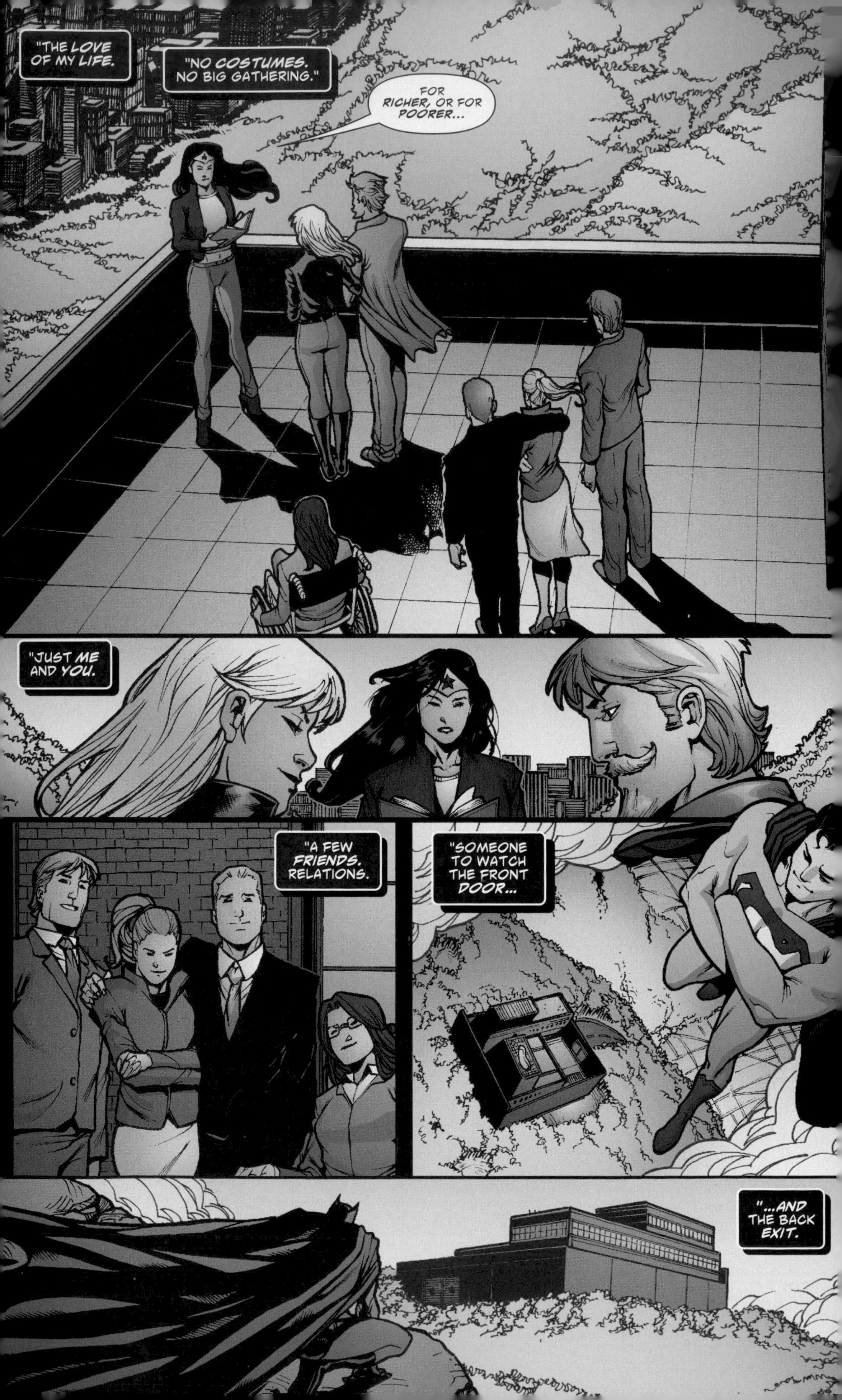

"THE LOVE OF MY LIFE.
"NO COSTUMES. NO BIG GATHERING."
FOR RICHER, OR FOR POORER...
"JUST ME AND YOU.
"A FEW FRIENDS. RELATIONS.
"SOMEONE TO WATCH THE FRONT DOOR...
"...AND THE BACK EXIT.

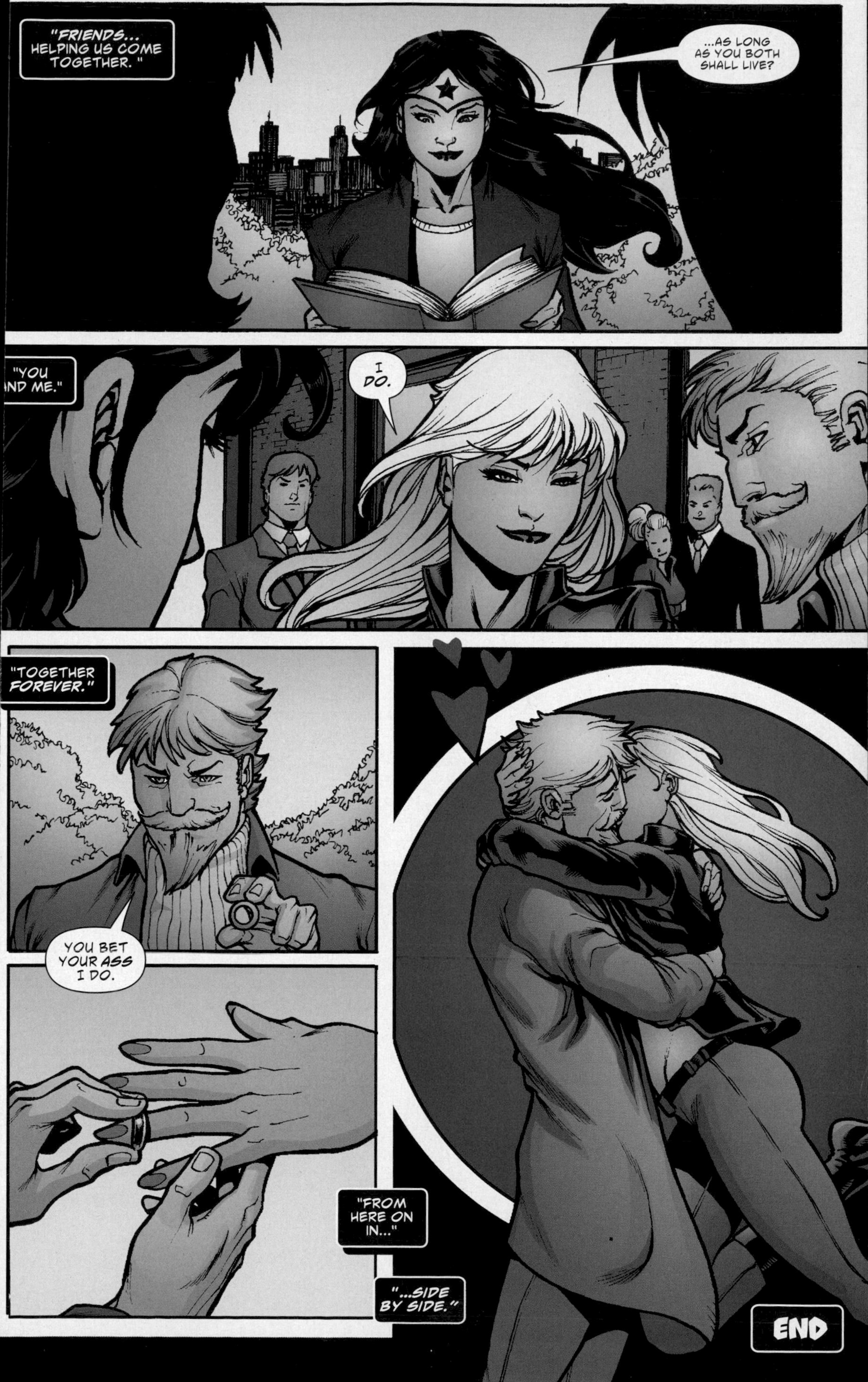
"FRIENDS... HELPING US COME TOGETHER."
...AS LONG AS YOU BOTH SHALL LIVE?
"YOU AND ME."
I DO.
"TOGETHER FOREVER."
YOU BET YOUR ASS I DO.
"FROM HERE ON IN..."
"...SIDE BY SIDE."
END

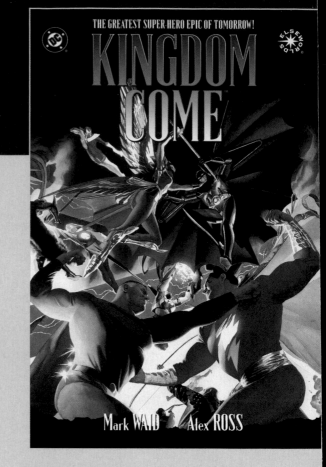
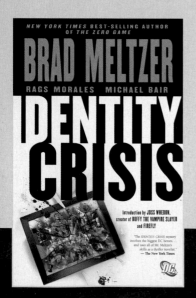